# ARGUING ABOUT SEX

# ARGUING ABOUT SEX

## THE RHETORIC OF
## CHRISTIAN SEXUAL MORALITY

# JOSEPH MONTI

*STATE UNIVERSITY OF NEW YORK PRESS*

Published by
State University of New York Press, Albany

For information, address State University of New York Press,
State University Plaza, Albany, N.Y. 12246

Production by M. R. Mulholland
Marketing by Nancy Farrell

**Library of Congress Cataloging-in-Publication Data**

Monti, Joseph
    Arguing about sex : the rhetoric of Christian sexual morality /
Joseph Monti.
       p.   cm.
    Includes bibliographical references and index.
    ISBN 0-7914-2479-0 (hard : alk. paper). — ISBN 0-7914-2480-4
(pbk. : alk. paper)
    1. Sex—Religious aspects—Christianity. 2. Christian ethics.
I. Title
BT708.M64 1995
241'.66—dc20                                        94-26956
                                                      CIP

10 9 8 7 6 5 4 3 2 1

Thus it happens that rhetoric is an offshoot
of dialectic and also of ethical studies.

—Aristotle, *Rhetoric*

# CONTENTS

# PREFACE

This book is about sexual morality, the Christian Church, and moral argument in late modernity. These four subjects are inevitably intertwined in the Church's modern discourse on sex. Gauging how they are interrelated is the project of this book. Removing any of these subjects from its proper contextual mix accounts for much of the dysfunction the Church is now experiencing in its discourse on sexual morality. To think and argue about sexual morality outside of a self-conscious concentration on the present state of the Church in the late modern world is to engage in an abstraction. Norms, principles, and rules become mere cants echoing above the material-historical realities of the Church and its congregations. The Church's moral rhetoric becomes repetitive, even obsessive, and its moral arguments unpersuasive. I have become convinced that, in Michel Foucault's terms (1978: 11), the "discursive fact," or the way in which sex is being "put into discourse" by the denominations of the Christian Church is now neither constructive nor productive of a life of responsible sexual virtue.

In terms of this text, there are a number of assumptions that need to be spelled out from the beginning. Even though I have assumed a general Christian and western cultural stance, I do not assume that the only sexual morality is Christian. According to how one envisions the realities of sex and sexual behavior in the wide course of human experience, other values, virtues, and goods can be upheld that are not in full concert with Christian ethics. For example, sexual expression may be without overt religious implication at all or without as much implication at the core of human personality as Christian ethics promotes. Consequently, sexual morality could be engaged according to ordinary canons of mature consent and prudent physical safeguards. Certainly, Christian sexual ethics would find moralities that reduced sex to a more superficial level of human experience deficient. But this in no way means that such approaches are bereft of all moral standards and are in every way corrupting.

Drawing from the long history of the interaction of sex and religion, Christian sexual ethics maintains a rather high and rich interpretation of the place and function of sex in human life and has a heavily laden moral standard for sexual behavior. In these critical interpretations and judgments, Christians have burdened and obliged themselves to make good on their claims—to demonstrate in their behavior that what they claim is true. There are positive and negative effects in taking on such burdens. In making sex and sexual behavior such an important part of the meaning of being human before God, Christians have invested human sexuality with a potential for positive growth of the human personality and for informing loving, just, and peaceful relations with each other. At the same time, sex has also assumed a negative potential to make Christians greatly neurotic. It is fair to say that, for good and for ill, the mutual intertwining of sex and religion is now complete in the Christian Church to the extent that sexuality in general, and sexual behavior in particular, have had a great deal to do with the Church's self-understanding and the identification of Christian character.

Still, the question of how important sex and sexual behavior are to a constructive and morally virtuous human life bears further investigation. Insofar as we can construe sexuality as an intrinsic part of how human beings engage their life-worlds—as an informing dimension of character identity—we can say that sex and sexual behavior are of the utmost importance. However, in a negative vein, this does not mean that sex is of such importance that the paradigm of human irresponsibility and sin is fully disclosed in particular sexual acts or that the physical pleasure attached to sexual acts indicates its orientation to moral perversity. Acts and policies rooted in structured and institutional violence and injustice are often far more manifesting of human perversity than sexual irresponsibility. By overestimating the potential of sexual behavior to manifest human perversity, the Church's obsessive conversations about sexual sin perform an unnoticed and negative service of distracting Christians from our more profound sins of violence and class-bound injustice. In this sense, it is not so much that we have repressed sex, but that we have used the modern discourse on sex to repress these deeper challenges to our Christian character-identity.

It may be somewhat paradoxical, then, that while complaining about the denominations' incessant and obsessive conversations on sex, I have written a good many words about sexual morality. My intention, however, has been to focus these obsessive conversations in more precise ways. In gaining precision about the Church's "problems" with historical change and modernity, about the terms and function of moral argument, and about the role of the norm of marriage, perhaps we can have less but better talk about sexual morality and put sex into conversation in more constructive communities of moral discourse.

I have attempted to enter a debate in process within the Christian churches, religious groups in general, and the culture at large. Rather than surveying in detail the official statements and position papers of the various denominations, I have focused on what I take to be the underlying issues of the Church's argument about sex. Considering that argument now to be at a state of impasse, I have searched for a way out of our rhetorical morass and suggest some new ways to think about sexual ethics in particular and moral argument in general. Even though this book is theoretical in nature, it has the practical intent of improving the rhetoric of Christian sexual morality and offering guidance for present debates. The book itself is informed by the classical rhetorical intention to clarify and persuade by way of an extended argument. Even so, I do not consider my intention to persuade the Christian denominations to consider new possibilities in their arguments about sex to be only ideologically informed, but rather grounded in an extended argument with theoretic content standing upon critically articulated foundations.

As *Arguing about Sex* makes clear, the rhetoric of sexual morality is rooted in the larger and more complex discourse of institutions in the late modern world. Certainly the implications of the historical, cultural, sociopsychological, and economic conditions of knowledge are now too acute to miss in critical moral discussions, even of a religious nature. I make no claims to "put sex into discourse" amid all of these complex and interlocking dimensions. I do claim, however, that critically examining the "discursive facts" of the rhetoric of Christian sexual morality in the late modern world provides foundations for better moral argument and possibly more responsible sexual behavior.

The initial work on this manuscript was supported, in part, by a grant from the Association of Theological Schools, for which I am grateful. Deneen Patton's efficiency and good humor were invaluable assets. I am also grateful to Harrison West, Dann Brown, and Ben Dixon who helped with various aspects of this project while they were my student assistants. Ken Herzog was meticulous in checking details. Susan Blettel prepared the graphic. Ellen Stallworth did the final proofreading. The editors and readers at State University of New York Press were most helpful and improved the manuscript. Patricia Templeton deserves special mention and much appreciation for applying her considerable editorial skills toward significantly improving a writing style that one reviewer found to be "baroque."

While, to be more precise, I might admit to a more scholastic than baroque style of writing, I am also convinced that complex issues require complex arguments. Reducing multidimensional phenomena to single dimensional analysis is much of the problem of contemporary moral debates. However, complexity is no excuse for lack of clarity in expression. Saying clearly what we mean—always an elusive goal—as well as understanding the full historical dimensions of that meaning and the cultural and societal foundations of our own arguments, requires probing depths beyond what Ronald Dworkin has called the "high rhetoric of the public debate" (1993: 21). Critical linguistic and rhetorical clarity are themselves more than only facility of expression. And even though this book was essentially completed before the publication of Dworkin's *Life's Dominion* (1993), we agree on the importance of "a now neglected genre: an argumentative essay that engages theoretical issues but begins with, and remains disciplined by, a moral subject of practical political importance" (p. 28).

The arguments of this book, and argumentative speech in general, are under their own, now equally neglected, ethical norms and moral rules—what Richard M. Weaver calls *The Ethics of Rhetoric* (1953). Once we leave, as Weaver says, a sort of "neuter discourse" that appeals "to those who expect a scientific solution of human problems" (p. 9), we enter not only into the realm of systematic verbal argument with all of its own diversity of logic but also into the emotive appeal of words themselves. A persuasive argument rests not only upon the grounds of logically constructed order but finally upon what happens to our affections when faced with a stimulating, well-constructed, or even simply an ideologically effective array of words, stylistically arranged. Consequently, Weaver argues that rhetorical language "must always be particularized to suit the occasion, drawing its effectiveness from many small nuances...." (p. 8). It is this particularization that colors an argument with rhetorical style and also makes it open, in its exciting of interest, to what Weaver calls "base rhetoric" (pp. 9; 11). Base rhetoric has exploitation as its end and "hates that which is opposed, or is equal or better because all such things are impediments to its will, and in the last analysis it knows only its will," keeping "understanding in a passive state by never permitting an honest examination of alternatives" (Weaver, 1953: 11; 12). In order to overcome these prevailing dangers of manipulation in the speech of persuasion, Weaver points out (1953: title page) that Aristotle's relation of ethics and rhetoric comes through the nexus of dialectic: "Thus it happens that rhetoric is an offshoot of dialectic and also of ethical studies." (See also Aristotle, *Rhetoric*, Bk I: Ch. 2, 25; 1973: 733).

It is here that the appropriate irony of taking a rhetorical approach to the question of sexual ethics comes into play. For critical argument, framed as dialectic, persuades legitimately only when it is open to the other in dialogue and willing to be touched and persuaded by a better argument. Not all issues or persons are open to this sort of critical engagement or the momentary suspension of judgment that both good argument and human intimacy require. But when critical dialectical engagement in word and gesture is appropriate, it is an uplifting and ennobling experience. It is such critical dialectics—the common pursuit of truth and right with others different from ourselves—that make and build communities of moral discourse and action. In bringing and binding persons together, language that intends to persuade, like sexuality itself, is "a kind of love" (Weaver, 14). Richard Weaver (1953: 14: n.7) concludes that "it is worth recalling that in the Christian New Testament, with its heavy Platonic influence, God is identified with logos, 'word, speech' (*John* 1:1); and with agape, 'love'" (*1 John* 4: 8).

I have received permission to quote from the following works: Reprinted with permission of Macmillan Publishing Company from *The Meaning of Revelation* by H. Richard Niebuhr. Copyright 1941 by Macmillan Publishing Company, renewed 1969 by Florence Niebuhr, Cynthia M. Niebuhr, and Richard R. Niebuhr; from *Reason and Conduct* by Henry David Aiken. Copyright (c) 1972 by Henry David Aiken. Reprinted by permission of Alfred A. Knopf Inc; from *Interpretation Theory: Discourse and the Surplus of Meaning* by Paul Ricoeur, copyright 1976 by Texas Christian University Press; from Donald Davidson, "What Metaphor Means," and Paul Ricoeur, "The Metaphorical Process as Cognition, Imagination, and Feeling" in *Critical Inquiry* 5/1, copyright 1978 by The University of Chicago Press; Reprinted from *Models of God* by Sallie McFague, copyright 1982 by Fortress Press. Used by permission of Augsburg Fortress; *The Reality of the Historical Past* by Paul Ricoeur, copyright 1984, by Marquette University; *The Body and Society* by Peter Brown, copyright, 1988 by Columbia University Press; *Moral Consciousness and Communicative Action* by Jürgen Habermas, translated by Christian Lenhardt and Shierry Weber Nicholsen, copyright 1990 by Massachusetts Institute of Technology. I am also grateful for permission to use short excerpts from my article "Dangerous Times and Obliging Places: A Response to the New Sectarianism" previously published in *Quarterly Review* 13:4, (Winter, 1993); and from "*Foreword*: 'The Church: A Community of Moral Discourse'" originally printed in *Sewanee Theological Review* 35:1 (Christmas, 1991), a quarterly journal published by the School of Theology of the University of the South in Sewanee, Tennessee.

# Introduction

## Being Faithful and Contemporary

It would be hard to deny that Christian denominations are having difficulty articulating a coherent sexual ethic that is both faithful and contemporary. In this age of foundational pluralism, not a few voices wonder about the possibility of any rational coherence at all in ethics and moral guidance.[1] In light of this, the recent moral rhetoric of sex often infers two choices: the relativistic option in which individuals somehow determine their own morality; or the demarcation of a separated moral life for specific traditions and groups—a "special ethic" that insulates and isolates the group and its members from the dangers of contemporary life. In both of these options pluralism has become the reason for concern. In the first, pluralism functions as a reason for relativism. In the second, pluralism is an enemy that must be confronted at all costs lest a particular group or tradition lose its sense of faithful continuity with its own past. The present state of the moral rhetoric of sex in the Christian denominations suggests some combination of both options.

Some individual Christians and denominational leaders, especially those educated in the most recent sexual revolution of the 1950s and 1960s, have adopted some variation of relativism in matters of sexual morality. While it is true that age and parenting often bring on more conservatism in moral rhetoric and guidance, the relativism of the formative periods of our youth in sexual matters is transmitted to later generations. At the same time other leaders, rightly concerned about the growing relativism, have turned more and more to traditionalist sexual morality. These traditionalist teachers claim a more faithful and coherent form of moral guidance. However, most often cast in opposition to the realities of contemporary experience, such claims can be neither verified nor legitimated. Framed in flight, any rational coherence gained is only internal, and ironically, also relative, limited by the "success" of their attempts to reduce complex worlds of human sexual experience to manageable proportions. In this type of moral rhetoric, the denominations are sacrificing significant claims to the "external" coherence of effective contemporary teaching. What is being taught is not being adequately heard, much less heeded. Unfortunately, such a vacuum in the Church's leadership and teaching makes some form of personal relativism in sexual morality more attractive, if not necessary. For all concerned, modern pluralism seems to be a paralyzing fear in the face of which no coherent sexual ethic is being articulated.

Certainly denominational teachers ought to be *concerned* about pluralism with any attendant moral relativism and conventionalism. All disjunctive relativism and conventionalism are inadequate and unfaithful expressions of the universal commitments that define the Church. However, any *retreat* from pluralism in sexual matters also cannot be confessionally and theologically legitimated if the Church is to maintain its evangelical commission as an effective guide to truth, right, and good in any and all possible worlds. Any reduction of the complexity of the worlds in which the majority of Christians live for purposes of only internal coherence, more efficient management, or to allay an anxiety-ridden institutional conscience cannot be adequately faithful.[2]

Plural threads in the fabric of Christianity will certainly appear in a sexual ethic that purports to be a faithful weave of faith confession, theological construction, and moral response. The recognition of such simple pluralism depends on a foundation of common interests, interpretations, and themes that claim an intrinsic relation of sexuality, sexual conduct, and the foundations of Christian life in the world. The biblical religions know that sexuality and sexual conduct ought to have something fundamentally to do with love of God and neighbor, with steadfast commitment and enduring obligation. Yet no matter how Christian denominations formally identify themselves as standing in an authentic line of "biblical" and "traditional" teaching, all also know that there is diversity in the Christian understanding of sexual morality. This is not to suggest that any Christian denomination has engaged adequately the dimensions of the radical pluralism of modernity or its implications for faith and theology.[3] Still, cultural, theological, and moral variety and diversity are not new in Christianity. The Church has lived and transmitted its traditions amid some condition of relative pluralism throughout the course of its history. Certainly, for *tradition* to be the act of *handing over* and *passing on* something continuous must also be present amid the discontinuities of pluralism. In one way or another, the Church has always understood its life amid both the continuities and discontinuities of history. While it is true that pluralism as diversity and the discontinuity it displays continues to be a problem for the Church, it is not the main problem.

A distinction must be made between *simple pluralism* as variety and diversity, and *radical pluralism* as a foundational structure and dimension of modern understanding and knowledge. Pluralism as diversity has been a common experience in all periods of the Church's life with a variety of responses, from disputation to council, from schism to reformation. While the traditional experience of simple pluralism continues in the contemporary Church, it is the radical and uniquely modern experience of pluralism at foundational levels of historical interpretation and substantive knowledge that now challenges the Church's articulation of a faithful and contemporary ethic.

In modernity, history can no longer be understood simply as a cohesive and coherent linear thread, with pluralism as only variations upon a single theme. Amid simple pluralism alone, all denominations have found ways to claim historical and moral fidelity. However, the more radical pluralism of modernity now presents special problems for the Church. The more pronounced and fundamental problem engaging the Church in the articulation of an adequate and responsible sexual ethic has to do with the meaning of fidelity itself in the now radicalized contexts of time and history.

If fidelity in Christian faith and life could mean only recapitulating the past or living morally within the clearly demarcated parameters of Christian sects, then problems of articulating a coherent sexual ethic amid radical pluralism would not be so pronounced. Being faithful to a tradition or a community could then be understood simply as a more careful and complete repetition of what we have received as norms and rules of sexual behavior. Critical moral discourse would be an on-going analysis of the strands of sexual morality received from the past or articulated internally by the small "faithful" group, combined with necessary critical theological and hermeneutic criteria for determining what counts as authentic tradition and teaching. If this rather anachronistic posture adequately described what "being faithful" meant in history and tradition, the problems now being experienced by the Christian denominations would not really be with *constructing* an adequate sexual ethic at all, but rather with its *reception* by congregations called to receive what we can assume would be clearly presented. The problem would not be one of constructive theology and ethics but of what is commonly understood as Christian education or pastoral communication. My suspicion is that some version of this scenario is mainly what is guiding the teaching voices of the denominations in the moral rhetoric of sex, albeit with a good bit of confusion that is quickly becoming major and classical anxiety since pastoral statements and educational programs built on this insufficient premise do not seem to be working in the guidance and care of souls.

It is a basic and fundamental misstatement of fidelity that has brought the denominations to their present difficulties in articulating a responsible sexual ethic. Critically engaging the obligation of fidelity without its dialectical twin of contemporaneity has led to the present malaise. To be sure, in projecting fidelity upon the horizon of the past, or within the narrow confines of a Christian congregation, the denominations are engaging in a common form of ecclesiastical teaching and moral guidance. Such commitments to continuity with what we have uniquely received are foundational and necessary, but finally insufficient. Throughout the history of the Church, an equally classic and traditional obligation of faith confession, theological articulation, and moral guidance has also been critical contemporaneity, including the relation of Christian moral standards to "all the nations." Without sufficient attention to this second obligation, the legitimate concerns of denominational teachers for the articulation of a faithful sexual morality lead to the restatement of teaching from the perspective of the past alone. Theological and moral arguments by reiteration, however, or by reduction of the universe of coherence are inadequate both theoretically and practically. Such attempts at only conserving Christian faith and life do not adequately bear the faith forward. In its biblical origins, Christian faith maintains a foundational and self-identifying involvement with history and all of its possible worlds, including all the issues of life and death in contemporary historical existence. There has always been a certain pragmatic consciousness in the Christian Church—a spirit of practical involvement and of making sense of the present, of speaking truth, and of engaging the right and promoting the good in everyday life. Despite stops and starts, sectarian detours, liberal misdirections, gnostic temptations, and institutionally self-serving sins, the Church has maintained at least a thin tie of obligation to human history that directs it to its own contemporary experience no matter how pluralistic and discontinuous.[4]

Even when the denominations teach sexual morality from the perspective of the past alone, their legitimate concern for how Christians live their lives and for what they will pass on to their children is, ironically, a pragmatic engagement with contemporary history. The problem is that this kind of teaching inevitably becomes a pervasively negative indictment of the present and therefore not adequately constructive and effective for guiding everyday life. In matters of sexual morality, the Church's pragmatic concern for contemporary life is involved in what looks very much like a classically vicious circle of institutional anxiety. Anxiety-ridden repression is not always manifested by reticence. Incessant and repetitive conversation is just as much a manifestation of anxiety in individuals and institutions as silence (Foucault, 1980). When the Church has been anxious and repressed about sex and sexual morality, more often than not the manifestation has not been through reticence but through incessant and repetitive speech.[5]

The Christian denominations are worried and anxious about sexual morality. They are worried about the assaults the modern world has wrought on the traditional norms and rules of sexual conduct. Denominational teachers know that the ways in which we conduct our sexual lives have much to do with our character identity, with love of God and neighbor, and how we understand ourselves as moral beings and people of steadfast commitment and obligation. Since it is the modern world that has brought these new threats to the Church's life, it is the modern world that has now become the enemy. Especially in their teaching on sexual morality, the denominations are forgetting how the obligation of fidelity must be dialectically engaged with the equal obligation of contemporaneity—how Christian life must make sense in its own time, must be truthful and right-making, and promote the good in whatever world we find ourselves. Certainly the time is long past when the Church could think of itself as the principal maker of the worlds of everyday culture. We may contribute to any given life-world, but we do not make it by ourselves. Rather we are called to live in cultures we do not make.

The split between fidelity and contemporaneity continues a vicious and enervating circle of anxiety expressed in a somewhat compulsive repetition of a sexual ethic that is neither being accepted nor lived by a significant number of Christians. Such anxiety-ridden repetition has serious negative implications for the authenticity of the Church's teaching voice in general. Classical anxiety has unconscious causes; and in this case, the teachers of the Church must feel a confusing tug between their conscious and clear obligation of fidelity and their now repressed obligation of contemporaneity. The fact that the issues under discussion are sexuality and sexual conduct make the tugs of the unconscious even more pronounced. We are dealing here with a somewhat distinctive phenomenon, at least for the modern liberal denominations, which have relatively accepted historicist and pluralist modernity in some sense. There is often more anxiety and concern with new theologies and moralities of sexuality and sexual conduct than with what they generally consider more directly identifying and defining teachings and practices, such as biblical criticism, Christology, and revisions of liturgy.

Despite all of our "new" conversations about sex, the fundamental challenge is an old one that pertains to the very core of the biblical understanding of "God with us" in any and all times and places. Biblical faith in general and Christian faith, made substantively material in the communities of Jesus Christ, are historical through and through. To be adequately faithful the Church must continually engage in the struggle, as H. Richard Niebuhr suggests, to be "time-full" (1963a: 90-107)—to engage the past from the perspective of the present in terms of the future.[6] If it has been the forgetfulness of the "time-full" dimensions of history and fidelity that has led the Church into its present circle of innervating anxiety about sexual morality, it will only be with a recovery of a full understanding of the historicity of Christian faith and life that we will break out. We must begin to self-consciously engage sexual ethics under the dual and dialectically equal obligations of fidelity and contemporaneity. Christian morality will certainly not affirm all that it finds in any given time and age, but if it is to be faithful, the Church must constructively engage its own contemporary worlds. Christianity is defined and identified as much by its present as its past, cast always upon the horizon of the future.

However, an impasse remains in the Christian moral rhetoric of sex. The Church, knowing at some level that the transmissions of its traditions of faith confession, theological articulation, and moral guidance finally demand contemporaneity, fears what is necessary for its own fidelity, and not wholly without cause. To call for contemporaneity and modernity is to call at the same time for a dangerous and risky engagement. What is new and contemporaneous is not necessarily better. In the area of sexual morality, as in all areas of theology and doctrine, fidelity can be just as compromised when engaged from the single horizon of the present as from that of the past. Quick claims for change by those who are persuaded by any new rhetoric of sexual morality also do not address adequately the obligation of contemporaneity, much less fidelity. H. Richard Niebuhr calls what seems currently like an impasse our "enduring problem" (1951).

## Summary and Outline

In this book I do not intend a comprehensive treatment of the intricacies of human sexuality in its philosophical, theological, sociopsychological and political/economic ramifications. Some discussion of these areas will be engaged from time to time but only as they apply to the central aim of the book; *to offer a precise and focused treatment of sexual morality from the perspective of ethical and moral argument in the context of modernity.* Even here, my aim will be finally narrowed to a centering question of the formal relation between the ethical norm and the moral rule, and to substantive applications of this formal relation to Christian sexual morality. I will apply this relation specifically to only three areas of Christian sexual conduct: marriage; heterosexual relations among single persons; and homosexual relationships.[7]

Part One: The Church and the Conversation of History

The presenting problems of fidelity and contemporaneity for the Church in the modern world introduces the foundational questions of history and cosmological worldviews. Historical cosmologies are frames for adequate rational discourse and for how that discourse can proceed in terms of the "permission" to say anything new. Formal discussions of the historical groundwork for plural methods in theology and ethics are related to the substantive claims of the Church's faith confessions and its commitments to history and society as such. The first part of this book gives an argument for breaking the Church's enervating cycle of anxiety with respect to sexual morality. Even though anxiety has deeper dimensions than can be examined through argument alone, reasoned discourse might at least begin to crack some of our more debilitating theological defenses against modernity. If this defensive armor is breached, and the possibility of saying something that is both faithful and contemporary is at least formally entertained in principle, then the ground is set for hearing substantive proposals about what new guidance in sexual morality might be. Part One suggests how historical change and the modern age present religious institutions with both difficulties and prospects for new and more critical moral argument about sex.

Chapter One, Sexual Discourse and the Problem of Modernity, locates modernity in the historical flow of western culture and discusses how the Church is responding to the "problem" of modernity with respect to sexual morality. Dividing historical time into periods, epochs, and worldviews enhances our sense of presence—experiences of our own time and place in comparison with what has gone before and what may come after us. More substantively, a study of cosmological worldviews provides a constructive framework for understanding why we say and do what we do, as well as offering "permission" or not—both epistemological and moral—to say and do different things. To begin with a discussion of "the problem of modernity" is to enter a vast and complex terrain. And if we are at the start of a transition to what is now being called the "postmodern world," the intricacies of analysis become even more pronounced. However, I am convinced this is where we must begin if we are to offer a constructive diagnosis and remedy to the Church's current impasse on matters of sexual morality.

Chapter Two, The Historicity of Faith and Life, begins a constructive response to the problems presented for the Church's traditional teachings by modernity's relatively optimistic view of historical progress and the priority of the new over the old. In this chapter, the modern notion and experience of progress is purged of its optimistic evolutionary claims while retaining modernity's discovery of radical historicity. I develop this particular understanding of history as progress as it pertains to faith and the moral life in general and to sexual morality in particular. In Chapter Three, History, Interpretation, and the Moral Life, I take up the questions of the historical nature of faith and ethics framed by substantive examples in Christian sexual morality and sexual conduct. In these chapters, the importance of the critical hermeneutic shape of the Church's moral rhetoric is discussed, as well as the continuities and discontinuities necessary for any adequate sense and experience of an historical faith framed by tradition. These chapters argue that the relativity, plurality, and conventionality of history do not lead necessarily to relativism in ethics and moral behavior.

Part Two: The Analytic Conversation of Moral Argument

It would be fair to say that Part One sets the major foundations of an argument that intends to be self-consciously, though not uncritically, liberal and modern. It is certainly at least a subtext of this work that the Church's present flirtations with illiberal antimodernism are perilous for Christian faith and life. Merely to set the groundwork, however, for the possibility of saying faithfully something new about sexual morality does not mean that anything new ought to be said, or what that something new should be. Part Two emphasizes how a concentration on the nature of moral argument, especially the meaning and relation of ethical norms and moral rules, makes the constructive suggestions of the last section of the manuscript possible and at least initially plausible. This is the most technical part of the book and offers an expansion of the work of Henry David Aiken on the levels of moral discourse, and assisted by the work of Paul Ricoeur and others, offers new understandings of the meaning, role, and function of moral norms and rules as they are used in moral argument in general and in the rhetoric of sexual morality in particular.

Chapter Four, Ethical Norms and Moral Rules, is a formal methodological inquiry that locates the relation of ethical norms and moral rules amid the general levels of moral discourse and ethical argument. Central to the Church's present moral rhetoric on sexual behavior is an analytic confusion between an ethical norm and a moral rule. This chapter addresses that confusion.

In Chapter Five, The Origin, Structure, and Function of Ethical Norms, I advance the central argument for the metaphorical and symbolic quality of ethical norms and their relation to moral rules. The thesis that effective ethical norms function primarily as disclosing and designating metaphors and symbols that, when mature, model values rather than directly regulating conduct grounds the substantive argument of the rest of the book.

Part Three: Substantive Conversations in Christian Ethics
and Moral Theology

Part Three encompasses the substantive recommendations of the book concerning Christian sexual behavior and the Church's discussions of sexual morality in general. Chapter Six, The Norm of Heterosexual Marriage, argues for the continuing pervasiveness of the norm of heterosexual marriage in the Church. After advancing a theory of how the historical past is brought forward, the chapter discusses what is disclosed in the history of Christian marriage and how it currently functions as an effective model for contemporary moral behavior. Next, the chapter critically engages substantive and specific challenges to the norm of marriage in the everyday lives of Christians in three selected areas: heterosexual marriage itself; nonmarital sexual expression among unmarried Christians; and same-sex relationships. Sexual behavior among the unmarried and those of the same sex will not be treated as necessarily an assault upon the norm, but as indicative of proper role and the inevitable limits of ethical norms, including marriage. Throughout, the formal thesis of Chapters Four and Five (ethical norms as disclosing, designating, and demonstrating core values) is joined with the substantive thesis of Chapter Six (the normative model of marriage) in discussions of the relation of rules of proximate and specific conduct to distant and general norms. Combining the correlative values, virtues, and goods modeled in marriage, Chapter Six argues for the necessity of both the general and distant disclosures of ethical norms, and the specific and proximate guidance of moral rules for responsible behavior. In the practical application of the theoretic perspectives discussed in the first two parts of the book, Chapter Six is the conclusion of the book's argument—*quod erat demonstrandum*.

Since rational arguments have both internal and external liabilities and limits, however, the book ends with a concluding chapter that functions somewhat as a postscript to take recognition of these facts. At the end of Chapter Six I recognize the internal limits of argumentation in a specific instance and then turn to Chapter Seven, Building Communities of Moral Discourse, as an overture to the new "communicative praxis" that must take place within institutions in order for more critical moral debates to take place. This chapter begins with a discussion of the "moral intentions" of rationality and rational discourse and then turns to an ecclesiological overview of how the engagement of new conversations that can, in principle, say new things about sexual morality pertains to the very nature of the Christian Church. Under the theme of the "praxis of communicative action," this final chapter suggests Jürgen Habermas's theory of "discourse ethics" as a useful guide for the Church in constructing the conditions of adequate moral debate on sexual matters. In so doing it responds to the challenge noted in the Introduction concerning the continuing loss of the Church's credibility in this area entailing a loss of credibility in all areas of the Church's life. Chapter Six connects the problems associated with the institutionalization of moral discourse in late modernity with a final statement of new possibilities. The chapter and book end with a recapitulation of both the classical and biblical relation of critical dialectic and communities of love and friendly affection noted in the Preface and Introduction.

### The Rhetoric of Disputation: Writing as Argument

Much of the contemporary brief against modernity that I will debate in this book has to do with the failure of rational speech that attempts to persuade in response to substantive problems and issues. This book, which is centered in argument, also intends to be one. To be an adequate argument, the book ought to do two things. First, it must make sense logically, phenomenologically, and pragmatically (Robert Johann, 1968: 35–53). By logical sense, I mean, "does the argument hang together?" Is it "systematic"—an organized body of interpretation and knowledge? Next, does the argument make phenomenological sense? Is it descriptive of the sense and meaning of our lives in the world, especially of the moral conduct of our sexual lives? Finally, does the argument promote practical forms and structures of individual and social living in ways that advance an orderly sense of everyday life—is it pragmatic?

The second thing that an argument ought to do is attempt to persuade, and perhaps, be persuasive. Etymologically, "to persuade" means "to advise utterly or thoroughly" as an "inducement" to "believe"—to "prevail on a person to do something."[8] To this extent, the book could be considered academically "old fashioned," since I will self-consciously and directly prevail upon the Church to receive the cosmological and theological permission to engage in new discussions and debates about

Christian sexual morality that can, in principle, say new things. A book of this length and about a topic that is more in the midstream of historical change than some others cannot hope to "advise utterly" or "thoroughly." At the same time, it can hope to be persuasive enough to promote further and more critically open conversation and to make a contribution to it.

To present an argument that intends to convince and persuade is not necessarily an attempt, as philosopher Robert Nozick puts it, to "coerce"—or "force" someone to believe (1981: 4–24). Etymologically, "convince" does have the force of "overcoming." However, what I want to overcome in this book is the cycle of innervating anxiety that afflicts the Church in its teaching about sexual morality. My general approach is to try to draw out, perhaps in some new ways, the implications of the Church's mission as a teacher in moral matters. Whether I say anything new or not is not really the issue. Rather, what finally is of concern is that the Church engage the contemporary and the new because of its own obligations of fidelity.

In any event, I remain convinced of the value of systematic argument, especially in ethics. I have been told that my arguments tend to be linear and informed by my gender. I see no particular reason to apologize for that fact as long as I am aware that there are other ways of knowing. Linear or not, I am convinced that argument is necessary in theology and ethics and that all good argument is, in one way or another, orderly and systematic. There is much contemporary debate on male and female ways of knowing and argument.[9] Such debates are important and disclose the pervasiveness of sexuality and gender at epistemological levels, a matter of no small relevance in a book of this kind. In general, the issue turns on the difference between what has been called "linear" and "contextual" ways of knowing—the difference between the grounding metaphors of "line" and "web," or network (Gilligan, 1982). My approach here is based on the conviction that system and order, making sense in the public forum, giving reasons for beliefs and views, being coherent and persuasive can and ought to be accomplished under the direction of any number of epistemological metaphors and models. The web is no less orderly than the line. All real lines have contexts, but all lines are not straight—projecting forward without curve or intersection, fracture or break. Being orderly in argument does not mean ruling out or trying to avoid the loose end, the more or less tragic unravelling that we all experience in the great dilemmas of the moral life. As I will argue, a critically adequate and effective historical consciousness will be marked with an understanding of discontinuity as well as continuity, of the cracks and flaws in the historical universe of human nature, as well as by its smooth coherence. This is no reason, however, to turn away from orderly argument that attempts to persuade in its rough coherence. An argument that accepts, when it inevitably must, the limits of thought and language and the tragedies of human existence does not become less of an argument. It is precisely because the moral life is so marked by fissures and breaks, inconsistencies and incoherences, losses and inevitable negative moral remainders, indeed by the tragic itself, that ethical and moral argument is so necessary in the first place. It is not so much perfect sense and order, or totally persuasive conviction we seek, but a "rage" after that order[10]—an ongoing pursuit of new and more responsible moral convictions.

In this sense, the book intends to be argumentative. The logical, phenomenological, and pragmatic senses I seek make anticipation of objections to my argument necessary. Thus, at times, the book will be polemical with the flavor of a disputation. Yet the success of a disputation is not necessarily winning the day by "knock down" arguments—a perfection seldom attained or even appropriately sought in ethical debates[11]—but in the understanding reached in the disputation itself. This kind of disputation—one that assumes that there is more to say than has been said[12]—is precisely what has been lacking in the Church's conversations on sexual morality, but it is precisely what the Church needs to be a more effective community of moral discourse.[13]

## On Reading this Book

I have never liked authors' directions on how to read their books. Like all writers, I will appreciate those who read my entire work in the order in which I present it. Still, the economic realities of publishing as well as the more welcome dispersal of expertise and interest make it much more difficult than in times past to direct a book to only one audience. I have divided this book into three parts entitled "conversations." In each section I had certain conversational partners in mind. In Part One's concentration on the turn to history in the modern age, I had in mind those readers who are interested in investigating a philosophy and theology of change. I remain convinced that engaging the question of change has become a major challenge, often not engaged, in the discourse of religion in general and in Christian theology and ethics in particular. Part Two is the most analytically technical part of the book and sets new ways of looking at the relationship between ethical norms and moral rules. In this section I am speaking most directly to those interested in the origins and inner working of the language of ethics. I believe that along with an inadequate understanding of change, mistakes in the analysis and use of the concepts and terms of ethics account for much of the dysfunction of the Church's debates. Along with all readers who rightfully expect the arguments of the earlier sections of the manuscript to be applied in practical ways, in Part Three I had specially in mind those who may be looking for guidance in specific areas of sexual morality. I raise again the question of historical fidelity and examine how consistent the Christian tradition has been in its moral teaching. Then, within the ordinary canons of moral theology, I offer some practical advice for consciences in specific areas of sexual behavior. In the last chapter, I call upon those who occupy positions of leadership in the denominations, both clerical and lay, to envision the Church not only as a place of doctrinal teaching and liturgical practice but also a community of moral discourse and action. I then offer a more technical overture toward a theory of rational argumentation in ethics within the context of a general moral theology of communication. The strains of communicating effectively can overwhelm institutions and communities and render them dysfunctional. Learning to speak and act together in rational ways is part of the informing ethos of care and respect that makes the gatherings of culture, society, and church possible.

# Part I.

## The Church and the Conversation of History

# 1

## Sexual Discourse and the Problem of Modernity

### The Church's Conversations on Sexual Morality

Theological discourse does not move in a straight line in the historical life of the Church. What moves a topic, issue, or problem to the center of the Church's collective mind at any given time is hard to measure. Such motivating forces can range from new and critical concerns about the meaning and practice of faith in contemporary life to accommodations of the latest intellectual and cultural trends. As I noted in the Introduction, in recent years I have become interested in the increase in the extent and volume of the Church's theological debates on sexuality in general and sexual morality in particular. Though this discussion has been marked by anxiety-ridden repression and ideological distortion, its movement to the center of the present conversation of Christian denominations is not without constructive prospect.

Anxiety, in both individuals and institutions, often signals a serious concern that something is missing: ordinary connections within the course of our lives and with surrounding and informing events are not being made. Consequently, anxiety can often be an opportunity for new discovery and insight. The Church's anxiety about the state of the modern discourse on sexual morality and about the state of its own teaching can be an opportunity for further reflection and investigation— a new search for meaning and a renewal of rational theological and moral speech that can, in principle, say something substantively new. Even though what is missing in the Church's debates undoubtedly has many dimensions, a significant missing dimension is a new and more adequate engagement of modernity in rational theological argument, particularly in ethics. The Church's problems with articulating an adequate sexual morality are symptomatic of its deeper problems with rational conversation in the modern world in general. Relating the Church's conversations on sexual morality to its situation in modernity can provide further explanation for its present deep-seated institutional anxiety about sex. It is for this reason that I have framed this examination of Christian sexual morality in the wider frame of the Church's conversation with the modern world. Removing the analyses of moral issues from their proper historical context has always led to ideological distortion. Practical moral reasoning is practiced critically only in the self-conscious reflections of history and culture. And few human phenomena are more deeply embedded in the psyches of individuals, cultures, and institutions than sex.

Since the Church generally understands sexuality and sexual morality to pertain to the fundamental exercise of Christian character, sex will always be a significant concern. However, neither this deep concern nor any perceived crisis in the present state of sexual morality are sufficient explanations for the distortions and ineffectiveness of the Church's present debates. The legitimate concern the Church must express for the state of sexual morality in the modern age cannot be adequately exercised unless attention is paid to the deeper cosmological roots of the Church's anxiety and problem. Challenges to the moral life wrought by the modern age are in many ways unprecedented in the Church's historical life. This does not mean that the Church lacks resources to respond to such problems; it does mean that such responses must be vital—must, in fact, engage the challenges of theological and moral debates at the level of their present occurrence. Unless the Church's deeper problems with the modern world are engaged self-consciously and critically, the cycle of innervating and ineffective anxiety about sex will continue.

Part One of this book concentrates on the form of the Church's current conversations on sexual morality as indicative of its problems with the historicity of theological and moral discourse and the historicity of its own life. Radical historicism and the challenges of pluralism, relativism, and conventionalism in theology and ethics are the Church's major problems with modernity and constitute *the problem of modernity* in general. The notation of "the problem of modernity" is not unique to the rhetoric of the Church, but cuts across all claims of the failure of reasoned discourse and critical argument at the end of the modern era and to a large extent accounts for the rise of the rhetoric of *postmodernity*.

### The Problem of Modernity

#### Cosmology and the Moral Life

The term modernity itself suggests the results of a critical hermeneutic exercise in the discrimination of worldviews. To discriminate a worldview is to suggest that periods of historical time—most often long periods—can be understood according to fundamental assumptions about how humans understand themselves in the entire expanse of the cosmos. To feel and understand ourselves as participants in larger and ordered locations of time and space is to see and interpret the universe as "cosmos" in the first place—a place of human location and presence, a universal world-frame for identifying ourselves as characters in a larger whole.[1]

I shall use the term "cosmology" in a broader and deeper sense than simply a systematic theory about the universe and our place in it, though eventually cosmology also performs such a task. Related to my use of the term are notions of the metatheoretic and preconceptual. In *The Critique of Pure Modernity* (1988), David Kolb offers a good summary of Martin Heidegger's description of "preconceptual understanding" and its implications for the grounding and orienting of worldviews. Kolb describes Heidegger's attack on "the supposition that concepts and propositions are the only way to structure an encounter with the world." On the contrary, "propositions select and make explicit meaning that is already lived with in another way." Therefore, "significance is found in the world in which we are always already involved" (pp. 131–32).

Understanding the role of the preconceptual introduces a point that has some importance throughout my argument. No intellect or conscience, no single event or grand discovery ever "makes" a cosmological world. However, neither are cosmologies simply forced upon us by some fate. Kolb goes on: "The world, as a texture of significance and possibilities, needs us as the 'place' where it 'happens'"—i.e., cosmologies are accomplishments of human imagination, interpretation, and understanding. "On the other hand, it is the world as a field of possibilities that solicits our projects and shapes lived time" (1988: 134).[2]

Such a preconceptual and existential dialectic between ourselves and our worlds makes cosmological discriminations very difficult. Still, such discriminations are essential works of historical study and an adequate historical consciousness. Without them, we fail to understand how we have come to think, speak, and act in certain ways and not others, and whether we have the permission, so to speak, to do any differently. The fact that history has at least phenomenological priority over the self insofar as it precedes and comes after us indicates that "our texture of possibilities is limited" (Kolb, 1988: 136). Since self-conscious historicity marks any cosmologically reflective theology and ethics in the modern age, no appeal to an ahistorical or transtemporal divine and/or metaphysical revelation of truth and right will overcome our informing dialectic of historical limit and possibility. Moral understanding and argument, and the limits and possibilities of character identification, are inevitably informed by our age. It has been a continuing problem of the Church in the modern age to understand how modernity's turn to radical historicism can be an adequate frame for faithful theological teaching and moral guidance.[3]

Seeing reality, then, as part of a relatively ordered whole, or cosmos, is itself an exercise of human interpretation grounded in prior and preconceptual experiences of time and place, location and presence. Arising then from preconceptual foundations, cosmologies orient reason and action and effect the rational frameworks upon which we weave our systematic theories about the nature of the world and our own human nature and moral character. It would be useless to try to determine precisely any narrow order of causal sequence in the fall of old cosmologies and the rise of new ones. The framework that sets a worldview occurs not from any one interpretation, theory, or event but from the entire fabric of factors that creates a paradigmatic set of assumptions about life in the world. When these assumptions no longer perform the work of cosmological ordering and location, no longer answer our necessary and practical questions of everyday life, or fail even to ask questions relevant to that life, a change occurs. Such changes are gradual and embedded in the dynamics of any particular cosmological world view from its onset. What sometimes looks like a world-changing event or complex of events is only the most proximate occasion for becoming aware of a new identification.

To speak self-consciously of the collapse of old cosmological frames is to understand the radical relativity of time and place, of rational discourse itself, and of our general quests for meaning and character identification. Such speech is a characteristic mark of the radical historicist turn in human experience emerging at the advent of modernity. A modern historicist self-understanding expects all informing cosmological worlds to have temporal duration. I am not speaking here only of particular epochs in history but of fundamental views, understandings, and feelings for and about time and place—fundamental experiences of human location and presence which, along with many other functions, ground the meaning and experience of moral character and its obligations. To talk then of modernity as a cosmological experience and view of the world is to suggest that with the birth of modernity something fundamentally new emerged to the surface of thought in western history—new articulations of human location in the universe, new experiences of time and place along with new self-understandings of moral obligation and character. This is likewise to suggest that the cosmological age of modernity has duration and may be coming to an end.

Therefore, any attempt to reflect ethically on the contemporary dilemmas of the moral life cannot avoid cosmological implication. Our challenge, and indeed obligation, pertains to the level of our critical self-consciousness. Such self-consciousness is especially necessary for a Church that is attempting to live faithfully and responsibly within a tradition spanning more than one cosmological world. To say that the character of human nature in general, and Christian character in particular, has remained exactly the same with only formal contextual differences over the expanse of history is to make a fundamental mistake. To appreciate adequately the historicity of moral character, we cannot argue that contemporary understandings of "human nature" are either essentially continuous or now largely discontinuous with the moral wisdom of the past. Cosmological and historical growth, development, and change are marked by both continuity and discontinuity. Any either/or thinking here misses the fundamental nature of the interrelation of history, ethics, and the moral life.[4]

To speak of *nature and human nature*, as has been done traditionally in ethics, is first to suggest an experience of ordered human location—of time, place, and presence—through self- and other-consciousness and the experience of intersubjective interaction. Such location and presence set the ground for the occurrence of character as the axis of the moral life. The term "nature," with or without metaphysical underpinnings, thus becomes a way of speaking about human experiences of participation and dwelling in a cosmos.[5] As we experience ourselves as being in a cosmos, we experience a relatedness and bonding with the physical world and with each other. It is from these experiences of relatedness and bonding that moral character and its ties of obligation ensue. We are now participants and moral actors on a cosmological stage and in an historical world-drama. The shape of the world-play and our part in it is intimately related to the cosmology that undergirds us with all of its cultural discriminations. Cosmology and the moral life are thus mutually intertwined. Change in an extant cosmology or world view will inevitably result in changes in our experience of ethical character and moral obligation—changes in our moral *persona*.

Nor do the challenges of understanding ourselves in historical place and time become obviated by any appeals to a supra-historical revelation. The revelations of biblical faith are fundamentally and contextually bound to place and time—to the temporal and historically embodied location and presence of God with us. Faith confessions and theological articulations are themselves finite and temporal, bounded by the cosmological views that frame them and to which they contribute.

Given the anxiety, even terror, we experience as finite beings, our longing for supra-temporal doctrinal and moral truths is understandable and probably unavoidable. However, it is not the way of a deeper biblical faith that suggests, within all the vagaries of time and place and the discontinuity and continuity of historical time and cosmological change, a more foundational certitude that the historically embodied presence of God remains with us amid the old and new, in both constancy and change (see Niebuhr, 1960).

There is a relativity here, but it is not relativism. Rather it is the universal "relatedness" of God to all that we experience at all times and places in the world—the critical relativity of a divine presence embodied amid any and all cosmologies. A Church that came to maturity in what we will call classical western cosmology cannot be limited to that cosmology for fidelity and responsibility.

Much of my approach in this book is undoubtedly motivated by a self-conscious intention to remain modern as long as I can.[6] While remaining cognizant of the so-called postmodernity theses, many of the cues and characteristics of modernity will remain present in this work: historicity, relativity, plurality, and conventionality, all couched within a certain faith that a responsible measure of truth and right can be relatively grasped by individuals and groups in any cosmological world through rational interpretation, discourse, and reflection. None of this, however, means that I will either accept all of the common self-understanding of modernity or reject all of what the past offers as wisdom to the modern world. In the classical cosmology that frames most of the Church's history we will find both wisdom and foolishness. Much of the Church's present problem with modernity, particularly in the discourse on sexual morality, concerns the challenge to see ourselves differently than in times past and is a residue of a classical problem. Indeed it was part of the classical view of history that continuity was always assumed and discontinuity always problematic. In many ways, the modern view of history has reversed that assumption.[7] Still, along with some formal continuity of the classical faith in rational theological and moral discourse, I will also stress a certain substantive continuity in modernity of the Church's classical norm of marriage.

Now in what many think of as late and moribund modernity, the Church is being pressed on all sides. In not being modern enough—in not engaging its own age—the Church is criticized for being archaic, anachronistic, and thus both inadequately faithful and ineffective in its moral teaching on sexuality. In being too modern, the Church is criticized for being equally unfaithful to its ancient and informing heritage, of becoming only another popularizer and morally rationalizing the statistical norms of the day. In a third and more overarching criticism, objections are raised when the Church continues to envision itself as a moral teacher and guide for culture and society at large, uncritically accepting a modern revision of classical notions of the value of rational and public moral argument that the end of the modern age has now supposedly disclosed as moribund. Here the growing rhetoric of post-modernity arises to question the substantive work of historically ordered reason in general. Amid all of these criticisms, the age of modernity, just as any self-consciously modern church, must now engage in a new defense of itself as a cosmological world that has now become a problem.

Certainly, to speak of modernity as a "problem" is somewhat para-doxical, since it is impossible to stand completely outside of an extant cosmological worldview in order to engage in its own analytic critique. Still, the term has some use in framing the difficulties modernity presents in ethical interpretation, analysis, and moral judgment from both a classical and postmodernist perspective. This is especially so if in fact we are now beginning to experience a transitional phase from modernity to what we can at present only euphemistically call post-modernity. While I will discuss certain aspects of the postmodernist perspective that are beginning to subtly influence the Church's teaching and guidance with respect to sexual morality, the Church's major prob-lems in the mainline denominations still concern residues of the conflict between the classical and modern ages.

This does not mean that a full engagement of postmodern criti-cisms of modernity can be postponed much longer. However, for the Church to fully engage the rhetoric of postmodernity and to understand itself when it too speaks in a postmodern vein, it must first come to terms with the remainders of its problem with modernity. More particularly, the Church must become a fully critical participant in the *modern* discourse on sexual morality. It is important to understand that cosmo-logical worlds are never skipped. If we are now in a time toward the end of modernity and poised on the brink of postmodernity, no benefit will accrue to the Church if we slide relatively unnoticed from what has been considered classical moral wisdom to a time that suggests major decon-struction in the ordered processes of reason and the identity of moral character itself. It is time for the Church to take modernity more seri-ously and constructively in its moral rhetoric of sex.

We will not like everything we find in modernity and its moral discourse; but the Church cannot hope to advance into whatever new cosmological worlds await unless it first has passed fully and self-consciously through the world in which it still, however marginally, finds itself. To fight only rear guard actions against the extant age is to rob the Church of its own part in world-making leadership, with the denominations ending up as teachers that are behind rather than leading those who are asking for guidance. In being a full participant in the critique and self-understanding of the age, we may at the same time find new possibilities for effective teaching and moral guidance. This is all the more necessary now, since in its depictions of the crisis of the so-called end of modernity, postmodernist rhetoric generally fails to meet the challenge of offering any substantive and practical moral guidance for life in the putatively new age.[8] In finally coming to terms with modernity, the Church will be better prepared for constructive leadership in whatever further cosmological worlds history has to offer. Therefore, upon the horizon of late modernity and in light of a possible contemporary period of transition to other and future ages, an historical location of the Church's present position in the current debates on sex must begin with a discussion of the major contours of the rhetoric of morality in classical western cosmology and its transition to modernity.

Classical Cosmology and the Rhetoric of Nature

In *The Idea of Nature*, R. G. Collingwood understands the classical Greek view of nature, or *physis*, as belonging to the internal and identifying reality of a thing "which is the source of its behavior" (1972: 44). F. E. Peters continues in the same vein describing the classical view of nature as an internal organizational principle that accounts for the growth process or genesis of a thing—its directional motion that guides it toward certain ends, and in later developments, purposes (1967: 158). By the time of Heraclitus, Peters argues, the Greek world had extended the idea of order from the intelligent motion of nature to the *kosmos* itself under the notion of *nomos*, or law, denoted as divine (*theios*) (1967: 108). Collingwood describes the Greek view of intelligent nature as a vital motion under the guidance of a mind or soul. It was not just ceaseless and random motion that the Greeks saw in the cosmos, or only motion that obeyed mechanistic laws, but a type of character that was "not only alive but intelligent" (1972: 3; 3–4). Thus the cosmos operated under a providence that held the secrets of the true, the right, and the good. Human character could be deflected from such purposes as could the universe; but such deflections were only temporary disorders and could be remedied by returning to the providentially ordered course. Natural tragedies, often radical in their effects, were seen similarly as more disorder than chaos. Moral tragedy was classically interpreted as the result of failures of knowledge and will, sometimes among the gods, but most often in humans. However, the negative consequences of such failures could be integrated through psychodramatic catharsis and moral instruction for the advancement of character.

Upon this experience and understanding of nature, classical ethics was shaped by a sense of ordered motion having a direction and purpose for the integration of the cosmos and human character. Greek philosophy grounded our western understanding of both the cosmos and of human nature in terms of character internally and externally directed by law, all within or under the providence of nature/divinity. Grounded by a variety of metaphysical discriminations, ethical interpretation and moral argument were archaeological expeditions to discover the values, virtues, and goods embedded in the cosmos. Even though there remained a plurality of such expeditions, it was endemic to the classical view that, despite all the irregularities and disorders apparent in the life of human beings, there was a natural and cosmological foundation for the true, the right, and the good. What was of nature and nature's law was good and right. To counter the disclosures of nature's order was to go astray. There was an intelligence and a will to the cosmos—a character. Guided by the biblical God, other gods, or by its own internal and organic dynamic, nature was a motherly intellectual and moral guide.

Collingwood suggests that the Greeks experienced an analogy between individual human beings and the world of nature. "The world of nature as a whole is then explained as a macrocosm analogous to this microcosm" (1972: 8). Such a classical moral cosmos had a double character of individuality and universality. Once the analogy was set, the moral life of an individual and society was obliged by the intelligent natural life of the universe, all brought together as a unity of character. A change in one denoted a change in the other. Ethics and the moral life were grounded in far more than individual taste or cultural and social convention. The stakes of a life of virtue were cosmological in weight and proportion. Within this sense of the whole, there was plurality but not pluralism of any modern variety. What classical cosmology held most dear was a sense of unity and foundational order that could *contain* the pluralities, irregularities, disorders, and vicissitudes of life. To bear these burdens and meet these challenges were no more than the obligations of character and the pursuit of wisdom provided for by the nature of reality divinely and metaphysically upheld.

I have concentrated, however briefly and in broad strokes, on the Greek origination of the classical cosmological vision of the world and the moral rhetoric of nature that it informed. Certainly this rhetoric was developed especially in Roman Stoic thought and later in Medieval understandings of natural law. However, by and large, such foundations for the relationship of cosmos, character, and morality were set by the Greeks and relatively sustained from the beginning of the Christian era until the sixteenth century in Western culture. These classical philosophical underpinnings framed the major contours for the foundation of the Christian tradition of sexual morality even when supernaturalistic norms were added to the Greek rhetoric of nature such as in the celebration of consecrated virginity and dedicated celibacy in the early Church.[9]

Even while concentrating on these philosophical foundations, we cannot leave out consideration of the Christian scriptures when speaking about these matters. The Bible also remains foundational for the Church's moral teachings even though its treatment of specific issues and rules of sexual behavior cannot be considered thematic. Still, it was not a unique biblical cosmology that grounded the rise of the classical Christian tradition in sexual ethics. Rather in the main, the Church historically produced its teachings on sexual morality from classical cosmological recipes, with biblical texts and references often sprinkled like pepper in an ethical stock distilled from essentially non-biblical sources. The high point of the classical tradition of Christian sexual ethics was undoubtedly the Catholic Middle Ages. And it is tempting to think that things changed radically in the Renaissance with the Protestant Reformation and its new turn to scripture and the priority of the individual believer. And yet, as I will argue, the present state of the debate across all denominations seems to indicate a relatively unusual attempt to remain continuous with the major contours and intuitions of the classical tradition of ongoing natural order in sexual morality, even when the overt arguments given are not of the classical natural law variety. It is often suggested that classical Greco-Roman cosmologies expressed radically different views of the world than the Biblical-Hebraic. Though I think such distinctions are often too sharply drawn,[10] my point here is only to suggest that by the time of the patristic age, the major contours of biblical and classical worldviews had become intertwined.

No major cosmological shifts in worldviews were required in the establishment of the classical traditions of Christian sexual ethics. As James Brundage argues in his comprehensive *Law, Sex and Society in Medieval Europe*, "Many sexual beliefs and attitudes common in medieval Europe were Christian by adoption, not by origin" (1987: 2). The basic contours of such an adoption were in place by the patristic age. "Detailed treatments of ideas about sex and a well-developed rationale to support them did not appear in Christian literature until the fourth and fifth centuries of the patristic age"—i.e., in the generation of Jerome and Augustine (1987: 2). Thus, the classical Christian tradition of systematic theological and moral argument concerning sexual morality is a product of the patristic, not the biblical age. Nor was any putatively unique biblical cosmology foundational for these arguments. Brundage suggests that the arguments of the patristic writers were in one sense both original and derivative, drawing from the understandings of their time, as well as an original recombination of ancient notions, both philosophical and religious.

> What was original in patristic sexual morality was its singular mixture of Stoic ethical ideas with ancient religious beliefs about ritual purity, supported by a theological rationale based in large part on the Hebrew scriptures. Christian sexual morality is a complex assemblage of pagan and Jewish purity regulations, linked with primitive beliefs about the relationship between sex and the holy, joined to Stoic teachings about sexual ethics, and bound together by a patchwork of doctrinal theories largely invented in the fourth and fifth centuries (1987: 3).

"Invented" may be an unfairly pejorative word here even though it is beyond doubt that classical theological doctrines were critically constructed within extant cosmological environments and cannot be drawn simply from distilled biblical texts. This, of course, does not mean that non-biblical resources make such doctrines and practices miscast or wrong. The point is that in the patristic age the cosmology of the classical secular world was finally not so foreign to the biblical "world-picture" to suggest a total corruption of Christian origins. This also does not obviate the historical and contemporary relevance of scriptural references to sexuality and sexual conduct. The entire range of biblical texts, from prohibitions of sexual behavior in specific contexts to more universal images, values, and norms can and must be part of any faithful attempt at reconstructing a contemporary and theologically grounded sexual ethic. Still, it is clear that biblical sources do not contain sustained *moral arguments* about sexuality and sexual conduct. When such systematic arguments were forthcoming in the later Church, they were built largely upon the cosmological framework of the classical Greco-Roman world.[11]

Two important contemporary implications can be gathered from this analysis. First, what is not contained in the biblical sources cannot be imported surreptitiously or uncritically. The spate of biblical references to sexual conduct, couched in either liberal or conservative exegesis, will not substitute for contemporary theological and moral argument. Even without the appellation of liberal or conservative, exegesis itself, though necessary, does not suffice for theological and moral argument. A broader hermeneutic is necessary that holds new and contemporary conversations with the biblical texts rather than stopping with exegetic reconstructions, however critical, of conversations in their original context. Second, if the major traditions of the Church's teaching on sexual morality—that is, systematic teaching as theological and moral argument—are woven upon the frame of classical cosmology, then the collapse of that cosmology will have major and foundational effects on that teaching.

The Transition to Modernity

As I have indicated, the suggestion that cosmological worlds collapse is neither histrionic nor moralistic. Worldviews do not end because they are ignorant or corrupt, nor do they explode violently without important and influential residue and remainder. Rather, cosmological worlds collapse gradually over time and for essentially pragmatic reasons.[12] Since cosmologies are born as foundational environments for identifying ourselves as human characters and moral agents in a life-world, when they cease to accomplish these tasks they will wither and eventually die. Our perennial and continuous historical inquiries after meaning, truth, and right are not being satisfied in ways that can support an identifying cosmological environment. New questions are asked and old ones asked again in new ways. Particular historical events, discoveries, and theories may focus our attention on the transition from one worldview to another, but in themselves, they are not causative.

For example, it is commonly suggested—rather moralistically—that abuses in renaissance Catholicism caused the Protestant Reformation. However, any adequate historical description of such abuses sees them as *occasions* for rather than *causes* of reformation and thereby refocuses our attention on the deeper and more radical reasons for the historical shift. The Reformation, in its deeper historical sense, was far more than a mere reform in theological doctrine or moral action. The Reformation was, rather, both a participant in and beneficiary of a transitional period of cosmological change from classical to modern. Its origins were in a transitional period between cosmological worlds. Consequently, it would be just as much an error to expect that all in Protestantism even now expresses a theology and ethic built on the framework of pure modernity as to expect that Roman Catholicism, in all of its theological reflection, is totally wedded to classical and medieval world views. After the Second Vatican Council, both Catholic and Protestant traditions have experienced curious recombinations of both classical and modern cosmologies in their debates about sexual morality, especially in the rhetoric of human nature and the search of both Bible and tradition for moral guidance. To speak, then, of the collapse of cosmologies does not mean that the residual dust of the past is not left in a contemporary age. Often such residue contains traces of continuous wisdom that can be recovered. Just as often, however, through a forced continuity of what is now discontinuous, such classical residue contributes to the confusion in the discourse of an age that must finally be engaged in its own place and time.

Collingwood dates the beginning of the critical age of transition to modernity with Copernicus (1473–1543). Collingwood is aware that this dating of the start of the transition to modernity in the sixteenth century can be confusing since its more common dating is with the rise of European humanism in the fourteenth and fifteenth centuries. Yet despite his apology for this departure from established usage, there is an important rationale involved. Because Collingwood sees the fourteenth and fifteenth centuries to be still intertwined with Platonic and Aristotelian cosmologies of nature, they remain classical. In order to indicate the transitional status commonly attributed to the Renaissance, Collingwood uses the later dating when the classical cosmological view of nature began to shift. In this scheme, Collingwood dates the beginning of modernity with the rise of historicism in the eighteenth century as originating and defining of our contemporary life-world (Collingwood, 1972: 4–5).

At the beginning of the sixteenth century, Copernicus' scientific discovery of a heliocentric cosmos challenged the classical analogy between the microcosm of human nature and the macrocosm of the nature of the known universe. The link of intelligent and willful character connecting human nature and the nature of the universe was broken. If the earth was not the center of the universe, then no intrinsic analogy could be made between the principal inhabiter of the earth— human being—and the universe itself. Thus, as Collingwood indicates, the beginning of the collapse of the classical view of nature starts with the change in the understanding of the cosmos as intelligent, exhibiting within itself an ordered rationality and directional will: in modernity "the movements which it exhibits, and which the physicist investigates, are imposed upon it from without." Consequently, the Greco-Roman view of human character, grounded in an intimate participation with an analogous character of the cosmos, was challenged. "Instead of being an organism, the natural world is a machine: a machine in the literal and proper sense of the word, an arrangement of bodily parts designed and put together and set going for a definite purpose by an intelligent mind outside of itself" (Collingwood, 1972: 5).

Copernicus, Galileo, and most scientists up to and including Newton saw no major incongruity between a mechanistic view of the universe and biblical faith in God as the intelligent maker and source of all order. As Collingwood argues, an analogy remained, but in a different arrangement. The mechanism of the universe was cast into a new analogical relation with human character. God, as the intelligent creator of order out of chaos, used the machine of the universe for moral purposes: "Everyone understood the nature of a machine.... As a clock-maker or millwright is to a clock or mill, so is God to Nature" (1972: 9). Human nature and moral agency were now to act in cooperation with the Creator in relation to an inorganic physical nature and cosmos.

However, analogies have a way of extending themselves beyond what is intended in their original use. Given life by either reason, God, or both, the intimacy of the classical analogy between humans and cosmos was substituted for a more disjunctive and less vital analogy of creation as forming and making inanimate objects for functional use. Thus both God and by extension human beings, as creators and fabricators of the universe were cast upon a lonelier more inanimate natural stage. The body of the cosmos—and later "body" in general—was separated from its creating and fabricating intelligence and mind. In the Renaissance, the cosmological stage was set for overturning the classical rhetoric of nature as an intelligent organism that contained the secrets of the true, the right, and the good as well as a stable divine depository for those secrets available for discovery by the graced human intellect.

In classical Christian cosmology, intellectual and moral character had been cast as a quest for life-wisdom deposited by God in the cosmos, which, in turn, provided clues for its discovery. Now with the relative breach between the new more mechanistic cosmos and human beings, moral character became equated with an individual agent-intellect and will. Divine and human character were now understood as maker/operators in a natural world extrinsic to them, but which they inhabited. A new mode of participation and dwelling began to emerge—a new sense of moral participation and obligation oriented around the individual moral actor. Experiences of creativity in the Renaissance were routinized under notions of artisan and artistic genius. The modern turn to the individual person and the individual conscience as autonomous and separated from nature had begun. Conscience came to be understood under a model of super-agency. The moral agent as maker, under the power of a creative conscience, could create and direct the affairs of nature and cosmos.

With the coming of the Reformation, the classical analogical and organically rational bridge that connected God, humanity, and cosmos gave way to a new biblical revelational bridge between God and the individual soul. The relatively sociological/structural cast of the Medieval world gave way to a more internal psychological one. In cosmological perspective, the creative virtuosity of the Renaissance artisan/artist was not totally foreign to the genius of internal confessions of faith of the reformers. Both highlighted the individual. Both were concerned with creating order and function in a relatively alien, sinful, and chaotic world. The challenge for Christian faith and life in this burgeoning cosmology would be to maintain this internal analogy of faith between God and the individual person now that the more organic and extrinsic analogies of nature and being were collapsing.

In the preceding I have stressed certain themes of a renaissance and early modern view of nature that were finally taken up and given new significance in the full birth of modernity in the eighteenth-century enlightenment. It ought to be recalled that any transitional period will contain great admixtures of the new and the old. For example, the same need and quest for order and regularity can be noted in this period as in the classical worldviews. If the nature of the physical and human cosmos could no longer display the ordered regularity and harmony of organic union, then to keep disorder and now chaos at bay required a new dependence on the orderliness of the divinely created human intellect and conscience and the regularity of the word of God spoken in the Bible and heard in the confidence of the moment of faith. If metaphysically grounded philosophical and theological speculation were no longer dependable, certainly one could cast one's cosmological lot with the providence of empirical science, the creative arts, and the evidence of the faith of goodly and godly people. As we have seen, the image of God was now expressed more in the creative genius of the human maker who *fabricated* the order of both nature and society, than in the speculations of metaphysicians or the incantations of mystagogic liturgies.

However, if God was, in the main, only extrinsically connected to the cosmos as its origin and first maker, eventually science rather than revealed religion would determine nature's laws whether first established by God or not. In this way, rationalistic deism presented a profound challenge to traditional religion. The intimate connection between faith and reason promoted in classical Christian cosmology would become more disjunctive, with a new and more radical combat emerging in what had previously been considered an organic and sacramental whole. In this transitional period, the seeds were sown for the later modern warfare between reason and revelation often polarized by both secular and religious positivism. In this polarization, either science and its method would claim all certainty of knowledge or religion would attempt to become more "scientific" and biblically and dogmatically positivistic in both theology and ethics. Even when the initial anxiety over the transition to the new age was overcome in new and critically modern interpretations of reason and revelation, and in the development of new critical-historical methods of biblical and doctrinal interpretation, the residue of religious, theological, and ethical positivism has been most long-standing in sexual ethics. Anxiety over the coming of modernity was exponentially increased by a renewed anxiety over sexual matters as another powerful energy and force of nature to be mastered by mind and spirit.

The Renaissance, as any transitional age, is a confusing period for cosmological discrimination. Any depiction of a trace of modernity can be countered with an equal trace of the classical world. Nonetheless, it was the Renaissance that set the stage for a cosmological shift from a moral rhetoric of organic nature to the rhetoric of individual genius and conscience whose challenge it was to *impose* order on the growing experience of historical relativity, plurality, and conventionality that would mark the modern age.

Historicist Modernity

Collingwood argues that the cosmology of modernity draws something from the classical and renaissance worldviews but differs in fundamental ways. By the eighteenth century, both organic and mechanistic analogies between the human microcosm and the cosmological macrocosm of nature gave way to the "analogy between the processes of the natural world as studied by natural scientists and the vicissitudes of human affairs as studied by historians" (1972: 9). The common demarcations of modernity as an age of relativity, plurality, and conventionality, of the boldly thinking individual, of science, technology, and finally, of an increasingly impersonal technocracy, while accurate enough, are finally encompassed and ordered in modernity's overarching historicist self-understanding. By concentrating on the studies of eighteenth-century historians, Collingwood noticed a new foundational theme for the age—a new way of dealing with "the very ancient dualism between changing and unchanging elements in the world of nature" (1972: 10).

Against the classical age, the historians argued that what had seemed unchanging in ages past was subject to change—had in fact changed (Collingwood, 1972: 10). Thus the rhetoric of historicism marked a new and more radical temperament and ushered the birth of cosmological modernity. If history and its progress also meant that fundamental and structural changes could occur in the nature of reality, then, as disclosed in the transitional Renaissance, it would seem that individuals and their reason and science—their technological control and political and moral ordering—could become the new dependability. Against this renaissance and later romanticist view, however, eighteenth-century historical study began to show that the inorganic mechanism of nature was not as manipulable as first imagined and that human intellectual, artistic, and moral genius could not in itself avoid the terrors and vicissitudes of history. No matter which analogy was used to address the wide breadth of cosmological self-understanding, being and nature were thoroughly involved with history and disclosed neither a clear and constant voice of motherly moral guidance nor an infinitely manipulable mechanism that could be directed toward clear moral purposes.

There were radical implications embedded in modernity's historicist turn even at the birth of our age. As I have argued, both the classical and renaissance worldviews bound the character of both nature and the self to a continuous experience of regularity amid the surface irregularities of life. In Christian traditions, all areas of life, including morality, had always demanded some sort of assurance that continuity in the universe could be guaranteed either through a divine deposit in nature or through the regularities of a creative intellect and conscientious will formed in and by faith. What was new was simply what had been there all along waiting to be discovered or fabricated from the given stuff of God-given nature: what seemed like radical change, even in the very fabric of nature and the cosmos was finally only an appearance. Even the reformers had argued that their reformation only seemed like a radical break from the authentic, biblical, and classical faith and that the Renaissance Catholic Church itself existed under only the appearance of fidelity. In the view of the majority of renaissance reformers, the Reformation was not a new strand of Christianity but only a recovery and re-creation of the ancient and constant identity. Protestantism was a faithful reformation rather than a radical revolution that would have been unfaithful in their minds. Catholics, of course, argued the contrary but on the same cosmological grounds. To some extent, in both classical and renaissance views what is older and closer to origins was in fact better, more authentic, and faithful. From a fully modern historicist perspective, this is the now archaic *genetic fallacy of origins*, which suggests that all radical discontinuities with the past are by and large either appearances or corruptions and that fidelity demands a return to core origins. Geneticist residues have remained influential in the theological and moral discourse of all Christian denominations.

Geneticist Residues

Despite all claims that biblical and Christian understandings of history had overcome the ancient and mythic understandings of recurring cycles, Christianity retained something of the cyclic view, at least in the priority given to origins. In this way Christianity resisted the full implications of modernity's historicist turn and its radical critique of such priority. I am not talking about general and necessary attempts to understand the past and the origins of traditions. The geneticism that has been transmitted to the modern age in the theological discourse and moral rhetoric of the Church exhibits a significant trace of the Platonic and neo-Platonic notions of exit from a former place of greater clarity, authenticity, and purity along with a constant need and moral obligation of return. Thus we are called always to judge the present in terms of the past—indeed, often with arguments rooted in the past. Even the interpretation of a linear historical frame for biblical eschatology suggests an originating deposit in the ancient past that is an adequate template for future fulfillment even when new and more critical understandings seem necessary for present guidance. Thus in terms of doctrinal and moral development, we are now only understanding more of what has always been there in the originating deposit. The biblical and Christian "answer" remains, only the questions change. Historical interpretation and the norm of historical response in the Church thus retained ancient cyclic characteristics rather than gaining the more radically modern dialectical and dialogical character wherein all questions and answers mutually change, transform, and decenter each other, and in that, become new. It is clear that such understandings of historical time directly confronted the radical and "progressive" view of history that Collingwood argues marked modernity in the middle of the eighteenth century (1972: 13).[13]

In the shift from the classical cyclic to the progressive view of history, modernity was searching for a new form of dependability—a new way to handle the question of order and change. If historical time is a progress of change, both continuity and discontinuity are real. Change is not mere appearance or a false step or detour from an originating source. One could "depend on" change, and therefore the wisdom and the burden of ethical interpretation and moral response must be shared and transmitted between and among the generations. Critical ethical and moral discourse about the values, virtues, and goods that frame individual and public character became an obligation of each generation. Modernity's historicism gave at least an implied permission that new conversations about the moral life could in principle say new things.

History as Progress in Modernity

Merely accepting a modern notion of progress over against the more ancient cyclic notions of historical return to past origins does not obviate the Church's problems with modernity. In fact, the character mark of progress in modernity is often suggested as a fundamental error of the age—a sign of the failure of the optimistic Enlightenment to account for the vicissitudes of time and history noted at the start of the age. In this sense the age has been failing since it can no longer account for itself to itself. With such a cosmological failure comes the rhetoric of the end of modernity. And indeed, if such progressive views of nature, cosmos, and history only mean the positive increase in knowledge and virtue within, as Johann Metz (1980) indicates, an "evolutionary optimism," this would indeed be so. This sort of evolutionism, taking hold most strongly in the nineteenth and early twentieth centuries, is often still the case in much of the contemporary self-understanding of modernity. Nor is this understanding of progress only an infection of secular modernity. The denominations of the Christian Church have not been immune from such theological/cultural optimism, even when we assume that we are only gaining deeper insights into the wisdom of our past. Certainly, from any number of sources, this sort of optimistic triumphalism is now being questioned.[14]

However, despite often trenchant critiques of modernity and the modern Church, questions remain for this genre of the Christian theological critique of Enlightenment modernity. Even if the Church's liaison with modernity has led to intellectual and spiritual failure, can we in fact simply remove ourselves from this cosmological body? Can cosmologies simply be exchanged without significant risks of naive illusion or retreat from all power and influence—a retreat often attended with self-congratulation at this self-styled purification of our faith? Or has the Church entered into only formal relations with modernity rather than now having been substantively changed by modernity in our own self-understanding? I have argued that we do far more than merely inhabit cosmological worlds, but rather are informed and identified by them. Even in Third World cultures, the substantive and identifying influence of modernity has not been prevented or even postponed by some putative standard of original simplicity in faith and life. Finally, and most importantly, if the Church has been and will continue to be substantively transformed by its own cosmological age, are we so certain that what modernity often says of itself is all there is left to say about the modern world? In terms of the modern age, has our ecclesiastical and moral discourse entered too quickly into a new rhetoric of crisis and dilemma between fidelity and contemporaneity without engaging again in a full critique that sees new possibilities for faith and action along with the now predictable catalogue of cosmological failures? The rhetoric of crisis ought to be engaged carefully, especially where there is no discernible exit. In light of this, David Kolb states a useful strategy: "the refusal to take as final the categories of modernity's standard self-description" (1988: xi). To understand the modern progressive view of history, then, a deeper probe is required into the broader cosmological context of modernity.

First, it is necessary to understand the novelty of the change in the modern age's understanding and experience of historical time compared to the classic vision. I have argued that the modern world was born when the visions of the classical age no longer accounted for the experiences of contemporary life. New questions were not adequately addressed by old answers. If one could no longer depend on the past, then turning toward the future was understandable. As Ernest Gellner suggests, eighteenth-century Enlightenment modernity captured a new form of "World Story." The historical temper of the modern age was one of "upward sloping, and, on the whole self sufficient. Its salvation was endogenous" and the modern commitment to progress based on a "kind of intramundane destiny" (1978: 9; 3–4).

As Gellner notes, there was a certain charm in the promise of salvation in the new rather than in the retrieval of past origins. The growth of science, technology, and industry marked a period of unsurpassed progress in Western culture in comparison with past ages and other cultures. In the nineteenth century, Darwin's evolutionary biology was seen as a further verification of such progress. Along with these charms, an analogy of progressive and evolving destiny fit perfectly with the growth of middle-class culture: "The period of the belief in progress was also, notoriously, a bourgeois period" with middle-class life being "essentially a *career*" (Gellner, 1978: 13)—an equal mark of modernity's common self-understanding. Like the advancements of bourgeois life, history was now marked with a sense of growing experience and expertise. For philosophy and rationalist theology, "the problem of the relativity of belief and value is overcome.... Though values and ideas differ, they form a continuous series, such that each later set encapsulates, per-petuates and transcends all earlier ones." (Gellner, 1978: 14) In moder-nity, the evolutionary progress of *the spirit of history* accounted for both the continuity and discontinuity of knowledge, belief, and morality. Physical suffering and evil could also be accounted for without the unbearable strains of classical theodicy as good or ill fortune finally subsumed into an inevitable and essentially positive progress. Gellner concludes: "The World-growth theory justifies this world in terms of this world" (1978: 14).

Gellner presents three objections to this understanding of historical entelechy; i.e., growth and development according to the internal form of time and history. Logically, only to place something—in this case the historical age of modernity and its progress—in an ordered and devel-oping series in comparison with what has come before is not to explain it much less to justify it (1978: 15; 15–32). Thus the evolutionary progres-sive view of historical time does not fulfill the primary cosmological obligation to explain, and indeed, to justify the age to its members. For example, few are persuaded, logically or ethically, of either moral pro-gress or decline (though this approach is often implicit in the modern discourse) by a simple comparison of change in sexual mores, customs, and habits with former days. As Gellner indicates, a story about growth is not an explanation, or much less, a justification of growth (1978: 15). To be logically and historically coherent, any argument that intends to persuade the Church of its permission to say something new about sexual morality will have to do much more than simply argue on the basis of changes in statistical norms of behavior.

Gellner terms his second complaint against evolutionary progres-sivism a factual "moral objection." In effect, this is an objection "to the moral use of the global entelechy doctrine," since "it is hard to conceive of anyone subscribing to the doctrine without employing it as a moral premise. Conversely, to attack the moral use of it is to attack the doctrine itself" (1978: 21). In this century, the objection to the crass use of the doctrine of global political and economic progress to justify all manners of moral horror is well-known and easy to advance. However, an equally necessary moral objection pertains to its more subtle adoption as the doctrine of the progress of the majority. In modernity such a doctrine has been most clearly expressed in utilitarian moral philosophy and contains a very questionable assumption that the progress of the majority even-tually and over time entails the significant progress of all minorities. Related to the partiality of the doctrine of progress toward the majority, Gellner also notes an objection to the implied partiality of time. In the doctrine of history as positive progress, in what temporal dimension is such progress to be determined: "Is it the victor of the decade, the generation, the century" (1978: 21)?

These problems of moral partiality raise Gellner's final "factual objection." The cultural pluralism that modernity itself discloses suggests that "the world no longer looks as if progress were either continuous or endogenous" (1978: 28). For example, what counts as progress in Western culture may not be experienced as such in non-Western cultures. The cultural pluralism that also marks modernity challenges the notion of a continuous strand of evolutionary progress defined only in Western cultural terms.[15] Exhibited in this sort of radical pluralism is the cosmological strain in modernity to account for itself to itself—a strain that leads some to indicate a fundamental and internal logical crisis that gives rise to forecasts of the coming of the new age of postmodernity.

However, a counter can be made that sociologically and culturally the political-economic "victory" of Western modernity is complete, with non-Western culture inevitably becoming increasingly Westernized—becoming increasingly subject to the lure of evolutionary progressivism. If this is so, and without enthusiasm I am more often than not persuaded that it is, despite the ongoing tragic and violent conflicts of modernity with remnants of traditional cosmologies, Gellner's last factual objection is only transformed into a question about modernity's ability to deliver what it promises and to make good on what the majority of humankind has come to expect—that is, the internal cosmological and logical crisis of sense and meaning becoming an external and moral crisis in verification and legitimation. Gellner concludes:

> Just how reliable, simply as factual predictions, are those prognoses of victory which are intended to also persuade morally? (Answer: not at all. In other words, do not lose your soul in order to gain the whole world—for you will not even receive your price. Our devils, unlike Faust's, are in fact quite incapable of delivering that with which they would tempt us. If they could, our virtue might well falter.) (1978: 21)[16]

Thus, historical time as evolutionary and optimistically progressive does not finally stand to logical, moral, or factual objection. Still, much of the lure of positive progressivism and the Enlightenment's priority of the future and the new comes from deep experiences of the inadequacy of the traditionalist cosmologies. Certainly no rehearsal is necessary of the sins of traditionalist approaches to the priority of historical origins. What has been offered as universal nature has all too often been only Western, white, male, heterosexual, and Christian. Even so, cosmologies should not be judged in an overly moralistic manner, though the entire variety of sins and virtues are committed within any cosmology. Cosmologies are finally judged in their function—how they account for life in the world, how they answer the very questions they themselves promote. The move to a progressive sense of time, even in its evolutionary dimension, was a way of dealing with new questions of stability and change, of newfound individuality and the relativity, plurality, and conventionality brought on by the critical engagements of intellectual, political, and moral life. Historical progressivism provided a new framework for order and the ordering of nature when traditionalist cosmologies became dysfunctional. Individuals, cultures, and societies were now connected to the totality of time and nature through an experience of progress that attempted to explain the past in terms of its development toward an open and optimistic future. Cultures, nations, and societies were participating in an evolving divine-human drama.

This rationale for the modern vision of positively evolving history and the moral progress of the new, however, does not adequately account for the vicissitudes of late modern history. This particular and often pervasive sense of history as progress has become as materially undependable and terrifying as the organicism of the classical period and its burdens as unbearable as those of the moral virtuoso of the Renaissance. Gellner's summary of objections stands:

> World growth stories will not do.... They will not do because entelechies are pseudo-explanations; because trends do not dictate norms, even if trends were clearly discernible, which they are not; and because to the newly emancipated majority of mankind, history does not even look like an entelechy (1978: 32).

Consequently, if evolutionary progressivism and its rationalistic optimism were all that could be made of modernity's notion of progress, then the verification and legitimation of modernity as a cosmology would indeed be at an end both intellectually and morally. In matters of sexual morality, as well as in all matters of faith and life, the Church would understandably begin to look for other frames of discourse from antimodern to postmodern. Fidelity and contemporaneity in sexual morality would be opposed to each other and the Church would have every right and obligation to pursue a brief against modernity.

## The Church's Brief Against Modernity

### Antimodernist and Postmodernist Discourse

In the *antimodern mode*, the Church essentially attempts to re-create among its members ways of belief and life of former worlds, or convince its membership that living faithfully must be radically different from living ordinarily in the modern world. I will discuss both of these modes of discourse under the moral rhetoric of *nostalgic return* and *neo-sectarian withdrawal*. Since postmodernity necessarily suffers as a euphemism, a truly *postmodern mode* of moral discourse for the Church is hard to gauge. I will discuss one possible strand as an *aestheticist* moral rhetoric that promises escape from the crisis and problem of modernity itself. Even though all of these forms of moral rhetoric are present in the Church's discourse on sexual morality, I will find none of them adequate as a response to the "problem of modernity." The hope in modernity that finally informs this book rests in our ability to avoid a modernist under-standing of evolutionary progressivism while still maintaining an historicist view of time and history. Consequently, I will argue that with a new and more critical understanding of its own modernity, the Church's engagement of new conversations about sexual morality that can in principle say new things would also be an exercise of the Church's obligation to be faithful in the age in which it finds itself.

In the context of moral argument, the rhetoric of the failure of modernity concerns, most specifically, the failure of the Enlightenment project of the progress of rational discourse. As I have indicated, the responses to this so-called failure run the gamut from nostalgic attempts to return to the rational discourse of past worlds; the neo-sectarian rendering of whatever worlds of discourse that occupy us as smaller and thus more coherent and putatively more faithful; or more radically, the aesthetic quest for a release from the deadly bonds of rational argument to a freedom of artistic-moral practice. Such responses can be ordered generally as *nostalgic, neo-sectarian,* and *aestheticist.*

Most often the Church's conversations on sexual morality are centered in an antimodernist discourse of nostalgic return to and repeti-tion of past modes of moral rhetoric and argument—argument whose coherence and persuasiveness are rooted in worlds of sense and meaning which no longer survive as effective guides to practical conduct. Imaged essentially upon the horizon of the past, the antimodernist discourse of faithful nostalgia becomes repetitive in the denominations' statements on sexual morality. At best, such statements contain a sophisticated repeti-tion of the arguments of past worlds. At worst, such statements are merely specious arguments by repetition. Nonetheless, even in this type of antimodern moral rhetoric, the Church is still understanding itself as a conversational partner with modernity—indeed still interested in the state of sexual morality in the modern world.

However, a new type of antimodernist rhetoric is now emerging among the denominations. Neo-sectarian rhetoric is growing in the contemporary Church with a seductive promotion of a form of rational theological and moral discourse of the faithful remnant of Christians who intend to live as modern people within the biblical injunction of being in but not of the world. In this approach, Christian sexual morality is not only substantively different from the morality of the world in which it finds itself, but formally different as well—that is, judged within ecclesiastical worlds of discourse and action that are disjunctive from modernity and without modernity as a major conversational partner.

I have called this approach "neo-sectarianism" to distinguish it from the more classical varieties of sectarianism in the Christian traditions. Essentially, the difference between the forms of traditional and *neo*-sectarianism pertain to the practice of "withdrawal" from contemporary culture. Neo-sectarianism calls for a more psychological and personal moral withdrawal from aspects of contemporary life deemed threatening rather than the more literal social, political, and cultural withdrawals of traditional sectarians. Because of this leisured selectivity, neo-sectarian ecclesiology in the modern Church remains bourgeois and class bound.

At first glance, the biblical warrants for such an approach have great appeal to many, especially for those who spend the majority of their life and work within the institutional confines of the Church. Yet it remains highly questionable that such a new sectarian option for articulating a practical moral life for Christians whose daily lives are not so ecclesiastical is responsible. We can question as well whether the ecclesiology of becoming a faithful remnant or "resident alien" underlying such rhetoric is an adequate theological rendering of a Church called forth biblically to be in and for the world.[17]

Finally, at the margins of the Church's moral rhetoric we can only watch, with some dismay, the emergence of a postmodern aestheticist discourse that seeks, in various ways, a kind of spiritual release from the bonds of finite, error-prone, sinful, and violent reason. Undoubtedly, modernity inherits an enlightenment faith in reason that has claimed too much—a rationalism itself involved in the ancient hubris of being self-creating and tending to diminish and negate every other who is not in conformity with the boldly thinking self, culture, or nation.[18] However, this is not the whole story of reason and moral argument in the modern age. Rational argument can be cast in ways that make it more critically aware of its own limits and more respectful of other partners and views. I will argue that a new commitment to this more historically critical form of rational discourse and argument is precisely what is called for in the face of threats by a more impersonal, narrowly self-contained, and fragmented technocratic ethos. The abuses of reason are not finally resolved by a new release of the aestheticist spirit of unknowing.

In the remainder of Part One, I will argue that when framed in a nostalgic, sectarian, or aestheticist way, the rhetoric of the Church on sexual morality will be neither persuasive nor effective. I will develop further my argument that such moral rhetoric finds its roots in deep misunderstandings of the nature of the Church itself and our obligations of fidelity. Even in a book about a particular aspect of the moral life, it is important to point out that not all failures to reach rational consensus are the result of disagreements about particular content and conclusions. Consensus first has to be attained about the formal nature of the conversation in question, its type and internal functional dynamics, whether it is appropriate or not, and whether it has any prospects at all of coming to a fruitful end, one that promotes understanding and frames critical judgments that have effects in the world. And even though I think that a nostalgia for past worlds of theological and moral coherence and persuasion still orders mainline denominational teaching on sex more than any other mode of moral debate, all of these failed models, often in strange admixtures, are growing in their negative influence upon the Church's present ability to discuss critically matters of sexual morality. I will conclude this chapter with a more thorough description of this typology of failed conversations the Church is now employing in its brief against the modern discourse on sexual morality and engage in a critique of each type, now re-ordered more specifically as *the new sectarianism, postmodern aestheticism* and *melancholic nostalgia*.

The New Sectarianism

Any ecclesiology of worldly engagement or cultural and societal transformation is not adequately maintained in neo-sectarian rhetoric. Here the shape of the Church's conversation itself changes to one engaged by a faithful remnant who work to develop a coherent discourse on sexual morality for Christians alone. Such moral rhetoric is most often cast upon the horizons of the Christian narrative story that, in its telling and ritualization, is relatively separated from the stories and rituals of secular society. I do not mean to suggest that narrative and liturgy are not

foundational in measuring the Church's theological and moral obligations in this or any other age. And certainly they are fundamental parts
of the horizons of remembrance and anticipation required in any
adequate Christian moral argument. However, what is troubling is the
sense that Christian narrative(s) and the use of Christian symbols and
rites of worship can be so easily distilled from the cosmological worlds
in which they are told and engaged. In the new sectarian discourse, there
is a strong sense that the Church's modern conversations about the
meaning and practice of Christian faith and life are not finally to be
extended to modernity itself, or that it is appropriate or even faithful to
do so. The attempt is to narrow and thus control modern challenges of
sense, meaning, coherence, and practical effectiveness. In the retelling of
our own story and in our liturgical practices, being a Christian in sexual
or other matters is construed as being fundamentally different from the
rest of modernity. In telling a radically different story, we become, in
effect, radically different characters. The major opponent of this new
sectarian rhetoric is most often cast as an enlightenment liberalism
whose optimistic rationalism suggests the modern world can and ought
to be rationally engaged and transformed. To engage the world in this
way, so the modern sectarian approach goes, is to accept false criteria for
a faithful theology and ethic. The ethic of Jesus is always compromised
by the ethic of the world. For rational speech in Christian ethics, the
modern world is not a constructive partner in the Church's conversation.

Certainly in sectarian rhetoric of all sorts, there is an important
dimension of prophetic confrontation of the Church's penchant for false
accommodation and theological and ethical dilution (see H. R. Niebuhr,
1951). However, even if one chooses to take little notice of the uncritical
priority given to origins displayed in sectarianism in general, the question would still have to be asked whether the neo-sectarian approach is
as close to the origins and contemporary needs of the faith as is often
suggested. The theological question at issue here, as it is in all of the practical moral discourse of the Church, is finally an ecclesiological one.
What is the nature of the Church and its relation to the worlds of its own
dwelling—worlds that inevitably and foundationally frame moral questions, problems, and dilemmas? Thus the fundamental question that
must be asked of the new sectarianism is how Christians in any age of
mass society are to understand their identity as formed only ecclesiasti-
cally. No matter how painful it may be, when the Church is truthful, it
gives up all understanding of itself as a sole maker of the world. When
it is more truthful still, it gives up the correlative idea that it can "make
itself" through telling a story that is not inextricably intertwined with the

story of its own age.[19] The narratives and symbols the Church has always used to inform its own identity have always been intertwined with the speech, symbols, and practices of the ages in which it has dwelled. Therefore, Christians will not remain unaffected by the sexual symbols, customs, and practices that go on around them and are, in part, made by them. The challenges of Christian sexual responsibility cannot be separated neatly from the same challenges of the so-called secular age that we not only inhabit but that is also intimately part of our identity. Any new sectarian discourse on sexual morality engages in something of the melancholic nostalgia noted previously but without the same dimensions of worldly engagement and transformation implied in any ongoing complaint against modernity. The new sectarianism does not complain against modernity for transforming purposes but by and large only to justify its own dynamic of separation and release from modernity.

Insofar as we are experiencing intellectual and moral crises, the new sectarian rhetoric is initially appealing and is even seductive as a way out of the current malaise of moral debate about sexuality. In its most extreme form, the new sectarianism suggests that the Church's involvement with the world, though necessary in part and finally unavoidable, is inevitably corrupting and not part and parcel of faithful character identity. It seems at first glance ironic that such radical rhetoric does not, as it did in times past, promote more literal political and societal withdrawal. However, with further investigation we see that the withdrawal proclaimed is more psychological—pertaining to internal and particular needs for personal self-understanding and identity. In the new sectarian view, the Church's story of its own life in general, and now of its sexual moral life in particular is in this sense radically disjunctive from the rest of the world. Thus, an adequately Christian sexual morality must be formed more singularly and personally on the basis of unique biblical and historical narratives of the Christian story and the grounding images and symbols of the Christian liturgy and sacraments. In this way, Christian sexual morality can become rooted in a separated and isolated Christian community of story and liturgy. However, even with initial success in its psychological, epistemological, and moral "separation," what such a neo-sectarian model does not account for is how the vast majority of "secular Christians"—those in the greatest need for guidance in sexual matters—are, in the long term, to live in the world in this overly "churchly" way. Furthermore, the fact that such a community does not set itself apart in the more radical ways of its more traditional sectarian predecessors leads to an almost irresistible lure of becoming satisfied with mainly an internal and self-approving rhetoric.

There is a legitimate sense of the unique as "special" in Christian ethics, but it is neither singular nor absolute, nor can it be based on any ahistorical and structural abstraction from the cosmologies that have not only accidentally but substantively informed Christianity in all of its ages. The unique quality of Christian character identification comes more by way of a *phenomenological dimension*—an identifying communal biographical heritage and historical course of life—that cannot be separated completely from the full material-history of its ongoing occurrence. Thus the Church, so historically and sacramentally embodied in the materiality of culture and society, experiences both continuity and discontinuity with wider secular worlds. If the Church's narrative stories are to function as ways of informing Christian character and identity, then we must read and listen to more inclusive stories of how our own *internal* confessions and self-understandings are always framed by the *external* stories of others—those different from us who challenge our penchant to claim that we have, so to speak, given birth to ourselves.[20]

Such criteria of inclusive expansion rather than narrow reduction must be applied even to the Church's own narratives and rituals as well. Christians gathering to celebrate the Eucharist, Holy Communion, or the Lord's Supper in the catacombs, or in the great cathedrals of Medieval Europe, or in Elizabethan England, or in the trenches of World War One, or in suburban North America, or in base communities in Latin America do not tell the exact same story or engage the ancient symbols in exactly the same way. There is certainly continuity here, but there is discontinuity as well. Such celebrations are not only internal exercises of a separate self-identification, but are also identifying statements about the meaning of life in the worlds in which we find ourselves—worlds that are also part of us and our biographical heritage. Consequently, over arching cosmologies, as well as their particular and plural cultural and societal manifestations, affect such liturgical celebrations and their meaning and implication for moral responsibility and action. Christian worship is far more than an internal act of self-identity for Christians who are somehow temporarily removed from the worlds they inhabit. Celebrated now in the context of modernity, Christian worship is a modern act—one that either advances the meaning, truth, and right of life in this age or does not. Christians do not liturgically celebrate marriage, for example, only because our forebearers did so, or only because we want to reiterate what marriage means for Christians, but because we also want to make a statement about the meaning of sexual and social relations in general, with all of their joys and vicissitudes, possibilities and limits. In this sense, liturgical, theological, and ethical statements about modern marriage are statements about modernity itself.

To call liturgy public worship is not only to suggest that it is a public and communal act of the Church's internal life. Liturgy is also a public act that participates in cosmological world-making—an act that is now performed in the cosmological environment of modernity and is itself a modern act. That such a claim for our liturgy is often more an ideal than a fact is clear. But if liturgy is to function as a ground of contemporary Christian moral life, then its cosmological implications must guide its form and substance. Paradoxically enough, such an understanding of the public world-making intention of Christian liturgy is closer to our ancient understandings of the daily life and death implications of worship than certain contemporary geneticist views that facilely assume the priority of older meanings and forms of liturgical celebration, or of the new sectarianism that tends to insulate Christian liturgy from the challenge of wider worlds of sense and meaning.

If Christian liturgy is to have foundational implications for the moral life in the worlds in which we find ourselves, it must symbolize and articulate modernity in a critical way. Certainly it is easier for us to think of ourselves celebrating an originating age of putative innocence and purity than a modern age of horror and rampant immorality. However, in this context, "to celebrate" means to remember and anticipate, "to frequent" our ancient stories and symbols in our present historical situation and to be grateful that they are still "famous"—can still be spoken about—because they continue to have something meaningful and truthful to say. To recognize our own present possibilities and limits, virtues and sins is the mark of vital and contemporary liturgy. Liturgy is as much a remembrance of failure as success, as much an anticipation of pain as joy—a remembrance of the inevitability of sin amid the continuing possibilities of grace. Christian narrative and ritual cannot be adequately maintained as a world-making praxis by attempting to separate the language and symbols of worship from the cosmological worlds in which they are invested with meaning. As our surrounding worlds of meaning change, so too will the meaning of our narratives, symbols, and rituals.[21]

More particularly, if liturgy is to function formatively for a Christian sexual ethic, then its symbols and practices must be open to challenge and possible transformation by the meaning and values experienced in the sexual lives of contemporary Christians. Again, it is not just crass statistical measures of behavior that will challenge the Church in its liturgy and moral teaching but theological and moral discourse that critically articulates responsible sexual meaning and behavior in contemporary life. If new ways of sexual interpretation and behavior can be sustained in theological and moral arguments that are both faithful remembrances of the past and effective anticipations of the future then, under necessary canons of pastoral prudence, liturgical rites and symbols ought to be initiated to incorporate and support these new rules of life.

Many of these same points can be made with respect to a Christian story that, in the new sectarianism, is somehow disconnected from the story of the worlds in which Christians find themselves. If narrative is to function adequately as a frame and praxis of character identification, then we must be open to and make thematic the wide diversities of human stories including those that pertain to sexuality and sexual practice. No individual or group can tell a single and isolated story, much less only an anachronistic one. Self-identity and group identity also depend on a wide diversity of stories from the entire expanse of historical experience and environments, including the contemporary. We often speak in a mistaken and falsifying dichotomy of subject and object, spirit and body, inner and outer, and the like. In such dichotomous speech, environment seems like only an external repository wherein the substantive self only accidentally dwells. Thus the story of that *substantive self* is told with only accidental overtures to the cosmological environments in which it lives. My argument throughout is to suggest that such environments have foundational and substantive implications for what is often mistakenly understood as only an *internal* story. In this sense, the cosmological and cultural environments of the Church are neither accidental nor only "external," but foundational for what is commonly termed "self-identification."

The stories of the modern world —in First, Second, and Third World varieties, Western and non-Western—are now intrinsically part of the Christian story, as are the stories of the ancient world, the medieval and renaissance worlds, and future worlds yet to come. Consequently, there is simply no pure and historically segmented story Christians can tell to ground a sectarian ecclesiology and ethic that is substantively removed from the story of modernity itself, in all of its complexity. Furthermore, the sexual lives of contemporary Christians, for good and for bad, is now part of the Church's story and must ground the denominations' continuing conversations with modernity about sexual morality. Any argument that the Church engages with modernity about sexual morality is finally also an argument with itself. Such conversations must include the variety of interpretations of sexual meaning and behavior that are extant in both modern culture and the Church.

More particular to our discussion, the story of heterosexuality—of happy and successful marriage and family—is not the full, modern Christian story of sexuality and sexual morality. Stories of accepting and supporting Christian communities and congregations that ameliorate the strain of moral dilemmas, no matter how much desired, are not the total story of the Christian Church either historically or currently. To be faithful, the Church must stop telling partial stories and begin to tell more complete and truthful stories of its own moral life and of the prospects for responsible and effective engagement in the foreseeable future. Even though I will present a more comprehensive discussion of the implications of H. Richard Niebuhr's *The Meaning of Revelation* for my project in the next chapter, his categories of "internal" and "external" history can be introduced here (1960: 59–66). My interpretation of Niebuhr suggests that the mere telling of an internal self-confessional story by the Church—"internal history"—is not enough for its self-identity. Rather the more public and material-historical "external history" of the Church—how the Church affected and continues to affect larger nonecclesiastical worlds is also necessary for its own internal identity. If we extend these categories, we can see that what we say of ourselves in terms of our own self-identity must be dialectically engaged with what others say of us—what others say has happened to them because of us.

My use of Niebuhr's categories are not exactly the same as his. Though eventually highlighting the importance of *the other* in the event of moral character, Niebuhr argues that internal history is foundationally initiating for character-identification. However, I find narratives of character-identity of individuals and groups in terms of this "external other" to be more phenomenologically initiating and historically compelling. Certainly, the identity of the Church in "first worlds" cannot be confessed without the completion of our self-narration *told to us* by Second and Third World cultures; similarly, stories of white males are relatively completed only when told by people of color and women—the stories of Christians completed by Jews and other "non-Christians," heterosexual by homosexual persons and so on.[22] In the same vein, if heterosexual marriage is to remain normatively identifying in the sexual morality of the Church, then it can only do so through critical conversations with those who are not married and not heterosexual. In this way heterosexual marriage as the Christian norm for sexual normality will find its identifying strengths as well as its limits—will have the "rest of its story" told.

We come to self- and character-identification through the primary call and challenge of the other. What seems so internal and private as a confessional story of identification is also external, phenomenologically and cosmologically public—dependent, in fact, on the experiences of those who are different from us and who decenter us from our own self-contained confessions.[23] If, in the progressive spirals of history, the story of modernity both contains and decenters the ancient and traditional Christian story of classical cosmology, then the praxis of a fully critical narration of modernity is necessary for the Church's contemporary identity, self-understanding, and faithful confession. The story of the Church's efforts to articulate a faithful sexual morality must also be engaged from the perspective of those who find themselves currently outside of but affected by the origins and major development of the Church's sexual teaching. Insofar as these traditional teachings have been mainly formed by men, this decentering praxis would include women. Insofar as the norm of the Church is now, as I will argue, heterosexual marriage, it would include sexually active unmarried and homosexual persons. Insofar as the teachings have been Western-European in origin, non-Western cultures will also have to be included.

In the new sectarianism's penchant for an insular and mainly internal Christian confessional narrative and liturgy, it seems that Christians, as *a faithful cosmological remnant* are becoming tired of their journeys through history, journeys that have been longer and more arduous than we ever imagined, tired of trying to transform a world that simply refuses to be transformed. Certainly such approaches are understandable in a century that began with such a gilded optimism of reason, science, and the technological control of our political-economic life only to be cast into the despair of the Great War. The terror of that war was recapitulated and increased in the next world war and its holocausts. Since then, there have been more wars, more genocides and internecine destruction—still cast upon the possibility of thermonuclear danger. After Freud, none of the recitation of the death-dealing of modernity can be easily separated from our sexuality. The drive to death and destruction of modernity and its frenetic quests for life in the contemporary sexual revolution are certainly intertwined.[24] Paradoxically, in response to this, the new sectarian "theo-logic" seems somewhat akin to forms of modern technocratic and functionalist reason in its questioning of why the Church should risk the corruptions of this bloody modern age to our own internal working and systemic function. Thus, so the argument goes, if the Church is to engage the moral discourse of modernity at all, it ought to do so from a distant perspective of the witness of a faithful ethical remnant.

Even in an overview of the new sectarian rhetoric, this motif of retreat cannot be avoided as a typification. However, a retreat from modernity is not only not possible for contemporary Christians, it is also not faithful. The rationalism and antirationalism, the death, destruction, anxiety, repression, frenetic sex, and all that goes into the modern age are now intimately part of the identity of both Christians and the Church. Having a conversation with modernity about sexual morality is finally having a conversation with ourselves. Being faithful Christians amid the inextricably intertwined Church and world means being willing to engage all that goes into the age in which we find ourselves. We will not approve of all that we find in our age or in ourselves; we must, however, accept it as part of our own, however guilty, identity. If any ethical transformation or moral change is possible, it will begin with this first phenomenological acceptance and religious confession.

Postmodernist Aestheticism

Such failure of reason and rational argument so clearly revealed in the death and sex of modern life, gives rise to a sense of an even more radical cosmological crisis and an attendant motive of aestheticist release from the standard order of rational discourse and argument and all boundaries upon our efforts to create and interpret ourselves.[25] Unlike the antimodernism of the contemporary sectarians who seek new forms of moral reasoning rooted only in the unique Christian story and liturgy, the postmodern, and at times, quasi-mystical aestheticists seek a way of release from the tyranny of rationality as a form of oppressive ordering in general. Certainly there is both sophistication and cause in many manifestations of this aestheticist way of unknowing, both in the mystical traditions of the Church, in various forms of negative theology, and in contemporary philosophical and literary proclamations of the deconstruction of the Western tradition of rational discourse—a tradition that has made false and often deadly promises to disclose and enforce the secrets of the true, the right, and the good. However, crucial questions must be asked of the adequacy of the deconstructionist description of the rational/moral crisis of the modern age and thus of the aestheticist release proposed from the bounds and sometimes terrors of such a rationalist history. Along with this we must also ask whether a general understanding of freedom and creativity as *release* from the bonds of orderly reason is an adequate rendering of either art or religion.

However critical or uncritical it may be, human reason is more than the intellectual history of its own speculations, interpretations, and theories and the political and moral practices they engender. Critical reason need not entertain a posture that there is something "out there" to discover as indicative of classical forms of metaphysical and "logocentric" reason; nor does critical reason necessarily imply that the self and its meditations are the certain foundations and source of human reflection as indicative of forms of renaissance and early modern Cartesian rationality. Furthermore, we need not ground our rational enterprise upon a mind that "contains" transcendental categories of reflection that can be known in the acts of perception and mirror categorical imperatives in the moral life, as in Kantian reason. Still less is it necessary to consider the *Geist* of history, and history as *Geist*, as progressing in its dialectical resolutions of antinomies as in Hegelian reason. The same lack of compulsion must finally be brought to bear upon any number of twentieth century rationalities in the physical and social sciences and humanities, including theology, that either accept, transform, or reject what has gone before and attempt to start ordered rational inquiry anew. Despite all the wisdom and foolishness disclosed in any and all of the historical forms of human reasoning and argument, what finally grounds rationality and what has brought humanity to its not altogether noble state of modernity has been "the question"—the experience of wonder and the praxis of inquiry.

To call human beings rational is to say that to be human is to engage in communal material inquiries from within given cosmological worlds, including the worlds of all other questioners. All human inquiries, then, are grounded in substantive practical, political, and moral interests—interests of body as well as of soul and mind. In light of these material human interests, we ask questions, search for sense, coherence, meaning, and truth in the particular contexts of everyday life (see Jürgen Habermas, 1971). To ask questions is to begin inevitably plural searches for answers, however tentative, limited, and incomplete—answers that inevitably lead to other questions and other answers in a moving and decentering spiral of the historical pursuit of wisdom. Certainly it is true that in our modes of rational speech, we have too often forgotten, at our peril, the corrigibility of such pursuits. Yet, such a forgetfulness of the limits and liabilities of rational inquiry, though deadly at times, can never be total. No matter how radical the critique of any arrangement of rational answers to substantive questions, no matter how moribund any particular intellectual tradition, the radically critical question always offers an invitation to begin a new tradition of human inquiry not totally discontinuous with what it criticizes. It is this praxis of the dialectic of question and answer that gives human history its shape as a metaconversation, indeed, as a metanarrative that frames rational discourse as the measure of meaningful time.

The story of reason is not told only by systematic theories, speculations and arguments. Emerging first and foremost as inquisitive conversations, reason takes any variety of forms and shapes and can be understood under any number of secondary metaphors. As I will argue,

it is indeed possible to view rational discourse in modernity, and the life
of reason itself—including the rhetoric of morality—through the root
metaphor of dialogical conversation. Shaped finally by the continuous
motion of history as a narrative progress of decentering spirals, critical
historical conversations decenter one another and bring the whole
human rational enterprise forward. To exercise reason critically, then, is
to be embodied and finite human inquirers who know the wisdom that
there is no single "answer" but rather an ever-expanding dialectic of
questions and answers—an ongoing inquisitive dialogue with both past
and future that is definitive of what it means to be rational and to have
rational conversations.

Casting rationality and rational argument in terms of passionately
engaged conversations about a common though diverse material world
suggests another wisdom, likewise seldom attained among philosophers, theologians, and moralists. Such a praxis upon a horizon of ongoing question and temporary answer is in fact enough even for the
Church. To inquire, to receive finite and temporary answers upon which
we advance *claims* of truth, right, and good, manifests the communicative praxis within which we continually come to identity as inquiring
rational subjects and acting moral agents. Instead of the individual and
institutional hubris that claims the final answer, we hold our truths more
lightly, always attentive to others whose perspective will always critically decenter our own. None of us come to self-understanding as
rational moral agents from within the dispassionate confines of our own
self-created meditations or categories of perception. Nor does history's
*Geist* disclose its secrets to us. Neither are we illumined by the internal
dynamics of language or writing, or simply living, but only through our
encounters in substantive conversations about the challenges of life in
the world. To this praxis we have always been called by others who have
gone before us and locate us materially in history's metanarrative. From
this sort of critical and dialogic rationality there can be no release
without violence to the human condition itself, nor is one necessary. The
insecurity of no final answer is matched by the inevitability of the new
question and the new answer as long as inquiring human subjects
survive. And even though we have no guarantee that any new answer is
an advance of the old, we can have enough faith in honest, respectful,
and open inquiry to bind us together into communities of rational
speech and action that make humanity a worthwhile enterprise in the
first place. Human inquiry is finally premised upon such an horizon of
faith—a faith that informs us of our own limits but that also tells us there
is always more to know than has been known, more moral wisdom to

attain than has been attained (see Gadamer, 1975; 1991). Such an anthropological faith also has a humbling theological dimension: the divine mystery both locates and limits all the theological and moral claims we make in God's name or in the name of the Church.[26]

I do not think that the horizon of critique I am proposing will lead to either a frenetic questioning that deconstructively, and indeed destructively, pushes every position to its own always problematic critical foundation, or to an infinite postponement of judgment and decision because other "critical" questions are always waiting to be asked. I am speaking here of the wide sweep of history and the horizon of history's discursive progress. Certainly, as I will argue in later chapters, the systematic work of theoretic discourse and persuasive arguments and appeals for particular action will be necessary. Substantive and effective answers need to be given to questions of critical and legitimate human interest—answers whose prospect for critical revision always remains but whose material and moral intent can lead to responsible discriminations and judgments. Constructive and particular judgments can and must be made that are related to the kind of conversation and level of critique appropriate to the content of the inquiry engaged. Thus, it is the material-historical content of the conversation itself, the kind of legitimate interest and particular need expressed in the inquiry that will be the lead in determining the proper mode and level of discourse at any given time.[27]

Lest the Church still fear such an historicist approach to reason and rationality as some sort of vacuous relativism, we are easily reminded of the metaphors in our biblical heritage of approaching the divine source of knowledge and wisdom with fear and trembling, without the hubris that thinks the final knowledge of good and evil—of God or humankind—is attainable in this life or that such attainment is necessary for living faithfully and responsibly. At the same time it is the substantive approach, the critical engagement rather than aestheticist release, that is enough—the search, the quest, the *seeking after* as the effective action of pilgrims who do not avoid the dangers of the way, nor run from the risk of positive decisions at problematic crossroads or ask for release from the burdens of the journey. The pilgrimage of reason enjoins substantive paths toward practical ends rather than only endless meandering through self-engendered mazes of texts and meanings. The rational pilgrim engages the problems, challenges, and dangers of the journeys of reason and morality and makes, when necessary, life and death judgments and decisions.

Postmodernist and deconstructionist claims of crisis in the deadly heritage of rational speech and argument are always partial and rooted in the forgetfulness of the deeper historical roots of critically inquisitive reason. Insofar as such radical aesthetic critiques work to demythologize any claim of rational closure and finality and confront the denial of the different and the other in claims of a self-constituting intellect, they participate in the recollection of reason's rightful place in the material origins of human experience. To deconstruct this sort of reason is a rational therapy for reason itself. A truly nihilistic aestheticism writes no books, paints no pictures, composes no songs, does not even indict what is finally not there for the indicting.[28]

Even if certain forms of art, philosophy, and literature entertain goals of aesthetic release from the confines and restrictions of material historical reason, an incarnational Church cannot. The freedom of the Christian Church is bound to the world and its needs and interests. The Church must engage the world's conversations as its own as an obligation of its character identity—not as a monologic proclaimer, but as a rational dialogic participant who listens as well as speaks. Even when proclaimed, the gospel must also be heard. All words—as well as the Christian logos as *the Word*—are transformed both in their speaking and hearing. Indeed, speaking, hearing, and writing words effect a partial and critical deconstruction of all assumptions of received and sacred meanings and judgments, but always for the purpose of a new and ongoing reconstruction.

The true aesthetic spirit is not the same thing as the religious spirit, yet the two can be related (Tillich, 1959). Art, by and large, searches for the freedom of creativity and expression amid the bonds of self and earth. Religion, by and large, ties together the infinite pluralities and relativities of human life in the world in identifying bonds of obligation with divinity. In this sense, one could say, perhaps paradoxically, that art starts with given matter and seeks the freedom of spirit while religion starts with the freedom of spirit and seeks the material ties of earthly obligation. Thus art can remind religion of its need for creativity and the freedom of expression while religion reminds art of its material-historical obligations—its ties to the earth.[29] When religion refuses the lesson of art, it becomes encrusted by obligations that kill rather than incarnate creativity and freedom of expression. When art refuses the lesson of religion, it seeks release from the material-historical home of its own creativity—becoming a self-creating and unbound aestheticism.[30]

Finally, only the rhetoric of aestheticist release from the burdens, bonds, and false promises of orderly reason makes any project in practical moral guidance in sexual matters hard to imagine. There is certainly an aesthetic dimension to the moral life just as there is a necessary foundation in the imagination for rational argumentation itself. I have set the concept of moral character within a context of a dramatic image of historical worlds and the temporal and spatial location of moral obligations and responsibilities. A visual aesthetic is also necessary since work in moral interpretation begins with the phenomenological description of what is appearing before us—asking, in H. Richard Niebuhr's terms, "What is going on?" (1963a: 63). However, the radical aestheticism challenged here questions any notion that something is being said or promoted in art, literature, philosophy, and theology that has any ties of meaning and practical effectiveness beyond what is experienced in the saying and doing. Beyond experiences that deconstruct and repeat themselves *ad infinitum* as the meaning of human experience itself, "no-thing" is going on at all. In this sort of aestheticism, the "play" of history is not about anything other than the playing; the book that has no meaning other than what was experienced in the act of its writing and reading; a writing that self-erases its own meaning in light of what is inevitably left out—a rewriting that is interminable. And while we can never step outside of ourselves and history to engage truth, right, and good objectively from beyond the limits of our own conversations, all conversations have topics and texts, are directed from and toward others, and are about some "thing"—a representation of something other than the process of conversing or the act of writing.

Under this motif of aestheticism, I have mainly in mind what is being called postmodern deconstructionism in philosophy, literature, and now, theology.[31] I do not intend in this book to advance a systematic argument that deconstructionism is completely and necessarily defined by this radical and finally invalid form of aestheticism, though I do think this motif is present throughout the rhetoric of deconstructionism and offers a helpful strand of interpretation and evaluation, especially in this context. In deconstructionism, there are certain defining intentions to escape from what are seen as the encapsulations of past traditions, from the narrow and imperious limits of the self in notions of "alterity"/ *altarity* or "otherness," and in notions of "difference"/*différance* and "erasure," from the encapsulation of speech and writing as mirrors of a "logocentric" cosmos and the "onto-theological" presence of reality— i.e., being, nature, and history waiting to be disclosed, fabricated, discovered, and told.[32] Since deconstructionism arises from within the rhetoric of radical crisis, critique, and the imminent collapse of modernity (Megill, 1985), it has been framed under the title of "postmodern." As I have noted, the term postmodern itself is necessarily euphemistic in terms of a new cosmology, and, like deconstructionism, is still dependent on modernity for the sense and meaning of its claims.

Certainly deconstructionism can present insightful critiques of the modern heritage of priority of both the microcosmic ego and the macrocosmic totality, as well as the often deadly heritage of history enforced as evolutionary progress, most often of the so-called "advanced" cultures and nations. If this is all that deconstructionism claimed, then it would be an important and radical moral moment in modern critical hermeneutic theory. However, it seems to claim more. What is finally problematic in this particular context is the motif—which finally may be definitive—of aestheticist release to self-verifying and legitimating experience wherein, despite all claims to "differance," "erasure," and "altarity," no critical and substantive ethical/moral engagement is effected with *what* is different, *what* has not been and now *ought* to be written and said, much less done, or with *whom* the other is as writer, speaker, or actor. Without such material-historical engagements, interpretations and actions that oblige moral character seem impossible. Insofar as deconstructionism can be transformed to engage in substantively critical speech that leads to action in worlds beyond the literary, it can remain connected to the praxis of character and the material-historic dramas of the moral life. Insofar as deconstructionism expresses a radical and aestheticist disconnection from the substantive and material-historical conditions of intellectual/moral character, its ethical nihilism can only function as a form of shock therapy and promote confession for the encrusted and sinful rationalistic spirit of both modernity and Church.

All such artistic, philosophical, literary, and indeed, mystical theological "ways of unknowing" are, as I have argued, necessary reminders of the penchant for deadly hubris of reason and its institutions and arguments. Sometimes such deconstructive ways of the negative are, paradoxically, often important pursuits of knowledge and life wisdom— ways of rational inquiry, however oblique. However, beyond this crucial therapy, if one is to take seriously the substantive import of the postmodern aestheticist critique, the only result I can presently imagine for sexual morality would be an adulation of sexual practice as a kind of writing of a self-deconstructing moral text that is beyond the pale of any obligation other than the experience itself.

Lest this imagination be thought too fantastic, we should take note that this sort of license for experience is not totally foreign to certain forms of Christian mysticism and other enthusiasms. Release from the impurities, corruptions, indeed sins of the bodily order of reason to the clouds of unknowing seem, in many of its descriptions, not alien to the release of sexual orgasm. Such mystical orgiastic release from reasoned theological and moral argument parallels in part the release of sexual tension. I do not want to make too much of this point or to be interpreted in an overly moralistic way. Nonetheless, a connection can be made between mystical orgiastic release to a playing in the cloud of unknowing that contains the way that is not a way, to truth that is beyond truth, and the adulation of sexual experience as a play and a text that is beyond the delimitations and obligation of the right and the good—a sexual text that has meaning only in the continual writing, a sexual play and playing wherein no rational moral conscience has any significant ordering and limiting role.

Certainly, I am not challenging the free play of responsible sexual joy or of so many of the spiritual traditions of the Church that oblige strong care and commitment to the building of the earth as a divine-human dwelling. Rather I am calling attention to a heavily romanticist aestheticism and unbound mysticism whose drive to an unconstrained and unobliged life beyond the ties of rational conversation has caused as much death and destruction as any hubris of rationalism. The deadly hubris disclosed in thinking that such an aestheticist release from the bonds of earth is possible is not qualitatively different from reason that thinks it can enclose and possess the true, the right, and the good that it seeks.

## Melancholic Nostalgia

Unlike the new sectarianism and aestheticism, the Church's nostalgic reiteration of a sexual ethic built upon past worlds of coherence and meaning does imply a deeper sense of bonding and obligation to modernity. The nostalgia noted here discloses more of a wistful melancholia about modernity than an outright rejection—an antimodernism by default in not knowing what else to say and do. In this moral rhetoric, modernity has gone astray and can be relatively returned to the path of moral responsibility in sexual matters, at least in the lives of Christians who are confused in the whirlpool of modern change.

Nostalgia is defined as a "severe melancholia caused by protracted absence from home"—a "homesickness" that is "brooding or poignant," an "enervating homesickness" that is a "wistful or excessively sentimental, sometimes morbid, yearning for return to some past period of irrecoverable condition." All of the elements in these dictionary definitions seem to fit the Church's anxious brooding about sexual morality. The majority of the Church's teachers, as well as some voices of modern society itself, are deeply worried about sexual behavior. Sharing in all of the other common conditions of power and insecurity that pertain to sexual matters in general, the Church is in a particularly poignant dilemma. What the Church has said in the past—what it thinks, not with total historical accuracy, was effective in the past—it now suspects to be relatively unpersuasive. That the Church feels itself to be unable faithfully to say new and different things about sexual morality only makes the poignancy of its situation more pronounced. There is a double homesickness here: first for a time when the Church's teachings on moral matters were taken more seriously; and then for a place where its teachings fit within a receptive—verifying and legitimating—cosmological environment. And so the Church wistfully, often with overly sentimental expressions of pastoral concern—rejecting the sin but loving the sinner— engages in a reiteration of its past arguments, often pressing them to fit where they will not, and indeed, cannot fit.

Sometimes a morbidity develops when the Church suspects that the time when it could engage in a faithful didactic and transforming conversation with its own age is forever past. Such may account for the initial appeal of the new sectarian and aestheticist rhetoric. However, most antimodern nostalgia has more pathos than morbidity—more authentic concern and care about the state of the world than either the new sectarianism or postmodernist aestheticism. Nonetheless, such care does not obviate the seemingly intractable problems involved in interweaving both a faithful and contemporary Christian sexual morality. The nostalgia that motivates the Church to reiterate a sexual ethic rooted in lost cosmological worlds leads more to enervation in the face of contemporary challenges than despair. It is a repetitive speech born out of a misplaced nostalgia that expresses the Church's longing and homesickness for days when its teachings on sexual morality could, in its own estimation, be both faithful and contemporary.

The double homesickness of this antimodernist nostalgia mirrors a further double bind insofar as neither the antimodern geneticist understanding of historical time nor the modern sense of positive and evolutionary progressivism in theology and ethics are adequate for teaching that intends to be faithful and contemporary. What is needed in the Church's rhetoric of sexual morality is a new engagement with historicist modernity. The legitimate and obliging interests of the Church in being a moral teacher and guide do not leave simple choices to engage the modern world or not. Rather the nature of the Church requires it to be sure that the resources of its own age for constructive moral and theological discourse are exhausted before it engages in melancholic and naive retreats to former or smaller worlds, or rushes headlong into a so-called postmodernity that it can experience only in anxious and hazy anticipation.

In the remainder of Part One, responding to the moral rhetoric of antimodernist nostalgia will claim much of my attention. As I have indicated, such nostalgia for former worlds rests finally upon an inadequate theology, epistemology, and social psychology of change. Nor do the Church's problems with change in sexual morality only abide in its ecclesiastical leadership. Many local congregations also resist mightily a complete and competent discussion on these matters. Be that as it may, the obligations of leadership and instruction within the denominations and across the body of the Church remain. Here we encounter the paradox of expertise that, while always necessary, is always also fictive. Even with all of the difficulties encountered in the present debates about sexual morality among the denominations, it is a fundamental mistake to concentrate only upon the rhetoric and arguments of theological experts or special interest groups. Despite the problems of such wide-ranging conversations on sexual morality, the wisdom of the Church finally emerges from and must return to the body of the faithful.[33]

In summary, I am suggesting that while none of the modes of rhetoric discussed above are adequate for the Church, their underlying theme—the Church's problem with modernity with respect to rational and faithful guidance in general and in moral matters in particular—is foundational for understanding the Church's situation as it faces the challenge of being a faithful and effective teacher of sexual morality. In the Introduction to this study, I raised the question that I think finally haunts the discussions and debates of the denominations in this area: "Can anything new be said?" I have also argued that it is a facile interpretation to suggest that the Church is only being adamant in the face of totally obvious evidence that something new ought to be said, or hopelessly archaic, or simply repressive, sexist, and homophobic. All of the above as well as other mistakes and sins are undoubtedly present in the Church's discussions and must be engaged. However, the question of the faithful possibility of the new in sexual ethics and morality points to much more complex grounding and involves deeper issues that pertain to the very self-understanding of the Church in the era of modernity.

In the next chapter I will offer a reconstruction of the understanding of history as progress in modernity and follow this lead throughout the remainder of the text. In so doing I intend to establish a foundation in modernity for the Church's exercise of faithful and contemporary moral teaching in sexual matters that avoids the problems noted in the three types of moral rhetoric discussed above.[34]

# 2

## THE HISTORICITY OF FAITH AND LIFE

### Modernity and the Progress of History

The Spiral of History

Modernity's historicist self-understanding and the critical rational discourse it promotes are not bound by a positive evolutionary understanding of an increase in wisdom and virtue. Instead of this evolutionary-linear view, R. G. Collingwood notes that initially the progressive view of history in modernity was envisioned as a "spiral movement, one in which the radius is constantly changing or the centre constantly displaced, or both" (1972: 14). We can expand upon Collingwood's metaphor and understand the progress of history in modernity as neither cyclic nor linear but as an advancing spiral that constantly loops back as a precondition of advancement. This looping remembrance sets a continuity with the past that is internally necessary for the shape of the spiral and its advancement toward an anticipated future. However, when set in motion, such advancing spirals create new and discontinuous centers and radii. With this continuing recombination of the dimensions of continuity and discontinuity that mark historical experience, an historical foundation and model for critical discourse and argument is attained. The problems of the priority of past or future in either the cyclic or the progressively linear model give way to a model whose contemporary acts of remembrance and anticipation integrate past, present, and future. The classical commitment to continuity and order, the renaissance commitment to the contemporary thinking and acting subject, and the modern commitment to the moving progress of history toward the future are all maintained without bifurcating separations and priorities or the sense that the forward movement of history itself is somehow redemptive.

A first moment of *remembrance* is the backward loop of the spiral that retrieves in a new way what has gone before. The loop forward indicates that all discourse is set upon the horizon of *anticipation* of a relatively unknown and open future. At the center of the spiral, the present is constantly decentered by new conversations of remembrance and anticipation obliged in every age. Advancement is achieved only in the decentering of the loops of the spiral. Progress is thus not simply the retrieval or further harvesting of the fruits of a seed planted once and for all as in the geneticist view. Neither can it be found in only the historically isolated and insulated inspirations of individual intellects and consciences, nor in the evolutionary unfolding of a world-soul or spirit, or of history itself. Rather history as progress in modernity is an accomplishment of critical hermeneutic acts of remembrance and anticipation—an accomplishment of critical speech and intellect. Consequently, critically reasoned discourse demands remembrance and anticipation upon dual horizons of past and future. What can be currently imaged at the critical center of any conversation is never complete or finished but constantly decentered as one conversation among a countless number within the spiral of history. Any single loop of memory and anticipation always stands upon the horizon of previous conversations and calls forth new ones. Neither the past nor the future are normatively prior in the decentering process of the historical present.

Within the obliging ties of heritage and tradition, acts of remembrance establish a relative continuity with the past, but not as mere repetition. Since our remembrances are active in the progress of history, *recall* has the character of the new as well as the old. Accomplished from new and moving contemporary centers, a remembrance of the past always entails new content and meaning. The future functions as a test for such remembrances—a test of the pragmatic moral imagination that transforms memories of the past into practical goals yet to be accomplished. Accordingly, our memories must advance beyond their own acts of simple retrieval to be faithful. Remembrance is always a moral/political act whose purpose is achieved in acts for the sake of the future. We remember the dead, victims of war, famine, and holocausts lest their lives and death lose meaning—they themselves becoming lost as historical persons—but also for ourselves and for future generations lest such evil happen again because of something we do or fail to do, something we fail to remember.[1]

In further notes on modernity's turn to history, Collingwood indicates that progress in modernity is functional rather than substantive (1972: 16–17). What we say in any present historical conversation is not necessarily better or worse than any previous or future one. The functional progress of history only requires that we have new conversations in every age that must in principle be capable of saying new things. Within the context of formal and functional history, critically modern discourse neither requires nor allows any understanding of nature as holding a deposit of truth and right waiting to be explored. Nor can nature be viewed mechanistically, available for infinite manipulation by individuals, cultures, and nations.

Such a nonvalorized understanding of progress does not mean that we engage history from within only an abstract spirit of change. Rather, the functional progress of history is oriented materially by the content of the remembrances and anticipations of actual peoples and cultures and is about real events whose interpretations stand in substantive traditions of discourse. The faith required in the functional cosmology of modernity turns on our ability to remember critically the content of both the foolishness and wisdom of past ages and to anticipate a future worth caring about. In theological terms, such a faith expects God's presence in our new conversations just as that presence was realized and confessed in ages past.

However, anxiety remains and total dependability is not guaranteed. Undoubtedly, all historical conversations are in danger of being inadequately critical, systematically distorted, ideologically obscured, narrowly self-serving, partial, noninclusive, off target, and subject to all of the risks that infect the human condition. In late modernity, as in all cosmologies that begin to experience the strain, stress, and the crisis of age, new commitments are required to work first within the heritage of meaning and truth in which we stand—in this case, caring for the present state of reasoned discourse and argument.[2] Certainly we may fail at rescuing reasoned and public discourse within the historicist commitments of the modern age. Modernity as a meaningful cosmology may be coming to an end. Yet, as I have argued, continuing and critical engagements of the world in which we find ourselves are far better preparations for whatever cosmological ages are to come than only archaic or futuristic fantasies of either a secular or ecclesiastical variety.

The progress of new functional conversations that meet material and particular human needs and interests, and respond to substantive human questions frame the teleology Collingwood claims as formally endemic to modernity (1972: 15–16). Though negative dynamics have indeed been part of the self-understanding of the age, the teleology of modernity is not necessarily experienced as a positive and evolutionary unfolding of an organic and genetic seed, or as a goal imposed by the overly romantic intellect, conscience, or spirit of any individual or group, or by history itself. Collingwood's depiction of the *becoming of being*— "the principle that the *esse* of a thing is its *fieri*" (1972: 16)—also pertains to the functional history of human conversations and action as the formal progress of the pursuit of knowledge and wisdom in general. The progress of history in modernity need not, though again it often does, have the characteristics of modern technocratic functionalism—i.e., a reduction of general human needs and interests to their service in specialized and narrowly based bureaucracies and systems.

Accordingly, discourse about sexual morality in the Church can be marked by a material and historicist functional teleology that progressively seeks faithful remembrance as well as an effective future of teaching and guidance. Dutifully remembering the values and norms of our heritage and tradition of sexual morality is finally for the purpose of promoting responsible sexual behavior in the future. Moral rhetoric that is both formally and substantively disjunctive from an entire range of experiences in the lives of Christians and the culture at large cannot hope to accomplish the ends intended by the critical remembrance of tradition. The material life-experiences of Christian people, though not "salvific" in themselves, are fundamental ingredients of any new conversations. Such narrations of life-experiences are not mere statistics.

For example, functioning within the narrow institutional interests of modern technocratic reason, part of the error of the official magisterial positions of the Roman Catholic Church on birth control, mandatory celibacy for priests in the West, and the ordination of women is methodological and lies in a confusion of the narrations of those whose lives intimately engage such realities with relatively crass statistics that the Church rightly argues cannot claim the center of its theological and moral discourse. Contemporary Roman Catholic practice expresses more pastoral sensitivity to these issues than in ages past, but the magisterium has not yet found a way to methodologically use these material narrations as a substantive part of its own theological and moral teaching. The significant promise of the Second Vatican Council for a new way of public theological and moral discourse—a new way of magisterial teaching in the Catholic Church that includes full collegial participation of its members—has not yet been successfully applied to these issues.[3] Similar confusion also marks the present discourse on homosexuality across all denominations. Finding ways of discriminating such material-historical narrations from only crass statistics of how society currently behaves remains foundational in the Church's new conversations about sexual morality.

Finally, Collingwood notes that in modernity's view of progress only a minimum amount of space and time will be given to the satisfaction of a functional human interest or question (1972: 17–20). The pragmatic functionalism promoted here means that conversations and arguments that do not in fact respond to the substantive questions of everyday life will in one way or another be rendered irrelevant. Still, the dangers of abuse of this unique principle of parsimony are clear. Often the sparse allotment of space and time for critical conversation and action is carefully controlled. In many situations of strict majority vote, as soon as the necessary votes for a position or policy have been gained, the discourse is stopped. Conversations that intend consensus are controlled as conversations that only intend victory. And when access and power to participate are similarly controlled, such a parsimonious use of space and time only compounds the dilemma. However, in conversations that are not so structurally unjust, one can see a constructive use of such a standard of allotment. In the rhetoric of Christian sexual morality, this can work as a legitimate moral/pragmatic counter to the Church's own penchant of obfuscation and irrelevance. The failure of the Church's discourse on sex in this particular respect is often marked by interminable debates and unrealistic expectations and goals.

I have introduced the discussion of new possibilities for modernity's progressive historicist self-understanding because I consider it a key to the present struggle of the Church in interpreting its own moral life as part of the age in which it lives. As I indicated in the last chapter, in its discourse on sexual morality, the Church is now involved in new forms of antimodernism and postmodernism. Historically, antimodernism has not been a new form of cosmological self-understanding, but rather a discourse of complaint against modernity.[4] I understand the present euphemistic use of the term "postmodernity" in much the same way. I have already suggested that such complaints are not completely miscast. Modernity, like all cosmologies, experiences stresses and strains, crises and self-contradictions, problems and dilemmas. One should not expect cosmologies to be logically and phenomenologically perfect—but rather to function as environments for only relatively successful verification and legitimation of meaning and action. Thus in the modern discourse on sexuality, the Church is also expressing its complaints against modernity and the liabilities that modernity presents for a faithful and contemporary Christian sexual ethic.

The Liabilities of History:
Pluralism, Relativism, and Conventionalism

In the context of historicist modernity, pluralism, relativism, and conventionalism present major liabilities for fidelity in the theological and moral discourse of the Church. In fact, this trilogy most often frames the Church's contemporary brief against modernity. It cannot be doubted that the modern age displays defining characteristics of the plural, the relative, and the conventional. To be persuasive, my argument must demonstrate that these benchmarks of the age do not necessarily lead to ideologies that make faithful and effective moral teaching impossible for the Church.

In some denominational traditions, simple pluralism as diversity does not necessarily present radical problems in doctrinal, theological, and moral teachings. Denominations oriented toward more Catholic magisterial teaching have more problems with diversity than those oriented around the more Protestant ecclesiology of the priority of individual believers and their consciences. But even Catholic denominations have always found ways to integrate simple pluralism into their lives and traditions and are often not as practically monolithic in teaching and practice as either their own rhetoric indicates or external interpreters think. Certainly, the worldviews of the classical and renaissance ages could and did contain diversity. However, as I suggested in the Introduction, pluralism in modernity is more radical than simple diversity. Understandably, the denominations worry that such radical pluralism inevitably brings a corresponding relativism and conventionalism that will make it difficult, if not impossible, to sustain sufficient identifying beliefs and practices to demarcate the Church as a recognizable institution and assembly. The Church's moral quandaries always have not only theological but sociological and psychological ramifications as well that pertain to the future of the body.

Pluralism as simple diversity suggests that the same thing or event is experienced but according to the varying modes of perception and judgment, is understood in a variety of ways and with different practical implications. Accordingly, the problems of simple pluralism pertain to a conflict of perception and judgment that, in turn, can be relatively ameliorated by fuller conversation and more critical attention and instruction. In a more radical vein, foundational pluralism suggests that the reality of the thing or event itself is transformed in the perception and interpretation—that historical *appearance* has something to do with *reality*, and thus the nature of the thing itself is not immune from fundamental historical change. As an example of a claim of simple pluralism, ecumenical discussions often suggest that it is the appearance of the same God, interpreted in different ways, that connects many world religions. However, at the deeper level of foundational pluralism we find that the "Gods" we experience are also different. That is to say, the ways of the appearance and revelation of God also affect—and indeed, effect—the reality of the God who appears and is revealed. Furthermore, in political ethics one would be hard pressed to sustain an historical argument that the understandings of liberal individuality in societies marked by the European Enlightenment are merely variant perceptions of the human individual in societies not so closely marked. Rather we would be forced to say that the very *nature* of the human individual as a center of rights and value appears differently in divergent cultures and societies. We might still claim that one perception and understanding is more accurate and complete than another, yet we will be unpersuasive unless we broach the deeper level of the plurality of the phenomenological appearance itself—that is, the level of rational discourse that inquires how God and human individuality have first "appeared" historically and have been described culturally by the conversing partners. Even at these levels of foundational pluralism—i.e., at the foundations of the first appearance of the reality—relative consensus can be attained, but only if the discourse moves to deeper phenomenological levels. By saving, sharing, and re-configuring these foundational appearances, it is conceivable, though not guaranteed, that new consensus can be gained about what we are talking about, what is going on, what reality is appearing historically and culturally. However, effective consensus at this or any level is never achieved by discussions that insist throughout that what we have initially seen and heard—indeed, what we confess—is all that there is to see or hear—that *our* experience of "reality's appearance" is total and final.

The foundational and historicist pluralism of modernity suggests that reality is multidimensional. In engaging the modern discourse on sexual morality, it will be of the utmost importance to understand that the experience of the realities of committed and steadfast love are not necessarily limited to how they have appeared and been experienced in our own lives—that love and commitment are multiple realities that materially and historically appear and exist across cultures and among peoples in both continuous and discontinuous ways.[5]

The progress of the history of multiple cultures, societies, and biographies drove modern epistemological pluralism to a more radical level. Nature and reality were not experienced as single and continuous wholes. History was not a single and continuous metanarrative—a tale that, despite variance in particular historical interpretations, could be told by simply stringing continuities together over time, either through the envelopment of organic nature, or through the continuous building of the work of one artisan intellect and conscience directly upon those who preceded. Modern history now told often disturbing and discontinuous stories as well—stories of the rise of new truths and realities and the demise of old ones. Nor were the tales of modern historical reason, and the realities they disclosed, only of one sort or embedded in only one culture: other cultures had different criteria for coherence and truth, knowledge and virtue—different experiences and different realities. And when we were wise in this new age, we understood, because of foundational pluralism, that the experience of the reality of one person, group, culture, or nation could not be forced upon another without political and moral violence or total annihilation. When we were not so wise, we courted and promoted great disasters. Many of the great moral debacles of the foreign and political policies of modern nations, including our own misadventures in Vietnam, could have been mitigated by the wisdom of radical pluralism.

In other areas of modern life, we have become equally disturbed and instructed to learn that the stories of women—their ways of thinking, feeling, and acting—were not just minor acts or simply variant interpretations in the generic story of Western male experience and reality; nor were the stories of Native Americans and African-Americans or other racial and ethnic minorities merely diverse subplots in a grand and singular historical narrative of the dominant white race. Nor were the teachings and doctrines of the Church immune from the radicality of modern historical pluralism. The full implications of historical-critical methods in Bible and theology suggested that our traditional symbols, stories and doctrines, even with proper exegesis, did not bear a single meaningful reality across every extant cosmology and culture. What are we to make, for example, of doctrines of the Trinity and the Christ woven on a classical Greek cosmological frame in an age when that frame had long since collapsed? The confession that the Son is *of one Being with the Father* does not now signify to modern Christians exactly the same experience of the reality of the Christ as it did in the patristic age. Nor does the single image of God as *Father* now say all that we want to confess of our new and modern experience of God. Foundational female imagery for God also transforms and makes new the reality of the God experienced. This accounts for why gender inclusive language in theology and liturgy is so threatening to some. And further, what are we to make of those who claim the experience of deep commitment and steadfast love outside of the rule of heterosexual marriage? Were the realities of past and ancient experience wrong? Are these new realities simply variants or mistakes in interpretation and understanding; or are they more vicious heresies and sins? The wisdom of radically pluralistic modernity counsels that we can live faithfully and responsibly with both old and new realities through critical conversations about the multiple appearances and experiences of truth and right—of reality itself.

I do not mean to be facile or to suggest that coming to terms with this new and more radical pluralism is an easy task for the Church. In responding to this overall task, this book presents a formal identification and location of the substantive work that needs to be done among the denominations, and a constructive overture of how that work might proceed with respect to sexual morality. Thus, in Part One I present a foundation for theological and moral discourse that is embedded in a more critical notion of the modern progress of history—a progress that frames the plural appearance of both old and new realities at foundational levels of shared historical experience. My argument seeks to persuade the Church that the tendency in all denominations to define pluralism as only simple diversity of interpretation, opinion, or theological and moral *point of view* leads to an avoidance of the deeper challenges of the foundational and identifying pluralism of modernity—a challenge that cannot continue to be avoided without risk of ineffective engagement of the realities of the modern world.[6]

Except in times of societal and personal crisis, Western denominations and their members most often exist in worlds that are far removed from the daily life and death implications of some of the Church's earliest teachings. Thus, especially in North America, churches are often able to relatively insulate themselves in denominational wombs from the challenges of foundational pluralism. According to its own rhetoric and self-understanding, a single denominational tradition can attempt to be so continuous with either an ancient foundational age—often interpreted biblically or metaphysically—as to envision itself as an anti-modern or supramodern subculture of truth and right. Or it can attempt to be so discontinuous from its ancient and "embarrassing" origins as to be an expression of the best and brightest of popular and "enlightened" culture.[7] With the establishment of such an insulating routine of denominationalism, the full impact of the collision of multiple realities disclosed in historicist modernity could be postponed in both conservative and liberal traditions, with enlightened Christians in enlightened cultures given a choice among an array of denominational options. Certainly by our own century much of North American Christianity had become an aggregation of voluntary associations. We responded to the foundational historicist pluralism of modernity by situating ourselves on a diverse methodological and sociocultural continuum in Bible, doctrine, and liturgy. Consequently, despite the distinct advantages of such denominationalism over the oppression of establishment churches, in modern denominations the facile acceptance of simple pluralism often served as a distraction from the more radical pluralism embedded in modernity.

Before the Second Vatican Council, denominational pluralism was more a phenomenon in Protestantism than Roman Catholicism. However, this is no longer as completely so. Paradoxically, since the Reformation, it has been the Roman Church more than any other denomination that has been experiencing the full tension and dilemma of the conflict of classical and modern cosmologies in doctrine, liturgy, and morality. It is true that the Catholic Church of the Counter-Reformation came to resist modernity mightily, epitomized in its nineteenth-century doctrine of papal infallibility. However, in the span of slightly more than a century, the "same" church has issued a syllabus of modernity's errors, including freedom of conscience in religious affairs; condemned "Americanism" and "modernism" as heresies; called the Second Vatican Council to bring the Church "into the modern world;" and issued a decree promoting religious liberty largely drawn from American Catholic experience. Although the official magisterium continues to worry about the serious challenges of modernity to classical Catholic Christianity, indicated in the most recent round of what can only count as antimodernist positions in discipline and morality (Curran: 1986), modern Roman Catholicism still exhibits clearly the entire range of challenges embedded in radical pluralism for Christian denominations in general.

Still, I am not suggesting that the simple pluralism of denominationalism nor the variety of plural interpretations and applications of common experiences and realities are negative in themselves. Variety in how one can creatively and responsibly "be a Catholic," or what type of Protestantism best calls forth one's Christian commitment is necessary and welcome. However, when such a concentration on simple denominational pluralism and the voluntary choices it entails becomes self-defensive and works to distract from the more profound challenges of foundational pluralism, the Church's teaching and moral guidance will be rendered ineffective.[8]

Issues are raised from time to time in the life of the Church, however, that make it harder to maintain the insulation of either conservative or liberal denominations from the full impact of modernity. The Church's present rhetoric has raised sexual morality to such a status. With the shock of the new realities of sexual practice and their claims for moral justification, I have argued that a common typology of the moral discourse of the teaching Church crosses ordinary denominational lines. It is not the case that the teaching voices of the denominations on sexual morality are simply polarized along ordinary liberal and conservative lines. In their rhetoric of sex, some liberal denominations are also trying to conserve modes of moral discourse that by and large do not take seriously the challenges of the foundational pluralism of modernity. It is also not the case that all conservative denominations consider sexual behavior of foundational concern in the lives of their members since bold sins are sometimes seen to bring forth glorious repentance. Nonetheless, even though other theological issues challenge the denominations' fragile truce with radical pluralism, for most it is now sexuality and sexual morality that are galvanizing the Church's problems with radical historicist modernity. Therefore a new and more critical engagement of the entire range of issues that underlie the Church's modern discourse on sexual morality will have wider implications than first envisaged. At some level the Church understands what needs to be done; but its resistance and postponement of substantive discourse leaves room for the onslaught of a general malaise of melancholic nostalgia and the constant repetition of arguments rooted in lost worlds of coherence and meaning. Moral rhetoric with such an enervated nostalgic and melancholic center makes understandable the attraction of the more actively moralistic sectarianism and escapist aestheticism that essentially attempt to side-step the Church's problem with modernity.

Radical pluralism produces in all denominations an initially legitimate worry about relativism and its cultural twin, conventionalism. If history's narratives of character and virtue are themselves foundationally pluralistic, how can the Church develop an ethic that is more firmly grounded than upon either the sincere opinions of individuals or upon only statistical norms of behavior? That the Church should look for more than mere relativism and conventionalism in ethics turns on its basic claim that religion has something truthful and right to say about human beings and their behavior. Despite the discontinuities that we have been discussing in the conflicts and progress of cosmologies in Western history, this classical and biblically defining characteristic of the teaching Church remains.

It is certainly not the case that such universal goals have ever been fully realized—that what the Church teaches is the total and final truth and right or that in any time and place the Church achieves a total experience of reality and thus closure in its teachings. A proper sense of historical plenitude and divine mystery, as well as our own finitude and sin, would prevent such ecclesiastical hubris. At the same time, despite and because of the inevitable pluralism both within and without the body, the Church defines its mission as one that is exercised in light of this universal horizon. Ironically, the radical historical pluralism that informs modernity also safeguards our quests for universal truth and right—i.e., grounds such quests as ongoing projects within the multiple experiences and interpretations of modern reality. Thus, this classical "world-building" (1969: 3–51) project remains continuous in the modern discourse of the Church as it does in religion in general. Such modern historicist quests for truth and right express both a desire for comprehensive universality as well as a knowledge of finite and limited plurality. The religious desire of limited and sinful creatures for certainty, though necessarily unattained, is nonetheless defining and worthwhile.

These classical characteristics of universalism, however, are challenged more severely by relativism and conventionalism. Radical relativism and conventionalism in ethics fractures the common horizon of history as a metaconversation and metanarrative. Consequently, all universal interests and desires will be reduced to an endless variety of particular and self-contained conversations and thus render null the cosmological implications of religion as a world-building project. Such fractured plurality has no motivation to pay attention to the realities disclosed by the experiences of others and, in its self-defining insulation, does not promote a communicative ethos of shared interpretation and meaning. If truth and right are defined on such narrow and individualist grounds, then the conversations and narratives of history will be separated into an infinite variety of disjunctive histories of individuals and groups. The worlds we build and make will be particular to us. We may be curious about other worlds of truth and right, but we will have no motivation to admit them as possible enhancements of our own experience or challenges to our judgments. Rational discourse that is not marked at the start by intentions of universal communication and sharing most often leads to a self-defensiveness and a negation of the experience of others. None of this is to say that historicist modernity does not include the "relative" and the "conventional" embedded in the history of humankind. Our challenge is to see the implications of the relative and the conventional in ethics in ways that are beyond this sort of isolating segmentation. Among the many ironies involved in the historical location of the typologies of negative discourse I discussed in Chapter One, is the realization that the "antimodernism" of neo-sectarianism often displays a more radical modernist rendering of relativism and conventionalism through its attempts to isolate the interests of the Christian community from the universal interests of the age.

The grounds for revision of this fragmented understanding of the relative and conventional were disclosed in our discussion of the functional progress of history in modernity. The progress of history's narratives is not grounded in the priority of any isolated inquiry, or in any dimension of time. The critical hermeneutic movements of remembrance and anticipation suggest not relativism, but *relatedness* that inevitably moves and changes with the movement of the center of the historical conversation itself. Similarly, the material circumstances and conventions of critical conversations are related contextually to the full dimensions of historical time. Consequently, the relativity involved is fully historical, not temporally partial or only individually personal. Decisions about what counts as true, right, and good at any given time are not self-generated by historically isolated and decontextualized interpretations of the individual ego or particular group. Ethical norms are not made from scratch by individuals or the narrowly defined conventions of special interest groups, but are themselves historical products mediated through a praxis of critical conversation.

In this light, marriage will neither remain nor give way as normative in Christian ethics simply because, in the isolated sincerity of their own consciences, any individual or group thinks that it ought to do so. Embedded in the historicity of modernity and the inevitable displacement of old by new conversations, traditional norms will either retain or lose their status on a more historically pragmatic basis. That is to say, in their ability to sustain or not the challenge of both faithful remembrance and effective anticipation of the responsibilities of Christian faith and life—their ability to disclose a contemporary set of historically effective values. New critical conversations always exercise a transforming function on traditional norms. Such transformation may involve the efficacy of the norms' response to new questions as well as, more radically, in the norms themselves. My argument in later chapters will be based in part on my description of the present state of Christian marriage. In that interpretation I will suggest some new applications of the norm of heterosexual marriage to rules of sexual behavior along with the judgment that the integrity of the norm remains intact, however, not without significant erosion.

Consequently, serious conversation about the moral norms of a given society are neither initiated nor sustained only by individuals or particular groups, but by the wider and deeper conventions of history and culture. Taken etymologically, convention means a "coming together," with the "conventionality" of history, culture, and society involving our intersubjective and public associations and relationships. In the circumstances of historicist pluralism and relativity, we do not adequately pursue truth and virtue in conversations fractured and narrowed by historical and cultural enclosure, but in the common discourse of the narrative of humankind. Relativity, as relatedness, and conventionality as the praxis of our coming together expand our universes of discourse and action, whereas relativism and conventionalism narrow them.

Similarly, adequate conversation is neither promoted nor prompted by events and subjects that are so homogeneous and continuous that they lead to no critical question.[9] Rather it is the discontinuity and plurality of history that most often frame the conventions of critical discourse and action. Paradoxically, relativism and conventionalism do not engage the discontinuity of history or its pluralism seriously enough. Pluralism and discontinuity are offered as excuses for a narrowing of vision and a segmentation of discourse. In thinking that pluralism and discontinuity can be so easily controlled and obviated, what is accomplished is only a false sense of continuity and coherence. Accordingly, it is not historicist pluralism that promotes relativism and conventionalism in ethics, but the failure of its engagement. Seen in this way, the pluralism, relativity, and conventionality of modernity can be more of a promise than a liability for the moral rhetoric of the Church.

I am not suggesting that crass relativism and conventionalism are not also part of the ordinary understanding of modernity or the practice of the moral rhetoric of sex. And if this is all that could be made of the moral discourse of historicist modernity, then a crisis in virtue would indeed be at hand and antimodern and postmodernist stances more understandable without necessarily being more effective. I have argued that the more accurate assessment of the state of sexual virtue in later modernity requires that we ask how, amid the relativity and conventionality of foundational pluralism, the Church in modernity can be faithful to its own traditions as well as to the realities of the contemporary world. Even though the Church has found ways to temporarily survive radical historicist pluralism by offering denominational choice, the more pronounced and fundamental challenges of articulating an adequate and responsible sexual ethic, as well as saying anything new at all in any given age, pertain to the very historicity of our faith and life.

### The Obligations of Fidelity

Following Collingwood, I have emphasized a radical and unique turn to history as a formally identifying characteristic of modernity. I have also suggested that the experience of modern history can be understood as a moving and decentering spiral that combines linear and cyclic motion. I interpreted history under this model as a counter to defining progress as only a positive evolutionary advancement in knowledge and moral enlightenment. In so doing I refused to take as final a major portion of modernity's own self-understanding, but I did not take the now common antimodernist turn or move completely into a postmodernist posture. Instead, I have called for a more critical examination of the cosmology of modernity and its turn to history. It is this renewed self-understanding that offers the best prospects for more coherent and effective public moral discourse in the Church precisely in the context of modernity.

Nonetheless, coherence and effectiveness alone are not enough to persuade the Church to engage in conversations about sexual morality that can in principle say new things. Coherence and effectiveness have to be marked also by a sense of fidelity. Given certain defining confessions and presuppositions, any number of approaches to sexual morality can stand particular tests of coherence as well as have prospects for effective adoption in the lives of some people. However, the Church will interpret both coherence and effectiveness finally in ecclesiological ways—ways that pertain to the Church's self-understandings throughout the course of its history. The Church's experience of its own character in history is the enabling context for its own faithful moral teaching. Ecclesiology is not only a study of the doctrine of the Church. Before the Church is a doctrine, it is a tradition and heritage of the experiences of communities of faith. Thus ecclesiology must also be a critical reflection on the nature and meaning of the Church's experience in particular historical contexts, including our own, and in the context of history itself. Underlying my approach in this book is the conviction that in its biblical origins, the faith of the Church is tied to history. In biblical understanding history is not an abstraction but is marked by the experiences of people coming together for common projects amid the conventions of cultures and societies. It is faith in the value of these common projects that connects the ages of the Church's life amid the discontinuities and change of history's progress. Through the birth and death of the ages and the rise and fall of cosmological worlds, the faith of the Church remains formed by and committed to history and history's material manifestations. The historicity of human experience does not threaten fidelity or moral responsibility in the Church, but rather defines it.

Fidelity to its historicist character requires that the Church not flee from the material conditions of its own age through nostalgic reconstructions of ages past or through sectarian segmentation of the worlds it inhabits. Nor can the Church opt out, so to speak, from the material content of the burdens and terrors of history through flights of aestheticist release to "freer" and "purer" but less incarnational worlds. For our theological and moral teachings to be coherent, effective, and faithful, they must be drawn from engagements of the world in which we find ourselves. The faith of the Church is materially historic and its teachings historicist, with all the continuity and discontinuity, plurality, relativity, and conventionality that history discloses. To be historic and historicist is to be incarnational. To be incarnational is to be in and of the body. And, for Christians, the body in question is the world.

The cosmological and universalist themes depicted in New Testament Christology are not accidental. Nor need they be interpreted in ways that reject the pluralism that ought to define ecumenical and inter-faith relations.[10] Rather, such Christology sets the cosmological and universal implications of the Church's life and work. In the Christian Testament, the Christ of the cosmos does not *ascend* to a place outside of historical time and place to usher in a new otherworldly narrative-drama separated from human history. The paschal events of the New Testament frame the Church's historical/ecclesiastical character on the one side by the sign of the cross and on the other by the promise of a new pentecost in human history. Though the biblical stories of faith and life are often particular in the form of their telling, they are cosmological stories—universal stories that not only engage old worlds but also make possible new worlds of meaning, truth, and right.[11]

Thus fidelity to origins cannot rest secure on an orientation to the past alone or in a fragmentation of the universal and cosmological in service of the narrow and particular. The projects formed in particular communities of biblical faith were worldly and universal from the beginning—historicist projects that intended to engage history in its full-ness as a time and place of the divine-human dwelling. To be faithful to those projects—to be in fact the Church revealed in our origins—is to be bound to history as a narrative drama and to the contemporary cosmo-logical worlds that tell its tale and mark its progress.

### The Obligations of Contemporaneity

As I argued in the Introduction, the time when the Church could think of itself as the sole or principal maker and transformer of cultural worlds is long past. Whether what we find in the cultures of late moder-nity seems at first glance to be welcoming to Christian faith and life or not, we are bound to our own contemporaneity. Still the question of crit-ical contemporaneity is complex and ought not to be interpreted in only a bourgeois sense. By remaining contemporary, I do not mean being merely up to date or following only middle-class statistical norms, whether liberal or conservative. The Church's obligation to be contemporaneous lies in its full historicity—that is, recognizing that our basic acts of remembrance and anticipation are engaged amid our present circumstances. Historical convention and circumstance are not external contexts that merely surround us, but rather they make up the vital ethos that frames and forms our character as actors and agents in a social world. Being critically contemporaneous in a fully historicist sense also means being inclusive, bringing to the center those who, in the moral presumptions of the age, have been rendered anachronistic and marginal. In this sense, being in step with the contemporary progress of history means that the Church will not continue, as Johann Metz says, to be an "accomplice" in bourgeois efforts "to safeguard the status quo" (1984: 170).

In his essay on "Productive Noncontemporaneity" (1984), Metz is by no means suggesting a formal principle of "withdrawal" from modernity as an ecclesiological ground for substantive theological and ethical work. He argues against both liberal presumptions and conservative reactions for or against modernity (pp. 169–70). Perhaps it is, paradoxically, this critical aspiration of a full engagement of contemporaneous life that is now, in bourgeois church and culture, being rendered so "noncontemporaneous." For it does often seem out of step with middle-class life to refuse to accept as given our present conditions of global violence, poverty, and injustice. In this historically effective sense, being noncontemporaneous means continuing such world-making engagements and aspirations.

> In fact a religion that has not been rendered superfluous through the abandonment of its aspirations is permeated with this atmosphere of noncontemporaneity, with this scent of the anachronistic. It comes from afar, from the depths of the history of humankind.... (Metz, 1984: 170).

It is most often only misplaced nostalgia, sectarian narrowing, or aestheticist flight that suggests that fidelity and contemporaneity are opposed. As definitive of the historical shape of Christianity, fidelity to the traditions we have received demands a constructive engagement with contemporaneity and the futures our present worlds will bear. We do not simply choose or not to live, understand, and act in the world in which we find ourselves, including its own patterns of sexual experience and conduct.

### Revelation and Historicist Modernity[12]

#### The Suspicions of Reason

If this book has intentions of being a relatively persuasive argument about the possibility of saying something new in sexual ethics then, under the twin obligations of fidelity and contemporaneity, more attention needs to be paid to the question of modern reason and classical revelation. Even when not articulated directly, in one way or another, confusion in the relation of reason and revelation disrupt the denominations' moral discourse. More often than not, either through biblical quotation or traditional teaching, claims of revelation are eventually used to trump any further critical debate. Throughout its history, the Church has been both attracted by and suspicious of the claims of reason to articulate a faithful doctrine and morality when cast against the traditionally revealed mysteries of faith and life. In an ironic twist, such suspicions have now been brought to some degree of canonization by more secular critiques of modernity's enlightenment faith in rational discourse.[13] While attentive to such critiques, the Church should not feel simply affirmed in its own heritage of suspicion of rational discourse in general. When the Church proceeded with care in its teaching, it was from a piety that revealed the limits and sinfulness of all human endeavors to know the truth, proclaim the right, and promote the good. At the same time, the Church always understood at some level its practical and material-historical commission to speak a substantively rational gospel however finite and sinful its articulation and consequent need for reformation—in H. Richard Niebuhr's terms, our "enduring problem" of relating God and history, reason and revelation, Christ and culture, and Church and society (1951: 1–44).

Throughout his works Niebuhr argued that in light of the plenitude of the divine mystery, it is finally our experience of finitude and sin that discloses the limits of reason and culture—indeed limits in the reception of revelation in any given time and place. The more critical its confession, the less the Church was tempted by overly irenic rationalism and self-serving accommodation. Still, "enduring problems" remained. As soon as denominations turned from false accommodation—in this case, to only popular sexual behavior—the correlative temptation ensued to avoid substantive and constructive engagements of faith and contemporary life in general. In promoting this sort of noncontemporaneity by appeals to a static "revelation," the Church only accommodated its own anxieties, fears, and confusions. With such an anachronistic posture, the Church's incarnational and historicist center erodes and the Church loses its vital contact with culture and society, with its teachings becoming abstract and largely irrelevant.

Certain knowledge of truth and right cannot be purchased by a return to what, from our distant vantage point, only seems like more coherent worlds of past revelation. Nor can we gain security by a myopic reduction of revelation to smaller worlds in the present or by expansion of our worlds toward unconstrained futures that claim, paradoxically, certainty in the revelation of uncertainty—a determinant revelation of indeterminacy. As I have argued, no aestheticist release from the earthly bonds of uncertain reason and history can be faithfully gained by appeals to negative theologies of mystical silences or "literary philosophies" of an uncontained and undemarcated spirit hurled toward an ever mysterious and open future—the revelation of an infinitely "self-deconstructing" discourse.[14] Absolute certainty and intellectual closure are not what we seek in our religious and moral lives, but rather substantive and constructive responsibility. Responsibility is our grounding metaphor (Niebuhr, 1963a: 47–68). A *responsive* and *responsible* Church will call forth the simultaneous and "time-full" engagement of past, present, and future in terms of critical decisions and actions in contemporary material-historical contexts.

Having God, Morality, and History

In *The Meaning of Revelation* (1941; 1960), H. Richard Niebuhr gauged the implications of confessional fidelity in the rational theological discourse of the Church from a modern historicist perspective—in short, he reflected upon how fidelity and contemporaneity must be conjoined. All of Niebuhr's work and writings finally reflect his struggle with his evangelical confessional commitments to the experience of biblical faith and his encounter with pluralism, relativity, and conventionality that mark the historicity of the modern age. I choose Niebuhr's work as a resource not because he totally supports my argument or because his engagement with this question is exactly the same as mine. I do not follow completely his neo-Kantian critical idealism, nor am I formed in his evangelical orientations, broadly interpreted, or in his pietism. At the same time Niebuhr's struggle with the meaning of history, reason, and revelation mirrors the continuing and contemporary struggle of much of the modern Church. Niebuhr was acutely aware of the substantive and particular struggles of the Church to be both faithful and contemporary. And he was aware that such a struggle, and its always relative resolution, must take place on the stage and within the narratives of the material-histories of people and cultures. Despite the differences in our philosophical orientations and theological approaches, he was similarly convinced that historicist modernity, critically engaged, still had much to offer as a way of dealing with these enduring problems.

It will not be surprising to those familiar with how Niebuhr engaged ethical issues to learn that there is little if any direct discussion of sexual morality in his writings. Niebuhr was convinced that unless adequate philosophical and theological foundations were laid for practical moral reasoning and argument, the results of any substantive discussion about any particular issue in the moral life would remain unsatisfactory to all concerned. In my attempt to "recover" modernity as a constructive cosmological venue for the substantive moral discourse of the Church on sex, I am to some extent following Niebuhr's lead. I have argued that the key to this recovery is a reinterpretation of modernity's turn to history, understood by Niebuhr to be the medium for the confession of our faith as material-historical and revelatory stories of our lives. In *The Meaning of Revelation*, not only does Niebuhr not turn from the relativity of history that has become definitive of modernity, he makes it foundational for his understanding of revelation itself and its claims upon the Church's fidelity.

Niebuhr writes: "I have found myself unable to avoid the acceptance of historical relativism yet I do not believe that the agnostic consequence is necessary" (1960: ix). He describes his effort as guided by three convictions. First, Niebuhr is convinced that "self-defense is the most prevalent source of error in all thinking and perhaps especially in theology and ethics" (p. x). Second, "the great source of evil in life is the absolutizing of the relative, which in Christianity takes the form of substituting religion, revelation, church or Christian morality for God" (p. x). And finally, drawing on the above convictions of the historical relatedness, plurality and finitude of all articulations of faith and life, Niebuhr describes his third conviction that "Christianity is 'permanent revolution' or *metanoia* which does not come to an end in this world, this life, or this time" (p. x).

Far from implying a reversal of the turn to history in enlightenment modernity, any faithful appeal to revelation, in Niebuhr's view, is historicist through and through. Even if we cannot say all of the same things our forebearers have said about revelation and thus stand in some discontinuity with them, we can come to a deeper appreciation of the continuity of the challenge to gauge the implications in word and deed of the divine-human presence as definitive of the Church. Niebuhr continues: "the revival of revelation theology is not due to a conscious effort to repristinate ancient ways of thought but to the emergence in our time of a problem similar to that with which the classical theologians dealt" (1960: 5). Consequently, simple appeals to revelation do not solve the problems of history, nor can we attain a purported past "innocence of vision by wishing for it" (Niebuhr, 1960: 3). Nor is such a nostalgic repristinization of the past necessary for standing faithfully in revealed historical traditions. Rather, fidelity means a contemporary engagement of the full historicity of the Church's life in ways that revitalize the past and lay open the future. The self-conscious quest for contemporaneity in the discourse of the Church cannot be merely something we seek occasionally but must be definitive of the "time-full" nature of Christian faith and its ongoing interrelation of revelational confession, rational theological articulation, and moral action.

Revelation and reason are joined dialectically in our historical quests for meaning. To speak of God's revelation as somehow apart from the progress of history is to eviscerate the concrete and incarnational nature of the Church. To be revelation, the words and acts of God must be received, rationally interpreted, and effectively understood in the context of historical circumstance.[15] That the Church believes that its relative ability to receive revelation historically is also by the grace of God only points to a prior grace that marks created time itself and the concrete historicity of divinity that lies at the heart of biblical religion. Revelation depends on history and the rationality it bears; just as history, despite its sinfulness, depends on revelation and thus becomes sacred. In light of this, modernity's turn to a historicist self-understanding does not indicate infidelity to revelation. In the decentering spiral of history, the old is encompassed—deconstructed and reconstructed—not lost. Continuity with our informing heritage is maintained in new and contemporaneous conversations that bring the past forward toward an effective future. In the present debates on sexual morality, Niebuhr's reminder of the full historicist character of the Christian Church is still timely for those whose voices are becoming shrill and self-defensive, who absolutize the relative, and who forget the meaning of the Church as permanent, albeit faithful, revolution.

> The patterns and models we employ to understand the historical world may have had a heavenly origin, but as we know and use them they are, like ourselves, creatures of history and time; though we direct our thought to eternal and transcendent beings, it is not eternal and transcendent; though we regard the universal, the image of the universal in our minds is not a universal image (Niebuhr, 1960: 7).

Humans are by nature historical and temporal beings—not just in time, as Niebuhr argues, but because of the time that is in us. And in a point that has significance for the remainder of his book, he continues that "the time that is in (us) is not abstract but particular and concrete; it is not a general category of time but rather the time of a definite society with distinct language, economic and political relations, religious faith and social organization" (1960: 10, parens added). This is the "sum of the matter:" we must begin with a historicist view of revelation because we cannot think about God or ourselves, "save as historic, communal beings." We must ask "what revelation means for Christians rather than what it means for all men, everywhere and at all times" (1960: 30–31). It is from the particularities of concrete history that the story of Christian life must be told. Thus, Niebuhr raises conventionality to the status of a characteristic of history and faith—Christian history as a narrative and record of our faithful coming together.

Here a critical point of interpretation arises in the discussion of Niebuhr's understanding of revelation and raises again the phenomenon of the new sectarian separations of God, morality, and history. The conventionality with which Niebuhr marks Christian revelation can and often does lead to sectarian claims that Christian ethics narrow its perspective to smaller worlds of meaning, coherence, and fidelity. The coming together of Christians can then be described by stories and enacted rituals that are separated from the larger worlds in which the Church finds itself leading to a segmented ethic unique to the Christian convention. A sexual ethic formed in light of this sort of conventionality can stress a coherence related to the particularity of its own internal and self-told story. A Christian's call to fidelity is thus bound to an experience of commitment and membership in the narrow body of the Church's institutional and congregational traditions. This does not necessarily mean that the ethic formed will be internally uncritical, but rather that the standards of judgment and critique will be rendered immune from the general rational conversations of the modern age. The criteria of criticism are wholly internal and particular to the Church itself and stand under no ordinary external norms of verification and legitimation. Such particularity and narrowness is not seen as a weakness, but the only way for any sense and coherence at all in the mass of confusion that modernity offers in ethics and the moral life.

In this same vein, Alasdair MacIntyre has argued that "modern moral utterance and practice can only be understood as a series of fragmented survivals from an older past and that the insoluble problems which they have generated for modern moral theorists will remain insoluble until this is well understood." Moral speech that stresses obliging duties appear now as "the ghost of conceptions of divine law which are quite alien to the metaphysics of modernity." Clear moral intentions and goals abide similarly as a "ghost of conceptions of human nature and activity which are equally not at home in the modern world." Thus, "we should expect the problems of understanding and of assigning an intelligible status to moral judgments both continually to arise and as continually to prove inhospitable to philosophical solutions." Framed against our classical heritage, MacIntyre argues that modernity is truly an age that is "after virtue" (1984: 110–11).

I have no quarrel at all with MacIntyre's understanding that cosmologies that "compete" as horizons for rational meaning and coherence in moral argument lead to confusion and failure. Yet in *After Virtue*, he presents a chilling "choice between 'Nietzsche or Aristotle.'" MacIntyre takes Nietzsche as one who understood the failure of modernity to sustain a heritage of rational moral virtue and who pointed out how the "irrationalism" in ethical theory left a necessary vacuum to be filled by a dominating and "supra-rational" will (pp. 113–14). Consequently, if we desire to continue within a tradition of constructive moral discourse grounded in a coherent sense of character and rational virtue, Aristotle is our "only choice." Yet, in a question that MacIntyre should understand, since the history of rational ethical debate is so intertwined with the cosmological and historical worlds that ground or not its meaning and coherence (pp. 264–78), how is "after virtue modernity" to *choose* "virtue-dominant" Aristotle? The answer lies in MacIntyre's own brand of philosophical and cultural sectarianism, albeit with theological and ecclesiological undertones. "What matters at this stage is the construction of local forms of community within which civility and the intellectual and moral life can be sustained through the new dark ages which are already upon us" (p. 263).

There are several reasons why MacIntyre's sectarian philosophical approach in his "choice" of Aristotle is also chilling. First, it is not obvious that modernity and its historicist conversations are so totally discontinuous with the classical age of virtue as to be totally alien to that rational heritage—i.e., that we no longer have enough historical, cosmological, and moral convention to understand and be moved by even a trace of classical moral reasoning. Second, and more importantly, no matter how critically and historically insightful rationally articulated philosophies of virtue may be in any given age, these are not definitive of experience of virtue itself. In the metaconversation of history, the moral life is not defined by any particular philosophic articulation. And even if modernity is an age that is after virtue, any "return" to Aristotle and his classical world is impossible both historically and morally. The local communities that MacIntyre seeks will remain modern only without the aspirations of a self-critical reflection upon their own condition. Finally, despite the wisdom of Aristotelian virtue, it also centered a classical hierarchy of valuations of persons and gender that critically enlightened moderns would find morally odious.

If modernity is an age that is "after virtue" it is, in the new sectarian ecclesiology, an age that is also "beyond redemption." Instead of the universal horizon of biblical soteriology and ethics, this new Christian story of redemption will be told within the confines of the local communities, and essentially, for those communities. The Church of the local community will be no longer defined by its interests in and conversations with "the world," but rather by internally defining confessional conversations with itself. Even in its witness to the larger worlds, Christian ethics will be framed by narrow congregational and institutional values and interests—an ethic that "belongs to us." In this ecclesiological rationale, those who entered the biblical covenant were particularly chosen by God and the intentions and obligations of that covenant remain particular and local.

And yet pertaining now especially to the question of fidelity, what remains inadequately addressed in only internally historical approaches to Christian existence is how such a God of the universe remains interested in local communities and traditions self-consciously separated from the larger discourse of the age. Similarly, how can such a God be seemingly so uninvolved in the "rest of creation" so to speak? This question becomes even more poignant if we recognize the first Covenant to be between God and creation upon whose horizon and for whose sake all particular and later "covenants" were formed.[16] Finally, such a concentration on the particular and internal at the expense of the universal and external falsifies how we find ourselves in the world. We can no longer, if we ever could, come to critical identity and virtue through internal self-told stories that are materially and methodologically marked off from the external stories of others who are different from ourselves. Moreover, history always discloses that the destinies of such chosen peoples always involve the fate of those not so chosen.[17] Moreover, Christians who live and work in the secularity of the world are aware that they are not simply defined religiously by the life and practice of their local congregations. No matter how couched, hard methodological separations between the sacred and secular in theology and ethics only increase the schizophrenic split that modern Christians experience. As it has always been, the challenge for Christian theology and ethics is to understand from the outset that its own particular rhetoric is bound to the universal discourse of history itself.

Despite some remaining ambiguity as he wrestled with these perennial problems, and his particular and often legitimate fears of anthropocentric and irenic accommodations, Niebuhr (1960: 13–31) understood that the Church's "internal" life is inextricably bound to the "external" life of the age in which it finds itself. Thus, neither in *The Meaning of Revelation* nor in his later work did Niebuhr take the new sectarian turn but continued to struggle with the full implications of the relativity, pluralism, and conventionality embedded in historicist modernity.

In *The Peaceable Kingdom* (1983), Stanley Hauerwas describes his attraction to "the Niebuhr of *The Meaning of Revelation*." Given Niebuhr's concentration on internal confessional history, Hauerwas describes a puzzlement that the same person "could write *Radical Monotheism and Western Culture*, since the God of the latter seemed to lack the characteristics necessary to be identified with a particular people and their distinct history" (pp. xx; xxi). Hauerwas goes on to say that "perhaps the tension between the positions of those two books witnessed to the tension in Niebuhr's life between the particular and the universal, the historical and transcendent, the church as sect and as universal" (p. xxi). Even though he has correctly stated the tension, one wonders why Hauerwas stops with *Radical Monotheism* (1960) and does not also note Niebuhr's similar movement toward the universal in all of his other major works.[18] It is the radical and universal historicity of the faith, which Niebuhr depicts so well, that makes what was received in a particular way no longer bound by that same particularity. The critical progress of history dialectically decenters both particularity and universality. Even in the ancient Christian Testament, the Jesus of particular historic faith and moral reference is decentered by the universal and cosmological Christ. And though Hauerwas says that he now no longer sees an "either/or" polarity here, if he had been forced to choose, he says he would have taken his stand on particularity: "Otherwise, I simply did not see how one could make sense of the significance of the life and death of Jesus for Christian life and thought" (p. xxi; 61–63).

I agree with Hauerwas that an either/or choice here is miscast. However, my understanding of the decentering dynamic of history, and how that dynamic immediately and foundationally casts any narrative of communal particularity in Christian ethics onto a more universal cosmological stage and in terms of a wider world-story, marks the difference in our approaches. We may claim initially to be formed biographically as individuals and communities in *the ethics of Jesus*, but we are immediately, even in the process of that formation, challenged and thus equally formed by the universal historical orientation of the cosmological Christ. Christian ethics does not just have implications first for us and then for the world in the face of which we can only stand in witness. At its Christocentric heart, the Church is historicist, universal, and worldly with all the critical burdens and challenges that such universal worldliness entails. In general, I think this is what Niebuhr is reaching for in his categories of "internal" and "external history," categories that Hauerwas rejects too quickly (1983: xx).

Internal and External History

As I noted at the outset of this discussion, I am not arguing that Niebuhr's approach is exactly the same as mine. Even though he does not take a sectarian turn in his confessional approach in *The Meaning of Revelation*, his emphasis on the recovery of the universalist meaning of Christian faith, theology, and ethics remains ambivalent. Throughout this text, Niebuhr's point of departure is the internal history of the Church—a story that seeks a "grammar...not of a universal religious language, but of a particular language" with a "method applicable not to all religions, but to the particular faith to which its historical point of view is relevant" (1960: 13). However, in the same passage Niebuhr notes that such language "can seek within the history of which it is a part for an intelligible pattern" (p. 13). The history of any age of which the Church is a part is also the history of the Church itself. Accordingly, the Church's conversations on sexual morality in the modern age are from the beginning—both in content and method—part and parcel of the discourse of modernity itself. My attempt to persuade the Church to become more self-conscious of this historical and cosmological reality is motivated not only by the desire for a more universal coherence and effectiveness in ethics, but also by the nature of the Church itself as a thoroughly incarnational world-making praxis.

The envelopment of the Church in history means that our quests for identity are dialectically engaged through the narrative histories of both self and other, the particular and the universal. Logically, one can enter a dialectic at either point and such points of departure serve orienting heuristic intentions. Stressing, as I have, the universal as a point of departure for the full dialectic is to counter the stress on the particular in Christian ethics of the new sectarianism. Without sufficient care, however, heuristic points of departure often lead to single and closed methodologies that are not sufficiently attentive to the dialectical dynamic of the material reality under investigation. Accordingly, if the particular self and its demarcated communities and worlds are taken as points of departure in Christian ethics, the challenge of the universal remains. If the universal is taken as a point of heuristic departure, the similar challenge of the particular remains. These questions do not turn on whether the Church purports a theology and ethic that, as Niebuhr decries, "prescribe what form religious life must take in all places and all times beyond the limits of its own historical system" (1960: 13). Rather the questions have to do with the limits of the Church's historical nature and identity. My argument does not negate the foundational importance of the Church's self-conscious heritage of its own uniqueness and particularity, but suggests that that heritage is not limited by the Church's internal self-consciousness and understanding—that is to say, what starts particularly has universal implication and intent. Our experience of confessional particularity is embedded in a wider historical universality. Consequently, the history of the Church cannot be told adequately from only within the limits of our institutional and communal self-understanding. The ongoing project of self-understanding and critical judgment is also dependent on others—others outside of and external to the Church's internal heritage and community. As this recognition of the individual and communal self's dependence on the voice of the *other* is necessary for the Church's identity in general, so too is it necessary for any interpretation and application of historical ethical norms and rules. Norms and rules are not products of our own desires and needs alone, but rather of larger historical contexts and conventions that are both prior to and other than our own personal and institutional biographies.

In Niebuhr's distinction and relation of "internal and external history" he focuses precisely on the implications of the conventionality and pluralism embedded in modernity's historicist relativity. He casts the internal and external histories of communities as narratives that become revelatory as stories of what has happened to such communities at any given time and through "the medium of our history." Therefore, he continues, revelation is "the story of our lives" (1960: 32–66).

Niebuhr is well aware that beginning with such a particular confessional orientation and rhetoric has led many to stop short and seek individualistic, relativistic, and aestheticist ways of circumventing the more global relativity, conventionality, and pluralism that define us. He argues:

We may be tempted, with the individualists of all time, to seek a direct path to what we mean through inner religious experience. Can we not say that when we speak of God and revelation we

mean events which occur in the privacy of our personal, inner life
of what we feel to be basic in our moral consciousness? Yet once
more we discover that visions, numinous feelings, sense of reality,
knowledge of duty and worth may be interpreted in many ways.
We cannot speak of inner light at all, save in ejaculations signifying
nothing to other men, unless we define its character in social terms,
that is in terms which come out of our history. The 'true' seed
within, the 'right' spirit, can be distinguished from false seeds and
evil spirits only by the use of criteria which are not purely individual and biographical. We discriminate between light within and
spiritual will-o'-the-wisps by reference to a 'Christ' within. But the
word 'Christ' comes out of social history and has a meaning not
derived from individual experience. Religious experience and
moral sense are to be found in many different settings and can be
interpreted from many different points of view (1960: 38–39).

There is no accommodating escape from Christian faith's "partnership
with history, however many other partners it may choose. With this it
has been mated and to this its loyalty belongs" (p. 43). However,
Niebuhr's own inclinations raise what is, perhaps for him, the hardest
question of all: "How can revelation mean both history and God" (p. 43)?
In the confrontation of the classical and modern senses of history, this is
only a variant of my question of fidelity and contemporaneity.

Niebuhr begins with internal history—the telling of our own story
of what has happened to us—because such history seems initially to
orient and identify us as belonging to a coherent world of meaning,
truth, and right. External history, he says, refers more objectively to
events as told by a disinterested and analytic spectator. In external
historical narratives, facts are interpreted as a series of cause and effects,
with value being the relative strength of the effect of one event on
another in the series. In internal history and narrative, value means
worth for the self and the group—a worth determined by the sustenance
of orienting and identifying memory that is productive of a story of our
lives. Time in external history and narrative is sequential, while in
internal history it is marked by the sense of duration as meaning remembered and thus transmitted. The past remains present in memory and the
future in imaged anticipation as an open potentiality. External history
analyzes and reports the external relations of a human association, while
internal history confesses the experience of subjects interacting in community (1960: 44–59). Accordingly, Niebuhr suggests that in narrating the
internal life-story of a community, we can "have" both history and God.
Revelation finally rests confessionally on what we say about ourselves—

what has happened to us in the transforming and identifying events of faith. Similarly, the moral life rests on norms that arise from the internal discourse and practice of the Church as it relates its story in and through history.

If this is all that one chose to stress in interpreting *The Meaning of Revelation* (Hauerwas, 1983), Christian ethical norms could be interpreted as the products of the Church's internal self-understanding and particular confessions. But in so doing one would still have to stop significantly short of Niebuhr's analysis and refuse to follow internal history to its historicist conclusion. Even if Niebuhr's depiction of such internal conversations and confessional stories in any given age set the foundation for the Church's norms, they would still exist within the flexibility of a narrative tale wherein old things are said in new contexts and thus relatively transformed, as well as new things being said in the ordinary *progress* of the Church's story. Even if interpreted initially in a confessional way, ethical norms in general, and norms of sexual morality in particular would still be set within an historicist dynamic. This inevitable conclusion of modern historicism as a viable and rich context for interpreting the meaning of revelation leads the Niebuhr of *The Meaning of Revelation* far beyond the merely internal history of particular and local communities.

In fact, Niebuhr advances a "two-aspect" view of history (1960: 60–61) without lapsing into a dualism that separates what is distinguished. He argues that one can neither collapse the distinction between the story of the life of the Church from that of the world nor can they be separated without relation. That is to say that there is a functional necessity of relating the Church's external to its internal history for adequately critical self-understanding. This is the existential working necessity of a faith that cannot live apart from the world it inhabits (p. 62). Thus, Niebuhr says, that even if we must begin with the "internal knowledge of the destiny of self and community, we have found it necessary in the Christian church to accept the external views of ourselves which others have set forth and to make these external histories events of spiritual significance" (p. 62). Furthermore, he makes clear that such spiritual significance is not to be understood apart from history but is, in fact, a fully material and historicist moral experience.

> To see ourselves as others see us, or to have others communicate to us what they see when they regard our lives from the outside is to have a moral experience. Every external history of ourselves, communicated to us, becomes an event of inner history (p. 62).

Alterity and The Moral Praxis of History

In the final analysis of internal and external history Niebuhr broaches the intersubjective phenomenological origin of moral character—an examination he takes up most systematically in *The Responsible Self* (1963a). While often narrated in the form of self-told stories of our lives, fully critical moral experience is born externally from the call and communication of an external other. If the internal and confessional stories that the Church tells as the narrative frame of revelation and faith are also to be ones of character and virtue, they cannot be self-born but remain dependent on *what others say has happened to them because of us.* These external histories become part of our internal history in the form of the "rest of our story." It is from the perspective of *the other* that moral experiences are initiated. Accordingly, in *The Responsible Self* Niebuhr adopts responsiveness and responsibility as root metaphors for the Christian moral life.

In a wider vein, the internal historical narratives of the Church's moral life are dependent on the external historical narratives of the worlds the Church inhabits—worlds that are necessary for the Church's internal identity. Thus the Church's rhetoric of sexual morality cannot be separated from the discourse of modernity in general. Cast in a historicist narrative frame, our norms are not only told in plots of single and self-interpreted continuity but are cast into the wider and pluralistic narratives of our age. To survive as a critically verified and legitimated norm, the complete story of heterosexual marriage must also be told by those others who are not married and not heterosexual. Stories of such external histories are necessary for full character identity.

> Such external histories have helped to keep the church from exalting itself as though its inner life rather than the God of that inner life were the center of its attention and the ground of its faith. They have reminded the church of the earthen nature of the vessel in which the treasure of faith existed (Niebuhr, 1960: 63).

In the narrative history of the Church's faith and life, it is the perspective and story of the *external other* that prevents any use of the confessional approach to theology and ethics from taking the turn of antimodernist nostalgia, sectarian segmentation, or aestheticist release. Indeed, Niebuhr concludes that the internal life of the self—either of the individual or the community—"does not exist without external embodiment.... External history is the medium in which internal history exists and comes to life" (1960: 65–66). In Niebuhr's critical piety, taking the standpoint of the other—or *alterity*—ultimately means an effort of the Church "to see the reflection of itself with the eyes of God," the ultimate *Other*.

Even though there is ambiguity in his relation of internal and external history, Niebuhr's efforts were born from the depth of a lifelong struggle to understand the relation of self and other, the particular and the universal, reason and revelation, God and history, Christ and culture, Church and society. However, challenged by the world events of his day and his deeper evangelical understanding of total human dependence on God as *Other*—what he will later call "radical monotheism"—leads him in *The Meaning of Revelation* to a text within the text that supports the primary obligations of external history and responds to all overdrawn promotions of particularity and sectarian methods in theology and ethics. In the end, Niebuhr recalls the temptation of the virulent egoism that abides at the heart of the Church's theological and moral rhetoric whether of universalistic or particularist emphasis.

> Egotism is not only a characteristic of the will but also of the imagination, and appears in the tendency of the person to impute to all other selves the same interest in itself which it feels.... The group also thinks of itself as in the center. So all nations tend to regard themselves as chosen peoples...(and)...that all the world is centered in their destiny. Such imagination can never enter into the knowledge of another self; it is always the "I" that is known and never the "Thou." The self lives in a real isolation in which others serve only as mirrors in which the ego is reflected. Moreover the picture of the self which the imagination uses is likely to be a wholly fanciful one, since it is not subject to the criticism of other selves (Niebuhr, 1960: 74–75).

Much of the present discourse of the Christian denominations on sexual morality suffers from the burdens of an enervated and defensive will rooted in a diminished historical and moral imagination.

# 3

## History, Interpretation, and the Moral Life

### Revelation and Reason

Gaining an adequate historical and moral imagination is a task of interpretation and an accomplishment of critical hermeneutic theory and practice. As we have seen, H. Richard Niebuhr presents the meaning of revelation (1960) thoroughly within the historicist context of modernity. Indeed, the Christian Church can "have" God, morality, *and* history. However, nowhere does Niebuhr argue that revelation in its historicist frame is self-evident or suprarational—that simply and solipsistically "confessing" something to be true and right makes it so. Confessions of what has happened to us demand interpretation, discrimination, and finally, in the external history of others, legitimation. What we claim to see and hear remain only distant *appearances*—incomplete human events—until primary hermeneutic acts of naming occur. Naming is the initial human act of rationally interpreting and morally relating what we have seen and heard to the entire course of our lives in both internal and external dimensions. Such acts necessarily occur within extant worlds of meaning and claim to be rational insofar as they offer *reasons* for what we confess as a *revelation* of truth and right. They accomplish a coherent image of named identity—one that both creates and sustains an internal historical story that Niebuhr says, "illuminates the rest of it and which is itself intelligible" (1960: 68). These referential and interpersonally oriented *reasons for belief* are what he calls "reasons of the heart" (pp. 67–100). Thus reason is hermeneutically bound to revelation at even foundational and confessional levels of the Church's discourse just as it is at later, more systematic levels of theological and moral argument. Having God, morality, and history is also having both revelation and reason.

The fact that the hermeneutic bond of reason and revelation is historicist indicates that the confessional stories we tell must be materially sustained over time and its personal and temporal distances. It is the burden of critical-hermeneutic acts of the rational imagination to initially and relatively bridge such distances so that a practical life and world-narrative can be accomplished, becoming the histories and stories of our own lives and those of others. In this way history itself is materially sustained as a metaconversation and metanarrative—the ancient progress of new worlds of divine-human dwelling encompassing and decentering the old. Being decentered rather than replaced, the old *passes* to new as the praxis of tradition. Our confessions of character, cosmos, and world are first accomplished as acts of the rational hermeneutic imagination—ones that can create stories and form narratives, indeed, that linguistically "make history."

Ethical norms first arise as images born from such historical narrative confessions of the meaning and identity of our lives with others. As the stories and norms of such interpersonal and communally formed lives *progress* historically, they become decentered by new events and challenges and thus become subject to change—the permanent metanoia that marks both life and Church in the historicist world.[1] In this, history is both burden and grace—the burden of retelling our stories, reforming our character, reconsidering our norms and the grace of the rational hermeneutic imagination to do so. The dual burden and grace of the metanarrative of history is the final meaning of revelation. "Revelation means the point at which we can begin to think and act as members of an intelligible and intelligent world of persons.... By revelation in our history, then, we mean that special occasion which provides us with an image by means of which all the occasions of personal and common life become intelligible" (Niebuhr, 1960: 69; 80).

To abandon history for the sake of revelation is to abandon both the form and the content of revelation itself. Likewise, to abandon reason is to tear asunder the material meaning of revelation as a practical and ongoing story of cosmic identification, participation, and presence.

Whatever else revelation means it does mean an event in our history which brings rationality and wholeness into the confused joys and sorrows of personal existence and allows us to discern order in the brawl of communal histories. Such revelation is no substitute for reason; the illumination it supplies does not excuse the mind from labor; but it does give to the mind the impulsion and the first principles it requires if it is to be able to do its proper work. In this sense we may say that the revelatory moment is revelatory because it is rational, because it makes the understanding of order and meaning in personal history possible. Through it a pattern of dramatic unity becomes apparent with the aid of which the heart can understand what has happened, is happening and will happen to selves in their community (Niebuhr, 1960: 80).

## The Labor of Rational Interpretation[2]

The phenomenological and temporal distances that separate the dimensions of history and the stories of individuals and groups frame the labor of rational interpretation. The reconstructed understanding of history in modernity—the movement of decentered spirals—focuses the work of the relative hermeneutic abridgment of such distances. At the same time, such an understanding criticizes any evolutionary progressive view of history as definitive of modernity. World history is the narratives of actual life-worlds in all of their variety, fracture, and sin. The conventionality of history in modernity needs to be seen in this light—people, communities, and ages coming together, amid pluralism and change, as participants in history's metaconversation and metanarrative.[3] In this practical and moral labor of interpretation, we are burdened to understand historical relativity and pluralism without being either relativistic or solipsistic. Consequently, we engage in the conventions of history with self-conscious understanding that our own narratives of moral character and ethical norms are always incomplete without hearing those of others—those most often cast to the margins of history's metanarrative. The wider hermeneutic conventionality of history does not narrow the moral life to a particular and conventionalist ethic whose coherence is only self-engendered and self-contained. Rather the conventionality of history and the labors of historical interpretation are linguistically framed. It is through language universally practiced dialogically—as speaking and listening, questioning and being questioned, telling our stories and listening to those of others—that we respond to the challenge of critical historical understanding. In coming together as communities and worlds of narrative confession and constructive dialogue, we experience the events we name as revealed and true and develop norms we claim to be right. These engagements in the universal discourse of any given age form rational and moral character. Beyond the narrow conventionalism of our own internal histories and norms, we become interested enough in our common worldly life to bear the burden and appreciate the grace of the labor of rational moral interpretation and judgment. This is the loyalty that revelation owes to history and the commitment that the Church owes the world and its conflicts.

When Niebuhr speaks of revelation in terms of a labor of the mind (1960: 80), he is speaking initially of the burdens of interpretation amid the relativity, plurality, and conventionality of history. Revelation and the confessions of our own experiences do not obviate the need for interpretation in the Church, but rather give to our minds an impulse and ground for the first principles we will use in our later and necessary theological and moral arguments. Becoming a vital community of moral discourse and action is to become a community of moral interpretation, systematic ethical argument, effective persuasion, and substantive action. Being such a community means that the Church will come to self-understanding and identification in a "time-full" historicist manner. As a fully historical community, when the Church speaks of *tradition* it will not be in a narrow and self-defensive manner that attempts to protect its past against the challenges of the present and future. Ironically, as the latest rounds of the denominations' debate on sexual morality exhibit, radical self-defensiveness does not protect the Church's tradition but renders it static and moribund. For the past only survives in acts of contemporary remembrance and anticipation when the old is recovered and set upon the horizon of the future. In such critical-hermeneutic conversations, the Church will engage with courage and faith the universal burdens and labors of history. The movements of history cannot be rendered timeless and absolute. To be an effective confession and proclamation of faith, revelation remains time-bound owing its loyalty to history and to the worlds that history frames. It is the incarnations of the divine-human presence in every time and place—history as permanent movement and change—that claim the Church's loyalty and measure its fidelity.

Consequently, in every age, the Church must inquire into the sense, meaning, truth, and right of its own heritage of theological articulations and ethical norms. This is not disloyalty to its past, but rather a deeper loyalty that allows the received stories of its internal history to relatively traverse the phenomenological and temporal distances that separate the past from the present and future. The material historicity of the Church—its own defining incarnational center—makes such critical and historically effective inquiry a foundational ethos and informing virtue for all methods of theological and ethical work. In this sense, critical-hermeneutic discourse and the judgment and action it engenders is not just one method among many but the defining ecclesiological ground for all methodology. In its historicist character the modern age still has much to offer the Church for a full understanding of the meaning of revelation and for more effective theological articulation and moral action. Relativity, plurality, and the wider convention of the metaconversation of history need not be considered debilitating threats to fidelity, but rather "grace-full" burdens that hold promise of renewal and vitality in the work of the Church in any age.[4]

## The Reality of Hermeneutic Burdens[5]

Even though I have argued that there is a defining grace in the practice of ongoing rational interpretation, the attendant burdens of continually *coming* to understanding are real. While necessary and foundational, the drive to understanding alone is insufficient. Once achieved, understanding provides only an initial ground for action. Finally, processes of systematic theological and moral argument and passionate rhetorical persuasion must intervene as a bridge that guides understanding toward judgment and action. In the remainder of this chapter, I will describe and gauge the import for moral argument of (a) the burdens of first and second hermeneutic moments in the critical interpretation of particular questions; (b) the burden of interpreting the material-historical state of any question as the informing context for the above hermeneutic moments; and (c) the burden of prejudice as "prejudgment" that forms the necessary horizon for all interpretive acts. In the next chapter I will describe in more detail the role and function of systematic/theoretic argument and the rhetoric of ideological persuasion. There we will engage the procrustean temptations of all systematic theory and argument and the temptation to self-serving obfuscation in all rhetoric of persuasion.

### Exegesis and Interpretation

Once the Church inquires into its own traditions, it often finds, in form if not degree, the same relativity, plurality, and conventionality there as in the contemporary age. Thus, even fully critical methods of exegetical recovery of the past seldom disclose single understandings of what was said and meant in any particular age or with respect to any particular point in theology and ethics. Nor does the past tradition of the Church itself appear without fracture and discontinuity. Even when exegesis of our heritage concludes in broad agreement, the hermeneutic task is only half done. For tradition to be vital and effective, the decentering progress of the metaconversation of history demands that what has been said and done in the past be submitted to new and invariably transforming conversations in the present. All interpretation of the past involves this two-step process. With all exegetical methods, broadly interpreted, at our disposal, we inquire into the originating historical conversation—the broad sweep of this aspect of the *story of our life* that produced the theological or ethical point under consideration. We attempt to come to an understanding of what was said or meant in that context. Given the realities of historical distance, even with such broadly based and historically contextual exegesis, we can only relatively accomplish an understanding of our own past.[6]

Still, past histories are never narrated adequately by simple recall and recitation of facts and language told in a literal manner. The narrative histories of individuals and groups are more deeply textured than that. What appears at the literal threshold and surface of fact and language is only an invitation to the deeper recesses of human lives and historical ages that must be probed and critically sorted out. In our own time, psychoanalytic theory and practice have certainly demonstrated that remembering and telling one's own story demands the most intense probing and sorting of an infinite maze of discontinuous and symbolic meanings—of literally unrealized prejudices and unconscious causes and motivations. The past also has its own deeply embedded prejudices that are not fully recoverable in any exegesis. Consequently, though valuable and necessary, exegesis alone, no matter how critical, cannot bear the historical burdens of total recovery of the mind of an author, the complete meaning of a text, or the universal informing spirit of an age. Nor do we need our exegetical methods to bear such burdens. Proper exegesis also does its work in an historicist way—knowing that there is always more to say and know about a text and age than has been said or known. Such knowledge enhances and enriches the past as a constant claim on the Church's ongoing remembrance. Exegesis will be necessary but insufficient—a *first hermeneutic moment*—in the praxis of the Church as a community of theological and moral discourse.

It follows then, that exegesis and its accomplishments are only half of even the initial burdens of interpretation. For this reason, I have deliberately avoided collapsing all methods of interpreting texts under the name of "exegesis." Our always relative recovery of a biblical text, theological doctrine or system, or ethical norm in its own originating and informing context does not lighten the burdens of interpretive understanding and judgment in our own time and in light of the future. This first hermeneutic moment of exegesis can be called "re-constructive" insofar as we attempt to reconstruct the informing and defining conversations of past history. The *second hermeneutic moment* involves the new "construction." Thus in our conversations with the past, we will want to know how much sense, coherence, meaning, truth, and right can be brought forward in terms of our own age and its challenges to the renewal of Christian faith and life. We cannot expect nor can we seek either total continuity or discontinuity between the present and the past. Our obligation of fidelity to the past must always be joined with our obligation of effective contemporaneity.

Whereas *literalism* and *fundamentalism* in Bible and *dogmatism* in theology will always necessarily pick and choose among methods of exegetic interpretation, what is more common among all of the denominations is both a tendency and a practice of what can be called *biblicism* and at least a functional ethical *doctrinalism*. Here, all the methods of contemporary exegesis are used—methods of the first hermeneutic moment—to discover as far as possible the original, and indeed, originating meaning of the "text." Once reconstructed, without further interpretation and argument, such an approach claims to achieve a biblical, theological, and ethical norm. Often what is called fundamentalism in conservative denominations is really only a relative biblicism. However, even in liberal denominations, biblicism and doctrinalism appear in much sermonizing and Bible study, especially those that pertain to the rhetoric of sex. For example, coming to either a relatively affirmative or negative moral judgment about homosexuality through only an exegesis of biblical texts and past Church teachings are forms of biblicism and ethical doctrinalism. The key difference between biblicism and doctrinalism and a more fully critical hermeneutic method is the self-conscious acceptance of the possibility of the accrual of new meaning.

When theological and moral discourse rest with only the first hermeneutic moment of exegesis, it can be related to the genetic fallacy of origins—the logical, epistemological, and moral priority of the past. Here the priority of the past guides exegetical reconstructions of the origination of a text, doctrine, norm, law, or practice—i.e., the narrative ethos of an "original" community as a singular guide in the present and future. This kind of geneticist priority of the past is not a phenomenological-historicist priority whose reconstructive remembrance always issues further invitations for new reconstructions. In its stress on the priority of the past, such geneticist and positivist understandings of the metaconversation and narrative of history lose historical integrity—are less than "time-full." Only exegetical efforts to recover the past in moments of reconstructive remembrance lapse inevitably into an uncritical traditionalism, primitivism, and antiquarianism.

If the conversations of the first hermeneutic moment of exegetic reconstruction are fraught with deeply embedded prejudices of origin, so too are the conversations of our new constructive efforts. Second hermeneutic conversations are also inevitably prejudiced toward our own place and time—to the deeply embedded and informing interests and conventions of contemporary life. These conversations too must be guided by a plurality of interpretations and self-conscious practices of full historicist dialogue so that a full array of contemporary interests and ideologies can be critically examined and then compared with the wisdom of the past in systematic argument and appropriate pragmatic tests of application. As informing horizons of rational speech, such past and present prejudices are unavoidable amid the relativity, plurality, and conventionality of history. But they need not be damning if we are willing to submit them to the light of adequately framed hermeneutic conversations.

The Material-Historical State of the Question and Its Prejudices

To be adequately critical, the work of the first and second hermeneutic moments and their horizon of prejudices must bear a prior and overarching burden of interpreting the material-historical state of the question. In short, we have to know what we are talking about and then proceed to talk about that subject and not surreptitiously import other agendas that distort our conversation from the beginning. It is not true that every opinion and prejudice, once disclosed, has as much claim on the praxis of constructive discourse as any other. Our orienting prejudgments are also under rational and moral norms of coherence and order— criteria that enable constructive rational conversation in the first place and prevent its systematic distortion, dysfunction, and trivialization. Even though rational discourse has much to learn from discoveries of an informing and motivating unconscious by psychoanalytic theory and practice, effective ethical conversations about the meaning and guidance of our public lives are not primarily psychotherapeutic or pastoral. For example, while prejudices that ground racist or sexist attitudes and practices are legitimate subjects for the work of psychotherapy, pastoral counseling, and moral confrontation, they cannot sustain claims to be taken seriously as substantive and positive contributions to the Church's life and work. What counts as a legitimate or illegitimate prejudice and, thus, what rules are to guide the type of conversation to be engaged are also subject to the progress of history's metaconversation.

Certainly in our reconstructive exegesis of the first hermeneutic moment, we must seek out the negative racist and sexist prejudices that inform the history of the Church's story—indeed the totality of the Church's self-understanding in this or any age. In the conversations of the second hermeneutic moment, however, we will find that such prejudices can only be indicted, confronted, and confessed as irrational and evil and cannot be admitted to constructive conversation. Both hermeneutic moments of construction and reconstruction must be guided by a prior and deeper interpretation of the material-historical state of the question. Indeed, in advance of all our particular ethical interpretations and judgments about contemporary questions of race and gender, we now know that color and gender have nothing either rationally or theologically to do with human worth or the negative discrimination of the character of individuals and their public lives. The fact that we can transform such negative prejudices of our own internal heritage and tradition by new external understandings confirms the constructive use of reasoned discourse. Particular questions of race and gender are now embedded in a deeper and more complete historical narrative—stories of women and people of color. Therefore, the rest of the story of "white men" will be told by people of color and women—what they tell us has happened to them because of us. In this way internal histories are materially challenged and complemented by the external histories of others. This does not mean that we will not engage the racism and sexism in the Church or in ourselves; but it does mean that such engagements will be through the critical exposure of the rational nonverifiability and illegitimacy of such prejudices as viable points of departure for conversation and debate. This is the present material-historical and moral state of the questions of racism and sexism.

When cast upon the historicist approach I have been suggesting, to discuss *with serious constructive intent* whether women ought to be full ministers or priests or bishops, or to make allowances in polity for the sorts of prejudices that inform such discussions, no matter how sincerely held, is finally to accept as open to discussion whether women are human enough to bear forward the images the Church seeks for its ministry, whether clerical or lay. It would be far more coherent (but no less misguided) for the Church, as it has in the past, to continue to confess directly its adherence to an archaic and wrongful theological anthropology—i.e, that women *cannot* occupy such offices because *they are* theologically and anthropologically deficient—than to propose such prejudices as possible constructive interpretations appropriate for the framing of serious debate.

However, at times the contours of such distorted conversation are not easy to discern. To argue that women *ought not* be priests or ministers because one sees this as the specific command of God or the will of Christ, or because one does not possess an adequate philosophy and theology of change may not initially seem to be a direct sexist argument, though the result, rooted in a nonviable theology, is in fact a negative sexual discrimination. Here, especially in teaching contexts, we should first attempt to confront the presenting issues and problems in question and not immediately conflate them with other arguments or personalities that are clearly more sexist at their core. In the end, however, it is most often the case that arguments that lead to sexist conclusions are also mixed with deeper, perhaps unconsciously formed, prejudices that are rooted in a negative anthropology and fear of women. For example, to "inquire" further into "the mind of God" for reasons for this supposed divine prohibition returns us to the negative anthropology and theology of core sexism. It is for this reason that even conscientiously held stumbling blocks for the acceptance of women into every venue of Church and society so quickly distort our conversations and render them incompetent.

However, when speaking of racism it is more difficult to make even these initial and relative "allowances" of misunderstanding God's will and historical change with respect to serious and rationally competent speech. Admitting into discourse similar stumbling blocks with respect to people of color distorts such conversations immediately. Part of the reason for this is that the state of the question of prejudice against people of color claims now a clearer historical record than that of sexism against women and it discloses with immediate certainty that no constructive rational debate can be even begun that accepts as open for discussion any negative prejudgment whatsoever in the context of race—as in religious racist rhetoric that God has willed the care of people of color to the white race. Even questions couched as statistically descriptive are morally risky. To admit for serious discussion whether an African-American *can be* elected president, for example, is not necessarily a sign of our intentions to search for equity in our political life but almost always a sign of our own continuing racism. If the above seems to be a statistical fact—that an African-American black cannot yet be elected on the basis of race alone—it is one that cannot bear the burden of rational and moral sense but only the fact of our continuing racism. Unless the contexts of such discussions are self-consciously and self-critically focused upon the racism that continues to infect our national and cultural life, they will be systematically distorted by the admission of an unverifiable and illegitimate racist prejudgment and prejudice.

Finally, to complete the comparison, I take no comfort that the violence produced from sexist attitudes against women may not yet have attained the status of the historical record of racism. Nor do I think that when it does, the record will be less virulent than that inflicted on people of color. This only alerts us to the work that needs to be done to bring this distorting prejudice of sexism to full attention in the writing and telling of women's narratives and histories. Making more inclusive decisions with respect to gender as well as to race in reforming the canons of literature at all levels of education and among all of the disciplines can lead to important intellectual and moral progress in this regard. The temptation that must be resisted, however, is the implication that racism as such is worse than sexism or vice versa. We will finally make no moral progress in comparing victims according to whose is the worse oppression. Therefore, conversations that intend to probe the possibilities of systematic construction and argument built on racist and sexist prejudices—not just conversations *about* race and gender, but those that, intended or not, are a rational association of negative worth on the basis of race and gender—cannot be critically engaged except by way of exegetical exposition and moral confrontation.[7]

Discussions of white racism and male sexism often bring predictable questions of "reverse" racism and sexism—the racism of people of color and the female sexist. Yet the material-history of these relations, especially noted in the metanarrative of our own culture, does not uphold the coherence of such terms and makes their conceptualization less than a serious foundation for constructive conversation. Logically, there can be racism and sexism among all races and in both genders. Nonetheless, no historical and phenomenological interpretation of the state of racism and sexism in our culture can sustain either internal or external historical stories of routine rejection and negative moral discrimination against Caucasians and men because of race and gender. One can note, discuss, and morally engage the rage, anger, hatred, even violence against Caucasians and men, but these realities can be neither rationally nor morally sustained as racist or sexist when interpreted according to the substantive narratives of our material histories. In such a comparison, the stories of white men do not compare one to one with people of color and women. Our own histories belie such logic. History most often tells materially asymmetrical stories among different people and cultures that cannot be balanced arithmetically despite our desire of perceived need for such logical uniformity.

Not every broad interpretation of the state of moral questions is as clear as the stories of race and gender. Many questions are in narrative midsteam so to speak—their material stories just beginning to be told, if they are told at all. Homosexuality is one of those issues. As the Church engages in primary exegesis to reconstruct biblical texts and traditional teaching about homosexuality, a sense of dissatisfaction emerges. Some of the dissatisfaction is formal, rooted in the necessarily incomplete nature of the first hermeneutic moment of reconstructive exegesis. Even when this necessary work is engaged, there is a tendency to skip the work of new interpretation and argument. Accordingly, on both conservative and liberal sides, the present debate on homosexuality tends to jump from a conflict of exegesis to the rhetoric of passionate ideological persuasion avoiding systematic argument altogether or attaching itself uncritically to whatever scientific and social-scientific opinion suits its interests. Even if these conflicts in exegetical study were to be resolved in the negative with respect to homosexuality, the theological and moral questions would not be resolved. The Church would still be obliged to engage in further theological and moral debate about whether such a traditional rejection can now be faithfully brought forward.

Along with this exegetical dissatisfaction in reconstructing the Church's understanding of homosexuality, there is a correlative dissatisfaction with attempts at new constructions. The state of our conversations about homosexuality discloses a horizon of essentially unexamined prejudices on all fronts. We are having difficulty in even introducing the subject of homosexuality into the serious and constructive moral discourse of the Church not only because the story of human sexuality is so hard to tell in general but also because from the perspective of the heterosexual majority the fully historicist story of homosexuality as *the stories of homosexual persons* is so distant and marginal to a point of being alien. The horizon of prejudice we bring to this conversation tends to distort it from the outset because we are not really sure what we are talking about in either hermeneutic moment. As homosexual persons were projected historically to the margins of culture and society— became inhabitants in fact of underground subcultures—both their internal and external histories became relatively impossible to tell and hear. With such character-stories only jotted in the marginal notes of heterosexuality, heterosexual and homosexual persons have had great difficulty understanding each other. Indeed, the point can be made that in their shadowy historical/cultural *persona*, homosexual persons have had a greater burden to bear in coming to understand themselves—no easy matter even for those who have not been rendered so socially and culturally marginal. Consequently, the question of the ethics of homosexuality remains confused in all of its historical dimensions. These now negatively prejudiced historical burdens slow and deflect the work of ethical interpretation and argument and fan the flames of an illegitimate rhetoric of moral persuasion from both conservative and liberal camps.

In the metanarrative of homosexuality and homosexual persons we are often dealing more with internal and external parody than historical narration. Much of the reason for such parodies is rooted in the inordinate fear of homosexuality as well as the fears of homosexual persons.

Overcoming homophobia and homosexual anxiety are material preconditions for moving the moral discourse of the Church on homosexuality
from its present state of stagnation and enervating repetition. Rejecting
homophobia does not necessarily mean accepting homosexuality as an
alternative ethical norm. It is, however, a demand of the state of the question—a deep hermeneutic and moral burden that must be borne as the
significant precondition for faithful and effective ethical inquiry.

The responsible interpretation of homosexuality requires listening
to the story of homosexual persons as they now participate in conversations of culture and society. And such listening can only be effectively
accomplished amid conditions and structures of justice and friendship.
Without sufficient appreciation of the present circumstances of the debate
on homosexuality, we will continue to find our interpretations so distant
from the realities in question that our discussions will remain structurally
distorted. All of our hermeneutic efforts will proceed under the weight of
a variety of distorting prejudices—from homophobic rejection to
homophilic acceptance—that are simply too great for our conversations
to bear. In homophobia, the distance for adequate interpretation is too
great; in homophilia, it is too close. Without an adequate line of vision—
one that is not too far to see what is going on or too close to gain the necessary perspective—attempting to reconstruct an adequate understanding
of the past and to construct new meanings in the present merely continues a parody of critical moral discourse. Denominational arguments
about homosexuality are failing because they are proceeding with
premises built on an illegitimate prejudice of knowledge in the face of a
present state of significant ignorance.[8]

I have engaged these examples of racism, sexism, and homosexuality to indicate that the burden of critical interpretation in theology and
ethics, while historically universal, is not only methodologically formal or
intellectually abstract. States of the question are not only of logical and
scholastic interest. The burden of critical interpretation is born by the
concrete and material histories of people, by a flesh and blood that provides the first obligation and necessary content of all of our rational ideas
and methods. History may be framed as meaningful by ideas, but history
is not an idea. To engage in the praxis of understanding, we must first
possess an inchoate feeling for time and place, images of location and
presence that ground and motivate all of our acts of rational discrimination. Historicist reason is not only, or in the first instance,"of the head,"
but also, as H. Richard Niebuhr suggests, "of the heart" (1960: 67–100).

Critical-historical interpretations are not relative, pluralist, or
oriented around the conventions of real people and their stories because

this might be the way we like to think or because such claims provide a rationale for changes in ethics and morals that seem to meet only a personal need or interest. Rather the reason why we think historically is because we first feel these dimensions of history's reality and experience—because this is the way we are formed biographically in our passage from birth to death as individuals, cultures, societies, and nations. Thus the relativity of history is not a gross and solipsistic relativism. Similarly, the inevitable plurality of interpretation and the horizon of prejudgment do not lead to a trivialization of conversation in the acceptance of every initial and personal prejudice as an equal claim to bear the weight of serious constructive intent. We cannot sustain a claim to enter the conventions of constructive conversation unless what we have to contribute has some initial and broad resonance with some state of affairs—somehow fits initially and makes sense in the narratives of history, culture, and society. And while we should take great care and be broadly based in our interpretations of what counts as serious rather than trivial, foolish, or destructive prejudices, the burdens of interpretation are not so great as to be unbearable, leading inevitably to the failure of all our constructive rational intentions.

I am not thinking of necessary constitutional rights of freedom of speech here. Within ordinary and liberal canons of individual and public security and order and the protection of others from violent intrusions, people have a general right to believe and say trivial, foolish, even self-destructively prejudiced things. However, the burden of rationally constructive and morally competent speech cannot be borne by any and every foundational prejudgment, no matter how sincerely held.[9] Despite profoundly serious dangers of the abuse of power and control over the subject and participants in the public discourse of both Church and society, the praxis of critical interpretation and systematic argument cannot avoid the prior burden of the interpretation of the historical state of a question—the state of our knowledge as well as of our ignorance and prejudice. I am arguing here for a deeper and materially thicker interpretation of the historical states of questions and issues, problems and dilemmas—for a formal norm of content that furnishes substantive criteria for the practice of rational interpretation. Unless we can also engage this deeper burden of interpreting our historical circumstances, the particular burdens of relativity, pluralism and conventionality will be too great to bear. Without attention to the state of our internal and external stories and the ethos they engender as cultural-historical frames for particular questions and issues, our conversations will fail in their constructive intent or not even be tried because of the history of such miscast debates.

In the broad course of history, prejudgments, including religious confessions, that do not have prima facie rational and moral verifiability cannot be made subject to competent moral discussion. It is not the case, as some forms of rationalism suggest, that reason will win out and such prejudices once admitted to critical conversation will be easily rejected. Material-history shows the contrary. Without substantive criteria to guide such debates at the outset—indeed, enabling criteria that frame and structure the discourse from the beginning—the conversation as such will be systematically distorted. Racism, sexism, antisemitism, and homophobia are examples of an entire range of feelings, opinions, systems, and practices that render speech situations incompetent because they are inadequately rational and moral at the outset—not capable of sustaining a competent conversation among free and equal subjects that holds effective promise for verification and legitimation. Once admitted to discourse, such prejudices tend to be only repeated as a substitution for rational interpretation: systematic argument gives way to "argument" by reiteration or ideological obfuscation and intimidation. In such states of affairs it would be far better to say nothing at all, to suspend for a time the work of systematic argument and judgment, until the prior work of gauging the state of the question is accomplished and an adequate frame of initial rational and moral criteria established.

## The Norm of Content[10]

I have taken some time with a discussion of the material-historical state of the question to derive what I now call *the norm of content*. Without guidance from effective criteria of content, we will misunderstand the praxis of critical interpretation and its conversations, and forgetting the necessary foundation of our discourse in the material conditions of history, engage in historically abstract speech. Once these substantive historical and cultural contexts are forgotten, the way is open to a global relativism, narrow conventionalism, and fractured pluralism. Any attempt at rational discourse inadequately framed by the actual conditions of its subject matter is easily reduced to the self-verifying and self-legitimating promotions of individual and institutional egos. Adequate rational conversations cannot be engaged through a logic of argument alone leading to conclusions abstracted from historical and cultural circumstances. Neither are such conversations guided only by norms of sincerity, deep commitment, or the abiding belief of the participants, however welcome. Adequately critical conversations must also attend at the outset to what such participants have to say, by their initial starting points and prejudgments, and how such *prejudices* fit, if at all, in prior interpretations of the material-historical circumstances of the state of the question being considered.

Hermeneutic circles of relative perception, interpretation, and judgment are not endless nor need they be vicious. Rational conversations are invited as responses to particular issues and questions. Such issues and questions have historical substance and duration beyond the language of any particular rational conversation. In recognizing the prior material-historical reality of the subject matter under discussion— letting the content take the lead so to speak—we can learn to be less historically abstract in our discourse. Ideas, principles, and norms have full reality only insofar as they are embedded in the material conversations of history. The hermeneutic burdens of moral discourse can be borne only by recognizing the full historicity of moral problems and issues as they appear in culture and society. This fully historicist epistemology implies that all theories of knowledge are social theories, that all cognitively informed practices are social practices, and finally, that all ideas, norms, and principles must be engaged and understood historically— i.e., as histories and cultures of rational ideas and moral practices.[11]

In light of such a normative historicist epistemology then, moral argument does not necessarily mean that anything goes or that all is "up for grabs" as possible grounds for serious conversation, or that internally coherent argument alone is our only guide to the right and the good. Letting the substantive content of history take the lead, after Nazism, Stalinism, and any number of other right- and left-wing dictatorships, we know, no matter how seductive any argument to the contrary, that we cannot morally order society in a totalitarian way. After the same Nazi murder of European Jewry, we now know—as we should have all along—that articulations of Christology that negate others cannot be a faithful rendering of Christian identification no matter how doctrinally "orthodox." In the same way, we know that all who are different from ourselves in race, gender, culture, nationality, religion, or sexual orientation are as marked by the grace and image of God as we claim to be. We know that talk of survivability in a nuclear war is a deadly foolishness and that apartheid is a moral evil and political failure that can have no peaceful future. And furthermore, we know all of these things in advance of our arguments through a sensitivity and awareness to the often tragic lessons of our own histories. Adequate rational debate and argument respond to realities already in place; they do not create reality from scratch. This is the prior "norm of content" that must guide all rational conversation and take the lead in all moral analysis and judgment.

Not all historical disclosures are as clear as the examples I have been using. To speak metaphorically, sometimes history's voice is clear and its narrative relatively singular and coherent; sometimes it is not and a cacophony of many voices speak multiple and often tragically conflicting stories. Sometimes history is simply silent or contains voices that have been rendered too marginal to speak. Even while accepting our obligations to recover what has been lost of our informing narratives, admissions of lack of knowledge and understanding about the state of history's conversation often contribute just as much to our moral debates as our claims of understanding and knowledge. Rhetoric that proceeds from such grounds of historical and cultural ignorance must be even more carefully attentive and conservative in argument than that which proceeds from relative knowledge. By conservative here, I do not mean that we necessarily hold on to the past, but that we recognize that all conversation framed by relative historical ignorance is necessarily of a thinner sort and thus more capable of being penetrated by only idiosyncratic and facile claims of new knowledge. At the same time, thick and dense interpretations and bold attempts at moral persuasion and judgment imposed upon situations of significant ignorance are intellectually and morally dangerous. Imposing "old knowledge" upon situations that admit "new ignorance" is excluded in the the decentering progress of historicist modernity.[12] To return to a previous example: it is under this ethos of significant material-historical ignorance that the moral debate on homosexuality ought to proceed. In all ethical interpretations and substantive moral judgments, the norm of content directs a prior probe into the state of the question—our relative state of historical and cultural knowledge and ignorance. With this direction, the Church's moral rhetoric on homosexuality is less likely to be short-circuited by a rush of argument to particular rational judgment.

## The Church and The Problem of Modernity

I have argued in Part One that the challenges of constructing and articulating a responsible sexual morality pertain to the critical understanding of history and the norms of rational coherence and argument that history contains or refuses to contain. We confess faith, construct and articulate theologies, make ethical judgments, and engage moral action within cosmologies and historically conditioned worldviews. We are formed as characters and engage our character roles upon historical cosmological stages. Such stages provide the dramatic venue and primary script for the development of moral character. The initial scripting of the scenes may not all be to our liking: character also demands creative engagement and critical ad-libbing. At the same time, such cosmological plays cannot be replaced according to our own desires or the basic contours of the play rewritten from scratch. We are now playing our parts on the stage and play of modernity. As the Church engages its own historicity, the problem of being faithful and contemporary is also now the problem of modernity.

I have argued that to speak of cosmologies and worldviews as *problems* is paradoxical and euphemistic: we do not "solve" cosmologies, but engage the problems they present and try to anticipate those that will emerge in any particular shift and change. However, problems are also opportunities. Engaging the problem of modernity with full force gives the Church the only opportunity it has to be a faithful teacher and guide in the area of sexual morality. For the denominations not to engage modernity's challenges to the conduct of a responsible Christian sexual life is to miss an opportunity of proportions that far outweigh the particular issues under discussion. Because of a misplacement of the meaning of fidelity, and an inadequate theology of change, if the Church fails to interpret, understand, and guide the sexual experience of ordinary people who are still interested in doing the right and accomplishing the good—fails to be a teacher—its own credibility will continue to erode to a point of new crisis in legitimation of the institution itself.

Crises in legitimation in cultures, societies, and institutions are not always understood as negative. From such crises, so the argument goes, new life can emerge from the encrustation and dross of the centuries. Voiced by both revolutionist and reformers, these arguments are engaged on a continuum from insight into the limits and duration of all human achievements, including religious ones, to overly romantic progressivism, utopianism, and radical anarchism. More mystical voices make not only a distinction but a separation between the *reality* of the Church as a mystery of grace and its embodiments in sociopolitical structures and ecclesiastical institutions. However, if we are approaching the evening of modernity and the dawn of postmodernity, any facile embrace of a crisis of legitimation of structures and institutions may lead not to a new and invigorated life at all, but simply to the end of the Church as a significant moral voice and guide. Theological and philosophical dualism that separates the reality of the Church from its own institutional embodiments cannot save the day. Christian faith by name and definition is thoroughly sacramental—incarnated in and with the material conditions and institutions of human history. Neither faith nor the moral life rest on incontrovertible self-evidence of either reason or revelation; nor does hope rest in a certain future, but rather on committed and loving engagements of the world as we find it.

Therefore, without further schizophrenic fracture, the Church cannot pick and choose those areas in which it is obliged to make sense, communicate meaning, say things that are true, truthful, and right. Failure here is a portent of failure in other areas as well—the Church continuing to lapse into a cultural convenience tolerated by the modern and postmodern world and supported by many of its own members precisely because it no longer takes the chance to say anything insightful, risky, or dangerously disturbing of the status quo.[13] Still, despite all difficulty and threat, embedded in modernity is the startling permission to do the risky thing. In the margin of its own cosmological notes modernity still contains a critical stage direction that the new can bear as much truth as the old and that our moral character is born on the progress of both the continuities and discontinuities of history. Despite all of its resistance and forgetfulness, the Church has in many areas accepted itself as also modern—accepted this cosmological permission that recalls the commitments of its own historicity to the contemporaneous present as well as to the revered past. Now is the time for the Church to accept in the area of sexual morality what it has, in relative ways and across all denominations, accepted in other areas of its faith and life—the challenge to be both faithful and contemporary, the permission to have new conversations about sexual morality that can, in principle, say new things.

# Part II.

## The Analytic Conversation of Moral Argument

# 4

# ETHICAL NORMS AND MORAL RULES

## An Analytic Mistake

My intention in Part One was to place the Church's conversation on sexual morality in its proper historical and cosmological contexts. I argued that without a proper sense of the foundational relation of history and ethics that draws together synthetically moral discourse and the moral life, the Church will not pay adequate attention to the shape and quality of its own debates on sex. Lacking foundation and location, the moral rhetoric of sex has become segmented, systematically distorted, and dysfunctional. From this lack of attention as well, and cutting across all strands and modes of the Church's conversations on sexual morality, comes a crucial analytic mistake internal to moral discourse in general. Arguments about sexual morality often confuse ethical norms and moral rules, and by collapsing the distance between them offer little guidance to their proper role and function. Correcting this mistake will advance the moral rhetoric of the Church in actual practice. In Part Two, then, we will engage in an analytic conversation about the meaning, function, and relation of ethical norms and moral rules.

This analytic mistake mirrors, in part, the substantive and cosmological confusions I discussed in Part One. The challenges of historical distance remain but are now disclosed in a more analytic way internal to moral discourse as such. When in their search for uniformity and continuity with past ethical teaching or in their desire for a more singular and certain moral guidance, the denominations do not sufficiently attend to the decentering dynamics of modernity, they will also tend to collapse the distinction and distance between norms and rules. The distant disclosure of general normative values for orienting the moral life are confused with proximate rules of behavior in particular situations and circumstances, and critical moral reflection becomes confused and dysfunctional. Ethical norms become too closely tied to decisions about particular behavior and fail in their project of value disclosure and orientation amid ever-changing material conditions and circumstances. Moral rules become too general and distant from particular circumstances to effectively regulate behavior in given situations and become similarly dysfunctional.

For example, a continuing and meaningful historical norm of truthfulness will become dysfunctional if I take it as an absolute rule of literal speech—a regulation of literal behavior in any and all circumstances. In confusing the norm of truthfulness with the rule to tell the truth, the goods intended by the value of truth are not attained and the norm of truthfulness fails to function. At the same time, if I develop a "norm" that says that I can lie in all situations and circumstances that meet my needs and interests—that is, create a norm from the context of rule—the rule to tell the truth itself becomes dysfunctional and lying becomes regulative. In the first instance, norms are too close to rules for an adequate line of orienting moral vision: the values disclosed by the norm are lost and the goods intended are not accomplished. In the second, the rule of behavior becomes too distant from the norm, becoming subject only to vague needs and interests interpreted by any person or group and not regulative at all. Norms are never categorically regulative, but generally disclose and orient. Specific and overarching rules never orient us to any and all situations and circumstances but only to those that are similar in their particularity. Unique situations call for special rules so that the values disclosed by the norm can be realized as goods. Rules intend positive material goods in given situations as achievements of the values disclosed by general and orienting norms.

In his famous essay "On a Supposed Right to Lie from Altruistic Motives" (1968: 120–26), Immanuel Kant makes this analytic mistake in confusing norms and rules. Against Kant's conclusion, common moral sense—what I have called in another vein, the norm of content—tells us that surely one ought to tell a "lie of simple fact" to save the life of one unjustly pursued. Precisely because of the values and intentions of a continuing norm of truthfulness, I may be called upon in a given time and place to speak literal untruths. To live under a rule of literal truth in any and all circumstances of life becomes in fact a violation of the values disclosed in the norm of truthfulness and its intentions to promote an effective, respectful, and caring commonwealth of moral persons. However, the value of Kant's essay in this context is its reminder of an equally serious mistake in the analytic confusion of rules with norms. In the Watergate investigations, witnesses for the administration, and the president himself, created their own norms in their justification for lying based on a rule for promoting the interests and needs "of the country," which they narrowly identified with the needs of the Nixon administration and themselves. The fact that the situation for the "Watergate lies" was framed by confusing the interests and needs of the administration with those of the nation suggests a further and more synthetic misunderstanding of how norms are properly born by the metaconversation and narration of history—in this case the narrative story of a constitutional republic—rather than by only the interests of the particular group in question.

Both norms and rules are governed by material history—norms by the general progress of value-meanings framed by history and culture; rules by specific challenges to bring these values to relative and material achievement as particular and specific goods. Consequently, norms relate most proximately to the historical and cultural mediation and disclosure of general value-meanings, while rules relate to the individual and societal good as the achievement of those meanings. The confusion of the distance and relation between norms and rules and values and goods retard both of these intentions. *Norms fail to disclose and orient our lives around values. Rules fail to regulate the particular circumstances and behavior of our lives toward the promotion of the good as achievements of these values.*

In failing to relate adequately values and goods, we fail in the exercise of virtue since it is the precise function of virtue to mediate values and goods. Similarly, in collapsing the historical distance between norms and rules, their function in moral discourse and the moral life is lost— the broad horizon of moral vision required of the ethical norm is rendered myopic, meddlesome, and moralistic; the particular line of sight required for application of the moral rule to a given situation is rendered too distant, general, and vague. In such analytic confusions, norms become dysfunctional and their intentions of value-disclosure unfulfilled because they seem impractical and unworkable. Indeed, they become "unlivable" because they do not meet the demands of the practical guidance of everyday life. The fact that such moral confusion is based on asking norms to do the work of rules goes unnoticed. When rules are asked to do the work of generally orienting norms, our moral discourse and life seems "normless"—with any person or group creating values according to the narrow interests, needs, and circumstances of their particular lives.

In such a state, I may think that moral virtue demands that I speak the literal and often brutalizing truth in any and all situations and circumstances; or I may think that moral virtue allows that my own norms can be created in the context of whatever circumstances I find myself and lie whenever it meets my own self-interpreted interests. In both cases, however, moral character fails in the exercise of virtue. As habits of interpreting values and responding to goods, virtues mediate the values disclosed by ethical norms to the moral goods of any given situation as relative achievements of those values. To tell a factual lie to save a life cannot be considered in every situation a violation of the norm of truthfulness and a failure in virtue; whereas a vague and general rule to tell the literal truth in all circumstances, however brutal—i.e., to interpret and respond to all norms as if they were in fact rules—can be such a violation and failure. On the other hand, to lie in any situation that suits my needs and interests—i.e., to treat a rule of particular behavior in a given situation, like lying to save a life, as a general norm of lying for all situations according to my own whims—is such a violation of virtue and fracture of character. The analytic reason why I cannot lie in all situations where lying meets my needs and interests is that such a rule of behavior is too broadly based, is in fact a parody of a norm. More substantively, if I were to make such a claim, I would have to give up the norm of truthfulness itself: I would become a liar. Taken analytically, the norm of truthfulness does not pertain directly to particular individuals and their individual situations. Such a foundational and informing sense of morality and truthful moral character applies first more generally and universally in the interpretation of what counts as acceptable moral character in individual and social life. If I were to lie in the way I have described, I could no longer maintain membership in a community identified by the norm of truthfulness, but would already have entered a community of liars not so identified and governed. One might strain common sense in this case and argue that I would still logically have a morality, but it would be the *morality* of the liar not the truth-teller.

In these examples from the ordinary occurrences of moral speech and decision, two important analytic principles have been introduced: (a) *Ethical norms are grounded historically and cannot be subject to individual choice;* (b) *though always related, the distinction between an ethical norm and a moral rule must be maintained.* Any critical discussion of the analytic meaning and function of norms and rules, and the related dynamic of values, virtues, and goods, must be framed within the context of the moral lives of individuals, cultures, and societies. Here in common speech and use we will find the historical embedment of ethical norms and the proper relation between norms and rules. It may be ironic, but by no means uncommon, that ordinary usage contains meanings so deeply rooted that formal retrieval is often difficult. When this happens our ethical and moral arguments become distant from common sense and practice. If this separation continues too long within a particular group, or about a particular topic, moral confusion abounds—both moral argument becomes dysfunctional and our behavior lacks adequate guidance based in part upon these analytic mistakes. The burden of analytic conversations in ethics is to work to say self-consciously and formally what we mean—i.e, to return moral speech to its practical and common use and function. Bearing this analytic burden offers no guarantee of right and good behavior, but it does offer a corrective to debilitating moral confusion. Analytic clarification helps moral discourse to become functional again with greater prospects for effective ethical teaching and moral guidance.

*Analysis* means, etymologically, to "unloose," to separate and "resolve into elements." An analytic conversation in ethics, therefore, attempts to break down the basic elements and concepts of moral speech and argument and to understand their meaning and relation. And yet something has to be there to break and separate. The basic terms of the language of ethics do not have self-engendered meanings and relationships but are rooted in the prior conversations and behavior of peoples and cultures—in how concepts and terms are commonly used based on their intended function; how they are related and rendered as arguments about the values, virtues, and goods of everyday life. It is in this sense that I have argued that close analytic examination of ordinary usage and practical function indicates that ethical norms are born historically and that their main function is to disclose and designate moral values. The precise function of the moral rule, however, is to regulate particular circumstances and situations so that the values disclosed by ethical norms might be accomplished as goods. Virtues stand at the center of the moral life mediating values and goods, norms and rules.[1]

To continue with the example of truthfulness and truth-telling; if truth is a value in our lives, it is because we have come to this initial character identification. We have been claimed by the value of truth and the norm of truthfulness born by history and culture. In this sense, to be obliged as truthful people, we will continually struggle with the meaning and challenges of moral character under the norm of truthfulness. To remove truth as an identifying value and to escape the norm of truthfulness would require a fundamental change in our own self-understanding—a change in character and the achievement of another identifying historical narrative.[2] We would have entered different communities of historical interpretation and meaning. Such conversions of character, whether of a negative or positive variety, are not subject to simple choices, but involve the entire range of elements that go into psychosocial identification of individuals and groups. We are not just cast crassly into worlds of time and history, but into moral-historical worlds of value-laden norms already in place.

Paul Ricoeur argues that values come to us as "a received heritage, therefore as transmitted and carried by a tradition." Values "orient action because they are discovered, not created" (1973b: 153; 154).[3] Amid the pluralism, relativity, and conventionality of such surrounding and receiving worlds, our characters are formed and obliged morally. In this sense, we do not advance in moral consciousness and conscience in ways that are disjunctive from the processes that form ego and character identity overall. We are not thrown into amoral and nonmoral worlds wherein we have to gain our morality from scratch; nor are any world-periods or cultures ever "after virtue" (see MacIntyre: 1984). "Amorality" is produced by a malformed ego and dysfunctional character identity, whether of individuals or groups—those that have profound difficulties making the connections with others necessary for morality in the first place. Consequently the meaning of the language of values, and the role and function of norms, are disclosed in the material-historical conditions of life: analytic conversations in ethics are grounded in this prior synthetic and "world-making" experience. Cosmology, history, ethics, and the psychosocial sciences are mutually informing disciplines.

The obliging claims of value-meanings and their disclosing norms are also for social and political purposes. Values intend to be realized as practical and positive states of affairs or goods in the public realm. The character-identifying value of truth, and its continuing disclosure in a linguistically framed norm of truthfulness, oblige us to promote the *achievement* of truth in our speech and actions. Thus, the values disclosed by extant norms of moral discourse require further ordering and regulation according to the particular challenges of the achievement of the good in particular and various situations and circumstances. For such historically effective promotions of values and norms, mediating habits of interpretation are required for understanding the full dimensions of the value meaning and the ways that these values can be realized. Initially claimed by obliging value meanings, human character and conscience work to understand the variations and implications of those meanings when challenged by the particularities of situation and circumstance. These are the habits of virtue that are also mediated by historical communities of conversation and narration. As the locus of character, virtue centers our moral lives and discloses the depth dimensions of value and the challenges for promoting good and avoiding evil in particular life-situations. Neither moral character nor virtue are formed by overly romantic claims of self-creation or simple choice, or in great stories and deeds heroically and nostalgically separated from common moral experience. In trying to either exaggerate or over-simplify the full range of challenges to moral character, we rob it of its common substance.

Under the theme of "an analytic mistake," I have presented the challenges of truth and truth-telling as a framework for this brief discussion of certain key concepts and terms of moral argument as well as for emphasizing common historical and cultural contexts of all analytic conversations in ethics. Often in the overly technical productions of their language, the analytic traditions in ethics forget what they claim in principle—that sense and coherence in ethics are rooted in the ordinary speech and practice of everyday life. Truthfulness and truth-telling also provided some comparative exemplification for our present task of clarifying the Christian rhetoric of sex. What has been discussed as the relationship between norms and rules of truth are directly pertinent to the Church's rhetoric on sexual morality.

In upholding the norm of heterosexual marriage as a rule of behavior in any and all situations and circumstances, many denominations are making the same analytic mistake of confusing ethical norms and moral rules. A similar confusion exists when it is argued that the particular needs and interests of individuals are enough for the creation of new or parallel norms in Christian sexual morality. And when all such teaching fails to persuade a significant number of Christians, the problem, no matter how sensitively portrayed, is interpreted either as a defect in character—a modernist turning away from the traditional values of love and commitment—or the authoritarian dictates of an archaic and anachronistic Church. Being unpersuaded by either side of the debate, many are left without theological and moral guidance at all, and the Church's teaching voice gives way to the even greater confusions of popular culture.

The Levels of Moral Discourse and the Place of Ethical Argument

Certainly all of this confusion does not come from a simple analytic mistake alone. As I suggested by my arguments in Part One, analytic mistakes are embedded in complex problems of meaning and understanding. Nor does analytic clarification come easily in ethics. The reason why analytic conversations are necessary in the first place is because the terms and levels of ordinary moral speech when applied to argument are seldom clearly understood. Before the analytic discriminations of this section of the book, I have been using the terms rational "moral discourse" and "moral argument" quite generically to indicate our most basic efforts to give reasons for our actions (see Richard Norman, 1971). I have also attempted to avoid any reductionistic rationalism by arguing that feelings must also be included and that critical and rational adequacy in ethics need not bear the burdens of overcoming all risks of ethical interpretation and moral decision. Because of these inevitable burdens and risks, I have suggested throughout that systematic ethical argument was necessary.[4] I will now offer a more precise schema for the levels of moral discourse, including a more defined place for systematic ethical argument. I will also locate more precisely the place and function of norms and rules and their relation to values, virtues, and goods. In later discussions I will fold into this analytic framework the more substantive moral theological relation of the norm of heterosexual marriage to rules of sexual behavior.

In an important article written in 1952, "The Levels of Moral Discourse," Henry David Aiken outlined four levels of speech about moral issues: (1) The Expressive Level; (2) The Level of Moral Rules; (3) The Level of Ethical Principles; and (4) The Post-Ethical Level (1962: 65–87). While my argument is informed by Aiken's analysis, I will make further and sometimes different interpretations and applications. Aiken suggests that in the complexities of human interpretation and judgment, moral speech will be called upon to exercise a variety of functions and thus will be engaged at a variety of levels (p. 65). An analytic discrimination of these levels will advance our understanding of the type of moral conversation going on at any given time and how other conversations will be necessary to meet other needs and interests disclosed by the question under consideration. At the same time, such analytic discrimination will aid in locating the place and function of the basic terms of moral discourse.[5]

Aiken understands that while we may enter moral conversation at any particular level, "any moral argument which goes on at any length is likely to proceed on more than one level.... This means that the context of moral discussion is, or tends to be, a *shifting* context" (1962: 67). He goes on to suggest that the discrimination of levels is correctly made on pragmatic and functional grounds rather than by some intrinsic logical necessity. That is to say, it is the practical and ordinary use of moral speech and its terms that guides all analytic discriminations. This does not mean that there is no order in the use and function of moral speech and thus no discernible criteria of "relevance and validity" (p. 67). Aiken indicates that this is especially the case at the levels of ethical principles and moral rules. At either end of the schematic continuum, however, the criteria of relevance and validity are different and "we pass beyond the bounds of 'propriety' or 'rationality' to the open sea of individual feeling or human aspiration" (p. 67). Because the ordinary canons of systematic rational speech apply most especially at the middle levels of moral discourse, I will locate moral/ethical argument there. By *ethical argument*, I mean the systematic interrelation of moral norms and ethical principles to rules of specific behavior in particular situations.

It is an important reminder, however, that while ethical argument centers the levels of moral discourse, it is itself necessarily bordered on one side by the speech of human character identification—what Aiken calls the *post-ethical* level of human aspiration—and on the other by the *expressive-evocative* speech of passionate persuasion to action. Thus to be adequately critical and practical, ethical arguments always need deeper and more existential-phenomenological grounding as well as a more proximate and applied rhetoric of persuasion. In the center of argument as such, our criteria of "objectivity" are limited and can only be applied according to how systematically and coherently we have related appropriate norms and principles to adequate rules for the guidance of behavior. Even such formal "objectivity" does not mean we have captured an ahistorical standard of logical argumentation removed from the hermeneutic burdens of plurality, relativity, and conventionality; rather, "formal objectivity" means that we have attained a good argument, one that is internally orderly, clear, systematic, comprehensive, and coherent. In no sense does formal objectivity mean that such internal achievements of an adequate argument in themselves guarantee that the "right answer" has been attained or the good promoted. Justification and legitimation of moral discourse also require conversations that probe what Aiken calls the "subjective" dimension (see 1962: 67–68). I will extend this category of "subjectivity" to the phenomenon of intersubjectivity, recalling my discussion of the dialogic nature of all critical pursuits of knowledge. Full consensus can only be achieved relatively and must finally be pursued according to the measure and experience of our intersubjective confessions and character identifications at post-ethical or *metaethical* levels of discourse.

Nonetheless, the goal of limited and formal objectivity in argument is a basic requirement of moral debate. The most egregious violations in decision making are not only made by a rationalism that suggests "good argument" always makes "right decisions" but also by jumping from a rhetoric of confession and aspiration to one of passionate persuasion without bearing the systematic and public burdens of clarity, order, comprehensiveness, and coherence of critical argument. Our passions of belief and action need to be contained and carefully directed by the more laborious process of systematic ethical argument. This is especially the case when levels of moral sensitivity are high. This does not mean that high levels of subjective and intersubjective involvement in any particular issue is necessarily inappropriate. On some occasions the level of moral passion for decision and action is too low and the intricacies of ethical argument go on too long and obfuscate responsible engagement and judgment. This has certainly been the case in arguments for regional jurisdiction over the civil rights of African-Americans throughout most of our national history. In such situations, more moral passion was necessary to speed up debate and decision and cut through obfuscation. The state of the question takes the lead to determine what level of moral discourse becomes most appropriate at any given time.

Emotion, Passion, and the Rhetoric of Moral Persuasion

A vertical graphic depiction of Aiken's levels would find the *expressive* level at the top, followed in descending order by levels of *moral rules*, *ethical principles*,[6] and the *post-ethical* level. The expressive/evocative level is the closest to decision and action, framing the final acts of emotion that move people to decide and act. The post-ethical level is foundational and closest to the depths of human reflection—to the deep metaethical recesses of imagination, belief, confession, and core character identification. In a phenomenological sense, passion and imagination—the levels of the two extremes—are closer to each other than to the middle and "cooler" levels of ethical theory and argument. Though our initial engagement of any particular level must be guided by the issue under consideration, all levels are finally required for a full implication of character and the moral life.

Describing himself as "a pragmatist of sorts" (1962: xii), Aiken starts his analysis from the expressive level. In this way one starts with a description of the decision and action and then reflects backward in a search for reasons and foundations. There is nothing particularly wrong with such an approach as long as we remember that one can just as easily start from the post-ethical level and proceed upward, or for that matter, at the middle stages of rational argument and proceed both toward foundations and the rhetoric of persuasion to act. Aiken's levels are functionally rather than speculatively architectonic. In the "top down" approach, we search through the levels to see if what we *feel* to be right, and what we *desire* as the good is grounded adequately. In the second approach—from the "bottom up"—our argument is in the process of being constructed from its foundations; not from scratch, but from the materials extant in the moral conversation of history no matter how variously strewn about in the relativity and conventionality of cultures, communities, and traditions.

By and large Aiken limits the expressive level to an emotive rhetoric of feelings of attraction or repulsion, pleasure or displeasure (1962: 68–69). In moral speech of this kind, we would want to know what close relation exists between the speaker and the event in question calling forth an entire array of evocative phrases. Then we would want to know the quality of such phrases in order to gauge the speaker's current state of attraction or repulsion. Is the speaker expressing only a nonmoral taste or preference; or is the emotion indicative of a deeper but inchoate and unexpressed reason or moral commitment? For example, if I say that heterosexual behavior "attracts" me and homosexual behavior "repels" me, am I just expressing a feeling rooted in my psychosexual identity or some other experience; or am I beginning to signify something deeper? It is especially necessary at the expressive level to search for further meaning that will call forth deeper levels of moral discourse.

Aiken gives six analytic distinctions for a "full account of the expressive level" (1962: 69).[7] The first three can be contained in what I have described above as "a feeling," with the fourth causing the turn to the more cognitive level of ethical argument. In the fourth distinction, Aiken suggests that we will want to know how symptomatic the expression is of deeper levels of moral significance: does the emotion expressed point to something deeper of a positive or negative nature? While emotion alone is not sufficient for a full moral interpretation and analysis of any issue or event, a negative emotion often discloses that further investigation is necessary—that something is out of balance in the relation of the speaker to the event. For example, if pregnant women or health-care professionals commonly experience severe negative emotions about abortion, then we can ordinarily surmise that deeper levels of moral conversation are required. In short, while emotions do not ordinarily need to be justified as authentic, their significance needs to be examined and should not be discounted as having no relation to cognitive meaning.

The final distinctions Aiken suggests at the expressive-evocative level pertain to "the incitive or rhetorical effect of the expression upon an interpreter, in virtue of which we speak of a relation of communication between him and the speaker; and the intentions of the speaker in thus giving vent to his emotion" (1962: 69). In these discriminations Aiken broaches, but does not develop, the more universal and public significance of this level of moral discourse. Passion and emotion—expressive-evocative speech in general—are what most proximately persuades and moves us, as individuals and groups, to decision and action. If such speech does in fact signify, however inchoately, in both the speaker and interpreter a deeper level of cognitive and existential phenomenological meaning, then it functions in ordinary usage as ideology.

I do not intend a full discussion of the complexities of ideology here, but merely to indicate that ideological speech pertains most proximately to moral decision and action through the power of the passionately persuasive word. Ideology engages our emotions and moves us to act. However, while signifying deeper engagements of moral conversation, ideology does not in itself promote such movement to more critical levels. Thus ideology both obscures and discloses. Without an awareness of the place of ideological speech in our moral conversations, we will miss its own pointer to the necessity of deeper and more critical levels of moral discourse. We will also miss the importance and necessity in its own right of a properly grounded rhetoric of passionate persuasion to move individuals and groups to decision. Though necessary for action, ideological speech is dangerous in its obscuring of vested interests in power and manipulation. Proper analytic discrimination allows us to know when we are having an ideological conversation and whether it has been appropriately grounded. To engage in a legitimate rhetoric of moral persuasion—indeed, to engage at necessary and appropriate times in moral preaching—means that we must always be open to further conversation and more critical inquiry. Left to itself, ideological speech never allows its own suppositions to be rendered problematic. Nonetheless, if we are willing and able to allow our ideological rhetoric to be challenged, then the dangers of ideology can be contained and its proper function engaged. If we are not so willing, or if no such critical grounding exists, then all such rhetoric is unverifiable and illegitimate. It is in this context that my previous remarks about racist and sexist speech ought to be interpreted—that is as ungrounded and dangerously inciting ideological rhetoric.[8] Still for those interested in moral action, there is also a positive role for ideologic persuasion. Consequently, in both positive and negative dimensions, I find, more than Aiken (1962: 70), that serious questions of the moral life also emerge at the expressive/evocative level and not just at the level of ethical argument.

Moral Rules and Decisions

Continuing downward, the outer edge of ethical argument abuts the expressive/evocative level and discloses the level of moral rules. In the ordering of moral rules in particular situations our major intention is to accomplish the substantive good—the realization of values in positive states of affairs. At this level, Aiken describes two further discriminations. First we will want to engage in "(a) factual appraisals of relevant means and consequences and (b) rules or procedures in relation to which alone the moral relevance of such appraisals can be established" (1962: 70). The moral relevance in question pertains to how such rules of procedure intend to accomplish the good. However, as Aiken indicates, facts of the case do not always and self-evidently entail the rules of procedure (1962: 70). For example, ought medical practitioners save the life of a seemingly competent adult—a value accomplished as a good—through an ordinary medical procedure like a blood transfusion when that procedure would violate the correlative value of the freedom of religious conscience of that person?[9] In this specific medical dilemma values conflict, with the achievement of one good entailing a corresponding bad. The proper contextual analysis of this case would lead us to understand that we are in the throes of a moral/ethical dilemma. We can no longer search for simple and narrowly determined rules of procedure. Rather, we are directed to larger frames of reference and argument that pertain to such things as the status of the claim of conscience being made and the degree to which such a claim legitimately obliges the medical practitioner; to the nature of medical practice itself and the character of the profession; and to the relevant universe of all participants in this decision who must bear the burden of its effects. Serious moral situations seldom entail self-evident decisions and conclusions, but rather materially frame what counts as the relevant facts for ordering rules of procedure. Aiken concludes that the particularities of situations and circumstances that call for moral conversation at the level of rules are filled with "ellipses and elisions" (1962: 70).

It is axiomatic that the closer one gets to the actual moment of action in complex and diverse situations the more conflict is likely to occur. In such situations the distance between norms and rules has become so great and the chance for divergence and splitting of the values, virtues, and goods so pronounced that the requirements of responsible decision require that our ethical argument become multi-layered and more complex. Full ethical/moral dilemmas occur most pointedly at the level of the application of moral rules, and the harmony we commonly seek at the beginning and even middle stages of our ethical arguments is less likely to be attained (See Aiken, 1962: 74). This does not mean that at the level of moral rules our speech will necessarily become dysfunctional, but that the particular burdens of precise application and decision cannot be avoided by moving immediately from the more distant levels of norms and principles to an entailed rule—i.e., by confusing a norm and a rule. In our medical dilemma, the priority of either the value of saving a life or respecting freedom of conscience is not immediately obvious nor are the rules of procedure that the health-care practitioners ought to follow.

Further compounding our analytic problems, the meaning and function of the term "rule" is not univocal and confusions can lead to ineffective application in argument. By moral rule we often mean that we should all act with regularity and similarity. And while this has some relevance when situations, circumstances, and people happen to be both formally and substantively similar, it is the special role of the moral rule to bear more proximately than the ethical norm the great diversity of situation and circumstance. Moral rules are closer to the actual realities of everyday life than ethical norms. When circumstances are similar and situations for decision less complex, regular habits of virtue serve: the distance between the norm and rule is not so great, and we depend on tried and true rules of moral response. At other times when circumstances are marked by specific and unique conditions, our moral assumptions no longer seem effective for the realization of values and the achievement of good. Therefore, even as moral rules function in their mode of "regularity," to be useful they must always be more flexible than ethical norms. In the same vein, ethical norms will suffer and become dysfunctional if they are engaged within the same canons of plurality and flexibility as moral rules. Moral rules must be flexible enough to regulate diversity and variety. However, once in place, norms that project a specific value or set of values toward realization as goods tend to resist or take no notice of alternative choices. In the medical ethical dilemma we have been discussing, the values of life and the freedom of conscience take no particular notice of each other in their disclosure and both vie for realization in the same instance.

There may also be crises and conflicts in the origination and narration of norms and principles and thus in the informing values of individuals and groups, cultures and nations. I have argued that these are the crises in the ethos or moral environment of a culture and society wherein more complete ethical narratives and moral stories need to be told, other values and virtues of character recalled, and new ones engaged. Still, the full recognition and engagement of the moral problem and dilemma pertain most proximately at the level of moral rules of behavior where we are challenged most practically by the claims of mutually conflicting values, virtues, and goods. And while the deep origin of our conflicts is often at levels of norms and principles, or of primary character identification, conflicts over what to do in the here and now instance are most initiating of the moral dilemma.

Not everything in the moral life is a profound conflict and dilemma. When the course between clearly interpreted and relevant norms and rules of procedure is direct—has not been deflected or complicated severely by mutually conflicting goods and values—we know more clearly what we ought to do. For instance, we would not call rape a "moral problem" or "dilemma." The route between ethical norms and moral rules is direct and easily traversed with the conclusion that rape is *ruled out* in any situation or circumstance whatsoever. The real problems in rape pertain to responding helpfully to victims, dealing with the rapist, and attending to those things that seem to encourage this immoral practice. I am aware that full acceptance of the fact that in any sexual situation whatsoever, whether married or not, "no means no" has not been achieved either morally or legally. But this only demonstrates the necessity of moving our moral conversation to the appropriate level wherein women are recognized fully as autonomous persons and where we come to a better understanding of rules of respectful sexual behavior.

The current debate on abortion discloses yet another example of the variety of material-historical terrains that must be traversed in the virtuous mediation of values and goods, norms and rules. If abortion, in any and all situations, is "killing a baby"—always innocent in my estimation—then we have no dilemma as such and ought to have strong prohibitive rules. Or in the presence of other moral values and goods of putative equal weight, we might have the dimensions of a tragic situation where ordinary rational moral speech and rules of procedure tend to fail. And while I think that abortion decisions are often marked by some experience of the tragic, the rhetoric of "killing one's baby" ought not to be engaged as a normal part of the moral debate. Such rhetoric will only be ideologically inflammatory and fractious unless one can offer sustainable grounds of the personal status of fetal life at any or all stages of its development. It is often with this question of the status of fetal life that the full moral problem of abortion ensues. Disclosed most especially but not only in the lives and narrations of women who face this choice, simple rules of procedure seldom function because of a profound conflict of values and norms focused materially around diverse interpretations of the status of fetal life. Whether fully realized in all communities of moral discourse or not, in the case of rape, the track between the norm and the rule is direct and without significant detour. In the case of abortion, it is not so direct and any norm and principle of the "sacredness of life" is immediately confronted with other paths that pit "life against life," including questions of the quality of life, or make discriminations between human genetic/cellular life and fully personal life.[10] Gauging the different terrains between norms and rules appropriate to particular moral situations is fundamental in understanding the types of discussions that need to go on. Even when agreement and consensus is not easily gained, understanding the appropriate levels of moral discourse and the meaning and function of moral terms will help prevent the systematic misplacing and distorting of our conversations from the start.

Another reference to homosexuality will further demonstrate the function and limits of moral rules in the entire spectrum of the levels of moral speech. If we understand the terrain between an extant Christian norm of heterosexual marriage and rules of heterosexual behavior to be so clear and direct as to make such a norm and rule correspondent, then homosexual Christians are left with a serious moral dilemma in sexual behavior. I say this in light of my conviction that there is no credible evidence to suggest that either heterosexual or homosexual orientations are simply chosen. To anticipate the discussion in Chapter Six of the substantive values disclosed in a Christian norm of heterosexual marriage, let us also assume that the homosexual Christians in question are committed, loving, and monogamous. In this case, a homosexual Christian must choose between two options. One is to live essentially a celibate life, never experiencing the intimacies of responsible sexual love that the Church, at least in its contemporary teachings on marriage, holds up as important for the formation of character. Or in their homosexual activity, they must stand relatively outside of the orbit of the Christian norm of sexual virtue and behavior—to become at least "material sinners."[11] Nor does jumping immediately to the rhetoric of "hating the sin and loving the sinner" make the homosexual Christian a full participant in the life of the Church. Without a critical discussion of the ethics of homosexual practice, such rhetoric functions only as a pastoral platitude that deflects from the full work that needs to be done. If they are forced to live as celibates, homosexual Christians may sacrifice significant goods that we will assume may be necessary for character development. One can argue, correctly in my estimation, that sacrifice is also part of the burden of character. Yet it seems that unless such sacrifices are either freely chosen or necessarily imposed by the material and moral conditions of our life-situations, then prospects for erosion in character and virtue are strong. The real question remains whether the material-historical terrain between a norm of heterosexual marriage and a rule of heterosexual behavior is in fact so clear and direct that it leads to a correspondence and a requirement of a single rule of life. Only by engaging in a full range of moral speech, including clearly disclosed rather than systematically distorted attention to the narrations of homosexual persons, will we find whether the burdens of celibacy now being *imposed* on homosexual Christians by many Christian denominations are morally necessary or not.

In this debate we cannot avoid a critical examination of the state of the Church's moral rhetoric of homosexuality. My argument throughout has been that the present discourse of the denominations discloses significant confusions. Christian sexual ethics is no longer as sure as it once was of the relation between norms and rules for moral guidance in sexual matters in general and especially with respect to the question of homosexuality. Therefore to assume that we are as clear about the ethics of homosexuality as we once thought short circuits the contemporary moral debate by forcing the question toward a pastoral admonition alone that homosexual Christians confess their sin, while at the same time offering to assist them to live by clearly ordered rules of celibacy. It is similarly distracting to assume, because of only sincere aspiration and desire, that the traditional norm of heterosexual marriage and its traditional rules of behavior have been overturned. My argument will be that the course between the Christian norm of heterosexual marriage and rules of sexual behavior is neither direct nor totally open and free and that heterosexual marriage is normative for all Christians but that rules of sexual behavior will be necessarily plural.

In this variety of examples, I have attempted to indicate that ethical norms and moral rules have different functions in our moral lives and that such variety is necessary because of the diversity of moral situations. To try to force a fitted course between any given norm and rule beyond the disclosures of historical and sociocultural circumstance is to deflect the work of the norm and make rules dysfunctional. In the question of rape to suggest indirection and complication in the distance between the norm and the rule because the participants are married, or for some so-called and surreptitious invitation of the woman, or assumption of the man is to misunderstand the material content of the moral terrain. In the examples of abortion and homosexuality, to force a direct line between norms and rules upon what appears to be a complex moral terrain filled with a plurality of paths to the good is to make a correlative mistake. Certainly one would have to demonstrate through accurate description and cogent argument that the terrain between norms and rules in abortion and homosexuality is not as direct and clear of responsible option as rape. Because our moral landscapes shift throughout the course of history, in the most serious and classic questions of the moral life we must check our moral terrain in every generation. Serious and classic moral questions and dilemmas recur in the human situation and must be interpreted again in light of how that situation has developed and changed.

Ethical Norms and Principles

As we move from the challenge of ordering rules of behavior for the accomplishment of the good in particular situations and circumstances, we approach the disclosure of normative values that orient and finally justify such rules. I have argued that the first function of the moral norm is to disclose such values. It is, however, important to understand the distinction between a norm and a principle. Though closely related to a norm, the function of the ethical principle is to linguistically articulate the values disclosed by norms and to direct them on their course toward realization as goods. Etymologically, "principle" indicates a source or origin. In this sense, principles are linguistic indicators of the source of the meaning of the good in interpretations and confessions of prior value-meanings. We say it is generally a "good thing" to save someone's life because human life has been previously interpreted in a given universe of discourse to be of the value—"to be of worth."[12] Such an interpretation is commonly articulated declaratively in a principle that says something like "life is sacred" or its functional equivalent. The values articulated by such principles are directed on their course toward the achievement of corresponding goods. But in the examples of the freedom of religious and moral conscience in medical matters as well as in abortion, I suggested that this terrain is often bumpy and the values directed by the principles of the sacredness of life and conscience can split and divide, often leading to a conflict of goods and a dilemma in rules of procedure. Even when ethical principles clearly articulate values the material realities in any situation can lead to divergence, splitting, and conflict. Aiken indicates principles "reside" at linguistic levels of universality and generality that initially seem far removed from the challenges of particular situations and conflicts (1962: 76–77). But as I will indicate, when used correctly, they do not remain at such levels nor do they finally arise with such seeming rationalistic impersonality. Principles also have a practical function and are always challenged by the obligations of particular decision and action.

Like values and goods, principles have a dialectical interrelation with both norms and rules. Principles depend on rules for ordering particular behavior toward the achievement of the good, just as rules depend on principles for their direction and justification. Principles depend on norms for disclosure of the values they are to linguistically indicate and direct on their course toward goods; while norms depend on principles for such value-articulation and direction. In our example from medical ethics, norms disclose the values of life and autonomy, while principles articulate the sacredness of life and the autonomy of conscience and direct those values toward realization as a life saved and a conscience respected. However, once our situation indicated the dilemma of a choice between saving a life or respecting freedom of conscience, the failure of ordinary rules of medical procedure disclosed a more overarching conflict of principles, norms, and values. In this situation, the challenge of decision casts us back to reexamine the terrain that ordinarily measures the course between normative principles and practical rules because of the extraordinary nature of our situation. In short, we begin to engage in the necessary ethical argument.

In the example of rape no such argument was necessary because the terrain remains ordinary and clear. In the examples of abortion and homosexuality, I argued that the terrain is confused and unclear and new explorations in argument are required. The formal purpose and analytic function of ethical argument is to bridge the distance between normative principles and particular rules. Taken more substantively, argument intends to show how the values at stake in any community of moral discourse can be advanced toward their realization in positive and material states of affairs, or goods. In its habitual interpretation of value-meanings and practical promotions of good, moral virtue functions as a relatively experienced guide over such distance and terrain. Virtue has both a "right and good-making" function, dutifully forming and guiding character-actors and historical moral agents—helping us as individuals and communities to see and understand what is of obliging and identifying worth and moving us along a *right path* to enact those obligations as *goods achieved*.

Being only relatively experienced as a guide, however, and given the variety and change in human situations, traditional virtues can also be challenged. Sometimes this means only that new and more rigorous arguments are required to move us over old terrain that has eroded and become more complex. Sometimes more radical explorations are necessary to find new paths because the ordinary terrain has become impassable and traditional norms and rules moribund—no longer disclosing, indicating, directing, and ordering our moral passage. In still more radical times and situations, particular virtues that have been dependable guides in the past are replaced and transformed because of radical changes of cosmos and character. But amid any and all of these challenges and strains, virtue remains our mediating though imperfect guide, making us into moral travelers, directing us along right paths, helping us over the changing grounds of moral interpretation and ethical argument. While virtue and character are not defined and formed by the practice of ethical argument alone, they are framed by its rational and practical intentions to promote value in the achievement of good. Moral discourse and ethical argument are also exercises of virtue and participate in the ongoing formation of character.

As my analysis indicates, norms and principles are closely related in the language and work of morality. I also indicated that because of this relation, as well as a rather notorious variety in the close analysis of the meaning and function of moral terms, norms and principles are commonly lumped together in the same phrase or sentence. Thus we spoke of ethical norms *and* principles as a "higher" level ordering and guide for the work and justification of moral rules—for the work of providing overarching reasons why we decide to act or not in a certain way. However, I introduced above a distinction between norms and principles, both in their function and origination. Norms first *disclose* values; principles linguistically *articulate* and cognitively *direct* the course that such values must traverse to goods. Principles thus depend on the prior disclosures of values by norms and articulate and direct the values disclosed from this prior source. In Chapter Five I will discriminate a second and third functional intention of *designation* and *demonstration* of values to add to that of *disclosure* for the complete analytic picture of the moral norm. According to their characteristic functions and intentions of *disclosing, designating* and *demonstrating* values, mature norms are more like models than sentences, and they function more metaphorically, symbolically, and sacramentally than declaratively and descriptively.[13] Before I turn in the next chapter to a discussion of this more discriminate work of ethical norms, their role as effective models needs more exposition.

If, for instance, we articulate as ethical principles that *life is sacred, human beings are autonomous,* or that *sexual behavior is a manifestation of committed love,* we do so because within our moral imagination we have certain models that effectively visualize for us the meaning and worth of life, humanity, and sexuality. As visualized images of meaningful worth, such models function as normative paradigms for the order, sense, and coherence of human life—demonstrating for us how life ought to be lived and displaying the values necessary for specified ways of life. Therefore, the at least quasi-religious ethical principle that *life is sacred* is rooted in a prior model of some relation of the origination and continual contact of human life with a font of sacredness or some benevolent divinity. In the West, God could be visualized as a universal craftsman and kindly and benevolent parent, and most traditionally, as a father. Similarly, to say that human beings are autonomous is to indicate, in Western cultural history at least, a change in a model of the relation of human beings to wider wholes. In the Renaissance and Enlightenment, human beings began to be imaged more radically than ever before as autonomous individual persons in their own right apart from their masters, either secular or religious. Such autonomy could be visualized in artisan workers, small-business owners, independent thinkers, and, most especially, in the citizen. Such normative models were not totally continuous with prior and more traditional models, and new values of autonomy, liberty, and freedom of conscience were disclosed. Finally, to say that committed love is the ethical principle for our sexual lives requires a similar model or models that function as foundational and material images of the meaning of sexual relations. Through a long and sometimes meandering journey, heterosexual marriage—monogamously engaged—has come to the fore as a material model for the visualization and demonstration of the values of love and commitment and their relation to sexual expression. In this sense I will argue that heterosexual marriage remains normative in the Christian Church.

In any discussion of norms and principles, it is important to understand their material-historical character—a quality necessary for their disclosure and articulation of values. As models and sentences extant in the discourse of cultures and societies, norms and principles are not finally formal, only theoretic, or historically abstract, but rather are fully embodied in imagination and language. As products of our historical moral imagination and actual moral speech, neither ethical norms nor principles exist in any ethereal world of pure and formal rationality. Being so materially grounded, they also run the risk of erosion and loss of meaning and demonstrate the need for maintenance. It is precisely the failure to understand and make use of the material origination and practical historical function of norms and principles that gives rise to often justified criticisms of over-generality and formality in ethical theory and argument.

At this level, Aiken indicates that we often think of their necessary generality as "empty," "trite," and "vague" (1962: 81–82). He indicates further that "such criticisms are based on a complete misunderstanding of what such principles are designed to accomplish." Aiken understands the work of ethical principles in the ordering and relative justification of substantive moral rules to be essentially procedural: "Their role is not to tell us what to do in particular cases but to provide us with standards of relevance or 'reasonableness' when appraisal of lower-order rules is required" (1962: 82). Consequently, if norms and principles have mainly a formal and procedural function and intent, one would not expect nor look for the substantive historicality and proximate applicability I have described above. Proper analysis would then assign only formal-logical criteria for their adequacy. We might ask for the logical sensibility and even internal effectiveness of a good argument, but we would not be able to demand further that norms and principles make phenomenological and historical-pragmatic sense—that is, that they say something meaningful, effective, and true about the world.[14] While I have argued that in their disclosure and articulation of values, norms and principles do not *entail* rules and that they have different functions appropriate to their own level of moral discourse, I do not follow Aiken completely in his argument about only their procedural formality. My analysis and understanding of proper analytic conversations in ethics remain more material-historical than his.

For example, Aiken says that the problem with Kant's procedural categorical imperative is not that it is an "empty formula but that the one he provides will not bear the burden of justification required of it" (1962: 82). Now if Aiken means that Kant's categorical imperative fails because it does not meet the requirements of a universal ethical principle as defined by Kant himself and is thus internally incoherent, then I think Aiken is mistaken. Kant has a formally good argument. However, even if I am the one mistaken here and Kant's various formulations of his categorical imperatives do not meet the internal criteria defined in his own theory of morality, this is still not the main reason why they fail when applied to many circumstances of the moral life. As Aiken indicates, Kant understood with "an unrivaled clarity...that moral criticism which is something more than an *ad hoc* expression of individual attitudes is impossible save on the assumption that there are ethical principles which are general in normative appeal" (1962: 82). But the question of the success or failure of Kant's categorical imperatives turns on the quality of this generality.[15]

In adequately critical ethical theory, generality and formality cannot mean that maxims and principles are empty—that is, of little substantive relation to the practicality of the moral life and its material-historical challenges. To the extent that Kant intended his principle of formal universalizability, and its various formulations and articulations, to function as a maxim or a "formula for testing rules of conduct" (Aiken, 1962: 82), it was not in fact empty either in intent or practical applicability. To the extent that Kant's origination of the principle was based on the internal requirements of his theory of knowledge rather than on the practical burdens of living the ordinary moral life, then it does appear to be empty at times—as Aiken indicates, "it had to be 'empty,' it had to be formal, if it was to do the job assigned to it" (1962: 82). But questions remain: who assigns the "job" and what is the job assigned? Is the job of an ethical principle and norm merely formally determined and assigned by the theorist and theory in question or are ethical theorists and theories in fact "assigned" their jobs by the material-historical circumstances of the moral life at any given time and in any given situation—in Collingwood's phrase, by "the vicissitudes of human affairs" (1972: 9)?

Paradoxically, Kant presents ethical principles that seem at times relatively empty and formal in their theoretic origination but material and substantive in their practical intentions. However, in ethics as finally in knowledge and theory in general, it is precisely the burden of the achievement in practice of a material and substantive intention that gauges the success or failure of a principle and theory. The failures of Kant's principle of universalizability informing the categorical imperatives has something to do with its mode of origination. Any ethical principle whose origination is bound by such strict and self-conscious requirements to be methodologically formal and substantively empty of material-historical content—content that Kant saw as generally heteronomous—will not, save by happenstance or luck, be able to meet very often its own intentions of substantive and material applicability.

Despite his self-conscious methodological intentions to the contrary, Kant's ethics are marked by the conventionality of his own culture and religious and philosophical heritage (see Norman, 1983). As we saw in our reference to Kant's now infamous example of not telling a simple lie of fact to save the life of one pursued by a "murderer" (1968: 120–26), his methodological formalism makes the categorical imperative dysfunctional in this case and not able to meet his intentions of ordering right-making rules of behavior to achieve the good either in the individual instance or overall. That Kant may have thought that such empty formalism was necessary to achieve the good universally and overall despite the evils effected in any given situation, suggests that, even with his vision of a "kingdom of ends," his view of the moral life tended to be too historically abstract and narrowly uniform. From Kant's mistake, we learn that if an ethical principle is derived in only a methodologically formal way, then it will not very often attain any substantive intentions of adequately ordering and testing rules of conduct. The reason why Kant's categorical imperative fails in its intention to order universally the moral life is not because it may or may not bear the burden of justification required of his theories of knowledge and morality, but because it does not bear the burdens of justification by material-historical experience. Despite the ongoing value of Kant's theoretic work in ethics, his Achilles heel is his overarching and pietistic distrust of our human abilities to bear the burden of substantive interpretation and judgment amid various situations and circumstances. Kant finally misunderstands the material-historical work of theory in general and the close and practical connection between knowledge and human needs and interests.

In general, then, Kant's theoretic foundations and formulations for the categorical imperative are too abstract—too distant to bear the burdens of everyday life. In the formalistic and methodological abstraction of his ethical theory from its proper material-historical conditions, Kant's principles and maxims stand as a reminder of the procrustean temptation of all theoretic work. Kant was certainly right to worry about our abilities to interpret and judge particular situations as given since we will fail as often as we succeed in bearing such critical hermeneutic burdens conscientiously. But as I have argued, we have no other choice. There is no escape from the fundamental, and indeed, methodological interrelation of history, ethics, and the moral life. Therefore, Aiken is wrong if he is suggesting that for ethical principles to function as a general direction, order, and test for moral rules, they have to be formally empty (1962: 82). Guided by substantive practical intentions and grounded in the values disclosed and articulated in normative models and common speech, norms and principles, even at their appropriate level of generality, always emerge from and must return to particular needs and interests.

We have now followed Aiken's vertical schematic to the mid-range level of ethical argument whose precise intent is to connect norms and rules. I have argued for the close functional interrelation of norms and principles. I have also argued for some distinction and discrimination between them as meaningful terms. In general, the relation and discrimination of norms and principles turned on how they work for the disclosure, articulation, and direction of values toward realization as goods. If value starts and directs us toward the good, and virtue is our mediating guide, we can say that the moral life originates in value, ends in the good, and is centered in virtue. But there is no logical or analytic priority here. Even with all of its separations and discriminations, proper analysis is framed and drawn by the work and function of the whole. Consequently it is a mistake to speak of ethics and ethical theory as "dominated" by values, or virtues, or goods. Nor is moral character adequately understood under any similar priority. While moral character is centered in our habits of moral interpretation and response as the practice of virtue, it is not just analytically related to virtue. Moral character is formed as much by understanding value meanings and achieving goods as it is by the practice of virtue. Moreover this entire complex of interrelationships and the phenomena of moral character itself do require further grounding. If moral rules that most proximately order behavior are guided and justified by appeals to ethical principles, and ethical principles justified in how they effectively articulate and direct the values disclosed by norms, how then are norms and the values they disclose to be justified? How does the character of individuals and groups, cultures and societies originate?

I will turn now to Aiken's final and grounding level of moral discourse and consider the origin of values and norms in the praxis of moral confession and character identification. The distinctions of analytic conversations always run the risk of losing sight of the synthetic whole. Consequently, it is important to reiterate that the levels, terms, and functions we have been analyzing are part of more complex life-experiences. We take risks of too precise an analytic discrimination because of the sometimes overwhelming confusion of synthetic complexity. We return to the check of synthetic complexity because of the equal dangers of sterile analytic simplicity. Understanding more precisely the form, structure, and function of moral speech and its basic terms does not ensure that the good will be accomplished and evil avoided. Being analytically articulate is a precondition for ethical *competence*, not a guarantee or a recipe for being a good person. In this sense, ethically competent people can be morally destructive—in fact have evil characters. Ethically incompetent people can by temperament, accident, or grace be good persons. This is not to discount the value of analytic ethical competence but only to suggest that what grounds a good and virtuous character—whether of individuals or groups—depends on more fundamental and informing value confessions and character formations that are "beyond" ethical argument. We engage in discussions of these foundations of moral character at what Aiken calls the "post-ethical" level of moral discourse.[16]

Foundational Confession and Character Identification

At the end of this schema we arrive at the grounding level that displays the most synthetic complexity. When all is said and done, any architectonic structure stands or falls according to the strength of its foundation. Thus the formal analytic structure we have been examining finally comes to its foundation with the question of the grounding of values, norms, and principles. All questions at this level are oriented by the related phenomena of character-identification and moral obligation as such. Accordingly, here we engage questions about the sources of our values and why any particular norm and principle ought to oblige us or why should we be persuaded by any particular ethical argument? Or still further we might ask the more universal question, as Aiken puts it, "why should I be moral" in the first place? (1962: 83). Why should I be interested in or care about norms and values at all? I will deal first with the more general question of moral sensibility and then with the specific question of how we come to be substantively obliged in any particular way.

Aiken is ambiguous in his treatment of the question of "why be moral?" On the one hand he suggests, somewhat facilely, that Kant has given such a question its "comeuppance" if not its "quietus"(1962: 83); on the other, he treats the question with some seriousness if not comprehensiveness. In my own rendering, a mid-range Kantian response to this question would read something like this: *Morality is co-terminus with rationality. We must be moral if we are to be rational. To question morality in this way is at the same time to question rationality, to which no rational answer would be satisfactory. Thus, in both moral and rational discourse, the question is meaningless.*[17]

Such a Kantian response—one that seems to attract Aiken—is not persuasive, however, on a number of levels. First, as Aiken knows, the question of "why be moral?" has meaning and can only be meaningfully addressed at the foundations of moral speech—one beyond the limits of any particular ethical argument. The question concerns the existential-phenomenological grounds of the moral life (see Aiken,1962: 86). Since my rendering of this response is within the confines of Kant's own substantive understandings of the relation of morality to his *theory* of knowledge, we find, in Kantian terms, that the question is meaningless. However, its lack of meaning is only related to a confusion of the levels upon which the question needs to be engaged. Asking and responding to a metatheoretic question at theoretic levels of discourse—i.e., levels of systematic rational argument—is what makes the question meaningless. And this our Kantian response has failed to notice. Secondly, even Kant's theoretic attempts to equate rationality and morality fail for two additional reasons: (a) rationality is not universal in the way Kant envisioned; and (b) to be rational is not necessarily to be moral.

Although an act may satisfy the internal requirements of logical and rational coherence, order, and universality at levels of theory and argument, it still may not be adequately justified since what grounds morality is not primarily the order of rational theory. Rather what grounds theory and its particular form of rationality are the imaginative models that we form and the values we confess to normatively identify our characters and our meaningful interactions with others. Even though I find Kant's approach to the question of the foundational relation between rationality and morality to be inadequate, this does not mean that such questions are beyond the Kantian imagination. Kant's own image and model for both rationality and morality were grounded in his often-noted analogical relation of the order of the starry heavens above and the rational moral law within.[18] This is a more foundational rendering of Kant's relation of rationality and morality that broaches the proper level of analogy and imagination, cosmology, and worldview that finally ground Kant's theoretic system. With the fall of Newtonian cosmology, such an analogy from the physical universe makes Kant's rationalist model for ethics less acceptable but still indicates the proper epistemological level to deal with such questions and at which they can be meaningful.

An example of a foundational inquiry into the prior and metatheoretic grounding of specific values, norms, and principles would be the query: "Is it right and good to take personal and corresponding vengeance upon another for an offense?" In other words, is vengeance rational and moral; and further, is it an obligation? Or am I obliged to forgiveness? Even in terms of ordinary common sense, such a question draws to the fore no immediate and single criteria of reasonableness. In anarchic situations of judicial chaos, it may very well seem reasonable to take such vengeance so that the offender will not have acted with impunity. In other situations of even relative law and order, it may not seem so rational and for the sake of order and justice, the state's right to punishment should take precedence. So even if we were to grant Kant his relative equation of rationality and morality, the real question becomes what rationality is to guide the moral life. However, in neither situation does it follow that "rational vengeance," either by the individual or the state, is necessarily moral. Given the varieties of what counts as rational, there is not as close or intrinsic a relation of rationality and morality as Kant thought. Furthermore, even if I were prepared to argue that with all due processes of constitutional law that state initiated capital punishment is rational enough to meet minimum standards of logical coherence, I could still claim that it is immoral. To argue for or against capital punishment because it is or is not a deterrent does not save the equation of rationality and morality because the rational motivation of such punishment is not only deterrence but also vengeance. What is at stake in any suggestion that capital punishment, or vengeance in general, is immoral is not rational argumentation as such, but the grounds upon which such argumentation rests—the models of human interaction that we imaginatively form as frames for the identifying values of character. And the informing model that I personally have in mind for refusing to envision capital punishment as moral is the radical forgiveness of Jesus and the redemption of Christ. Capital punishment is immoral in Christian ethics not primarily because of any argument but because vengeance is unimaginable as an identifying dimension of Christian character.

Moral discourse in general, and ethical argument in particular, are not complete unless such foundational levels of discussion are appropriately engaged. It is true that misplacing or over-concentrating upon foundations can be distracting and seriously obfuscating with respect to the needs and interests of the specific discussion at hand. For example, in situations of medical emergency where a moral decision is required immediately, to take the time to engage in foundational discussion can be irresponsible. However, it is as equally irresponsible not to have had such discussions in advance of such emergencies so that morally responsible protocols can be set. Therefore, in the broad scope of our critical conversations in ethics and morality, foundational or "post-ethical" discussions are necessary and must always be possible in principle lest the entire house of moral debate and ethical argument collapses because of inadequate foundation.

At times our presumptions in favor of the values, norms, and principles upon which we base our common ethical arguments are so strong that we fail to see the import of what often look like distracting or less than serious questions. Thus we might well want to know why anyone in this day and time, and in light of the violence of our own century, could possible hold that "life is sacred," or, similarly, that in our technocratic culture that human beings are autonomous and that freedom of conscience is of fundamental worth, or that love and commitment have anything at all to do with the current realities of sexual expression. In these inquiries, serious questions about the real or continuing existence of normative models and disclosed values are raised in light of the strong and contrary evidence of everyday life.

In the last chapter, I argued that to entertain seriously racist and sexist prejudices as premises for constructive argument was to engage in a racist and sexist discussion—discussions that would be systematically distorted as arguments from the beginning. At the same time, I suggested something else was going on in such discussions and that rather than engage in a systematically distorted ethical *argument*, one should search for and confront the racism and sexism that informs this speech—that is, move to a post-ethical level of conversation that discloses the racist and sexist images and models that normatively inform and oblige persons attempting such "arguments." One could say the same thing about premises for arguments rooted in such claims that AIDS is an affliction from God for immoral behavior. I would hold little hope of rationally and systematically persuading another that such negative prejudices are not so. Argument is not what is called for here, but a deeper probe of the imaginative models that normatively inform these pernicious convictions. It is these normative models and related images that inform principles of such specious ethical arguments that ought to be the subject of our discussions. In discursive situations such as these, it is the foundational and post-ethical moral imagination and confession that are directly at issue rather than the requirements of substantive ethical theory and argument.

What such serious foundational inquiries disclose, and what even trivial ones indicate, is the existence of a deeper level of conversation that grounds ethical theory and argument and its functioning norms and first principles. Norms and principles, and the values they disclose and articulate, may function primarily at the midrange level of ethical argument, but they are born at post-ethical, or literally understood, "metaethical" levels of confession and character identification. If we reverse our direction on Aiken's schema and start from this foundational level rather than from the top levels of passionate moral persuasion and rules of behavior, *metaethical discussions* would be the first rather than the last level of moral discourse. In this context the term "metaethical" would not be taken literally as "after the ethical argument," but more generically, as "before" all ethical argument and moral persuasion. In both approaches, such a level is grounding and foundational—necessary for the analytic discrimination of the origin and justification of our models of ethical norms and their informing values.

Even though we have located this foundational level, the question still remains how such informing values are confessed and normative models formed—how they come to be obliging, and how conflicts of confession, obligation, and disputes among the imaginative models themselves could ever be brought into constructive conversation. Aiken is on the right track in his analysis of this challenge, yet perhaps according to the purposes of his essay, he does not follow the path he indicates to its synthetic and proper conclusion. For whatever reason, Aiken stops short:

It is at this point, it seems to me, that the existentialists, for all their strange way of saying things, have really understood a fundamental fact of the moral life. When they speak of man's "freedom" in the moral situation, what they mean, I think, is that no purely logical or metaphysical "reason" can bind a man to any obligation whatsoever, that only by a gratuitous decision can one in the end even answer the question "Why should I be moral?" I am more than my commitments. I am bound by my commitment only so long as I continue to be moved by it. No existential situation can compel my loyalty unless, for *whatever* reason or for no reason at all, I choose to be bound by it.... The continual possibility of rejection or indifference thus renders the authority of moral rules constantly dependent upon what I, as an agent, elect to be or to do.... Decision is king (1962: 86–87).

Aiken has located the proper existential-phenomenological context for the occurrence of moral obligation and commitment. Such a context frames the necessary grounding for all ethical theory and argument as well as all legitimate rhetoric of meaningful moral persuasion. And it is correct to say that, in a certain psychological sense, we do feel ourselves to be moved by "chosen" loyalties. Finally, at the foundational level of moral discourse, amid all of its complexity and conflict of values and normative models, we do seem to stop the debate of conscience with choice and decision. Yet if, like Aiken, we end at what has every appearance of simple choice and decision we will have stopped short. Like some forms of existentialism, Aiken's sense of moral character and agency is too individualistic and not adequately historical in a material sense. Amid what can be endless debates and conflicts about our moral imaginations and the normative models that oblige us, we may think we stop our debates by choice and decision, but further probes are necessary to understand why we "choose" and "decide" in any particular way. As John E. Smith indicates, this particular sort of existentialist error lies in the claim that not only do we "seek freedom" but that "we are freedom" (1984: 43–54)—i.e., relatively unbound ahistorical beings who form history in our choices and decisions rather than also being formed by history and the possibilities history offers for freedom at any given time.

Freedom is born from interdependency and is always intrinsically related with how history's conversation and narratives form and inform us at any given time and place. At foundational levels, we do not merely choose what to confess as values or what models to use as normative images for disclosing such values. The material conditions of history are not just static environments within which we choose identity and character, but are rather active and materially informing contexts that locate, identify, and oblige us. I have argued throughout that we do not come to moral identity and obligation only along internal historical, intellectual, and psychological journeys but through initiating and external ties of obligation to others. Such ties are born in our remembrances and anticipations extant in the imagination and language of culture and society. Thus our moral obligations and commitments are first mediated to us through material-historical expectations and experiences. Accordingly, the same plurality, relativity, and conventionality that mark history in general will also mark the foundations of the moral life. With a critical openness to being informed by others, conflicts at this level can only be adequately handled through a sharing of the variety of confessions, imaginations, and models that ground and frame our values, norms, and principles.

At this foundational level, we do not just confess monologically how we have "decided" to become obliged—the kind of moral character we have "chosen"—but rather how we have *come to be obliged* and how *we have been chosen*. Moral character does not give birth to itself. In allowing our value confessions and normative moral imaginations to be informed dialogically by the conversations and narrations of others, we do not give up all criteria of judgment; rather we merely allow a different sort of criteria than that of systematic argument to guide us. The criteria we seek at metaethical levels is of a confessional-phenomenological variety. Such criteriology pertains to our descriptions of how we have been formed as valuing human beings in relation to others. At metaethical levels of moral discourse, we will investigate by what normative obligations and principles and in what traditions and communities we have been claimed and how, amid the diversity of history and culture, we are being transformed and changed through our interactions with others. At such foundations we will also find that the norms we image as models and the values they disclose, designate, and effectively demonstrate are materially present in historical traditions that precede us. We never create morality—even our most deeply felt convictions—from scratch. In our interaction with other moral subjects, such values and models are flexible and malleable in the ongoing revelations of old traditions and in new and different historical conversations and narrations.[19]

Throughout this book, I have indicated this historicist context of moral obligation and the importance of informing and identifying cosmological worlds for the event of moral character. Experiencing moral character and obligation in the time-full dimensions of historical remembrance and anticipation make human history the medium for all critical conversations in ethics and responsible moral judgments and decisions. Telling and confessing the material-historical stories of our lives in the presence of others—in the context of alterity—cast the whole dynamic of character and obligation within existential-phenomenological ties of intersubjective relationship. Ethical norms arise as ways of designating and disclosing the nature, meaning, and obligations of human relationship with an intention of virtuously effecting value-meanings as goods of social life. No adequate and foundational sense of morality can emerge within the context of self-engendered choice. Norms cannot finally oblige individualistically or privately, but only in the context of historical experiences of relation with others.

In the next chapter I will continue this analysis and argue that the origination, structure, and function of general ethical norms, and the measure of their course toward moral rules of particular behavior, display a three-fold functional intention of metaphorical disclosure, symbolic designation, and effective/sacramental modeling of value-meanings in the context of material-historical experience. In this way, when successful, ethical norms become cultural and societal models for the moral guidance of everyday life. The arguments of Chapter Five will ground more completely the substantive argument I will make in Chapter Six concerning the present state of the norm of heterosexual marriage in the Christian Church.

# 5

## THE ORIGIN, STRUCTURE, AND FUNCTION
## OF ETHICAL NORMS

### The Origin of Ethical Norms

#### The Ethical Norm as the Moral Ideal

Ethical norms emerge by way of a prior moral sensibility that seeks the ideal in human relationships—how we in fact ought to live together. Implicit in the birth of an ethical norm is the distance and tension between the "ideal" and the "real."[1] We recognize that the realities of our everyday interactions with others are not what they should be and need ordering and guidance by ideal images—i.e., normative relationships that are different from the realities of everyday life yet are intimately connected to them. Accordingly, ethical norms come about through exercises of our practical moral imagination. Norms elucidate values, ground ethical principles, and function as motivations for change. Born as imaginative ideals, ethical norms order our moral engagements of everyday life, but they are not literal descriptions of moral facts. To interpret and understand an ethical norm as a literal description or to expect in ourselves and demand in others a literal accomplishment of any moral ideal is to rob the norm of its practical effectiveness. This point will be quite important in our later and substantive discussions of the Christian norm of marriage and rules of sexual conduct.

As imaginative ideals, ethical norms are also qualitatively different from statistical norms that mark, measure, and describe how we ordinarily think and act. Ethical norms cannot be accomplished in only measurements of demographic standards. This is not to say that the social sciences will not have an important role to play in measuring the moral beliefs and practices of individuals and social groups and, most especially, the distance between the ideal and the real in our moral conduct. It is to say that ethical norms, and critically constructive ethics itself, cannot be reduced to only social scientific measurement. Even though the influence of extant peer behavior is strong in the formation of character, something of the imaginative ideal must be added to create a sense of personal and communal obligation beyond the statistical measurement of numerical majorities.[2]

In the next chapter I will address the question of the historical origin of the Church's norm of marriage. I have already argued that ethical norms are substantively born through the narrations of history and culture. I also suggested a schema for their location amid the levels of moral discourse. I indicated that ethical norms are grounded at post-ethical and metaethical levels of prior value interpretation and character identification and that our claims of character inform all subsequent arguments and our attempts at moral persuasion. I argued further that such norms, and the values they model, are finally measured as virtuous in the effects they promote in the material worlds of human relationship. Such practical effectuation remains a constant challenge and check to our initial claims of character and conscience. In this chapter I am interested in exploring the origin, structure, and function of ethical norms as images and models of ideal values that ought to be promoted in our intersubjective relationships. Norms emerge in the context of intersubjectivity because insulated and isolated egos do not possess enough moral sensibility to feel the primary dissatisfaction with "the facts" that is necessary to pursue imaginative ethical ideals. It is this intersubjective experience of being tied to others—across vast and tense distances—that first signals the event of ego and character identification and makes us interested in normative ideals in the first place. The same is true of the moral histories of cultures and societies whose moral breakdowns occur when their ties of intersubjective obligation begin to fail and the norms that order them fade as imaginative ethical ideals.

Such ties of foundational moral obligation cannot be taken literally but must be understood first metaphorically and then symbolically. We are not bound by chains and ropes into moral cultures, societies, and communities. Any forced moral relationships at primary levels creates not an intersubjective bonding of free response to another but a binding moral prison. Obligation in this sense is a parody and sham of morality. This does not mean that law and sanction have no place in morality. It does mean that at primary levels of character identification forced relations assault the freedom necessary for moral engagement and bonding with another. Thus the platitude "one cannot legislate morality" applies only here and not at levels that politically establish in constitution and law the values, norms, and rules deemed necessary for the character identification of the group. A virtuous moral life also requires legislation and law to protect and promote the values that have normatively informed character identification. In this sense the formal purpose of rule and law is to make the terrain between value ideals and realizable goods passable for all, especially those who are the least experienced, least advantaged, and "weakest" travelers. Properly grounded in the freedom required of foundational character identification, rule and law are also exercises of virtue.

This relationship can be seen most clearly in the recent history of civil rights legislation in our country. Such legislation was necessary and required to make the ideals promoted in the images of American citizenship practically realizable to all. What was finally at stake was the nature of American character itself—the metaethical grounding of all civil rights legislation. No amount of legislation will accomplish its task unless it is sufficiently grounded in these prior imaginative and normative ideals. While sufficient clarity and consensus in normative ideals are necessary to enjoin constitutions and laws in the first place, such documents and legislations also serve to educate and advance our corporate moral imagination.

The imaginative ideals disclosed by ethical norms are both drawn from and return to the literal realities of everyday life. Norms function by relatively abridging the distance between the ideal and the real, the self and the other. Without such distances and correlative moral dissatisfaction, ethical norms will be moved by no particular and practical purpose. Thus, if individuals envision themselves without significant ties to others, or correlatively, if institutions engage the world as totalitarian personalities without adequate individuation, then the necessary contexts for the exercise of a normative moral imagination will not be present. Ironically it is diversity, separation, and dissatisfaction that prompt our practical moral imaginations in the formation of ethical norms.

### The Structure and Function of Ethical Norms

#### The Dual Journeys of Functioning Ethical Norms

We can describe traversing the distance between the "literal real" and the "imaginative ideal" as the first journey of the ethical norm. Through this first mediation norms attain their original analytic quality of metaphor. In "twisting" the imaginative ideal from the literal real, the metaphorical *disclosure* of a new and different value-relation of self and other gives birth to the ethical norm. As the norm matures and gains regularity in the moral discourse and rhetoric of culture and society, as it attaches the new metaphorical disclosures to nonsemantic images as well—to persons, states, and things—it attains the quality of a symbol that *designates* new forms of moral knowledge. Rooted in conscientious disquietude in the literal realities of intersubjective life, these metaphorical and symbolic qualities of ethical norms attain full maturity when they effectively demonstrate and *model* the values as goods achieved.

This primary mediation of the ethical norm calls forth a second journey of return to the literal realities of everyday life. Thus claims for a new metaphorical disclosure of the moral ideal in face of the literal real, as well as for a new symbolic designation of moral knowledge must be tested according to dual intentional structure of the norm itself. Born in disquietude, its journey from the literal to the ideal becomes challenged by a final intent to return to direct the literal in better and more "perfect" forms of human interaction. The work of ethical norms can consequently be framed as dual journeys or, better perhaps, as a single journey with two discriminate but related phases. This final modeling and effecting of its own values as goods of sociopolitical life completes its sacramental function and double intentionality.[3] When fully mature, the structural qualities and functional characteristics and intentions of ethical norms are marked as *metaphorical, symbolic,* and *sacramental.*[4]

Yet in their journeys of exit from and return to the literal, normative ideals retain something of the distance and tension of their laborious birth. Journeys always imply a leave-taking. In taking leave of the literal realities of everyday life, imaginative ideals tend to become distant and remote. It is the burden of all proponents of moral values to keep literal realities in sight. Ethical norms and principles that forget the literal realities of everyday life quickly become impractical fantasies rather than deep moral commitments that intend effectiveness. For example, a norm of familial love for the ordering of the public life of nations could easily be judged impractical and thus a pseudo-norm. This does not mean that other images of love, metaphorically designated and symbolically disclosed as friendship or hospitality (see Ogletree, 1985) could not be woven into a normative model of justice for such practical ordering. Still the distance and tension between the imaginative ideal and the literal real create an abiding challenge for the practical work of ethical norms.

In the completion of its return journey to literal application and "sacramental" effectiveness, an ethical norm gains distance from the metaphorical and symbolic images of its birth. Here the challenge of the ideal comes into play again as the encrustations of the literal surface of everyday life tend to erode, block, and absorb the transforming work of the imaginative ideal. If such encrustation succeeds and norms are deflected from their intentions to model and effectuate change, they become equally impractical, but on different grounds. In the first instance, norms were impractical because they failed to keep their literal origins and intentions in sight: now, they are impractical because they no longer have their ideal images in view—have in fact become too close to the literal realities of everyday life and enter into collusion with them. In this latter instance, norms have become impractical because they have given up on the imaginative ideal—have failed to maintain the critical dissatisfaction between how things are and how things ought to be. In such an ethical vacuum, it is often the case that the essentially demographic language of sociological measurement and description become substitutes for the fully ethical norm. This sort of confusion of the ethical and the sociological suggests, for example, that marriage ought not to be normatively modeled any longer as a life commitment because of divorce rates or that nonmarital or even extramarital sexual relations and homosexuality ought to be included in the Christian norm because of similar statistical evidence. If critical and practical effectiveness are to be maintained, the distance and tension between the ideal and the real cannot be collapsed in these ways. Indeed, in the metaphorical birth and symbolic maturation of the ethical norm, the literal is changed by the imaginative just as the imaginative is transformed by the literal. To be effective in moral speech, ethical argument, and moral decision, norms cannot bear the burden of either complete "ideality" or direct literal applicability. To be effective, they will be framed by dialectical intentions and functions of mutual interaction between the ideal and the real.

A norm that is framed too literally—such as, to return to a previous example, "In all my relations with others I must tell the literal truth"— fails to image the deeper dimensions of intersubjective life and experience, in this case, the deeper dimensions of truth and truthfulness. As I have argued, truthfulness becomes confused with simple and, at times, brutal frankness. Not being able to live literally the values disclosed by such a norm, it hovers abstractly above the realities of everyday life as a moral *idea* rather than an *ideal*. On the other hand, if I can tell lies in any situation that meets my self-interpreted needs and interests, I have no norm of truthfulness at all, but only one of lying because I have no ideal image of how truth ought to order my life in ways that are beyond my own isolated determinations. Since I have no way of morally ordering and directing my needs and interests, I have no line of distant moral vision that is wide enough to include my situation in the general characterological context of my relations with others. I lack a constructive moral imagination. I am deficient in character. Nor would another norm *chosen specifically* to fit my situation function any better. It would only be a pseudo-norm because it would lack historical credibility. Such credibility can only be achieved by the disclosures, designations, and demonstrations of the public moral discourse of culture and society. Development, progress, and change in ethical norms do not come from individual choices but from their record of material-historical and sacramental effectiveness. *In their imaginative mediation of the distance between the ideal and real in the life of a culture, society, or community, norms are born not chosen.*

For the ethical norm to be effective—to avoid a stillbirth or moribund state—the ideal and the real, the imaginative and the literal must coexist in mutually informing tension. We know, for example, that the norm of truthfulness always exists amid structures of lying and deceit and is paradoxically dependent upon such structures when the overt moral speech of culture and society expresses moral dissatisfaction with liars. At the same time, the moral rhetoric of a community must be materially truthful in its expression of dissatisfaction and not use its rhetoric of ideals as an obfuscation and misdirection—i.e., to complain about liars only when particular needs and interests are negatively affected. Such a materially untruthful rhetoric would function as an abstraction and segmentation of morality from the fully political and public realm— would in fact render morality an obfuscating and manipulating ideology. This is what Karl Marx essentially claimed about the moral rhetoric of justice in capitalist societies (see Tucker, 1963: 306–25). In Marx's sense of capitalist morality as ideology, the minority powers use a false rhetoric of justice to feed the appetite of the majority cultural imagination for moral ideals in order to keep at bay their moral outrage and dissatisfaction with the realities of everyday life. In a similar vein, we can notice how promoting the Church's norm of marriage can also be involved in a similar rhetoric of falsifying ideological obfuscation. Amid claims of an abiding norm of heterosexual marriage, to suggest that there is a crisis in sexual morality because of the behavior of those who are not married and not heterosexual without at the same time suggesting a crisis in marriage itself is to be either naively judgmental or to engage in a disingenuous masquerade wherein we claim more satisfaction with Christian married life than we in fact have. If the Church is in moral crisis with respect to sexual values overall, such a crisis is finally grounded in Christian married life. Norms do not work in the abstract, but only in the symbolic and sacramental concrete. For any foundational Christian norm of marriage to work effectively in the disclosure of moral values, Christian married life must work as well.

For the moral ideals to achieve historical and sacramental effectiveness there must exist an expressed dissatisfaction with how we are living our moral lives. At the same time there can be no project of abstract perfection that suggests that such ideals can be literally and fully realized. In this instance, all are distant from the center of the values disclosed in the norm of marriage. Norms continue to be effective if the values disclosed and designated are sufficiently approximated as goods not absolutely and perfectly realized. In light of the ideal, we realize that we ought to relate with each other in certain ways, but very often we do not. It is amid such a mix of relative success and failure that we realize further that no one lives out literally imaginative and normative ideals, and that the guilt we feel when confronted with the distance between who we say we are and how in fact we live is not necessarily destructive and neurotic, but rather can be a precondition for moral motivation and practical and effective change—a new way of being in the world.

Ethical norms as moral ideals always exist within the context of their own failure—the norm of truthfulness amid lying and deceit; the values of love and commitment, amid anger, hatred and infidelity. Norms come to life and maturity not in spite of the morally disquieting facts of everyday life but because of them. The return of norms from what we often, but mistakenly, think of as the historically purer realm of the ideal to the more complex worlds of context, circumstance, and situation is only the completion of their characteristic journey. The metaphoric and symbolic structure of the norm are both grounded in and completed by the literal moral realities of everyday life. Nor does this recognition of negative realities dilute normative ideals, but rather points out their meaning and purpose of engaging effectively the situations and circumstances of everyday life. Adequate and effective norms do not hover abstractly above literal realities nor are they only a reduction of our interests in how we *ought* to live to how we *are* living. Even a preliminary analysis indicates what I argued in the last chapter: *an ethical norm cannot be reduced to a literal moral rule, nor can moral rules do the imaginative and ideal work of ethical norms.* Rather, once the metaphoric and symbolic characteristics of norms are understood, we realize that they model formally the tension and only relative mediation of the distance we experience in our lives between the real and the ideal, the "is" and the "ought."

As models of the value ideals of intersubjective interrelation, norms are not properly configured as points of location or places in which we can stand or abide. The realization that no one embodies a norm gives the necessary shock of recognition of our own failures. Shocked from our own moralistic slumber, we can be drawn into renewed worlds of value and valuation. When ethical norms remain vital, they can be envisioned existentially as revolving centers with extending and flexible orbits whose outer edges are formed and measured by the material-historical conditions within which sometimes conflicting values must be received and embodied as goods. Even when the ideal values imaged at the center remain constant for a time—are not being radically decentered and transformed—the orbit of the norm is flexible enough to sometimes change what has traditionally been included and excluded. For example, it is possible to argue that in principle, and on the basis of abiding and effective values of love and commitment revealed by the norm of marriage, that sexual intimacy may be morally responsible in certain material conditions and situations other than marriage and heterosexuality because the same values are being effected as goods. In these cases, the sacramental effectiveness of the Church's norm has been extended functionally to these states of affairs. However, an argument that is analytically possible in principle must still bear the burden of substantive accomplishment. We will need to know in any particular situation and circumstance whether such values are actually being effected. Nonetheless, it seems that a recognition of this analytic possibility—how ethical norms are in fact structured and used in ordinary speech and behavior—is a precondition for even considering this and listening to further argument.

Before taking up at least my fair share of this burden of substantive moral theological argument in the next chapter, a more precise analysis of the structure and function of an ethical norm is necessary under the dynamic characteristics of metaphor, symbol, and sacrament. Our goal here is to discover how these characteristics can themselves bear the burden I have assigned them of moving moral discourse and practice across the vast distances between the ideal and the real, the imaginative and the literal in an historically effective manner—how, in fact, ethical norms become mature and effective models for the guidance of·practical moral behavior.

Throughout this analysis, I will avoid the stronger claim of identifying ethical norms as metaphors and symbols. If such a claim could be sustained, it would require more analysis and argument than is necessary to support the substantive discussion in Part Three on the status of the norm of marriage and its function and limits as a guide for responsible sexual behavior. Rather, all I need to demonstrate here is that norms in general and marriage in particular have identifying qualities of metaphor and symbol and that successful norms function sacramentally in their effective modeling of ideal value meanings as goods of social and political life. When these three characteristic qualities work effectively, ethical norms appear in the historical and culture conversation of any age as models for the responsible engagement of character in a particular aspect of the intersubjective relations of the moral life.

It ought to be axiomatic in argument that stronger claims should not be engaged when weaker claims will do. In making the weaker claim and trying to avoid the temptation to lapse into "all is metaphor and symbol" language, I am also rejecting any reductionist interpretation that suggests the work of metaphor and symbol lessens the practical applicability of the ethical norm or makes ethics into only a semantic and ritualistic exercise—in effect, language without a clear material-historical and political referent. Without due emphasis on political and sacramental completion, metaphor theory especially and symbol theory to some extent run great risks of remaining abstract or "only literary." This is the main reason why I am emphasizing the sacramental intentionality that I find to be ingredient in the structure and function of metaphor and symbol and thus in the ethical norm. Even though such literary reductionism is a misunderstanding of the structure and function of metaphor and symbol, it remains ubiquitous.

While fundamentally rooted and continually intertwined in speech and language, ethics and the moral life are not only semantic or ritualistic. In *The Philosophy of Literary Forms* (1967: 8–9) Kenneth Burke warns:

> Still there is a difference, and a radical difference, between building a house and writing a poem about building a house—and a poem about having children by marriage is not the same thing as having children by marriage. There are *practical* acts and there are symbolic acts (nor is the distinction, clear enough in its extremes, to be dropped simply because there is a borderline area wherein many practical acts take on symbolic ingredient, as one may buy a certain commodity not merely to use it, but also because its possession testifies to his enrollment in a certain stratum of society).

An adequate understanding of the structure and function of metaphor and symbol discloses the moral/political dimensions of their sacramental intentionality thereby maintaining the distinction between symbolic and practical acts without undue separation. In other words, while it is true that any normative model of marriage (the "ideal") and being married (the "real") are different things, they must be related if moral discourse and ethical argument are to be brought to bear as guides for everyday life.

The Metaphoric Quality of the Ethical Norm

In analyzing the metaphoric qualities of ethical norms, I have no intention of entering, as Paul Ricoeur has noted, "the somewhat boundless field of metaphor theory" (1978c: 143), or to engage fully the similar range of debate about symbol, sacrament, and model. At the same time, I must present enough analysis to make my substantive claims about sexual morality plausible and, perhaps, persuasive. In our investigations of metaphor, the work of Paul Ricoeur will be the most helpful.

Ted Cohen has noted that "these are good times for the friends of metaphor. They are so salutary that we are in danger of overlooking some very thorny underbrush as we scramble over the high road to figurative glory" (1978: 3). The particular "thorny underbrush" I want to engage in this discussion of metaphor theory is any tendency to reduce moral speech and ethics to only *a linguistic disclosure of meaning*. Thus, as I have indicated, my basic reason for introducing the somewhat unusual category of "sacrament" in this analysis is to point to the necessary social and political referent that finally grounds and completes the moral life. Even though we must begin with the metaphorical quality of an ethical norm, we cannot stop here. Ricoeur helps us see that metaphors themselves do not merely indicate a deviant linguistic denomination, or introduce only an enigmatic semantic clash between the literal and figurative meanings of words, but rather disclose a "*new* predicative meaning which merges from the collapse of the literal meaning" (1978c: 146). For Ricoeur, a "metaphor is not an ornament of discourse. It has more than emotive value because it offers new information. A metaphor, in short, tells us something new about reality" (1976: 52-53). As predicative, the new metaphoric disclosure proclaims, declares, and affirms something new— a new meaning not disclosed by the literal referent even though it is the "failure" of the literal referent that gives birth to the metaphor. As I have argued, in the metaphoric birth of the ethical norm, the literal realities of how we are living our lives fail as adequate moral guides.

The second and related layer of thorny underbrush I want to engage in the thicket of metaphor theory pertains to the phenomenon of *being captured* by metaphor. I have argued that in our engagements of material-historical existence, the structural dynamics of norms indicate that metaphor is only one of the characteristics of the human quest for critical meaning, truth, and right. Again, Ricoeur's analysis of symbol and its relation to metaphor will assist us (1969; 1976; 1978b). Ricoeur indicates that from a comparison of the work of metaphor and symbol, we can learn of the internal structural dynamics of both as well as understand the unique work of symbol in designating the necessary return of what he calls the *logos* of metaphor to the *bios* from which it was born. In this analysis, symbol testifies more clearly than metaphor "to the primordial rootedness of Discourse in Life" (Ricoeur, 1976: 59). It was this exit from and return to *bios* that I have related as the "dual journeys" of the ethical norm. While necessarily rooted in language, ethics and the moral life are not simply linguistic, semantic, or ritualistic, much less only metaphorical, but are defined by their sacramental intentionality to affect—and indeed, effect—the social and political structures of material-historical existence. It was within such structures and because of them that I argued that the historical drama of moral character is formed and practiced. Within this dialectic of material-history—*logos* and *bios*—the event of moral character is intertwined with the drama of its worldly engagements. Thus there is no need to oppose metaphor and symbol, *logos* and *bios*, or the figurative language of moral ideals and the demands of practical action, but merely to see their interaction. Once the proper relation of metaphor and symbol is understood, the "re-bonding" of metaphor, via the work of symbol, to the nonlinguistic dimensions of culture and society (see Ricoeur, 1976: 61–62) can inform a theory of ethical norms as historically effective models for the practice of moral virtue.

Both Philip Wheelwright (1968) and Paul Ricoeur adopt "tensive" and "interactive" (see also Max Black, 1962; 1979) theories of metaphor as the transitive relation of the literal descriptive and figurative imaginative. Indeed, Wheelwright adopts Wallace Stevens's understanding of metaphoric speech as "'the symbolic language of metamorphosis'" (1968: 71). Wheelwright describes the twin dynamics of metaphor as *epiphor* and *diaphor*. In the work of *epiphor*, the new figurative meaning "appears upon, over, near, and after" the old literal meaning; in the work of *diaphor*, the new meaning is completed, appearing in one sense, as its own disclosure and drawing us into an "accomplished transition." It is important to remember, however, that even in the completion of this transition, the bonds of the new figurative meaning are not entirely severed from the literal from which it was born. Wheelwright argues that both the movements are necessary for the metamorphosis—"the one standing for outreach and extension of meaning through comparison, the other for the creation of the new meanings by juxtaposition and synthesis" (1968: 72). Wheelwright concludes that "the role of *epiphor* is to hint significance, the role of *diaphor* is to create presence" (1968: 91). Ricoeur notes with approval Monroe Beardsley's description of this dynamic as the "metaphorical twist" (1976: 51)—the twist of the new figurative meaning from the old literal meaning. Such a dynamic is far more than mere wordplay, but draws us linguistically into a new way of seeing and being in the world. Through the metaphorical utterance, we are drawn into new worlds of meaning, truth, and obligation. When successful, the work of metaphor is not a mere substitute denomination—saying the same thing or disclosing the same meaning in a different way—but rather signals a new way of knowing and acting (see Ricoeur, 1976: 50-51).

Even though the event of metaphor is more than merely saying the same thing under a different name, metaphor theory does not need to discount the quality and power of a new name. In its deepest dimensions, to name something or someone differently is to *disclose* and *designate*—"open up" and "reveal," "mark out" and "delimit"—new forms of interrelationship and meaning, knowledge and reality. In this sense, naming, like metaphor, is an original act of predication and affirmation of a way of being and acting in the world. In both positive and negative moral dimensions, naming has something fundamental to do with the full birth of human personality and moral character. In a more negative vein, it is not hard to see how derogatory names—those that reduce the worth of human personality and character—function metaphorically and when embodied in cultural and societal symbols are so inviting of evil and destruction.

In engaging perhaps a third layer of the thorny underbrush of metaphor theory, we cannot be reminded too often that the analysis of figurative speech does not obviate the substantive work required along the whole range of moral/ethical discourse to discriminate between good and evil confessions, imaginations, and character identifications. Metaphors and symbols effect evil as well as good, and through the same structural dynamic. The value-ideals modeled by even effective norms can also be evil images—values of an evil imagination. This is the most substantive reason why all our confessions, claims, and imaginative figurations must be submitted to the scrutiny of their sacramental efficacy to see what they produce and have produced in the literal realities of everyday life. Evil is also a category of the moral life and, like the good, begins in the imagination. If there is any way to break out of this circle, it is through open and public conversation about the practical implications and effects of our value ideals and habits of virtue measured first in the context of alterity—i.e., through the effects on those different from ourselves.

The interactive and transitive theory of metaphor adopted by Wheelwright, Ricoeur, and others—the origination of new meaning from the collapse of the old—makes it tempting to think of metaphorical language as extraordinary and emerging at the limits of ordinary speech. And in one sense this is true.[5] The rise of metaphoric speech and language indicates that what we have claimed as meaningful experience and now want to linguistically communicate and predicate of ourselves and others—indeed, of the world itself—can no longer be born by literal and surface description. In sum, we are dissatisfied with the power of literal speech and language to circumscribe and communicate depths of meaning and understanding or to sustain our new claims for truth and right. Facticity is no longer enough and what even most people believe, say, and do at any given time are not, in themselves, sufficient renderings of ethical norms.

In another sense, metaphoric speech and language are not extraordinary at all but rather are ordinary exercises of the human imagination that make critical thought and action possible in the first place. Like metaphor, critical speech itself confronts the limits of descriptions of literal and surface realities, "sorting them out" (*krinein*) and "digging deep," so to speak. In this sense and running the risk of, as Ricoeur indicates, speaking "metaphorically about metaphor" (1978c: 145), we can speak of *heights* and *depths* beyond the surface of everyday life.[6] What is important to note here is that the new metaphorical disclosure and the ubiquity of critical speech require and depend on the regular failure of ordinary literal usage. Thus the linguistic matrix within which metaphor and critical speech in general arise and become ubiquitous is grounded on the regularity of ordinary literal speech to fail. We might say that literal descriptive speech is *designed* to fail when it meets the limits of its own function. Consequently, the new worlds of meaning disclosed and invited by metaphor are extraordinary only in one sense and quite ordinary in another. This may help account for why metaphors, symbols, myths, poetic and religious discourse, and the language of ethical ideals have, in one way or another, informed all cultures and societies. If there are such universal and implicit dimensions in ordinary experience and language, it is because literal description *ordinarily* reaches its own limits and calls forth genres of the entire range of critique—limits first noticed and disclosed by metaphor.[7]

As extraordinary as their disclosures and invitations may seem in contrast to literal description, metaphoric speech only hastens the course of language in its regular course of creating critical meaning, understanding, and knowledge. It is this ordinary course of language that informs our dissatisfaction with "how things are" and our subsequent search for new metaphors of "how things ought to be." When metaphorical utterances "negate" the literal, they do so not only to substitute a new description for an old one, but rather to engage in a transformation of the literal and the so-called facts themselves. In this way, metaphors predicate a new and extraordinary relation and experience in terms of ordinary and everyday existence. Accordingly, metaphoric speech and language are not to be considered a super-aestheticist rhetoric that attains release from the bonds of ordinary description through either substitution or permanent negation. Ricoeur argues that the suspension (*epochē*) of the literal—the release of the metaphoric utterance into the "already purified universe of the *logos*" (1976: 59)—is only a "moment of negativity" (1978c: 151). Metaphorical and poetic language in general

> is no less *about* reality than any other use of language but refers to it by means of a complex strategy which implies, as an essential component, a suspension and seemingly an abolition of the ordinary reference attached to descriptive language. This suspension, however, is only the negative condition of a second-order reference, of an indirect reference built on the ruins of the direct reference. This reference is called second-order reference only with respect to the primacy of the reference of ordinary language. For, in another respect, it constitutes the primordial reference to the extent that it suggests, reveals, unconceals—or whatever you say—the deep structures of reality to which we are related as mortals who are born into this world and who *dwell* in it for a while (Ricoeur, 1978c: 153).

Therefore metaphorical utterances do not disclose or create new and different worlds of the *logos* hovering above the *bios* of everyday life. Rather metaphor is born within the confines of material-historical existence—an existence which regularly and ordinarily discloses the limits of its own literal description.[8]

Curiously, the growth of contemporary metaphor theory is dependent on the historical progress of modernity that marks our own time, especially the rise and fall of scientific description. In commenting on the comparison between literal and figurative speech in Medieval and modern times, Owen Barfield argues that in the Medieval environment, it was the literal that was problematic, and in modern times, at least in some dimensions, it is the reverse. Because of this reversal, he continues, we find the emergence of a *modern idolatry* of the literal alone and the need to save the entire range of the appearances of reality from scientific hegemony (1965: 74; 71–78). With the coming of the modern world there has been a change in the relation of first and second order referents of speech and language. At foundational levels in the Medieval world, primary speech and language was more mythic, metaphoric, and symbolic than literal. With modern scientific description, however, figurative speech began to lose its power to order and account for human experience. Literal descriptive speech removed figurative speech from its place of primacy, and the new cosmology of modernity was born. Modernity thus experiences different problems in its discourse of meaning and knowledge than the Medieval world. In modernity, what had been disclosed and designated by metaphoric and symbolic speech became problematic and figurative language.in general was challenged for a more critical account of itself. However, the victory of literal speech was short-lived, and moderns began to realize that the descriptive speech we depend on to order and explain so much of our daily lives in modernity also ordinarily and regularly failed. Nor can we change this new modern cosmological priority of the literal and bring figurative speech to priority again. In modern times, the language of metaphor and symbol will remain second order. The irony is that the modern and post-modern future of the now *second-order* discourse of religion, ethics, and the arts as predicative of meaning, truth, and right beyond what can be described literally, depend on the scientific speech of modernity to fail at some level. The future of religious, theological, and moral discourse, and of the liberal arts in general, is now bound with the future of literal/scientific speech.

Figurative speech and language have been ubiquitous in the course of human history and culture but for different reasons in different periods. Indeed, in the comparison of the different priorities of the order of reference of the figurative and the literal in Medieval and modern times, we find critical speech itself taking on different meanings. By and large with the rise of modern scientific method, critical speech implied only what could be verified and falsified by literal description and experimentation. The speculative, metaphoric, symbolic, and mythic figurations of metaphysicians, religionists, poets, and the like were rendered noncritical. With the regularization of scientific speech and theory over the course of modernity, however, a predictable crisis of all such epistemological hegemony ensued, and their singular promises were found as relatively wanting as the old figurations.[9] Consequently, the meaning of critique in late modernity has been gradually migrating from science back to the now-transformed humanities, including religion. Still, this late-modern dissatisfaction with the literal and primary scientific description is not simply a return to the epistemology and metaphysics of premodern ages where literal description was never primary for articulating and communicating cosmological order and location. Metaphoric, symbolic and, most especially, the mythic speech of religion will never assume a premodern priority especially in an aestheticist or romanticist sense. Scientific speech will remain primary in its functional descriptions, but it will continue to fail in all claims to be the comprehensive language of universal human experience. It is this regular failure that has given rise to the new critique. Any contemporary concentration on the disclosures and designations of figurative speech and language—on metaphor, symbol, and myth—as a critique of primary literal description and the *scientific spirit* will remain in the context of *second order* discourse in the sense described by Ricoeur.[10]

It is in this context of late modernity that metaphor theory has arisen again and anew to speak of the *heights* and *depths* of everyday life beyond the vision and notice of the literal description. Such *re-creations* of metaphor require only a temporary negation and release from the literal so that they might disclose a new cognitive and moral predication. In this way, metaphorical utterances draw the practicalities of everyday life into new and deeper lines of vision beyond what can be seen in ordinary descriptions. This effective drawing together of *logos* and *bios*, spirit and matter—the *critical figurative* and the *non-critical descriptive* and "factive"—is the formal work of metaphor and symbol. Within such dynamics, ethical norms work to effect and embody new and ideal worlds of meaning and understanding, truth and right, amid the realities of sociocultural and political existence.

It is this intentionality of metaphor, and of all critical language, that prevents any rest in moments of release or celebrations of the negation of the literal. Ricoeur argues that attempts to retain permanent release from the *bios* of the literal only "redirects language toward itself to the point that language may be said, in Roland Barthes' words, 'to celebrate itself' rather than to celebrate the world" (1978c: 152–53).[11] The *logos* of all forms of critical speech, including the metaphoric, is not for its own sake, but for the *bios* of everyday life—most specifically, to articulate, communicate, and invite participation in the "something more" we sometimes, but with universal regularity as cultures and societies, find there. The new creations and constructions of the metaphoric utterance are always *re-creative* and *re-constructive*.

In the metaphorical utterance "a new signification emerges which embraces the whole sentence" leading to "a new extension of meaning" (Ricoeur, 1976: 52). In the context of a sentence as a predicative utterance, the metaphorical disclosure is a "contextual action" that "creates a word-meaning which is an event"—a new relation with the world and a new world of meaning. Thus, Ricoeur argues, metaphor partakes of *mimesis* as "world disclosure" rather than merely a "duplication of reality" and is joined with *poiesis*, as "fabrication, construction, creation" (1978a: 138; 147).[12] In the same vein, Ricoeur asks, "Why should we draw new meanings from our language if we had nothing new to say, no new worlds to project? Linguistic creations would be meaningless if they did not serve the general project of letting new worlds emerge" (1978a: 148).

Still, as Max Black indicates, metaphor theory is "tantalizingly illusive" (1979: 143) in its attempts to account for the emergence of such new worlds and the "something more" that is going on in the metaphorical utterance beyond the literal description. At its deepest levels, I have argued that such an account would be necessarily confessional—that, in one way or another, sensitivity to metaphor requires experiencing material-historical reality as multidimensional. With "more going on than meets the eye," literal description will be regularly unsatisfactory. From such regular and ordinary dissatisfaction comes the birth of the critical mind, soul, and character, and our need for "sorting out" and searching for new linguistic modes of world-disclosure, reconstruction, and re-creation. Illusive though this "something more" may be in metaphorical disclosure, its anthropological ubiquity suggests a strong burden of explanation on any who claim the regular and universal adequacy of literal descriptive speech. Why literal speech and language regularly and ordinarily fail is what is illusive—the nature of the "something more," more illusive still. That literal speech and language do in fact *fail* over time and overall in every culture and age and that this accounts for the universality of metaphor and symbol seems beyond argument.

From this universal anthropological failure of literal description and the ubiquity of metaphor, symbol, and myth, carefully circumscribed in the context of modernity (see Ricoeur, 1969:5),[13] Philip Wheelwright extrapolates three sets of characteristics of "reality in so far as it is an object of tensive language and of the responsive wonder that expresses itself through such language" (1968: 154). His use of the term "wonder" is only a more positive rendering of what I have called our dissatisfaction with the failure of literal description as the grounds for critique. We wonder about and wander from literal speech and language because they fail to universally account for how reality is appearing to us. Thus Wheelwright's characterization of reality takes its cue from how we regularly speak and write about new worlds of experience. In this way, the characteristics he indicates participate in the "shy ontological claim" he attributes to the successful imagist poem (1968: 162).

From this standpoint the principal characteristics of living reality appear to be three: it is presential and tensive; it is coalescent and interpenetrative; and it is perspectival and hence latent, revealing itself only partially, ambiguously, and through symbolic indirection (Wheelwright, 1968: 154).

Wheelwright's "ontological claim" is not grounded in a systematic and speculative metaphysics but in how we ordinarily use language. For Wheelwright, metaphor and "living reality" mutually inform and describe each other. He concludes:

Reality is ultimately problematical, not contingently so; for to grasp and formulate it, even as a set of questions, is to fragmentize it. There is always, in any inquiry, something more than meets the eye, even the inner eye; the permanent possibility of extending one's imaginative awareness has no limits (1968, 172).[14]

The Symbolic Quality of the Ethical Norm

At this point of the disclosure of "new worlds" of meaning and experience we can conclude this brief analysis of metaphor and set the proper transition to symbol. With respect to ethical norms, the limits of metaphorical speech and language emerge when their *disclosures* of ideal value meanings are challenged by the requirements of cultural and societal sedimentation necessary for *designations* of new moral knowledge. To sustain any claims for moral knowledge, the value-ideals disclosed in the dynamic metaphorical structure of the ethical norm must become regularized in culture and society—indeed, "demarcated" and "deposited" as part of the noetic foundation of individual and social character. It is this work of new designation that is essentially performed by symbol.[15]

Though predicative of new meanings with cognitive content, metaphors are essentially semantic events (Ricoeur, 1976: 45–46). Ricoeur argues that within the metaphoric utterance the new "contextual action creates a word-meaning which is an event...a linguistic creation.... Only genuine metaphors are at the same time 'event' *and* 'meaning'" (1978a: 138). Even as successful metaphors shock and twist us predicatively into new recognitions and new worlds, when regularized and deposited in the linguistic sediments of culture and society, they tend to diminish and lose their force. Wheelwright argues that it is precisely here that "symbol is distinguished from metaphor by its greater stability and permanence" (1968: 98). To survive, metaphors require a continuation of the surprising dissonance created by the clash between the literal and figurative meanings; yet metaphors tend to die by repetition. Ricoeur claims that "there are no live metaphors in a dictionary" (1976: 52). Therefore, if the work of metaphor is not merely for the celebration of its own *logos* but finally for the *bios* from whence it came, then something more is needed. The work of metaphor is taken up and extended through the symbol. At the limits of metaphor symbol begins.

Knowledge requires not only the dramatic disclosure of new meaning but also the regular assimilation of meaning in routinized and regular patterns and judgments. In the context of the sedimentations of culture and society, knowledge requires a communal and public assimilation that what has been disclosed as meaningful is also "tried and true." With respect to ethical norms, whereas metaphors *disclose* new worlds of value-relations, symbols specify, indicate, and mark out—i.e., *designate*—regular communal understandings and judgments of the identity and character of both individuals and groups. Indeed, Ricoeur suggests a necessary dialectic for knowledge between the disclosure of new worlds of meaning and our assimilation to such worlds. However, "the metaphor is too short a discourse to display this dialectic between disclosing a world and understanding one's self in front of this world" (1978a: 146). Knowledge requires both a disclosure of meaning and a designation and assimilation of understanding leading to habits of regular judgment.

I am using the term knowledge here in a functional and analytic sense—i.e., what we think of, experience, and use as fact and truth in everyday life. "True knowledge" must still bear the continuing critical burdens of verification and legitimation, especially the critique of ideology to disclose false and obfuscating "knowledge."[16] Meaning and knowledge can be further distinguished respectively in terms of insightful experiences, and the regular and sedimented designations of some fact, state, or condition upon which we depend for functioning as cultures and and societies. In their predicative functions, metaphors and symbols can be similarly distinguished through their respective work of disclosure and of designation and assimilation. Metaphors "apprehend," "seize," "grasp," and "make us aware" of new worlds of meaning— indeed, new presentations and re-presentations of reality. Symbols assimilate and "take us in," not just to new worlds of meaning but to the regular and sedimented cultures of their own effective signification. As Ricoeur argues, "the symbol assimilates rather than apprehends a resemblance.... It assimilates us to what is thereby signified" (1976: 56).

For example, despite a metaphorical origination, to call government "the ship of state" or the Church "the body of Christ," is now to speak symbolically—novel apprehensions that have become sedimented assimilations. In the context of culture, symbols designate and demarcate the limits for what counts as knowledge for individuals and groups— limits for the identification and location of how self and world are engaged in any place and time. The semantic innovation of metaphorical apprehension and the assimilating function of symbol show "new possibilities for articulating and conceptualizing reality" (Ricoeur, 1976: 57). Indeed, the disclosure of metaphor and the designation of symbol mark the emergence of conceptual thinking. In this context, we can situate Ricoeur's well-known claims that the symbol "gives rise to" and "invites thought"—*Le symbole donne à penser* (1978b: 37; 1969: 348; 347–57). Unlike metaphors, symbols demand duration, regularization, and sedimentation. "A meditation on symbols starts from speech that has already taken place" (Ricoeur, 1969: 348)—that is to say, speech that has become sedimented in the material-historical life of a culture and society. Thus, we "become implicated" in the life of a symbol (Ricoeur, 1978b: 45) socially, politically, and morally.

It is this public and sedimented implication that is necessary for the transition from meaning to knowledge. Metaphor semantically discloses a new world of meaning, while symbol designates and marks out a culture of knowledge through its unique recombination of semantic and nonsemantic elements—in this sense, *logos* and *bios*. Returning again to the ethical norm, we can say that the metaphoric disclosures of a new world of ideal-value meanings—for example, the association of sexual behavior and committed love—must, via the symbolic designation, also effect a regular sedimentation of character identification and its expression in sexual acts. Whereas the metaphorical disclosure may be a new way of framing ideal values of sexual intimacy in the face of literal realities, in the developed norm committed love must also become implicated in the actual practice of sex. Under normative symbols and models of committed love, various practices and manners of life serve to politically embody the linguistic value-ideal in regular and sedimented ways. Accordingly, marriage can become a model and its symbols of home, hearth, and children part of the material and normative structure of culture and society. In the context of both these linguistic and nonlinguistic disclosures and designations, we find the emergence of our ordinary ritualizations of sexual intimacy, love, and marriage—what Niklas Luhmann calls "the codification of intimacy" (1986). With effective symbolic designations of metaphoric disclosures, the normative ideal of committed love in marriage can model not only meaningful but truthful knowledge about sexual intimacy and sexual conduct.

This is the analytic point that will guide the substantive argument of the next chapter concerning the present state of the norm of marriage in the Christian Church. There I will discuss the important substantive implication of this analysis. But even here we can say that the present state of marriage in the Church, or any norm at all in culture at large, depends on the continuing force of metaphorical disclosures—in this case foundationally, but not only, biblical ones—and the state of our historical symbolic designations. Again, it is important to remember that norms are not chosen but are woven into the fabric of material-historical situations. They exist in sickness and health in cultures and contexts. Gauging the state of any particular ethical norm as it exists in its larger moral environment is an essential part of any substantive ethical analysis—what we can call ethos-criticism.

Even though the most proximate informing environment of Christian sexual morality is general Western culture, formal analytic points concerning metaphoric disclosures and symbolic designations for the normative direction of sexual intimacy can apply to other cultures as well. While there is a marked degree of substantive relativity, plurality, and conventionality throughout the cultures of sexual morality, there is also some formal commonality. Relating our present analytic conversation with our arguments for the historicity of knowledge in Part One tells us that meaning and knowledge have deep and common cultural roots—indeed, in the root metaphors and symbols that identify and define cultures and societies. Ordinary cultural diversity in sexual morality does not mean that there can be no formal engagement of cross-cultural discussion; but rather that substantive metaphors and symbols are not easily interchangeable. Neither does the cultural embedment of root metaphors and informing symbols mean that no major shifts in consciousness or morality can take place within given cultures themselves but only that such radical change happens over time, not overnight, and implies some change in character-identity.

Given its history as an informing symbol in Western and Christian culture, I can argue analytically that for some other norm to replace marriage in the Christian Church would require a change in character and identity of that body. Failure to understand this analytic point leads to major and structural dysfunction in the Church's conversations on this matter. However, to finally ground this argument substantively, I and others would have to be willing to assume the significant burden of determining at what level the norm of marriage abides and functions as part of the identifying nature of Christian life and the Christian Church—that is, if and how the metaphorical disclosure and symbolic designation of committed love now come together, both in theory and practice, in a normative model of marriage as part of Christian character-identity. All discussion of sexual morality in the Church has deep theological and confessional roots that finally call for fully developed theologies of sexuality and marriage. In my substantive discussion of the norm of marriage as such in the Part Three, I will only engage the edges of such a foundational theology.

Still, in light of historical relativity and cultural diversity, symbols—including those experienced in the long history of the Church—do not always survive and seldom remain unchanged. Like metaphors, symbols stand under an obligation and pragmatic test of double effectuation. Initially metaphors and symbols are effective in their disclosures and designations—i.e., their own successful birth means that they have in fact disclosed and designated new meaning and knowledge. However, what is especially clear in the metaphoric and symbolic qualities of ethical norms is that such meaning and knowledge must finally be regularly received in the lives of people in ways that inform and affect their behavior. Consequently, judging the continuing health of the norm of marriage will include gauging how ideals of committed love and knowledge about sexual intimacy are functioning in sexual behavior. Are we in fact being implicated in the life of this normative symbol? Is marriage a functioning and practical model for the guidance of sexual behavior? No simple recitation of statistics will suffice for such an analysis. What is at stake is how the norm is metaphorically disclosing and symbolically designating ideal-values that intend to be effective across the wide spectrum of sexual behavior. In this sense, to continue to confuse the *norm* of heterosexual marriage with a single *rule* of heterosexual behavior in all situations and circumstances will finally strain this norm beyond its capacities for endurance as well as distract us from attending to the true source of our difficulties. If we are behaving badly with respect to sex, along with whatever other causes we may discern, it is also because our norms are becoming dysfunctional.

This is not to suggest that the transition from disclosing metaphor to designating and routinized symbol is simple, easy to measure, or without overlap and mergence. Ricoeur argues that "the semantic dimensions of literal and figurative meanings in tension is common to metaphor and symbol" (1976: 54–57). Even in their symbolic dimensions, images of home, hearth, and children stand as ideal value-figurations in tension with the literal realities of broken homes, homeless families, cold and loveless hearths, and indeed, abandoned children. Nonetheless, if we are implicated in the symbolic life of an ethical norm, such negative realities can stand convicted and possibly transformed by the ideal figuration.

Often symbolic figurations themselves become overly regular and too routinized—in fact, lose touch with the effective tension that mutually implicates literal reality and the life of the transforming ideal. This is what Philip Wheelwright calls the "steno-symbol" (1968: 93–94). Wheelwright indicates that symbols have their own range of function in the material-historical life of a culture and society—from *steno* to *tensive* (1968: 93–110). In this analysis, I am emphasizing Wheelwright's further and broader denomination of tensive "symbols of cultural range"—"those which have a significant life for members of a community, of a cult, or of a larger secular or religious body" (1968: 108–9). Here we find the symbolic range intended and needed for the Church's norms. It is the case, however, that even symbols of a broader cultural range can become, over time, only steno symbols. To expect a steno symbol to function as one of broader cultural range is to court anxiety, frustration, and confusion. We say the same words—"marriage is normative"—but we do not get the expected results: sexual behavior continues to deteriorate morally. For marriage to function as a designating symbol in the Church's modern discourse on sexual morality, it must retain its vitality as a tensive symbol of cultural range. Whether heterosexual and monogamous marriage has attained the function of an "archetypal symbol"—Wheelwright's final category—and has an "identical or similar meaning for (humankind) generally or at least for a large part of it" (Wheelwright, 1968: 110, parens added), awaits more cultural anthropological report.[17]

Ricoeur emphasizes that metaphors are initially "dispersed events,…places in discourse,…a semantic innovation" that only exist "in the moment of invention," with the result that

> when a metaphor is taken up and accepted by a linguistic community it tends to become confused with an extension of the polysemy of worlds. It first becomes a trivial, then a dead metaphor. Symbols in contrast, because they plunge their roots into the durable constellations of life, feeling, and the universe, and because they have such an incredible stability, lead us to think that a symbol never dies, it is only transformed. Hence if we were to hold fast to our criteria for a metaphor, symbols must be dead metaphors (Ricoeur, 1976: 64).

Yet metaphors save themselves from any moribund transition to symbols and their own death by repetition when they become implicated in networks of inter-signification—with one metaphor staying alive by retaining its power to evoke a whole network. Such networks engender "what we can call root metaphors" and have "the power to bring together the partial metaphors borrowed from the diverse fields of human experience" (Ricoeur, 1976: 64). In this sense, the norm of "committed love" may be counted as a root metaphor for the array of values disclosed as we claim to be loving and "in love" in our relations of sexual intimacy. As a root metaphor, love would "assemble subordinate images together"—such as steadfast affection, care, kindness and friendship—and "scatter concepts at a higher level" (Ricoeur, 1976: 64). In this way *love* becomes a dominant and normative value-ideal "capable of both engendering and organizing a network that serves as a junction between the symbolic level with its slow evolution and the more volatile metaphorical level" (Ricoeur, 1976: 64).

Still Ricoeur indicates that, despite the somewhat hazy transition from metaphor to symbol, there is "something in a symbol" that

> does not correspond to a metaphor.... Metaphor occurs in the already purified universe of the *logos*, while the symbol hesitates on the dividing line between *bios* and *logos*. It testifies to the primordial rootedness of Discourse in Life. It is born where force and form coincide" (1976: 57; 59).

If the linguistic network engendered by root metaphors prevents metaphors of regular linguistic use from dying by repetition and becoming symbols by default, so too does symbol's sacramental nexus between *bios* and *logos* prevent its passing back over into metaphor (see Ricoeur, 1976: 59). The symbol joins both semantic and nonsemantic moments such that it "brings together two dimensions, we might even say, two universes, of discourse, one linguistic and the other of a non-linguistic order" (Ricoeur, 1976: 53–54; 57–63).

Ricoeur marks poetry as the form of metaphoric language *par excellence*. Poetry "operates through language in a hypothetical realm. In an extreme form we might say that the poetic project is one of destroying the world as we ordinarily take it for granted" (1976: 59). Accordingly, when we speak of love as normative of sexual intimacy, we are speaking initially metaphorically and poetically. In its metaphorical dimension, love promotes moral ideals rather than literal realities. Like a poem, the metaphorical dimension of the ethical norm creates a mood of "the inversion of ordinary language" (Ricoeur, 1976: 59). Consequently, "poetry is liberated from the world" (Ricoeur, 1976: 60) just as I have argued, the ethical norm accomplishes a necessary liberation from the literal realities of everyday life to the world of moral ideals. This is the poetic dimension of an ethical norm. However, Ricoeur goes on to indicate that neither the poem nor the poet enjoy boundless freedom:

> But if it is liberated in this sense, in another sense it is bound, and it is bound precisely to the extent that it is also liberated.... The poem is bound by what it creates: if the suspension of ordinary discourse and its didactic intention assumes an urgent character for the poet, this is just because the reduction of the referential values or ordinary discourse is the negative condition that allows new configurations expressing the meaning of reality to be brought to language. Through these new configurations new ways of being in the world, of living there, and of projecting our innermost possibilities onto it are also brought to language. Therefore to limit ourselves to saying that a poem structures and expresses a mood is not to say much, for what is a mood if it is not a specific manner of being in the world and relating oneself to it, of understanding it and interpreting it? What binds poetic discourse, then, is the need to bring to language modes of being that ordinary vision obscures or even represses (1976: 60).

The mood of the poem and the ideal value of the norm are both introduced predicatively into speech through a deconstruction of ordinary language and literal reference. At the same time, this flight of the *logos* beyond the *bios* of everyday life is only for the sake of return, which refers not only to new ways of speaking or to new meanings but also to new ways of being and acting in the world. In this sense, metaphor necessarily sets the stage for the occurrence of symbol but, in the production of new claims for truth and right, cannot be its substitute. In this sense, too, neither metaphor nor the aesthetic moment of release accomplished in the successful poem can be a sufficient foundation for knowledge in general or for ethical knowledge in particular. Ricoeur's emphasis on the interest of a metaphoric and poetic mood and meaning to relate to a specific manner of being in the world is an expression of the prior and overriding obligation of language to bind critical figurative speech to action. Indeed it is this sense of urgency for political and moral effectuation that brings the dimension of full symbolic designations of ethical norms to the fore after their initial metaphorical disclosures. The same can be said for aesthetic and religious language. Only when the same sacramental and world-bound character of art and religion, and of poetry in particular are emphasized can we find the proper relation of the aesthetic and the religious. Anything less leads to a mode of unbound aestheticism.

In this coincidence of force and form, symbol engages more intentionally and publicly than metaphor the intention of material-historical effectuation. Necessarily initiated by metaphor, the power of symbolic designation in the sedimentation of culture and society is what Ricoeur calls the "efficacity *par excellence*" which "does not pass over completely into the articulation of meaning" (1976: 61). Here Ricoeur engages in his own ontological claim, which, like Wheelwright's, may be only a "shy" extrapolation of a thick phenomenological description of how our worlds of reality appear to us linguistically, historically, and culturally—in this sense, the term *being* itself taken as a metaphor for what Wheelwright calls "presential and tensive reality" in all of its interpenetrative complexity, ambiguity, and always only partial revelation (1968: 154). While Ricoeur does not use the term "sacramental" to describe this work of the symbol, it remains appropriate.

> Symbols are bound within the sacred universe: the symbols only come to language to the extent that the elements of the world themselves become transparent.... This bound character of symbols makes all the difference between a symbol and a metaphor. The latter is a free invention of discourse; the former is bound to the cosmos. Here we touch an irreducible element, an element more irreducible than the one that poetic experience uncovers. In the sacred universe the capacity to speak is founded upon the capacity of the cosmos to signify. The logic of meaning, therefore, follows from the very structure of the sacred universe. Its law is the law of correspondences, correspondences between creation *in illo tempore* and the present order of natural appearances and human activities (Ricoeur, 1976: 61–62).

Whether these claims of the rootedness of symbolic and metaphorical speech in the *sacredness* of nature are metaphorical or not, they are fully sacramental, and in that, religious. "The sacredness of nature reveals itself in saying itself symbolically. The revealing grounds the saying, not the reverse" (Ricoeur, 1976: 63). Through the function of metaphor and symbol, the material and the literal can bear normative, and indeed, sacred signification with possibilities for full sacramental effectuation.

The Sacramental Function of the Ethical Norm

I have already indicated Owen Barfield's suggestion of a shift in priorities between the figurative and the literal in the classical and modern worldviews (1965: 74; 71–78). In classical metaphysics, the literal was a cover for the deeper metaphysical structure of reality. Thus, in the medieval environment sacramentality was framed by a dualistic metaphysics—the literal being mainly a vehicle for the metaphysical and mystical. However, with the relative collapse of dualistic metaphysics, modern metaphor and symbol theory envisioned the literal as integral for the manifestation of the multileveled "heights" and "depths" of everyday existence and ordinary language. With the literal and the material taken more seriously, sacramentality in modernity—now unlocked by hermeneutic critique—could also be taken more seriously. We can speak of sacramental *appearances*, not because of a separate essential structure of reality underneath the material and literal "accidents," but precisely because of the powers of critical interpretation and construction to engage in metaphorical and symbolic disclosure and designation. Such sacramental words and gestures can transform the surface realities of everyday life and inform powerful motivations for change. In the context of modernity, then, sacramentality is not dependent on metaphysics or mysticism but on metaphorical and symbolic signification that, ironically enough, can be taken more seriously than in former ages because of its proximity and integrity with respect to everyday life. Modern religious and theological discourse are sacramental modes of metaphoric and symbolic speech.[18]

Being bound more directly to the literal and material rather than the metaphysical and the mystical leads sacramentality in modernity to new criteria for justification and legitimation. Modern sacraments can no longer claim to "effect what they signify" as realities in the cosmos in any metaphysical or mystical way through the act of signification itself—as medieval sacramental theology would have it, *ex opere operato—from the work worked*. Rather, the signification of metaphor and symbol now becomes fully sacramental through a more direct effect in moral and political change in the character and action of individuals and groups. In the context of modernity, metaphors and symbols work sacramentally— can be justified and legitimated in their apprehending and assimilating power—only when their disclosures and designations, drawn from material-historical reality, become politically and morally effective in the lives of individuals and groups.

Nor is this sacramentality only positive. The symbolism of evil rooted in the metaphor and symbol of the stain, for example (see Ricoeur, 1969: 33–40), becomes fully sacramentally effective when such stain gains political and moral reality in the actual physical shedding of blood. Similarly, the metaphor of death for sin becomes a vital symbol when *mortal sin* becomes effectively sacramental in ritual-technical acts of killing (See Ernest Becker, 1975). Metaphors and symbols function fully as apprehending and assimilating reality only when they attain the level of historical sacramental effectiveness. They continue as vital disclosures and designations in culture only because of the material-history of sacramental efficacy in this political and moral sense.

This point of the sacramental intention and function of metaphors, symbols, and ethical norms is worthy of further attention especially given the current danger of stopping short with metaphor—the danger in fact of an aestheticism, indeed of a depoliticized mysticism, that finds a refuge from *bios* in *logos*. In a curious way, the question of sacramentalism also marks a continuing debate between even modern and thoroughly reconstructed forms of Catholic and Protestant theology and ethics. In her *Metaphorical Theology* (1982), Sallie McFague opts finally for a precisely metaphorical and, in her estimation, nonsacramental "protestant sensibility," with "catholic sensibility" remaining symbolical and analogical (1982: 13). While McFague presents a clear exposition of recent work in metaphor and model theory, and by presenting trenchant critiques of the tradition of patriarchy that underlies so much of Christian theology and ethics, offers insightful new constructions for a metaphorical theology, her relatively disjunctive premise essentially separates metaphor from symbol and sacrament and runs the risk of the aestheticism I have noted throughout. In concentrating first on metaphors and then directly on models for her theology without any intervening steps, McFague suggests satisfaction with metaphor as an *illuminating mood*, a *shock of meaning* and *discovery*, a rather *internal insight*, collected systematically in groups of like-minded and like-souled individuals. In turn these effects of metaphor become elements of the "empirical fit" (see Ian Ramsey, 1973) necessary for justifying and legitimating religious and theological speech (1982: 141–44 ).

McFague does not argue that "everything is metaphor." Quite the contrary, she suggests there are nonmetaphorical dimensions to reality—something before and after metaphor so to speak. However, she does suggest that metaphor is "a highly suggestive and fruitful way...to understand particular aspects of human being, especially those pertaining to expression and interpretation, creation and discovery, change and transformation" (1982: 36). Metaphor is limited on the one side by the meta-linguistic dimensions of feeling, sensation, and affection that ground our primary metaphorical expressions and interpretations: "we feel more than we can express, we know more than we can interpret. Metaphor deals with expression and interpretation, not with the depths of human existence that lie beyond even words" (McFague, 1982: 36).

The other limit to metaphor pertains more directly to rational discourse and the necessary completion of the work of metaphor in the model (McFague: 1982: 22–23). However, as I will indicate, even here McFague understands model upon the direct horizon of metaphor.

In the initial statements of her positions, McFague gives an end note reference to Ricoeur and his discussion of the relation of metaphor and symbol in terms of *bios* and *logos* discussed above (1982: 202–3 n.12.). McFague agrees that there is an initial rooting of metaphor/*logos* in *bios*—my rendering of the first journey from the literal to the figurative. However, both in her discussion of metaphor as such and in metaphor's relation to model, she gives inadequate attention to the need for metaphor/*logos* to return to *bios* by way of symbolic mediation and sacramental effectuation. Because of this McFague's grounds for verifying and legitimating religious, theological, and ethical language are not stable. Even when she turns to model, her "metaphorical theology" stops short with metaphor and grounds religion and theological speech on what is, in effect, a way station of language. All may not be metaphor, but McFague's metaphorical theology seems trapped upon its horizon.

One reason for this is her initial and distracting disjunction between the metaphorical and the symbolical/analogical. Though the following quotation does not discriminate between the often conflicting Aristotelian and neo-Platonic stands, McFague is generally accurate in her rendering of the Medieval and classical Catholic sacramental mind.

> The analogical way, the symbolic way, rests on a profound *similarity* beneath the surface dissimilarities; what we see and speak must be the differences, but we rest in the faith that all is empowered by the breath of God, Being-Itself. The vision of God, the goal of all creation, is the belief that one day all of creation shall be one. The many shall return to the One, for the many are in secret one already (1982: 12).

I agree with McFague's premise (1982: 13) that the cosmological harmony of the Medieval world picture has not survived the birth of modernity. However, even though she suggests a complementarity between her metaphorical theology and renewed forms of analogical sensibility—i.e., "catholic" theologies that are not heavily or sentimentally sacramentalist in their over-stress on harmonious order (David Tracy, 1981 is offered as an example)—McFague finally opts for a form of "Protestant sensibility," which she sees as relatively disjunctive from the Catholic sacramental imagination (pp. 13–14; 198 n.16). She presents metaphorical "Protestant sensibility" as a functional counterpoint to Catholic sacramentalism, which has not and, seemingly, cannot completely uproot itself from its home in the classical Catholic synthesis. In sum, the reason why "metaphorical theology" is necessary, McFague argues, is the inability of sacramentalism to see adequately "dissimilarity, distinction, tension, and hence to be skeptical and secular, stressing the transcendence of God and the finitude of creation" (p.13)—in effect, the inability of sacramentalism to have the necessary "protestant sensibility."

My hesitation about this approach is not in what is affirmed about the metaphorical foundations of theological language but in what tends to be denied or at least overlooked. She fails to envision adequately the continuing necessity of symbolic sedimentation and sacramental effectuation for verifying and legitimating the claims of religion and ethics. Indeed, unlike Ricoeur, McFague argues that

> symbolic statements...are not so much a way of knowing and speaking as they are sedimentation and solidification of metaphor. For in symbolical or sacramental thought, one does not think "this" *as* "that," but "this" as *a part of* "that." The tension of the metaphor is absorbed in the symbol (1982: 16).

Thus, without the tension required for full and ongoing critique—for example, Tillich's "Protestant principle"—symbolic and sacramental theology and language are "priestly" and conservative, celebrating what is already there as an original unity whose fractures and discontinuities are only accidental and in whose worlds nothing new or fundamentally critical and prophetic can occur (McFague, 1982: 17). However, in emphasizing almost exclusively the necessary metamorphic moment of new linguistic creation, McFague's metaphorical theology runs the risk of failing to notice the necessity for symbolic sedimentation and sacramental effectuation of the proclamations we make amid the political and moral realities of everyday life. In taking the first journey away from *bios* to, as Ricoeur says, the "already purified universe of the *logos* (1976: 59), McFague does not pay sufficient attention to the need to return.

Even though priestly sacramentalism has been and often is conservative and not sufficiently prophetic in its celebrations of the given, it is not structurally so. In the context of modernity, priesthood, liturgy, and sacraments do not only celebrate how close our lives are to God, but also confess and symbolically designate how distant we are from God and each other and the moral ideals we confess. The Christ celebrated sacramentally is not necessarily sentimental and unaffected by the vicissitudes of daily life, transcending all diversity, fracture, infidelity, and pain. The priesthood of Christ is a victim's priesthood, and like the body of Christ it symbolically "re-presents," the bread taken in the Eucharist is broken for us and like us. The sacramentality referred to here is embedded as much in the material realities of sin and chaos as those of grace and order.

Liturgy is not simply worship of a God who is totally congruent with the universe but is also a ritualization of a consolation for God and ourselves who must equally bear the effects of sin, violence, anxiety and loneliness in the life-worlds of creation. The symbolic ritualization of such victimization calls forth more than new linguistic *apprehensions*, but also new sedimented and effective *implications* in the political and moral lives of all victims—not only a revolution in predicative language but also a revolution in material-historical and political existence. The prophetic dimensions McFague correctly notes in the metaphorical language of the parables of Jesus, whose shocks and twists call forth a revolutionary potential (1982: 17), must also be designated as action through the sacramental language, symbols, rituals and moral practices of a priestly people. Nor are prophetic apprehensions via metaphor, and priestly and political implications via symbol and sacrament disjunctive. It is precisely the role of symbol and sacrament to complete the work of metaphor's return from *logos* to *bios*. Priests and priestly people are called to mediate what is apprehended metaphorically to the political and moral realities of everyday life. In the context of modernity, it is clear that priestly sacramentalism must take on a more explicit political and moral character.

While ever-watchful of the penchant of symbolic sacramentalism to only celebrate the status quo, metaphor cannot rest with its own apprehensions and disclosures. Metaphors enact new revolutions in predicative language so that what is apprehended linguistically can become a fact of political and moral existence. Metaphors that become symbols gain new power for the sacramental effectuation of both good and evil. It is in this sort of political/moral sacramentalism that metaphors and symbols complete their material-historical course. Here too our religious and ethical language and claims find the proper grounds for their verification and legitimation. To be complete, religious and ethical language must be sacramentally performative—*logos* in solidarity with *bios*.

To name metaphorically "bread" as the "body of Christ"—broken and distributed as food for us—is not enough. In the movement from initial metaphorical disclosure to symbolic designation, the challenge of sacramental effectuation remains. The failure of eucharistic language is not necessarily a failure in metaphorical disclosure, cathartic emotion, or symbolic designations of new understandings. We may understand a contemporary theology of the Eucharist or anything else all too well and, indeed, be deeply moved with new intentions to renew our faith and life. However, the language and rituals of eucharistic celebrations remain incomplete until what is disclosed and designated becomes materially effective in our lives—in this case, starving people fed in body as well as soul. When all is said and done, McFague does not address adequately the complete journey of metaphor to symbol and sacrament necessary for the critical foundations of theological language she seeks. To remain vital, metaphorical theology must become materially performative in moral and political solidarity with the world. Theological metaphor and language that do not successfully traverse the distance to political/ ethical sacrament, fail because they stop at feeling and understanding, which, though necessary, are still short of action. Like arrows let with great promise but miss their mark, theological and ethical metaphors that lead to new insight without new action ultimately fail the functional and pragmatic tests of truth and right that mark modernity. Thus, our metaphorical disclosures are always wagers upon the promise of symbolic designation and sacramental effectuation in the material conditions of history and culture.

Religious language is more than disclosures and designations of new meanings and understandings. Religion and its theological articulations and moral convictions are finally material ways of being in the world. Mere claims of personal experience or individual obligation, however authentic, are not enough for verification and legitimation but must stand the further test of sacramental effectuation—the test of what is materially and politically engendered and accomplished by the words we say and the claims we make. Being performative, our speech is finally judged true and right by the material performance effected. It is in this material-pragmatic sense that religious and theological speech and the language of ethical norms remain sacramental in the modern world.

Thus, in modernity, the sacramentality of religion, theology, and ethics will be materially functional rather than mystical. These sacramental effects are not accomplished as suggested in classical sacramentalism—i.e., by their simple signification or sincere and faithful acceptance and reception (see Leeming, 1960: 7–10), but by the material-historical performances engendered by their significations. Now, the sacramental signification present in all religious, theological, and ethical language, as well as in liturgical ritual, arises as claims and intentions waiting for full realization. Indeed, because this sort of political sacramentalism is so dangerous and obliging in its ability to routinize and sediment both good and evil, we are often tempted to abstract religious speech and liturgical ritual from the contemporary challenges of life as a whole. New interests in mysticism and spirituality abound along with claims that sincere confession, authentic witness, and insulated and aesthetically coherent Christian "life-styles" are our last best hope for change.

Even McFague, whose tendency to aestheticism in this book I find more by way of implication than intention, argues that "the most basic context (although not the working context) of theology ought to be worship, for the reasons the mystics display. In prayer one knows the inadequacy of all one's images" (1982: 131). While prayer, worship, and "spirituality" in the Christian life remain informing, I am arguing that the political and moral sacramentalism I have been describing is a clearer and better way to confront the dangers of religious and theological hubris than any sort of disjunctive mysticism. Paying attention to what our metaphors and symbols sacramentally intend and what they actually effect in material-history is the surer path to both a critical theology and a profound and humble spirituality. Implicating and prayerful meditations on the material conditions of life will disclose our own course of intimacy and distance from God far more surely and quickly than mystical abstractions. Only in this broader and political sacramental context can worship and liturgy be seen as an informing context for theology and ethics. Such political and moral sacramentalism will inform our deepest implication in the material realities of God and history. Here we can know more completely the simultaneous "yes and no" Christian character must speak in its transit between the moral ideal and literal real, first disclosed by the metaphorical quality of the ethical norm.

Without this sacramental-political orientation, religion, theology, and the ideal language of norms remain only imaginative and linguistic exercises capturing the mind and affections of individuals and groups but offering no way to test that necessary imagination in the full material and political realities of history. Religion arises as a suspicion and wager that there is more to life than meets the eye—that there are depths and heights of divine presence *within* material-historical existence. But like all suspicions and wagers, religion and its languages must be tested pragmatically and sacramentally in terms of what they engender in the world—how they make worlds and become world-making. Theological language may arise metaphorically, as McFague maintains, but unless it runs its course through symbol and becomes fully sacramental, it fails in its performative intentions and becomes irrelevant to the human enterprise of cosmological world-making. Short of this, religion, theology, and ethics will become privatized in an aesthetic and linguistic prison with little public significance.

Ethical Norms as Sacramental Models

Both Ricoeur (1976: 66–67) and McFague (1982: 23–24; 37–38) refer to Max Black's (1962) notion of the relation of models and metaphors. Ricoeur suggests a mutual and critical interrelation between metaphor and symbol and relates his discussion of models as part of the mediation between the two. I do not follow Ricoeur's relation here and consider models integrated and paradigmatic configurations of metaphor-informed symbols rather than mediators between metaphors and symbols. Thus the progression is from metaphor to symbol to model. This is why I argue that mature and complete ethical norms function as models. In terms of either configuration, however, McFague pays little attention to symbol at all and moves rather directly from metaphor to model. Despite our differences in the location of model in relation to metaphor and symbol, I agree with Ricoeur that the movement of metaphor toward symbol advances its necessary referential function. In moving toward symbol, metaphor begins to realize its intention not only to disclose new sense and meaning but also to say something about reality, "in short, its truth value...its pretensions to say something about something" (Ricoeur, 1976: 66). Ricoeur is thus instructed by Max Black's argument that metaphors are related to models via a referential function. However, Ricoeur asks:

> What is this referential value? It is part of the heuristic function, that is, the aspect of discovery, of a metaphor and a model, of a metaphor as a model.... In scientific language, a model is essentially a heuristic procedure that serves to overthrow an inadequate interpretation and to open the way to a new and more adequate one.... It is an instrument of redescription (1976: 66).

Ricoeur, as does McFague, adopts Black's depiction of three types of models:

> scale models, as for example, a model boat; analogical models, which deal with structural identity, as, for example, a schematic diagram in electronics; and finally, theoretical models, which from

an epistemological point of view, are the real models which consist of construing an imaginary object more accessible to description as a complex domain of reality whose properties correspond to the properties of the object. As Max Black puts it, to describe a domain of reality in terms of an imaginary theoretical model is a way of seeing things differently by changing our language about the subject under investigation. This change of language proceeds from the construction of a heuristic fiction and through the trans-position of the characteristics of this heuristic fiction to reality itself (Ricoeur, 1976: 66–67).

If we were to adopt Max Black's categories as given we would describe the ethical norm in general and the norm of marriage in partic-ular as "an imaginary theoretic model," although in another under-standing—beyond Black's schematic/diagrammatic rendering—the analogical model will not be lost to us. I will begin to reconfigure Black's understanding of models in this chapter and continue in the next.

Working first from the paradigm of scientific knowledge, Black and, to this point, Ricoeur, see models as essentially heuristic. While not denying this heuristic "aspect of discovery," I also emphasize the special and *sacramental* intention of models to demonstrate and effect social and political life. Models in ethics intend more than discovery; they also intend to inform, frame, and direct action. Because Ricoeur places models in the middle space between metaphor and symbol, he tends to emphasize, as does McFague, the model's close relation to metaphor and its general intention of discovery of new knowledge, and he leaves to symbol the intention to accomplish knowledge that frames regular habits of behavior and action. Because I relocate models and consider them a maturation and congregation of metaphor-informed symbols, I place the intention of action closer to models than to symbols and find their heuristic/epistemological function transformed by a more direct political and moral one. As we will see, however, in her location of the relation of metaphor and model, McFague only goes part way with Ricoeur and stops short of his understanding of even the initial advance of the work of metaphor by the symbol.

Staying with Black's discriminations a moment longer, in any modern interpretation of biblical religion we do not have a paradigmatic ideal marriage of either the gods or of any human "holy family." God-Yahweh has no consort (see Blenkinsopp, 1969). The holy family of Nazareth is not structured as a model for a sexually active life, nor is the "marriage" of Adam and Eve more than proto-historical. This lack of analytic utility, however, did not prevent Christians from constructing models of sexual behavior based on metaphors of the sexuality or lack of sexuality of God, the "marriage" of Adam and Eve, and "the holy family of Nazareth" in ways that look very much like scale and schematic/ analogical models. In this usage, such models were often couched as at least quasi-myths and allegories of sexuality and marriage. The challenge of contemporary interpretation would be to translate historical scale and schematic/analogical models to theoretic ones or, as Ricoeur indicates in another sense, to see in the context of modernity myths in terms of symbols. To understand myth in a modern cosmology is to understand its revelatory and designating function as a symbol informed by metaphor. This critical-hermeneutic translation is necessary because of our time and place in modernity—"because mythic time can no longer be coordinated with the time of events that are 'historical' in the sense required by historical criticism" and "because mythical space can no longer be co-ordinated with the places of our geography" (Ricoeur, 1969: 162; 3–18; 161–74). Consequently, we currently have no actively constructive myth or *scale model* of marriage nor any *analogical/schematic* model to function adequately as an ethical norm though we live under such a "false" inheritance and are affected by it. The norm of marriage in modernity can only be visualized adequately as a model by a complex interrelation of imaginative ideals and actual practices.

In introducing the category of model as a third functional quality of an ethical norm, remaining clear about the interrelation of model, metaphor, and symbol is difficult. I have argued that norms become models when the regular transit from metaphor to symbol is completed—i.e., a normative model in ethics becoming a political and social configuration, a demonstration of a symbol-set as the third phase of the evolution of an ethical norm. To say that the metaphoric quality of a norm pertains to the counterpoint between the literal and the ideal is clear enough. To say that its symbolic quality pertains to its historically effective sedimentation in the language, rituals, and habitual expectations of culture and society is also clear. When it comes to the notion of the ethical norm as a model, however, there is some confusion in the actual use of the term "norm" in moral discourse itself. For example, I can say that love is *normative* in Christian sexual ethics. But "love" as such is not a model, but more of an imaginative value-ideal and value-set that has assumed normative weight and force, and thus, only an incomplete norm until it is systematized and visualized as a model. This makes the language of normative love easy to say initially because it is oriented by imaginative ideals. It does not, in the first instance of language, carry the existential visual weight of a model and runs the risk, as is often the case, of becoming platitudinous and abstract. What we also want and need to know is *how to love* sexually and what such love *looks like* in practice. However, marriage and all attendant configurations of steadfastness, constancy in good times and bad, sickness and health, family, home, and the like can have full visual effect only as a normative social and political model that has become sedimented as an ideal praxis of sexual order and stability in culture and society. To call *heterosexual marriage* a norm is to emphasize its dimension as a visual model of moral life and behavior. Unlike the linguistic *ideal of love*, the social and political *reality of marriage*—its visual role in culture and society—is analytically a more complete and mature norm.

To interpret marriage as "an imaginative theoretic model"—"a way of seeing things differently" (Ricoeur: 1976: 67) has much to recommend it. I have already discussed how imaginative ideals, metaphorically disclosed in tension with literal realities, form the initial structure of an ethical norm. In some dimensions, norms function precisely under this heuristic "aspect of discovery" by "changing our language about the subject of our investigation." In terms of literal realities, norms are initially like theoretical models and, though necessary and critical, they are in their first instance "heuristic fictions" (Ricoeur 1976: 66; 67), but ones with profound visibility and thus impact.

Models, metaphors, and symbols are always in some degree fictive—recalling Kenneth Burke's admonition, "a poem about having children by marriage is not the same thing as having children by marriage" (1967: 9). However, amid this fiction lie new facts and truths about our sociopolitical and moral lives. The visibility of models frame their historical and practical effectiveness and complete the transit of these literal *fictions* back to the realities of everyday life. In a successful model there is an "isomorphism between the model and its domain of application. It is this isomorphism that legitimates the 'analogical transfer of a vocabulary' and that allows a metaphor to function like a model and 'reveal new relationships'" (Ricoeur, 1976: 67). Nonetheless, it is here that I have some hesitation with using Black and Ricoeur's description of a theoretical model as one that is adequate to describe an ethical norm. Certainly in its metaphorical sense—in the way Ricoeur places and uses models to mediate the work of metaphor and symbol—norms do *reveal* new ideal value relationships. Still, according to my relocation of the place and role of model as a completion of the work of metaphor and symbol, their singular designation as theoretic models begins to fail. When norms become symbolically sedimented in the material-historical life of culture, and when they become effective and mature and function as models, they attain more of a sacramentally pragmatic than only epistemological and heuristic intent and function: they do more than *reveal* new relationships but also *effect* them. Once routinized, what could previously be taken analytically as an epistemological/heuristic model is now an activity of social and political life. Marriage, epistemologically designated first as a theoretical model, is now a social and political practice. We have now not only a "model" of marriage for heuristic disclosure, we also have people who are married. It will be these actual marriages and what they demonstrate and effect or not in public life that finally measure both the maturity and the future of this ethical norm.

I do not deny the theoretical dimension of normative ethical models but suggest that once routinized as effective in the moral activity of culture, such models are more sacramental than theoretic—that is to say, they begin to actively and practically order, demonstrate, and effect ways of behavior and become life-practices themselves. As full sacramental models, ethical norms complete their transit to rules of moral behavior in actual social situations and gain their energy and power more directly from symbol than from metaphor. Certainly, this is not all "good news" for the norm of marriage since its burdens of political and moral performance is now greater than only that of the disclosure and designation of values. Values must not only be disclosed and designated but also realized as goods effected. Once an ethical norm has become a sacramental model, it will retain its status only insofar as it performs its work—a work that must be measured finally on moral/political rather than epistemological grounds. As a mature ethical norm, marriage bears substantively the same threefold burden we have been describing analytically as the work of metaphor, symbol, and sacrament: the values of Christian sexual morality must be *disclosed* and *designated* and their goods effectively *demonstrated* by the actual practices of married Christians. To the extent that actual marriages fail to accomplish these tasks, the future of heterosexual marriage as an effective norm will be in jeopardy.

Even though Ricoeur does not speak of this *sacramental* function that completes the character of a model beyond the "theoretic," he does underscore how symbols are more directly and actively implicated than metaphor in the material activities and practices of everyday life.

The metaphorical order is submitted to what we can call a request for work by this symbolic experience. Everything indicates that symbolic experience calls for a work of meaning from metaphor, a

work which it partially provides through its organizational network and its hierarchical levels. Everything indicates that symbol
systems constitute a reservoir of meaning whose metaphoric
potential is yet to be spoken (Ricoeur, 1976: 65).

Though Ricoeur consistently argues that "there is more in the metaphor
than in the symbol" insofar as metaphor critically orders this material
and moral/political work of symbol "in the sense that it brings to
language the implicit semantics of the symbol" (1976: 69), there is also

> more in the symbol than in the metaphor. Metaphor is just the
> linguistic procedure—that bizarre form of predication—within
> which the symbolic power is deposited. The symbol retains a two-
> dimensional phenomenon to the extent that the semantic face refers
> back to the non semantic one. The symbol is bound in a way that the
> metaphor is not. Symbols have roots. Symbols plunge us into the
> shadowy experience of power. Metaphors are just the linguistic
> surface of symbols, and they owe their power to relate the semantic
> surface to the presemantic surface in the depths of human experi-
> ence to the two-dimensional structure of the symbol (1976: 69).

We may differ somewhat in our location and thus function of
models in relation to metaphors and symbols, but my argument for the
fully sacramental rather than only theoretic character of the model in the
mature norm is still within the spirit of Ricoeur's intent to relate both
metaphors and symbols to the practical realities of everyday life—to "the
shadowy experience of power" and "the depths of human experience"
(1976: 69). Our differences lie in my argument that symbol's "request for
work" of metaphor is completed in the model.

It is just this plunge by symbol into the depths of power, politics,
and work that McFague misses in her metaphorical theology and that I
am emphasizing in my indication of the full development of ethical
norms as *sacramental models*. Symbols and models are more politically
and morally dangerous than metaphors since they are closer to the
powerful sedimentations of images, language, and rituals that most
proximately inform action. Nonetheless, religion and theology do not
attain a higher, and indeed, more aesthetically and morally purer state
by failing to notice their own sacramental power to effect both good and
evil in the world. Failing to notice is the more dangerous state.

McFague understands that the foundation of theological discourse
in metaphor does not complete the systematic interpretations necessary

or avoid what she calls the twin dangers of "idolatry and irrelevance in religious language." Thus "metaphorical theology does not stop with metaphor.... *Moving beyond* metaphors is necessary both to avoid literalizing them and to attempt significant interpretations of them for our time" (1982: 22–23). But it is here that McFague moves directly to a discussion of models that she describes as "a dominant metaphor, a metaphor with staying power" (1982: 23). She continues to suggest that the transition from metaphor to model in theology is for the sake of empirical *illumination*, conceptual *clarification*, and *systematization*. Upon these grounds, we are to find whatever tests we can of the verifiability and falsifiability of religious and theological language. McFague argues:

> Since there are no empirical tests of the verifiability or falsifiability of theological statements of the order which we find in science, it is models which provide the explanation of theological concepts, without which concepts would be empty and unintelligible (1982: 105).

Theological models order what is discovered and disclosed by metaphor (McFague, 1982: 107). They illuminate and light up "our experience in the world in profound ways." Models provide something similar, McFague says, to the metaphorical "'shock of recognition' we get from reading a fine poem or seeing a good play" (1982: 141):

> 'yes,' we say, 'life is like that'—not life as conventionally lived or usually understood, but at its deepest level, or as it could be, ought to be, might have been. The basic structure of experience is illuminated and we feel the transformation that is the secret of the linkage between discovery and creation at the heart of great poetry and at the heart of great religious traditions (1982: 141–42).

Even when McFague moves "beyond metaphor" to models, her eschewing of the symbolical and sacramental as relative archaic forms of speaking and thinking of a lost world, or one that cannot be reconstructed except under the dominant aegis of metaphor, remains troublesome. Her turn to model also exhibits aestheticist tendencies. Certainly theological language and Christian ethical claims cannot stand the same tests of verifiability and falsifiability as empirical science. However, this does not mean that we need rest our obligations of verification and legitimation on only conceptual clarification, or personal or communal illumination and recognition of how we think or feel the world is, or might, or ought to be and become. There are conceptual and aesthetic dimensions to religion, but religion is not completed by either the intellectual or the aesthetical (see Tillich, 1959). In fact "fine poems" and "good plays," like "good religion," not only illuminate us but also change us and our world—effect new sacramental modes of political-moral existence. We not only see and imagine things differently, we become, as it were, different people and in some significant ways attain different characters. Just as we need the initial shock of recognition provided by new metaphorical disclosures, we need models in religious and theological language to systematically conceptualize and "empirically fit" (Ramsey, 1973) what is disclosed into our individual and communal experiences. However, it is not just theoretic coherence or an aesthetically illuminating fit alone that ground the verification and legitimation of theological models but finally what such models effectuate in the world. Verification, including all criteria of falsifiability, are also subject to the test of *legitimation*. Truth in all of its dimensions, and especially in religion and theology, is more than aesthetical and intellectual, but also moral and ethical.

For example, even in the absence of any other reason or feeling, we *know* that a Christology, no matter how theoretically coherent or illuminating, which negates the religious traditions of others is false because of the material-historical effects of its negation of other human beings (see Monti, 1984). Similarly, we know that racism and antifemale sexism is not true, much less a divine mandate, no matter how perversely illuminating it might be to some, because it likewise effectively diminishes human personality and worth. I am not arguing here for a *reduction* of religion and theology—the wagers of knowledge, language, and art—to the political and moral, but rather for their *completion* in material and historically effective action.

McFague is aware of the danger of comparably reducing theological language to the aesthetic and suggests that her description of "illumination" as the most basic characteristic of a theological model is not to be understood as principally an aesthetic category (1982: 142). She indicates that her sense of the term is descriptive and re-descriptive of reality. Models "are not reality, but a construct or interpretation of it, which must, however, be in some sense isomorphic with reality" (1982: 142). However, her sense of this necessary isomorphism of theological models is indirect. As faith statements, "we do not *know* that our models of father and mother, of liberator and friend, of creator and redeemer, really reflect the structure of the divine-human relationship" (McFague, 1982: 142–43). Thus, an aestheticist dimension remains central to McFague's understanding of theological models since, in terms of modern science, their verifiability and falsifiability rest insecurely on our own individual and communal constructions and interpretations of reality—our own relatively artistic description of how we think or feel reality to be, or wish it to be.

Such claims and feelings about the worlds we inhabit are necessary first steps to truth and right. They cannot, however, be only internally self-verifying and legitimating. To stop short of the now modern pragmatic, and indeed sacramental tests of material-historical and public verification and legitimation, lends an overly aestheticist flavor to our religious and moral language. In seeking the first release of *logos* from the *bios* of everyday life necessary for critical distance, we fail to adequately return.

Feeling the effects of scientific criticism in modernity, much of modern theology—especially in its stress on metaphor and language—opts for at least quasi-aesthetic grounds for verification. We think that all we can finally say about our theological language and models are that they are true and right because *we intensely feel* them to be so, because they make sense of and *illuminate our experience*, and make *our lives more coherent, systematic, and livable.* Thus, we accept uncritically the modern grounds for the philosophical and scientific criticism of classical theology and redefine our discourse less scientifically and publicly—less as public knowledge (*scientia*)—and more aesthetically, internally, and, in effect, privately. Because we have such trouble in scientific and pragmatic modernity in giving an adequate account of how religion, theology, and ethics are also knowledge about the world, we imply, if not say, that religion and theology have more to do with personal and private feeling and meaning than with public truth and fact. In light of this, and with no hope for return to the ancient and classical systems wherein true knowledge was defined more mythically, metaphysically, and mystically, it is no great wonder why, most particularly in the industrialized West, we are having such difficulty stopping the slide of religion to the level of cultural "life-style enclaves" (Bellah, et al.: 1985: 72), even when those enclaves are baptized as more intense forms of sectarian Christian community and assembly.

In these retreats from criticism, we have been too fearful in the face of the modern grounds for scientific and pragmatic verification and falsification. We have more than aesthetical and quasi-aesthetical means for verifying our theological and ethical models. Ironically, the new wedding of science and technology that marks so much of the modern age offers a new and more political pragmatic vision of the classic sacramental dimensions of religion—a modern sacramentality that offers better and more public prospects for verifying and legitimating our theological models than only personal, private, or insulated sectarian appeals to internal coherence and illumination. If contemporary scientific knowledge demands public and pragmatic tests for truth and right, then modern sacramentalism in religion can relatively provide it, not in the same way, but within the same modern epistemological spirit.

I have argued that religious and theological language are not finally verified and legitimated in their metaphorical disclosures or symbolic designations alone but also in their sacramental effectiveness. Like models in modern science, theological and ethical models are not judged true and right only by the power of their personal or communal illumination and conceptual clarification, but also by what is accomplished in the material-historical world—accomplishments that can be seen and relatively measured. Before material-pragmatic tests, models in both science and religion are mainly hypotheses and claims. Consequently, our basic question ought to be a pragmatic one: "Do our metaphors and symbols effect in the material-historical circumstances of the world what they signify and claim?" There is no avoiding the danger, however, that what we signify, claim, and effect can be evil instead of good. Nonetheless, such risks need not throw us into an aestheticist panic, abstracting religion and theology from its proper grounding in material-historical circumstances.[19] With a focus on concrete material existence, we can learn deeply embedded historical lessons of how our metaphors, symbols, and models have led to both great good and ruinous evil. With the pragmatic wisdom of history, we stand better prepared to promote the former and avoid the latter.

To name God as "father," "mother," and "friend," as McFague indicates (1982: 152–92), may be a significant metaphorical disclosure and symbolic designation that ground models for the relation of God and world.[20] The fact that we are not sure that these names "really" reflect the "structure" of the divine-human relationship—or the divine reality in itself—is not central. The real question is do they empirically, theologically, and morally fit with our confessions and faith-claims about the divine presence in ways that are effective in our lives and in our relations with others. Biblical religion is not really about the nature and "structure" of God alone, but rather about our claims of God's relation with the world. In calling God "father," "mother," and "friend" we are not "defining" God, but rather advancing claims of the divine-human relationship and presence which is all we can know of God in the first instance. The questions of verification and legitimation that we must ask pertain to the effects upon our own character and upon our relations with others—what they effect in the world in general. Are and how are they materially-historically performative?

If we call God father, mother, and friend, we, and especially others, will want to know if these metaphorical disclosures have become effective symbolic designations and models of ways of life. Are we actively relating to God as our *father, mother,* and *friend* and effecting material conditions and structures of political and social existence under models of parental and friendly obligation? Are we allowing ourselves to be loved and cared for by God as our parent, and do we parent our own children and all children in this way? According to the obligations incurred by these names of God, do we treat all others as offspring of the same divine parent and as our own brothers and sisters? Do we like each other's company and are we friendly with others, especially strangers and those most different from ourselves? Such are the material-historical and sacramentally pragmatic tests that tell the tale and the history of our religious and theological language and models. Without such continuing verification and legitimation, our metaphors, symbols, models, and norms inevitably become untruthful and illegitimate.

I do not intend this argument to be a new call to moral and ethical perfectionism in the sense that we must act completely and perfectly according to what is disclosed and designated in our metaphorical and symbolic speech. Rather, verification and legitimation come also indirectly from negative convictions and confessions of how far we are in our behavior from the names and ideals we claim.[21] Our claims can be verified and legitimated in both positive and negative ways. When such verification and legitimation of either sort is not forthcoming, the lack of material-historical and sacramental effectuation makes changes necessary. I can argue, for example, that the traditional metaphorical disclosure and symbolic designation of God as "almighty"—a model and norm of mainly power over the conditions of life in the world—can no longer be verified and legitimated in terms of modern cosmology and history, especially in the face of our experiences of physical and pervasive moral evil. Now we can continue to use untruthful and illegitimate significations and images of the divine-human relationship or draw upon new imagery and models that can be verified and legitimated in their material-historical performance. It only strengthens this point to note how often such a physicalist model for God's activity gave a not-so-subtle direction for our *will to power* over each other precisely as "Christian nations" and "Christian people."

McFague's book has much to recommend it. In this particular context, however, I have engaged it in order to provide a venue for describing further the sacramental intentionality I see as ingredient to metaphor and symbol and how symbols and models further the overall sacramental intention of metaphor. I have indicated how I see the interrelation of the metaphorical and symbolic qualities of the ethical norm creating effective sacramental models for the ordering of the rules of moral behavior. In this vein, I criticized the tendency of McFague's metaphorical theology, and metaphor theory in general, to remain aesthetically and methodologically aloof from the material-historical and cultural sedimentations of power that are necessary for political and moral change. Indeed, language in all its dimensions has power; but its power to initiate political and moral change is only in prospect when it rests upon the horizon of metaphor. Thus metaphor and metaphorical theology need the work of symbol and model to accomplish their own intentions. Indeed, symbol without metaphor runs great risks of over-sedimentation and encrustation—becoming as McFague indicates, only conservative celebrations of the status quo. Without symbol, however, and the social and political effects of sacramental models, metaphor and metaphorical theology will remain in the "already purified universe of the *logos*" (Ricoeur, 1976: 59) and in that retain strong aestheticist tendencies.

In referring to McFague's functional counterpoint between Protestant and Catholic "sensibilities," I did not mean to suggest that I completely agree with these characterizations. Historically, sacramentalism has been closer to the surface of the Catholic traditions in theology. McFague's characterizations of a general suspicion of sacramentalism of the "Protestant sensibility" displays the same sense of continuity with the main contours of the surface of the Protestant traditions. However, deeper probes of these traditions will find, albeit more hidden, important and effective dimensions of both sensibilities in each of these major stands of Christian theology. McFague is clear throughout her text that she is interested in ecumenical work and dialogue among all branches of Christian theology. I am not sure, however, that her characterizations of these two sensibilities essentially in counterpoint is only a presentation of a methodological alternative.

Her own powerful portrayal of the necessity of overcoming the traditions of antifemale patriarchy that infect Christian theology in all of its forms contains a not historically unfounded suggestion that Catholic sacramentalism must bear a major share of the blame for such a false and illegitimate theology. I am convinced, however, that the theological and moral imperatives associated with the feminist critique of Christian theology will not be brought to full verification and legitimation by a metaphorical theology that stops short of symbol and sacramentally effective models. McFague's approach tends to counter only the classical rendering of sacramentalism and pays insufficient attention to its modern possibilities. I am arguing that precisely in the context of modernity, and a renewed understanding of the role of symbol and model, we can find the sacramental effectuation and *implication* in political and moral history that McFague seeks, but does not find, in only metaphorical *apprehensions* and *disclosures*. In this sense, her metaphorical theology is a necessary first step. However, both methodologically and practically, her relative and functional separation of metaphor from symbol and sacrament distracts from the next steps necessary to not only prophetically proclaim but politically and morally accomplish the feminist critique. It may be a relatively unnoticed and tragic irony that the Catholic sacramental traditions which have been the most resistant to the feminist critique may have the best methodological tools for its political and moral effectuation.

## Marriage as a Normative Sacramental Model

The sacramental intention and function of metaphors and symbols we have been discussing are necessary ingredients in the final analysis of the structure and function of ethical norms as models of moral behavior. I will argue in the next section that the use and limits of the norm of marriage in the Christian Church has a direct relation to the continuing sacramental and pragmatic effectuation of the ideal values of sexual intimacy disclosed metaphorically and designated symbolically. I will offer a reading of the present state of this norm and argue that the values it discloses and designates continue to be effectively modeled—i.e., continue to demonstrate, effect, and promote the good. However, I do not think that this normative model is unscathed and meets completely or simply the ongoing sacramentally tests of verification and legitimation. Thus the problems the Church is noticing with sexual irresponsibility pertain directly to how marriage itself is faring in contemporary life. As marriage fares as an ethical and moral *sacrament*, so too will its effective disclosures and designations of the values the Church proclaims as necessary for guiding responsible sexual behavior in all dimensions of our lives. I will not argue that heterosexual marriage is a rule of life for all situations and contexts of sexual intimacy in the lives of Christians. I will argue that in the context of the present state of Christian tradition, heterosexual marriage, however fragile, is still the model for the central disclosure and designation and demonstration of the values required for responsible sexual expression and is in this sense still capable of effecting the normative good in Church and society.

The metaphorical and symbolic qualities of ethical norms will survive as models of human behavior only as long as they sacramentally effect what they proclaim. When and if they fail, it will be because they have become untruthful and illegitimate in this effectuation. In such situations long periods of moral confusion may arise. In such times we have the hope, but not the assurance, for the rehabilitation of such norms by a return to a more sacramentally effective way of moral life—in this case, the political and moral rehabilitation of marriage itself. Still, any extant norm can be beyond sacramental rehabilitation because of radically changing conditions and practices—the changing contexts for verification and legitimation. In such times we become implicated in a new, and indeed, intergenerational process of normative moral reconstruction with no guarantee that any "new" norm will be better or worse than the one lost.

My present estimate is that the Church has entered a time of serious but not total confusion about the possibility of saying anything new about sexual morality, a time of formal analytic confusion concerning the proper relations of norms and rules, and a time of substantive confusion about the changing conditions of sexual intimacy and practice. In its contemporary disclosures, designations, and demonstrations of the values the Church proclaims as necessary for responsible sexual behavior, the normative model of marriage is not being as sacramentally effective as it should be. However, I do not think that the prospects for rehabilitating this norm are completely bleak nor do I foresee any other norm taking its place or offering a viable and responsible alternative. The norm of marriage in the Christian Church and in culture in general is in jeopardy, but it is neither moribund nor dead. In the first two parts of this book I have attempted to outline the present situation of the Church in its modern discourse on sexual morality and to suggest certain avenues for the engagement of the work that needs to be done and the type of conversations that need to take place. Now, in the final part, I will present an overture to the substance of that work in a discussion of the norm of marriage itself and an application of that norm to rules of moral behavior in three instances of sexual intimacy. The book will conclude with a brief discussion of how such substantive discussions need to take shape as the Church engages this question in terms of its own identity as a community of moral discourse and action.

# PART III.

## SUBSTANTIVE CONVERSATIONS IN CHRISTIAN ETHICS AND MORAL THEOLOGY

# 6

## The Norm of Heterosexual Marriage

### Historical Remembrance and Moral Obligation

I will begin this third conversation with a discussion of how particular historical traditions and communities can call forth normative models and anticipate their future—how in fact they become attached and obliged to these models. After this analysis of how the contemporary Church remembers the norm of marriage and draws it forward into the present, I will turn to a substantive moral theological discussion of the implications of such retrieval for the Church's teaching and guidance with respect to sexual morality. Even though I intend that there be a coherent and logical progression among the three sections of this book, I will not attempt to rehearse and refocus all previous arguments in their specific application. I am building an argument that comes to conclusion in the applications I will make in this section.

The initiating act of moral character is remembrance—that is to say, our relative and critical retrieval of the historical images and models that inform and frame how we ought to be related to others. In critical hermeneutic acts of remembrance, the past is transformed and rendered alive again in the present with prospects for effective transmission to the future. Combining my arguments of Parts One and Two, we can conclude that mature and effective ethical norms are mediated historically to contemporary cultures and communities within a dynamic of significant metaphorical and symbolic function. Since they are dependent on communal acts of historical remembrance, norms can neither be private nor can they be created from scratch. Rather ethical norms manifest and model the ideal character-identity of a culture and community—what the community claims to be and wants to become, and how its members are obliged. As part of an informing and identifying heritage of moral ideals—short of myth and archetype—no single person, couple, or group of the community defines or manifests completely this common tradition of character-identification. One might find in premodern cultures or subcultures not directly influenced by modernity the presence of, so to speak, a "living archetype." Similarly, norms can function as paradigmatic myths in cultures that have not self-consciously transformed such ancient myths to modern symbols. However, neither mythic nor archetypical representations of ethical norms are possible in the modern Christian discourse on sexual morality.

I have argued that there is no paradigmatic Christian marriage or *holy family* that can sustain our present remembrance of an historically effective norm for the moral guidance of everyday life; nor was there ever at least in our monotheistic past a specific myth of divine marriage among the gods (see Blenkinsopp, 1969). In the context of modernity, successful norms must function more generally and figuratively than specifically and literally. This means that to be effective as an ethical norm, heterosexual and monogamous marriage in the Christian traditions cannot be remembered as a myth whose values are embodied in the specific narrative of a paradigmatic couple—ideal or real, divine or human—whose "life-experience" becomes an archetype and rule of life for all. On the contrary, the Church recalls metaphorically and symbolically its identifying and informing norm, and remains obliged by it so that the values required for all responsible sexual expression can be disclosed, designated, and modeled effectively as goods in the life of the Christian community and overall.

If, through the discourse of its own tradition, Christianity has been cast into an historical and identifying narrative, the images, metaphors, symbols, and models critically remembered and propounded will necessarily inform moral character and obligation. Accordingly, the values confessed will be disclosed as normative and obliging according to the contemporary state of such conversations and narrations—in this case, how the norm of marriage continues to be presently remembered and anticipated; and how it is functioning and actually directing Christians toward the good of a responsible sexual life in all of its multiple manifestations and dimensions.

No matter how analytically precise and systematic our theories and arguments, the progress of history continues first as contemporary acts of remembrance upon the horizon of the future. Ironically, in such critical-hermeneutic acts, new theories and arguments will decenter old ones; and old ones will become new again. We become obliged in both new and old ways. This is not, however, a vicious circle or a numbing and enervating historical-dialectical game. The reason why new arguments and theories emerge, or old ones become reconstructed, is because their coherence and effectiveness are relative to the contemporary circumstances of their engagement and occurrence. Character-identity and its obligations are not formed amid historical abstractness but within the various and often conflicting movements of material-historical time and place—in fact, formed maturely, more in the context of heterogeneity than homogeneity. It is in critical-hermeneutic conversation and action amid the relativity, conventionality, and plurality of material-historical circumstance that we engage each other in projects of understanding and responsible action. The individual and communal self is always coming to its character-identity and attendant obligations in the context of diversity and variety—in the context of the other.

Consequently, even when cast upon an horizon of universality, our rational discourse and arguments are never totally continuous in any tradition or totally applicable to all members of a tradition-informed community. Values and norms emerge from prior assumptions and interpretations of meaning and truth contained in the conversations and narrations of history, but to remain vital, must always be submitted again to verification and legitimation in every generation of the life of a tradition and community. This is the way that historical tradition is brought forward, progresses, and the past is made "real" again. Thus adequate ethical theories and moral arguments, and the obligations they promote, are built upon critical acts of remembrance, engaged in the present and submitted to the challenges of contemporary life upon the horizon of the future.

Before I turn to the more particular discussions of the substantive norm of Christian marriage and its relation to rules of sexual behavior, I will discuss how the historical past can be effectively remembered and what our deepest memories of the relation of sex to faith and life disclose. Here we will gain a perspective on how norms rooted in the Church's historical past, and how marriage, in particular, can be rendered contemporary as a present disclosure of the values necessary for a responsible Christian sexual life.

## "The Reality of the Historical Past"[1]

In *Time and Narrative*, Paul Ricoeur claims that "if, in fact, human action can be narrated, it is because it is always already articulated by signs, rules, and norms. It is already symbolically mediated." Symbolic forms are "cultural processes that articulate experience" and accentuate "the public character of any meaningful articulation" (1984b: 57). Our symbols and acts of symbolization are not "in the mind, not a psychological operation destined to guide action, but a meaning incorporated

into action and decipherable from it by other actors in the social inter-
play." Our symbols are thus situated into larger and structured symbol
systems (1984b: 57; 58) and are mediated to us in material-historical
cultures. Connecting meaning and action, Ricoeur argues that symbols
further introduce

> the idea of rule, not only in the sense...of...rules for description
> and interpretation of individual actions, but in the sense of a
> norm.... They give form, order and direction to life.... As a function
> of the norms immanent in a culture, actions can be estimated or
> evaluated, that is, judged according to a scale of moral preferences.
> They thereby receive a relative value, which says that this action is
> more valuable than that one. These degrees of value, first attrib-
> uted to actions, can be extended to agents themselves, who are held
> to be good or bad, better or worse (1984b: 58).[2]

For our purposes the question now becomes how such historically
mediated norms come to present experience. More particularly, how
does the traditional norm of marriage come to engage the challenges of
the present and at the same time maintain its own historical integrity? In
attempting to render the past contemporary, we can expect to encounter
the enigma of history itself—of time and its narrations. We will, therefore, stand in both continuity and discontinuity with the norm of marriage. Similarly, this norm will claim us with obligations both similar and
different from Christians who have preceded us. Our specific problem in
this instance is the same as Ricoeur's general problem of discerning "the
reality of the historical past" (Ricoeur, *The Reality of the Historical Past*:
1984a).

Through a variety of documentary evidence, an adequate moral
theological history of this norm will both represent, as Ricoeur says, "a
debt of *gratitude* with respect to the dead"—"*what once was*," as well as
configure what is now no longer. "This is the conviction that is expressed
by the notion of the trace. Inasmuch as it is *left* by the *past*, it *stands* for
the past, it 'represents' the past..." (1984a: 1–2). When we remember and
narrate historically, we both return to and take leave of the past. The *trace*
of the reality of the past stands in the present not "in the sense that the
past would appear itself in the mind (*Vorstellung*) but in the sense that
the trace takes the place of (*Vertretung*) the past, absent from historical
discourse" (1984a: 1–2). Adequate history thus bears a dual burden of re-
presentation and configuration. Ricoeur will argue that such configuration is joined to re-presentation by way of the indirect trace that remains

present for us through the effective mediation of rhetorical tropes. Our problem is trying to give an account of our "thinking of history rather than historical knowledge" (1984a: 2).

> Authenticated testimony functions like a delegated *eye witness* account: I see through the eyes of someone else. An illusion of contemporaneousness is thus created which allows us to place knowledge through traces along the line of indirect observation (Ricoeur, 1984a: 39 n.2).

Consequently, quoting Marc Bloch, Ricoeur suggests that history is "the science of men in time" (p. 39 n.2).[3]

While the past is rendered "alive" again in our own acts of remembrance and narration, the remaining illusion of contemporaneity pertains to the fact that we have not literally but figuratively brought the past to the present. In being unable to bring the past literally forward in any remembrance of obliging ethical norms, we can expect no transmission of literal obligation simply in the act of narration alone. The verification and legitimation of any ethical norm accomplished in the historical past needs to be accomplished again in each generation of remembrance. This task, however, remains our abiding obligation as long as we claim to stand faithfully within a particular historical tradition or community—our continuing debt to the dead. If, in fact, marriage has come from our past to center the Church's moral discourse on sexual morality, then we are obliged to remember this norm and to narrate its history adequately. Discerning what present obligations are now disclosed by Christian marriage requires new critical interpretations in every generation. In historical remembrance and narration, continuity with the past is always relatively achieved upon a horizon of understanding that knows that our reality is not in every way the reality of our forebearers, nor our obligations in every way the same as theirs. Becoming contemporaneous with our past is both an accomplishment of effective historical memory as well as an illusion. "What is no longer, one day was" (Ricoeur, 1984a: 3–4; 4): the past limits as well as guides.

The next and central set of questions we must engage pertain to how to go about such thinking and retrieval—what of our past remains both contemporaneous and noncontemporaneous with us. Under what categories, classes, and signs are we to proceed as we attempt to gauge the reality of the historical past? What are our methods of procedure? Ricoeur frames this method under "the incomparable categories that Plato in the *Sophist* called 'the great classes'" (1984a: 4).

I have chosen the three great classes of the Same, The Other, and the Analogue. I do not claim that the idea of the past is constructed dialectically by the very interconnection of these three classes, I merely hold that we are talking sense about the past by thinking of it, in turn, under the sign of the Same, then of the sign of the Other, and finally under that of the Analogue (pp. 4–5).

Under the *sign of the Same*, Ricoeur considers our attempts to reenact the past through entering, as it were, into the events that produced our documentary evidence—to attempt to think with the agent/actors of any historical event or period by way of this evidence. Under this sign, we engage our historical imagination and attempt to get "inside the events," not only in an intuitive way but always in terms of our texts, artifacts, and the like. In rethinking in our "own mind what was once thought" we might claim that "knowing *what* happened is already knowing *why* it happened" (1984a: 6–8).[4]

However, Ricoeur notes remaining problems. First, the reenactment claimed under this method is not *reliving* but *rethinking*, and "rethinking always contains the critical moment that forces us to take the detour by way of the historical imagination" (1984a: 8). Thus, for example, to try to "enter inside" any particular biblical text pertaining to the status of marriage does not create total and straight-line continuity with that text. Under the sign of the same, we are "reenacting" only by way of rethinking, not by reliving the contexts and conditions that produced the text in the first place. And while thought is intrinsic to life at all levels, thinking cannot simply replace living. A text about marriage is not a married life. Norms need to be verified and legitimated not just by thinking but also by lived experience.

The second problem with this essentially idealist method is that, in its claims for reenactment, it tends to abolish the distance between past and present (Ricoeur, 1984a: 8–12). In being drawn forward by the thoughts of the historian, or the person or community remembering, how does the past retain its own reality—the integrity of its own time instead of being consumed in the assumptions of the present? Other times and places, events and norms of our past can become captured in the present and the temptation emerges to consider these distant others in every way like ourselves. We establish continuity with them under the sign of the same, but we tend to lose the sense of distance necessary for retaining the reality of history as *past*. While attempting to establish the continuity necessary to live in a heritage and tradition by rethinking and remembering the norm of marriage, the temptation will be great to impose our own experience upon that of the ages of our past.

Under the second "great class," *the sign of the Other*, Ricoeur considers the possibility of "passing from the thought of the past as *mine*, to the thought of the past as other" (1984a: 14).[5] If the past does not retain its own reality under the sign of the Same, then perhaps it will fare better under the sign of the Other—i.e., "under a negative ontology of the past." Such an ontology will stress "otherness" and "a restitution of temporal difference, even an apology for difference pushed to the point of temporal exoticism." Still, Ricoeur wonders what such a history in terms of "this pre-eminence of the Other" would look like and how it would be accomplished (p. 15).

How can we remember or even be obliged within a tradition when we emphasize distance and difference rather than seek an empathic connection? When problems predominate over "received traditions" and the "simple transcription of lived experience in its own language," will not the past become only remote from the present with "an effect of strangeness in contrast to the desire to make the unfamiliar familiar again" (1984a: 15)? Ricoeur argues that insofar as this method of remembrance of difference stands in service to a necessary decentering of ethnocentric hubris (1984a: 16), or as a therapy for remembrance only under the sign of the Same, it has been effective[6]—for example, correcting the Church's history of sexual ethics through the narrations of mainly male and heterosexual voices. Beyond this imperative self-correction, Ricoeur wants to know how else we could remember the past in this way. Under "the sign of the Other," he finds remembering history as the thoughts and experiences of "other people" to be the best analogue (1984a: 16). Before it passes over into our ideas and thoughts—or to the theoretic constructs of argument including "ethical norms"—the reality of our historical past pertains to *other* people.

In centering the remembrance of our historical past now under the sign of the personal other, Ricoeur hopes to accomplish more critical retrieval than what can be accomplished in stressing only similarity or difference alone. In terms of our interrelations with others, epistemology and ethics can be joined in our acts of historical remembrance and in historical knowledge as such.

> The understanding of others today, and the understanding of men of the past shares the same, essentially moral dialectic of same and other: on the one hand, we know basically what resembles us; on the other hand, the understanding of another person requires that we perform the *epochē* (cessation; suspension) of our own preferences in order to understand the other as other. It is the suspicious

attitude of the positivist historian that prevents us from recognizing the identity of the tie of friendship that exists between the self and the other today, and between the self and the other in the past. This tie is more essential than curiosity, which, in fact, pushes the other back into the distance (1984a: 44 n.17, parens added).

Therefore, even when we remember our difference and discontinuity from *other people* in our narration of the Church's historical discourse on sexual morality, we engage terrain that is *similar* though not identical to our forebearers, and like them, seek ways of faithful and responsible Christian life. In our contemporary moral debates we are engaging in the same moral tasks even when our conclusions and consequent obligations are different from theirs.

We learn both an epistemological and moral lesson when we remember our historical past under "the sign of the Other." Even in their difference others do not stand in total discontinuity from us. When these lessons of *alterity* carry over to our contemporary conversations, others retain their unique reality and moral integrity precisely in their difference—a difference that both separates and then interpersonally relates them to us. This ought to be a defining mark, for example, of conversations between heterosexual and homosexual Christians who are different in their sexuality but similar in their personality and Christianity. Still when it comes to the historical past, as Ricoeur points out, we cannot abolish the difference between others of today and others of yesteryear and the temporal distance remains (1984a: 17). This means that even those who find themselves cast upon sociocultural and moral margins cannot find a simple correspondence between their position and those of others on the margins of the distant past. Accordingly, female and homosexual Christians cannot consider the dimensions of their own relative marginality in the Church to be exactly the same as those "others" of ages past. Some historical correlation can be drawn in these relationships, but it cannot be a simple correspondence. For example, in our mistaken desire for *only* historical correspondences between the place of women of the past and present Church it would be a mistake to think that dedicated women of the early Church felt obliged by virginity based solely upon a male sexist bias against the status and sexuality of women. While such bias certainly existed and has been continually pervasive, such women often made their own conscientious decisions and refused to allow themselves to be controlled by any dominant male prejudice. Even though the histories of homophobia and sexism in the Church are marked by past and present violence and tragedy, to assume only a historical correspondence between past and present marginality is to make a category mistake.[7] In both of these examples, the history of alterity displays more complexity and distance in the relation of past and present than only ideologically framed debates can encompass.

If historical remembrance and narration under "the sign of the Same" tends to collapse difference and distance under similarity and contemporary retrieval, and such remembrance and narration under "the sign of the Other" tends to either transform difference and distance to the strange and alien or to offer overly facile historical correspondences with others in similar situations, then, as Ricoeur indicates, "we return to the enigma of temporal distance" (Ricoeur, 1984a: 19). Yet we have made progress: the inadequacy of the sign of the Same called forth the sign of the Other. Proceeding under the sign of the Other in the remembrance of *other persons* raised the challenge of finding a more complete relation and "sign" of past and present, similarity and difference, self and other. "One way of 'saving' their respective contributions to the question of history's ultimate referent is to join their efforts together under the sign of the 'great class' which associates the Same and the Other. The Similar is this great category. Or better, the analogue which is a resemblance between relations rather than between simple terms" (Ricoeur, 1984a: 25).

Historical remembrance and retrieval under *the sign of the Analogue* will be a tropological approach; that is, historical remembrance and obligation by way of rhetorical figuration—how we speak about the past and the ways our figures of speech inform and oblige us in discourse and action. In comparisons and relations across temporal distance under the sign of the Analogue, we will want to know *"what* things are *like*— forcing us to make a metaphorical use of the verb 'to be' itself in the form of 'being-as,' corresponding to 'seeing as'"* (Ricoeur, 1984a: 28). For example, given our discontinuity with its originating and distant past, through the major tropes of rhetoric we can search for a proper and historically accurate and fitting analogy between the way that the norm of marriage modeled values and goods in the past and the way it is doing so in the present. Through such literary tropes,[8] the reality of the norm of marriage can be analogically mediated into the present and we can begin to plot the narrative history of the norm in terms of its past, present, and future prospects (see Ricoeur, 1984a: 28–29). Using a variety of rhetorical figures, we will be able to discriminate how we relate to this norm under the sign of the Same as well as under the sign of the Other and work toward a more adequate moral theological history of marriage. Standing in a faithful tradition demands that we envision and hear the story of our past with historical accuracy and effectiveness and not use our rhetoric of sex for negative ideological purposes of persuasion and power.

I have already spoken of the *re-presentational* function of the trope of *metaphor* in the structure of an ethical norm. Since the values disclosed by metaphor are drawn across the dialectical relation between the literal reality and the moral ideal, when we remember and speak of the norm of marriage metaphorically we will know that we are all "off the mark," married or not; and that no paradigmatic couple exists in the Christian Church such that to be unmarried, not heterosexual, or celibate would make one "abnormal." If we speak of our memories of marriage under the trope of *metonymy*, we equate the part with the whole and tend to reduce the complexity of the whole into a single dimension. Thus, when we equate Christian marriage, as the state of monogamous, committed, and faithful love, with heterosexuality we are thereby reducing the complexities of such love to heterosexual relation and expression. In stressing a single dimension for the complex of the whole, we at the same time seek an easier continuity with our past. However, metonymy immediately calls forth the trope of synecdoche. *Synecdoche* speaks of the whole in terms of the part but performs a more integrative function than metonymy, expanding the meaning of the part so that it might speak for the whole, epitomizing it as it were. We speak in the trope of synecdoche, for example, when we talk of marriage in terms of a single value or set of values disclosed, such as, "marriage is commitment" or "love;" or when we integrate the whole of marriage under a figure of a basic praxis, such as "marriage is communication." While inaugurated by metaphor which, as Ricoeur argues, in one sense holds the tropes together in their function as figures of speech that transmit the *reality* of our historical past, Ricoeur also points out Hayden White's (1978) reference to the trope *irony* as "metatropological" inasmuch as it provokes the awareness of the possible misuse of figurative language and continually recalls the problematic nature of language as a whole. Irony reminds us that in any figurative use of language under the sign of the Analogue, we must remain aware of the "negative note"—"something like a second thought"—which gives rise to hesitation and "suspension" of judgment and "gives preference to contradiction, aporia, by stressing the inade-quacy of any characterization." Irony serves especially as a corrective to "the naivete of metaphor" (Ricoeur, 1984a: 30–31; 48–49 n.32). Conse-quently, we must always also speak of marriage under the trope of irony to overcome historical naivete and recall that its present reality as an obliging norm is not the exactly same reality of any other expanse of time and place in the Church's historical past. What we now only partially and inadequately remember and become obliged by is not simply identical to the realities that obliged each and every generation of Christians past. Following Ricoeur, we can say that under the sign of the Analogue, there is a "resemblance" between the relations of past and present norms but not a simple correspondence. To interpret the traditional norm of marriage analogically does not, therefore, create a simple identity but rather a similarity of obligations between ourselves and our forebearers. We stand in fidelity through resemblance to their task of coming to moral responsibility and virtue, but not in singular identity and continuity with their judgments. Ricoeur concludes: "Only the complete route from the most naive apprehension (metaphor) to the most reflective (irony) authorizes us to speak of a tropological structure of consciousness" (1984a: 31).

In this analysis of remembrance under the tropological sign of the Analogue, we have recovered analogy as a frame for understanding fidelity to our past from Max Black's overly schematic and diagrammatic understanding discussed in Chapter Five. Still, tropes are *figures* of speech and must come together in some way to become designated as ingredient in the fabric of a culture, society, and community—to become standard ways of speaking and representing our past and effecting present and future meaning and action. Here I have found the work of the sacramentally effective symbol and model to be essential so that our speech is not so disjunctive from our action. In the conversations and life of a culture and community, when speech and action come together in a critical way we can gain the sacramental model necessary for demonstrating and effecting a responsible moral life. In terms of our remembrance and narration of our historical past, our analysis suggests that the tropes that inform the sign of the Analogue come together in a similar form—as Hayden White says (1973), in historical discourse "that purports to be a model, or icon, of past structures" (in Ricoeur: 1984a, 47 n.28). Within such a method of remembrance and narration we make use, self-consciously and critically, of the variety of tropes. Now centered in the praxis of analogical remembrance, the moral theology of sex and marriage will speak of fidelity by way of a set of resemblances, not identifications. Nor should we, in Ricoeur's words, "confuse the *iconic* value of representation of the past with a...scale model, like a geographical map, for there is no original given with which to compare the model. It is precisely the strangeness of the original"—in our case, the absence of a literal original and originating marriage—which makes the tropological/figurative forms necessary (1984a: 32).

Though somewhat analytically technical, none of this argument should be completely unfamiliar to the Church, whose originating theological images of marriage are identified and brought forward to us also through familiar biblical *figures of speech*. We have always spoken of and remembered faithful marriage and sexual behavior under the *resemblances* of configurations, such as God's *betrothal* of Israel and Christ's *love* for the Church. Our theological and faith-informed reality of the norm of marriage comes from the deep recesses of our history and remains real for us in these analogical resemblances.

## The Norm of Marriage

To make a claim that marriage remains normative in the Christian Church is to say at the same time that this norm survives analogically and relatively intact, though not unscathed, in the conversation and life of the Christian community—i.e., as a *normative analogue* that focuses our remembrance and models our obligations. Our discussion of the reality of the historical past indicates that to sustain such a claim one does not have to argue that marriage is universally and ahistorically normative, or that no matter what happens to the material history of heterosexuality and marriage it will remain the central focus of our remembrance. History teaches that the values and norms of communities and institutions—their character and virtue—rise and fall, are born and die. On the other hand, any claim of present viability will have to be based upon a relatively accurate reading of the present self-understanding of the Church and the practice of Christians—that is to say that in the general speech and praxis of the Church, marriage would still be understood and received as an identifying and effective norm that orients our character toward responsible sexual behavior.

This is the present state of the Church's memory and attendant claim: *heterosexual marriage is our single orienting norm for sexual activity.* As their character and life-experience is drawn into the orbit of this norm, the majority of Christians will find an experience of formal continuity between the norm and the rule of monogamous heterosexual marriage. Like people of most cultures and communities, the majority of Christians will marry heterosexually and monogamously. However, other Christians will find more formal discontinuity than continuity: they will either not marry or will find an integrity of heterosexual sexual expression to be functionally and morally impossible. Despite this variance within their own membership, the denominations can still claim, by and large, to stand within the tradition and the history of the norm of marriage as an identifying character mark of the Church. Even where there is a necessary discontinuity between this *norm* and a corresponding *rule* of heterosexual married life, as members of the Christian Church those who are unmarried and not heterosexual become obliged under the values modeled by this single norm and are not simply free to choose their own norms and values.

At the same time, those who enter Christian married life take on a profound obligation to protect and enhance the values disclosed by this norm of Christian existence. Being married in the Christian Church is a public act for the good of both the couple and the community. No matter how the denominations theologically articulate numbers of sacraments, marriage is called to function in this effective sacramental way, and is in this sense, if no other, a sacrament. This point of special obligation of married Christians should cause no special concern, since according to the gifts and strengths of each, all members of the body work for the good of the whole. Married Christians are not "more normal" than other Christians, they simply have taken upon themselves special obligations to protect the Church's norm of sexual life and to demonstrate the values that marriage discloses. The good of the body requires and the Church expects such Christians to model responsibly, not perfectly, the values required for responsible sexual behavior for all.[9] In keeping these values alive, such Christians keep the normative model of Christian marriage alive in concrete ways. In this way, too, marriage can attain the sacramental visibility necessary for the guidance of the body of the faithful toward responsible rules of sexual behavior amid the variety of circumstances, situations, and possibilities.

The decentering that takes place when heterosexuality and marriage confront other ways of sexual existence and expression does not call for the "creation" of multiple and parallel norms—for example, that the Church ought to proclaim that when it comes to sexual expression there are a variety of equal norms: for heterosexual and homosexual persons, for the married and unmarried, for celibate Christians, and so on. Even accepting the conditions of the radical historical change and pluralism I discussed in Part One, foundational norms and models of character-identification do not exist easily in multiple configurations within the same specific tradition and community at the same time. Plurality at the foundation often creates fractures and splits within the internal life of a community and often causes more crisis and confusion than any particular denomination can handle. This leads to an often inchoate, but largely accurate, fear that claims for parallel norms for heterosexual and homosexual Christians will fracture the integrity of the

Church and its denominations. For this reason debates in this vein are almost always relatively dysfunctional, with some members arguing isolated issues of sexual ethics and others, in effect, arguing in terms of the future of denominational order and the tradition itself. I am arguing here that the present conversations of the denominations indicate that the norm of heterosexual marriage is now extant in the Church at a core level of confessional and character identity—that is, this norm, and the values it discloses, designates, and models is part of what the Christian Church stands for and what it means to be a Christian and live a Christian life. Consequently, in the self-conscious discourse, argument, and life of the Church, informing *ethical norms* need to remain singular whereas the situations and circumstances that call forth specific *rules of life* must remain inevitably plural.

Rather than calling forth a multiplicity of norms to meet any and all occasions, when heterosexual marriage confronts the severe challenge of other rules of sexual expression and life, the decentering that takes place ought to be understood as contributions to "the rest of the story" —how marriage is, in fact, disclosing or not the values of its own normative status; how it is serving or not the total Church in this way. This is the constructive manifestation of the heterogeneity and diversity I have been speaking about. Heterogeneity and diversity are manifest in the work of character-identity at all levels of our discourse, but such manifestations are not without special and attendant challenges and dangers relative to any particular level. In the *rhetoric of passionate persuasion* we will ordinarily hear conflicting appeals intending to move us emotionally and persuade us to act. However, in such a conflict of ideologies our constructive response will be also to ascertain whether our feelings about any given issue—for example, whether or not we ought to liturgically "bless" homosexual unions[10]—has stood the test of critical argument and confessional integrity. At levels of *systematic rational discourse,* diversity and difference ought to be promoted so that all sides of any issue can be given critical rational attention. However, at levels of speech and reflection that probe the very *narrative* and *confessional foundations* of character-identity—our received heritage of remembrance, including core norms that frame that heritage—we cannot promote so easily a critical environment of diversity and difference. When there is divergence of foundational narration and confession, the issues at stake are the nature and character of the self and community in question. Indeed, such discussions are necessary at times but need to be engaged self-consciously— that is, with a full awareness that continuing and unresolvable differences at this level mean a change or split in the identity of the community in question or the conversion of an individual to a new self-understanding. Thus, I have argued that on the basis of my own confessional "self-understanding" to maintain a racist and radically sexist posture within a Christian community calls not for critical rational discourse about possible moral options, but rather for either a change in the character-identity of the Church or the functional conversion of such a person to an other than Christian self-understanding. Certainly there can be debate about what issues broach this foundational level, and we are constantly challenged to be self-aware about the kind of conversation we ought to engage about any specific question. I have suggested that in some significant dimensions questions of human sexuality rest at this basic level of Christian character-identity.

In arguing for the singularity of the norm of marriage, I am not engaging in an argument against heterogeneity and diversity. I am, however, suggesting a way to prevent what has every prospect of becoming a source of core-division and fracture at the very heart of some denominations and in the Church itself. If such a crisis can be avoided by more precise and critical engagement of the issues surrounding sexual morality, then our obligations are clear. In my argument, responsible nonmarital heterosexual and homosexual sexual expression—expression guided by the requisite Christian values—are never threats to marriage or to the Church itself; whereas pervasive irresponsible sexual expression of any kind among Christians can be a diagnosis of the failure of Church's norm to be working effectively. Merely to claim the norm of marriage as singular and informing is not enough. The material-historical future of Christian marriage is finally bound to its own sacramental effectiveness. The denominations' worry about a major lapse in Christian sexual morality is often addressed to the wrong audiences—those who are engaging in homosexual and nonmarital heterosexual behavior. If it has been the historical tradition of the Church and its remembrances that has raised marriage to its contemporary status as a singular norm in the Christian moral life, failure in sexual responsibility in all of its dimensions must also have something fundamentally to do with the failure of this norm to disclose and display necessary and identifying moral values. This should be the center of our discussions.

## What Our History Discloses

In *The Body and Society: Men, Women and Sexual Renunciation in Early Christianity* (1988), Peter Brown demonstrates how notions of the human person and society set a broad horizon upon which the significant writers of the early Church engaged themes of sexuality, sexual behavior, and marriage. Brown's theme of sexual renunciation is necessary for any adequate study of the norms and rules of sexual behavior promoted formally in the early Church based on the historical realities of the time and the documentary evidence. Brown's study indicates that in the beginning, the Church had no unitary and clear idea that marriage was the single and dominant norm for modeling sexual behavior. Nor was this lack of a central and constructive theology and ethic of Christian marriage a mere liability of the age. Even with the tensions common with times of transition and new beginnings, the contrary will prove to be the case. These earliest writers and teachers, in various ways and with various degrees of intensity and argument, held that the most significant values necessary for leading a Christian way of life were disclosed, designated, and effectively demonstrated most clearly, and in epitome, more by sexual renunciation than by marriage.

Two significant cautions are necessary when probing ancient sources of Christian antiquity to learn contemporary lessons. The most important caution pertains to the documentary evidence. Even though other evidence by way of archaeological artifact and parallel writings of other than Christian culture is necessary, we most often depend on the direct documentary evidence of the early Christian writers. Thus we depend on the writings of highly intellectual and literary experts. According to the rhetoric and needs of the day, such writers engaged in both argument against opponents and adversaries, often within the body of the Church itself, and in pastoral counsel. They often spoke in universal terms and, more often still, for the privileged few who were literate enough to read or to understand them when they spoke. (Brown, 1988: 24). Given this, and especially with respect to the most radical rhetoric of sexual renunciation, it is important to remember that "the silent majority of those who awaited the coming of the kingdom were careworn and decent householders, long used to the punctilious rhythms of Jewish life." Such a majority were not immediately ready to allow their lives to "evaporate" by calls of radical renunciation. (Brown, 1988: 44).[11] "Although many of their clergy, prophets and spiritual guides were continent, the average Christian congregation maintained its numbers through children begotten by the laity" (Brown, 1988: 143). However, whether the average Christian was willing to follow literally the counsel and, at times, command to sexual renunciation or not, Brown also indicates that "behind even the most extreme statements of many of the leaders of the second and third centuries—highly articulate men, for the most part—we can usually sense the mute assent of whole churches, even of whole Christian regions" (p. 86). What ordinary Christians often did not follow in practice, they assented to as an integral part of the Christian ideal and Christian cause: there were, in effect, not only hierarchies of class but also of virtue.

The second caution in this matter concerns gender. The "highly articulate" voices read and heard in our documents are essentially male. Women did occupy significant roles in parts of the early Church—for example as consecrated virgins and dedicated deacons. And some aristocratic women, more committed to the life of the Church than ordinary Roman men, participated in the intellectual life of Latin Christianity (Brown, 1988: 140–59; 259–84; 369–71). Brown warns, however, that overall, "given the harsh values of the Greco-Roman world, it is a comfortable and dangerous illusion to assume that, in much of the evidence, the presence of women is even sensed by its male authors, as might well be the case in later periods of European history" (pp. xvi–xvii). When male Christian authors did "sense" their presence and spoke of consecrated women, it was most often as a vehicle for their own idealized theological vision of a Christian life purified from the contamination of matter and calling forth the new spiritual city of Jerusalem to replace the present dispensation or to gain some release from the heavy penalty imposed upon the disordered human will manifested in sexual desire.[12] Still it is fair to say that in these writings, and certainly against the intentions of their authors to argue for a place of total equality of males and females, a significant trace of the burgeoning independence of mind and spirit emerges among these "daughters of Jerusalem" and "brides of Christ," some of whom also had in mind breaking the male hold over their own cycle of child-bearing (see Brown, 1988: 259–84). It was most often left to these Christian treatises on virginity to "speak in public on the physical state of the married woman—on their danger in childbirth, on the pain in their breasts during suckling, on their exposure to children's infections, on the terrible shame of infertility, and on the humiliation of being replaced by servants in their husbands' affections" (Brown, 1988: 25). Even when highlighting the new, more purified and orderly way of religious sexual renunciation, some of these texts indicated that the state of virginity would be a more blessed state for women even "if there were no Kingdom of Heaven for them to receive" (Eusebius of Emesa, in Brown, 1988: 25). To be sure, not all continent women were dedicated as virgins from their girlhood; rather most had been or continued to be heads of households and now, as widows, were neither shy nor retiring, often using their positions of wealth and influence in paraclerical roles in the Church (Brown, 1988: 150).

All this being said, our cautions remain. Brown indicates that in the second century of the common era, "a young man of the privileged classes of the Roman Empire grew up looking at the world from a position of unchallenged dominance. Women, slaves, and barbarians were unalterably different from him and inferior to him" (p. 9). The "natural hierarchy" had placed women at a lower level based on this difference and the insecurity of the labile nature of the female. Women could, and in the minds of ancient men, often did corrupt and destabilize societal order; thus, they needed to be placed under strict controls of the household, the Church, or, in Christian sexual renunciation, the more spiritualized and orderly virginal or continent states. This "instability" of women never left men with total confidence about their own status and position. Being constantly in social intercourse with women, the male position in the natural and divine hierarchies was also subject to a constant temptation toward destabilization: "It was never enough to be male: a man had to strive to remain 'virile'" and "to exclude from his character and from the poise and temper of his body all telltale traces of 'softness' that might betray, in him, the half-formed state of a woman." Men needed to maintain their grip on the world (Brown, 1988: 11; 22). Such are the ancient roots, including its defective anthropology and sometimes misogyny, of our contemporary debates on this subject, as well as the broad material-historical horizon of much of our present discourse on gender, male homosexuality, spirituality, and of our paradigms for authority and governance in the Church.[13]

With these cautions in mind, we can now summarize the argument of these ancient teachers for sexual renunciation rather than marriage as the dominant norm for sexual behavior in early Christianity. It is important to remember that we are engaging the earliest developmental period of the formation of Christian theology and ethics and that we will encounter variety in practice and argument. Still, as Brown indicates: "By the year 300, Christian asceticism, invariably associated with some form of total or perpetual renunciation, was a well-established feature of most regions of the Christian world" (p. 202). Our discussion will necessarily be brief and in outline, but the importance of this understanding of the reality of our own historical past cannot be overstated when the selective memory of so much of our present debate implies the simple continuity of the norm of marriage as the highest expression of the values of Christian sexuality.

The key point of departure for the argument for sexual renunciation in early Christianity pertains to the state of marriage and sexual relations in the late Roman world. In late antiquity, "the Roman ideal of marital concord had taken on a crystalline hardness: the married couple were presented less as a pair of equal lovers than as a reassuring microcosm of the social order" (Brown, 1988: 16–17). In this way, marriage and sexual relations in general had become implicated in the regular course of the state, the world, and by extension, the cosmos itself. Born with a biblical apocalyptic sensibility, however, early Christian rhetoric was intent on demonstrating that the new creation in Christ had overcome this old and moribund stability. With the implication of sexuality into the order of the state and cosmos, there was an open invitation for the radical Christian rhetor to argue against the old and proclaim the coming of the new on the basis of the destabilizing of sexuality and its familiar family relations. Sexual renunciation thus became a sign that not only pointed to the fall of the old and the coming of the new, but a way of sacramentally effecting it as well. With no new citizens for the city and the state, the coming of the "new Jerusalem" could be hastened. Upon this apocalyptic horizon, sexual renunciation came to the status of the normative ideal in much of early Christianity. Certainly, arguments in support of such a norm were shaded by negative dualisms of body and spirit, intellectual and social privilege, and of what we think of more simply, and when it comes to this period, more facilely, as the sexism of the male Christian rhetor. Nonetheless, the more dominant horizon normative sexual behavior had to do with the hastening of the new Christian dispensation. In Clement of Alexandria, Brown finds the argument that "sexual renunciation might lead the Christian to transform the body, and in transforming the body, to break with the discrete discipline of the ancient city" (p. 31). Other writers saw even more direct apocalyptic and cosmological implications and "believed that the universe itself had shattered with the rising of Christ from the grave" and that "by renouncing all sexual activity the human body could join in Christ's victory: it could turn back the inexorable" cycles of birth and death. "With marriage at an end, the huge fabric of organized society would crumble like a sand-castle touched by the 'ocean-flood of the Messiah'" (Brown, 1988: 32).

In this same vein, the preaching of Jesus was taken to involve "a break with the normal patterns of settled life." There could be no single continuity between the settled structures of either Roman or Jewish life but only a "stark contrast" (Brown, 1988: 42; 44). Not all understood such a contrast in terms of sexual renunciation and the dislocation of marriage and family, but all understood that some radical break with normal patterns of social living was required. Paul had preached a "new creation," but he did not think it necessary to renounce the human body itself. Rather it was "the power of the flesh: the body's physical frailty, its liability to death and the undeniable penchant of its instincts toward sin…(that)…served Paul as a synecdoche for the state of humankind pitted against the spirit of God" (Brown, 1988: 48). In later Christian writing, however, Paul's distinction between body and flesh was often collapsed. The new creation also became signified by a bodily life lived in the spirit rather than in the flesh—the universe itself transformed by the power of God (Brown, 1988: 48–49). In the *First Epistle to the Corinthians*, Paul had argued against dissolving the Christian household during the meantime before such a total transformation. However, even as the deutero-Pauline *Ephesians* (5: 25, 28–30) presented its famous and important comparative configuration of relations in marriage with Christ and the Church, Pauline theology remained suspicious of the power of sexuality (Brown, 1988: 57). The body could be distinguished from the flesh, yet lest this distinction be only in our minds, the "body" also participated in fleshly sexual desire. Brown summarizes:

> What is notably lacking, in Paul's letters, was the warm faith shown by contemporary pagans and Jews that the sexual urge, although disorderly, was capable of socialization and of ordered, even warm, expression within marriage. The dangers of *porneia*, of potential immorality brought about by sexual frustration, were allowed to hold the center of the stage. By this essentially negative, even alarmist strategy, Paul left a fatal legacy to future ages. An argument against abandoning intercourse within marriage and in favor of allowing the younger generation to continue to have children slid imperceptibly into an attitude that viewed marriage itself as no more than a defense against desire (pp. 55; 53–55).

Along with the collapse of Paul's distinction between the body and the flesh and an increasing moralistic attitude toward the body, even more important for the continuance of this slide to the negative were the various responses to the implication of sexuality and marriage at the heart of the stability of empire—or the interrelation of sex and secularity in general. In *First Corinthians*, Paul is concerned with keeping stable the order of the households of Christian Corinth. (Brown, 1988: 55). Here the order of society offers some prospects for ordering sexuality, at least in the meantime, and Paul is less radical than the rhetoric of sexual renunciation of later centuries that called, precisely, for a social disruption. In another vein, and even with his own negative suspicions, Paul was also less radical than those of later centuries, even our own, who depoliticized and overly moralized sexuality and made it prone in every way to unique and deeply sinister sin. Such a moralizing posture—one that essentially removes sexuality from the fabric of ordinary secular interaction—has come to occupy a major share of our contemporary and selective Christian memory wherein we commonly speak of *morals* and *immorality* to pertain to sexual matters alone.

Interpreters of Paul's new creation in late antiquity struggled to find a way of "single-minded" contrast between Christianity and the extant Roman and Jewish orders; and sexual restraint seemed to fit the bill (Brown, 1988: 57–64), being radical enough for contrast, and different enough to call forth and effectively symbolize the new creation. Yet in this renunciation, there had to be some continuity with times past. Prophecy and the ability to receive the divine inspiration had often been associated, in some way, with continence in biblical traditions. Continence was also not an uncommon feature of advancing age when the preparation for death was foremost on the mind. Considering sex always a "permanent weakness," Tertullian had argued for a "Spirit-filled gerontocracy" wherein sexual desire, under strict control for the young, would lessen in age so that in renunciation the "Spirit might flood unimpeded into the hearts of widows and widowers" (Brown, 1988: 66–69; 79–80).[14] Such a moderated asceticism on this point, however, did not prevent Tertullian's conviction that the ways of sinful flesh were deeply and inexorably implicated in the body and, more precisely, in the bodies of women who were always "seductive, and Christian baptism did nothing to change this fact" (Brown, 1988: 81).

Still, in one way or another, sexual renunciation was also a plea for freedom of the human person from the bondage of the powers of the age and of the body/flesh. Such pleas were as diverse and radical as the Marcionite claim for freedom in the dissolution of all bonds of marriage and family, as well as the Encratites' myth of original freedom over death manifested in Adam and Eve's spiritual marriage with God before the Fall. But all were associated in some way with a sense of new freedom (Brown, 1988: 86–95).

Nonetheless, freedom rooted in sexual renunciation alone was too easy. In relating the Fall with the sexual activity of Adam and Eve as their collusion with the bondage of death, the Encratites implied such bondage could be broken by sexual renunciation. Once accepted, such a myth, so they thought, would work to detach themselves from both the sex and death ingredient in secular society (see Brown, 1988: 95). These Christians thus engaged in a facile denial of the powers of death and sex in the propagation of society. For the same bonds of death that claimed the human condition also framed the polis, which, in turn, often asserted its own physical powers over life and death as a claim and sign of its own immortality. However, while always tinged with sex—as Freud indicated in our own time—the death-dealing practices of societies, ancient or modern, could not be countered by mere sexual renunciation. There was more than a touch of Gnosticism in many of these arguments for sexual renunciation: the search for new enlightenment and freedom of spirit and "an end to the ache of doubt" and insecurity. "The Gnostics claimed to be able to bypass, through a moment of instant 'redemption,' the long moral and intellectual discipline required of every Christian" (Brown, 1988: 107; 125)—indeed of every citizen of every secular state.

Clement of Alexandria presented the more rationally balanced and stoic view. For Clement, sex demanded another *reason* beyond desire or even love. Within the bounds of Christian marriage and household, the reason for sexual activity was children. Clement offered sexual guidance for the "moderate Christian;" but he also presented marriage as the place where the ancient contest between reason and passion would be worked out rather than the more traditional banquet, tribunal, or "highly public deathbed." He thus made sexuality and marriage the center of a life of public stoic virtue. In this way, amid the radical voices for sexual renunciation, Clement's was "a faint image of divine providence" but one soon drowned out by the louder cries for the more extreme way. Still, voices like Clement's were necessary since the pagan conviction that Christians met only "in order to indulge in sexual promiscuity died hard" (Brown, 1988: 122–39; 140).

If Clement presented only a faint image of divine providence, Origen's was bolder with a stronger call to "be transformed" (Brown, 1988: 162; 160–77). The Platonism of Origin was applied to sexuality as a paradigmatic case of the diversity of matter and its shadowy reflection of an original and spiritual unity. Thus we ought to be discontent with our present state. The body was in service to the soul only as a reminder of our need for spiritual transformation. All were called to maintain in "themselves, the huge momentum of their spirit's longing for God." The body was fluid, capable of motion and transformation. Sexuality was part of a "short interlude" and our bodies were "poised on the edge of a trans-formation" (Brown, 1988: 166–68). Virginity was not a state removed from the world of social-exchange but a sign and symbol of the far more intensely sociable world of spirit—the divine and harmonious commu-nion. Sensuality was not to be repressed but transformed and "reawak-ened in the mystic's heart" (Brown, 1988: 171–73). As much as the need to radically reverse the state of the polis to a new life of freedom, what also was at stake in sexual renunciation was the sign of where to find the holy in the visible world (Brown, 1988: 176). Physical pleasure alone coarsened the true spiritual delight of the soul.[15] In an even bolder call than Origin's, the Manichees argued that more than merely coarsening our souls, consorting with our body was a way of deep imprisonment. Our bodies and spirits were in cosmic warfare and sexuality was a mighty force but one that could be totally transformed—even repressed and conquered—in the lives of the enlightened discipline of the elect (Brown, 1988: 190–209).

Perhaps the boldest claims of all came from "the desert fathers" of the Eastern empire. "The desert was a 'counterworld,' a place were an alternative 'city' could grow" (Brown, 1988: 217). Still, to interpret these monks as only negative dualists with a clear hatred of the body is to miss the overriding radicality of their theological and political proposal. In their strange and violent practices, the lives of individuals and of the body-politic—souls and bodies in general—were deeply implicated with each other. Transforming the one would lead to the transformation of the other. Within the practice of sexual renunciation, women, as they had been traditionally, were especially implicated in the dangers of the body as a "source of perpetual temptation to which the male body could be expected to respond instantly" (Brown, 1988: 237; 242). Always in danger of bondage to these dark powers of sin and women, "the virgin body of the monk was called to act as a landmark. Its untouched state spoke of a barrier between the Christian laity of the towns and villages—the *kosmikoi*, the men and women 'of the world,' who were most usually married persons—and the monks" (Brown, 1988: 243). Even where eastern churches were not under the influence of these desert defenders, assaults on the hegemony of the cities continued. Both Basil the Great and Gregory of Nyssa believed "that through a reformed social life of a monastic 'brotherhood,' individuals set free from the demands of a family-based, conventional society could create a Christian society in miniature beside the city" (Brown, 1988: 303). In his own rhetoric of sexual renunciation, John Chrysostom aimed "to rob the city of its most tenacious myth—the myth that its citizens had a duty to contribute to the continued glory of their native Antioch by marrying." On the contrary, "their bodies belonged to themselves, and no longer to the city." Contributing children to the city ought no longer to be the reason for marriage, rather young Christian women and men would marry, if they must, to control their urge to fornication, or concupiscence (Brown, 1988: 307–8). In Chrysostom, "the last of the great urban rhetors of the ancient world," the theopolitical rationale of the ancient writers took a major shift toward moralistic argument. As Brown indicates, toward the end of the fourth century many of the great ancient cities of the East were in decline, and most serious urban Christians strove to explain how the powers of the present age, now in a care-worn state, were to be related to the spirit-filled Christian body and its households (pp. 306; 305–38).

The final phase in our brief tour of the struggles of Christian antiquity to find acceptable norms of sexual life brings us to the Latin West, coming to ascendancy at the end of the fourth century. This period is closer in influence than time to our own remembrances, and as Brown says, the thought of its greatest figures, Ambrose, Jerome, and Augustine "still appear, for good and ill, to run in the bloodstreams of Western Europeans" (p. 338).

In Ambrose, we find a bishop who is preoccupied with the role of the Catholic Church in Roman society—with noble women, and nobleman catechumens who often postponed the radical demands of baptism because of the needs of public life and the teachings on sexual renunciation. Even as Ambrose was intimately involved in Roman life, he fought against any admixture of the clear boundaries between the Church and the polis. Surrender to the secular powers would be to grow soft, to create an "effeminate" Church (Brown, 1988: 347; 341–65). Paradoxically, at the same time the question of celibacy for male clergy came to the fore in a way unprecedented in the ancient world. "Never before had Roman public men been expected to appropriate, in this way, virtues usually delegated to women" (Brown, 1988: 359). The virginity and celibacy of consecrated women and men were for Ambrose signs of a clearly demarcated integrity for the Catholic Church in a hostile society.

More paradoxical still was Jerome, whose associations with highborn and intellectual women of Christian households did not prevent him, in his argument against Jovinian, to claim that not only were married couples not to be placed at the same level of hierarchy as consecrated virgins, but that all marriages were somewhat regrettable (Brown, 1988: 377). The shock to common sensibility of this rhetoric, both then and now, should not distract us from Jerome's deeper rationale. Jerome finally did not accept anything like Origen's spiritualization of sexuality and the body nor were the rewards of sexual renunciation to be considered immediate in terms of any individual and social transformation. Sexual differences of male and female would remain and so would our temptations and disorders: there was no nondifferentiated sexual state either in this life or the next. Heaven for Jerome was not a materially abstract state, but more like a Roman society purged of its impurities (see Brown, 1988: 377–84). With Jerome, we see a final turn in the rhetoric and practice of sexual renunciation in the ancient Christian world. While often intemperate in rhetoric, Jerome is neither overly moralistic, much less spiritualistic, about sexual concupiscence nor was he totally negating with respect to the value of life in the polis and the necessity for an ordered society for the Church—an apologetic challenge Augustine would take up with much more complexity and rigor. Perhaps because of the need for patronage and his own advancing age, Jerome, in later life, became more realistically balanced than some of his predecessors. Brown concludes:

> Jerome, for all of his fashionable misogyny and his sharp sense of sexual danger, would never for a moment have doubted that the minds of Paula or Marcella, and his other female allies and clients, did not have their full share of 'male' bone and muscle (p. 385).

Finally, the great, and often unjustly maligned, Augustine emerges in North Africa to cast an ambivalent shadow forward on Christian sexual morality well into the present age (see Brown, 1988: 387–427).[16] Augustine's long reflection on the nature of the human personality and the role of intellect and will amid the passions is grounded biographically in his thirteen-year relationship with a woman who bore his son, Adeodatus. His relationship was strictly monogamous and loyal—as Brown describes, a "fragile spark of *fides* in the topsy-turvey world of a young professor on the make." He enjoyed sleeping with this woman and came to value her friendship (p. 389). The fact that he came to view sexual experience as more and more ambivalent did not lead him to the radical ascetic denials of earlier writers. In fact, during this time, and for some time after in the history of the Church, concubinage itself was seen as morally ambivalent. Brown argues that a "strictly monogamous relationship with a concubine" was common in many public circles and even accepted as valid by some Christians. For them, the essential and finally not unimportant difference between a relationship of monogamous and faithful concubinage and marriage had more to do with the intention to bear legally legitimate offspring for status, inheritance, and the like than the quality of the relationship. "Augustine chose his companion because he loved her; and he slept with her because he loved to do so, and not so as to produce grandchildren for his mother or citizens of his home town" (p. 390). As he grew older, Augustine's own ambivalence about sex increased. Brown indicates informing experiences on the fringe of the Manichaean movement, and more importantly, after his conversion, a brush with Origen's "wild Platonism." The pleasures he had enjoyed seemed more shadowy compared with the spiritual joy of Christ and the wisdom of God. "A deep sense of sadness lingered with Augustine for the rest of his life. Sexual love remained, for him, a leaden echo of true delight" (Brown, 1988: 394).

Despite the conflicts he engaged as bishop of a church in North Africa, Augustine was not an alarmist. His church was not traditionally an ascetical one, and he was realistic about the needs for order in the empire for the work of Christian apologetics. The Donatist controversy threatened the unity of Church and empire, yet it was unsettling in other ways as well. Augustine found himself arguing for the right of the empire to force conformity through punishment upon the Donatists. More than ever before Augustine was implying not only a toleration of empire for the order of the Church, but a thought process that begin to view the church from a "point deep within the structures of the settled world" (Brown, 1988: 398–99). In this process Augustine signaled the beginning of the quest for the medieval synthesis. He was too nuanced a thinker to call for either a flight from or a total collapse of boundaries between Church and state; however, like a good many who took up his challenge of reflecting on the relationship between the *secular* and the *sacred*, in later life Augustine became melancholic about the prospects for a *Christian society*.

Upon this horizon of the mutual implication of Christianity and world, Augustine offered a radically different interpretation of Genesis than ascetic exegesis. Before the Fall, Adam and Eve had not been in an angelic state purified from the lures of the body and the flesh; rather they were physical human beings called to sociality, though still somewhat hierarchically arranged with male over female. Marriage and continence were both forms of human social concord and friendship, the one producing children, the other not. Sexual desire remained ambivalent, however, and to some degree suspicious, not finally because of its physicality as such, but because it mirrored something far deeper as the source of our original fall and continuing bondage to sin (Brown, 1988: 400–4).

Even though his brush with "wild Platonism" continued to have some effect in the disordering of human rationality by passionate orgasm, Augustine finally argued his sexual theology on the basis of the disordering of the will. "What remained a dark enigma to him was the distortion of the will of those who now made up society. The twisted human will, not marriage, not even the sexual drive, was what was new in the human condition after Adam's Fall" (Brown, 1988: 404). Like death, sexual sensation mocked the orderly will and was the most proximate sign of something else—our primal dislocation or *discordiosum malum* (Brown, 1988: 408). Thus it was not strange that some of his most polemical debates were over understandings of the place of the human will in the Christian dispensation. Both Pelagius and Julian of Eclanum were far more sanguine about the human will, and in Augustine's mind, dangerously mistaken. As manifested clearly in the power of sexual passion, our wills are in bondage to sin. The attitude of Julian that sexual desire was easily amenable to the "salutary ointment of the Gospels," or Pelagius' "robust" and moralistic faith in the power of the will to guide us to virtue (Brown, 1988: 413), challenged Augustine to engage more in crucial debates about the foundations of faith itself and the relationship between grace and sin than to arguments about sexual ethics. Augustine was convinced that neither Pelagius nor Julian had looked deep enough into the human psyche/soul, and thus their advice was dangerous. While not the central subject of his argument, Augustine held that sexual desire not only manifested our disordered will, but in many ways was a major mode of its perpetuation—it was our *poena reciproca* (Brown, 1988: 416). In engaging in such a long polemic against anthropological naivete, Augustine would become more shrill in his warnings about sex. Nonetheless, our *concupiscentia carnis* had more to do with the disordering of our souls than with our bodies. Finally, however, as Brown indicates, Augustine came to understand that "sexual desire was no more tainted with this tragic, faceless concupiscence than was any other form of human activity," and, in his later years, to see more clearly the other, even more serious, signs of "ignorance, arrogance, malice and violence" as indicative of our fall from orderly grace. Still, sex would continue to be "a disturbingly ageless adversary" (pp. 418; 416; 419).

In fact, the historical ages themselves had become adversaries for Augustine. His later preaching and writing became more somber. The body could not be fled—either his own or the body of culture and state— and both were disintegrating before his eyes. His Christian humanism remained with no radical ascetic nor aesthetic posture of release. Nor did he retreat into sectarianism; but he did become melancholic, not so much for times past but for a time yet to come, though the distance was great and our sight dim. If, in a Platonic sense, one can be nostalgic about the future, this was Augustine's state of faith and hope. "Only in a city at the end of time, and in no city of the Western Empire in its last century, would the ache of discord, so faithfully mirrored in the flesh by sexuality, give way to a *pax plena*, to a fullness of peace" (Brown, 1988: 427).[17]

With Augustine, Brown ends his study of sexual renunciation in the early Church. The debates of the early Christian rhetors and teachers over the meaning, place and role of sexuality were varied and heated.

They were also complex and highly sophisticated. From them, even when they argued radical sexual renunciation, we learn that, in one way or another, our sexuality and sexual behavior is deeply implicated in our individual and social lives; that it has social and political ramifications; and that it indicates important things about our faith and our hope for the future. Their debates also tell us that what we now think of rather unambiguously as the Church's traditional norm of marriage was born more toward the middle and end of the fourth century than in the biblical or early Patristic worlds, and comparing their debates with "the rest of the story" of Christian marriage, that this norm had a long way to go to gain maturity and staying power.

In this study we cannot trace the continuing journey of the norm of marriage much further into its maturity and in some significant ways its decline. James A. Brundage's *Law, Sex and Christian Society in Medieval Europe* (1987) is another important guide through the development of the penitential, legal, and canonical codes of marriage and sexual morality of early and late medieval Europe to the sixteenth-century reformation.[18] During these often turbulent times we also find shifts in the shape and status of marriage and family life until the beginning of the tenth century when "Churchmen had reached agreement...that only married persons should have sex and that they should do so primarily in order to conceive children" (Brundage, 1987: 173). Yet, a thorough going theological, moral, and legal rationale was still needed for marriage and the important *Decretum* of Gratian (circa 1140) labored to provide it (Brundage, 1987: 234; 229–55). Was marriage legitimately and canonically rooted in consent alone or was physical consummation necessary? While stressing consent, Gratian, in effect, argued for both, and thus marriage *ratum et consummatum* could not be dissolved by the Church, whereas, on principle, a merely ratified—*ratum non consummatum*—or consensual marriage could be rendered null (Brundage, 1987: 235–36 and Schillebeeckx, 1965: 293). Even more importantly, and against prevailing social realities that he accepted overall, in this specific instance, Gratian also argued for the complete equality of women with respect to sexual rights within married life and before the law, especially where sexual crimes were concerned, including adultery (Brundage, 1987: 255). However, even in the "twelfth century of love," the prevailing biology and anthropology of sexual inequality between men and women among the decretists still had serious negative effects (Brundage, 1987: 324). By and large, the canonists were attempting to free marriages from "the control of parents, families and feudal overlords and to place the choice of marriage partners under the exclusive control of the parties themselves" making marriage "easier to contract and more difficult to dissolve." By the beginning of the thirteenth century couples generally engaged in marriages of free consent, and by mid-century Western "churchmen" had attained some degree of consensus concerning goals and judicial procedures (Brundage, 1987: 332–33; 414; 485).

Brundage summarizes that the period between the "black death to the Reformation (1348–1517)" saw little change and no major alterations in the Church's sexual policy until the sixteenth century, though social changes were challenging the consensus (pp. 487–550). The reformers generally argued against the inclusion of marriage as a sacrament and undercut the Church's overt canonical authority over it. Nonetheless, much of the framework (or at least substantive intention) of medieval sex law remained intact and in force even to modern times (Brundage, 550), especially the central role and normative status of marriage.

Eric Fuch's *Sexual Desire and Love* (1983) presents a good study of the similarities and differences of the reformers' views in comparison with the dominant Catholic positions of the medieval church. By and large, by wrenching marriage away from the canonical control of the Church, the reformers both recognized and spoke for the relation of marriage to growing middle-class life (see E. Fuchs, 1983: 136). Sexual renunciation as a "higher" Christian way of life had come to an end. Now it was marriage that was the sign of a stable Christian/secular order—an ordinance of God's creation itself—rather than sexual renunciation being the sign of the destruction of the state and the rise of a new Christian order. This reassertion of a more positive implication of marriage into middle-class life and secular order was much like the claims for marriage in much of secular antiquity that the radical Christian treatises on sexual renunciation had rejected. On this point, the reformers had not fled from pagan and secular "corruption" and returned to "original Christianity" as much as they might have thought. Fuchs summarizes:

> Finally restored to the created order, marriage became a matter of moral and social responsibility. What is lost as to the aspect of the sacred mystery is regained in the awareness of what is relevant on the human moral and social level. It seems certain that the countries influenced by the Reformation were the first to attempt basing a social order on the family as the primary nucleus of all social life (p. 146).

Paradoxically, however, in taking marriage away from the Church's canonical regulation, Protestant pastors reinserted themselves into the process in ways that Catholic clergy had not.

The direction of the evolution of the religious ceremony was exactly inverse in the two faiths. The Catholic priest was deprived of active intervention given to him by custom (to now become only a witness to the marriage). With the Protestants, the evolution developed logically and resulted in marriage being created only through the religious ceremony and the preponderant action of the pastor (François Wendel, in E. Fuchs, 1983: 147).

With the publication of the decree *Tametsi* (1563) of the Council of Trent, the Roman Church of the Counter Reformation reset its course for the canonical and moral theological regulation of marriage well into the modern era. The major concern of Trent was with the so-called clandestine marriages—those without record or protection, especially for women and children. After the promulgation of *Tametsi*, a priest and two witnesses were required for valid marriage.[19] Clerical celibacy was also hotly debated—"As the Bavarian representative put it: 'chaste marriage would be preferable to sullied celibacy'"—but no change was forthcoming and old punitive canons were reinstated (see Brundage, 1987: 568; 551–75). As John Mahoney (1989) makes clear, it was at this time too that a significant ambivalence occurred in the meaning of the scope of Trent's teaching on "moral matters," one that was to have major repercussions for interpreting the nineteenth-century decree of papal infallibility with respect to "faith and morals," and the role of the papal magisterium in the current day. What was unclear was Trent's use of the Latin terms *mos* (usually translated as "practice" or "custom"), and the plural, *mores* (usually translated as "morals"). Did such terms have a generally religious—referring to sacramental and devotional practices— or a specifically moral referent; or if both, which was operative in any particular use? What in fact did Trent mean when it claimed its authority to remove abuses and correct *morals*? What was the status of the authority of the magisterium over "faith and morals," especially with respect to dissenting opinion and the wisdom of the faithful? In all contexts, were they speaking of what we ordinarily understand as *morality*, or were they also, at times, talking more about customs and religious practices (Mahoney, 1989: 120–23)? In the pertinent decrees, Mahoney goes on to indicate that if *mores* referred in all cases also to *morals*, it was strange that Trent appealed to tradition and not to scripture; whereas such an appeal to tradition made sense as the most proximate criteria for judging religious custom and practice. Furthermore, the major debates with Protestantism were not over the morality of sexual practice even when Protestants pointed out abuses of Catholic clergy, but

rather over doctrine and religious practices broadly understood. Thus
Mahoney concludes, it might be more accurate to identify the agenda of
Trent "not as 'faith and morals' but, in the phrase used by both Cardinal
Campeggio and the Diet of Augsburg, as 'faith and religion'" (pp. 131–
32). This leaves us with the question of whether the magisterium of the
Roman Church has always had as much certainty as it now claims about
whether it speaks with the same authority on moral questions as it does
on doctrinal matters and religious practices. Few envision in the foreseeable future an "infallible" papal pronouncement on moral matters nor is
one even conceivable by many theologians.[20] What we now have in the
increasing hegemony of the Roman magisterium over even the traditional teaching authority of theologians as well as over the *consensus
fidelium*, especially in sexual matters, is, in Charles Curran's phrase, more
of a "creeping infallibility." (Noted in Gustafson: 1978: 133. See also
Mahoney, 1989: 164–74).[21]

### The Values and Goods of Marriage

This brief historical survey has indicated that the rise of marriage
to its normative status in the Church has neither been totally continuous
nor the product of a singular and clear memory. In learning even these
few lessons of our history, we can also see discontinuity, forgetfulness,
and, more importantly perhaps, selective memory. For a norm to be both
effective and faithful, however, it is not necessary to find total continuity
or singular and consistent memory. What finally counts is how the
Church remembers and understands marriage in light of the entire scope
of Christian history and how this norm presently functions. Although I
have addressed part of the substantive history of marriage, I have not
tried to engage its complete history nor have I made much use of important nonecclesiastical resources. Much more interdisciplinary research is
necessary. Nor have I intended to engage a full theology of sex and
marriage that would frame the reasons why the Church has come to
depend on this norm to disclose the faith-informed values that are to
orient normatively our sexual lives. Though I will make no claims for an
exhaustive list, I will now discuss what I take to be basic value sets
disclosed, designated, and modeled by functionally successful marriages
and advance the argument that marriage remains our best prospect for
normative guidance. Amid the radical changes in sociocultural life, the
description and state of these substantive values is also an essential part
of the Church's ongoing discussion of sexual morality.

To speak so pragmatically of the *function* of marriage is still not to
say that the Church can merely *choose* its norms. Rather heterosexual

marriage *became* normative because over time it came to symbolically embody and metaphorically disclose sets of values that identified Christian moral character in the dimension of sexual experience—became in fact a normative model. Even with this specific function, the values disclosed by marriage are not limited to the guidance of sexual behavior alone. It would be a mistake to think that there is a unique morality of sex. Rather marriage has become one model of virtue among many wherein we see how to engage in responsible human relations in general, bringing values to social realization as goods. Thus ethical norms serve an effective historical function with respect to the disclosure of values within particular dimensions of our lives and for the foundation of character in general. The *function* of ethical norms ought to be understood under this sort of *effective sacramental pragmatism*. Still, as a final overture to the lessons of our history, we must keep in mind that in coming to its present state, marriage as a norm had a somewhat curious start in the Church, and by no means was it a head start.

In *Human Sexuality: New Directions in American Catholic Thought* (1977), Anthony Kosnik, et al., argue "that it is appropriate to ask whether specific sexual behavior realizes certain values conducive to creative growth and integration of the human person." The value-sets that they find "particularly significant" in the order of their listing are: *Self-Liberating; Other-Enriching; Honest; Faithful; Socially Responsible; Life-Serving;* and *Joyous* (pp. 92; 92–95). These authors conclude that

> when such values prevail, one can be reasonably sure that the sexual behavior that has brought them forth is wholesome and moral. On the contrary, where sexual conduct becomes personally frustrating and self-destructive, manipulative and enslaving of others, deceitful and dishonest, inconsistent and unstable, indiscriminate and promiscuous, irresponsible and non-life-serving, burdensome and repugnant, ungenerous and un-Christlike, it is clear that God's ingenious gift for calling us to creative and integrative growth has been seriously abused (Kosnik, 1977: 95).

I have no particular argument with the substantive values listed by these authors, but I do suggest that in beginning with the value set of "self-liberating" they may imply more of a phenomenological priority of the "self" in moral experience than I do in my orientation toward *alterity*—though it is true that *self-liberating* can be presented as the first value-set precisely in order to engage another lovingly, constructively, and freely. They are rightly concerned with overcoming the notion of the "total giving" and the attendant "loss of self" by one of the partners—

most often the woman—in Christian marriages. Since I start from the other direction, so to speak, I will be challenged in my account to overcome the false notion that "Christian love" entails the sacrifice of the self. In their descriptions of the meaning of each value, there is also a tendency to over idealization and perfectionism. In their discussion of fidelity, they note that "in marriage, this fidelity is called to a perfection unmatched at any other level" of relationship even though they indicate that any "crippling possessiveness" ought to be avoided. Overall these authors speak in superlatives insofar as the value-ideals are described in their fullness. This may be understandable in the speech of a Church whose intention and rhetoric is often cast in terms of "Christ-like" character formation. However, when the analytic point of the necessary dialectical relation between the *ideal* and the *real* in ethical norms is not made thematic, we run this risk of an abstract perfectionism. The most important point these authors make is that debate oriented toward values rather than "absolute categorizations of isolated, individual sexual actions" arrives "at a much more sensitive and responsible method of evaluating the morality of sexual patterns and expressions" (Kosnik, 1977: 92–93; 95). The only remaining thing to keep in mind, and these authors do not deny it, is that it is through the mediation of virtue that the ordinary and regular course of values is advanced toward their effective realization as goods. While values are primarily orienting, virtues and goods must also be part of the foundations of adequate moral discourse.

In taking up the task of describing the values and goods at stake in the norm of marriage, three patterns of a morally virtuous sexual life can be discerned: *love, fidelity, and creativity.* As patterned-sets of virtue, love, fidelity, and creativity are habits of interpretation and response that set an array of respectively informing values on their course toward the good. At the present time in the life of the Church, and relative to any other alternative, these patterns of virtuous life and the journeys of value to good they center are most effectively modeled by the norm of marriage.

Love

Sexual behavior in the Christian churches is morally evaluated first under the virtue and value-set of *love.*[22] "Love"is not a univocal term but indicates a pattern of various valued relationships. Paul Tillich discusses the classical Greek denominations of love as *epithymia, eros, philia,* and *agape,* with *agape* appearing most consistently in the literature of the Christian Testament. For Tillich, all love involves the dynamics of completion, reunion, and relationship.

While distinct in manifestation and function, none of the expressions of love can be conflated or counterpoised with the other in mutually exclusive ways: all are related. *Epithymia* encompasses our physical states of desire, including sexual. We seek satisfaction and pleasure not necessarily for pleasure's sake, but for our own "natural/biological" fulfillment (Tillich, 1960: 18–34). *Eros* is not the same as *epithymia*—nor is it the opposite of *agape* (See Nygren, 1953). In *eros* we seek reunion with that from which we have been separated. If *epithymia* is our "drive" to fulfill and satisfy a physical force or urge, *eros* is a dynamic toward reunion of something from which, in classical Greek thought, we have been separated. *Eros* implies an original unity now metaphorically interpreted as something with which we ought to be united. This "knowledge" of an original unity leads *eros* to a passionate flight toward reunion. As Tillich indicates, *eros* has a "transpersonal quality" that is complemented by *philia*. In *philia* our separation "from which" becomes a separation "from whom." *Philia* introduces the interpersonal dimension to the experience of love. As love among friends, *philia* is love among equals. Here Tillich warns against an overly narrow understanding of equality in terms of only esoteric or "in-groups" (1960: 31–32). Finally *agape* continues the interpersonal quality of *philia* to the point of decentering the necessary self-orientation of the other dimensions of love and upholds the principle of radically "other-regarding" love. In *agape*, *philia* is perfected and all others are equals of the self and because of this can be rendered prior. Both *philia* and *agape* disclose that to be adequately interpersonal, love must be free. Even though we ought not think of *epithymia* or *eros* as over-powering *daimons* ("fated spirits"),[23] there is a sense of transpersonal and ontological determinism in their dynamics. However while obliging, the interpersonality of *eros* and *agape* demand freedom more directly. We cannot force friendship nor the *other* to become prior in our lives, but rather they emerge as *gifts* of successful interpersonal relationships.

While Tillich does not use terms such as "decentering" and "alterity," he is clear that *agape* challenges and "cuts into" love, so to speak, insofar as it "enters from another dimension into the whole of life and into all qualities of love." This "other dimension"—or dimension of the *Other*—is the divine ground of all life: the *Other* who calls us forth (1960: 33). In *agape*, our focus on the other does not imply "giving up" the self, but rather an entrance into the dynamic of interpersonal relations at their depth. Initially, the other has priority in *agape* because in the context of a necessary and risky faith, the other decenters the false personality of self-centeredness and brings us "out of ourselves" toward a new and more complete identity in relationship.[24] In this context, Tillich suggests "it is hard to speak meaningfully of self-love…(for)…within the unity of self-consciousness there is no real separation, comparable to the separation of a self-centered being from all other beings" (1960: 33). Tillich is at some risk in understanding even "other-regarding love" for the purpose of our own self-fulfillment—i.e., we regard the other as prior and necessary so that we can come to our own identity. While it is true that maturity in *agape* suggests a loving regard for the other for his or her own sake, and not as a mirror image of the self or for some other self-service, the self must still be implicated lest the other or "stranger" become only alien to us.[25] *Agape* does not rule out the experience of "self-acceptance"—"the affirmation of oneself in the way in which one is affirmed by God." Thus "self love is a metaphor and it should not be treated as a concept" (Tillich, 1976: 34).

It is not very difficult to apply these descriptions of love to the values and goods of a responsible life in general and to see how they can be modeled in marriage specifically. Rather than a sinister and overpowering force, marriage models a virtuous and humane frame for sexual desire, disclosing it as a value and offering relatively stable ways for effecting sex as a good in our lives. At the same time sexual desire is more than physical (*epithymia*) and also signals a sense of noncompletion and fracture—a *loss* of value—at the core of our personality and the need for reunion. In *eros* we enter upon a passion-filled search for what we have "lost." Such a search develops into a more interpersonal desire to find friendly companionship with an equal (*philia*)—another person *like* us but who is also *different* from us. This difference is made a priority in the other-regarding quality of *agape*. The *other* who finally calls us forth to a new relationship of character-identity, becomes, in this sense, prior. In discriminating love in all of its variety, we stand in less risk of perfectionism insofar as we become less single-minded about any one facet or dimension of love that must be attained in its fullness. Nor need we suggest any hierarchy. Marriage requires *epithymia* as much as *philia*; *eros* as much as *agape*.

Tillich is somewhat ambivalent on this point. He does not describe *agape* as "the last and highest form of love" (1960: 33) and intends no structural hierarchy, but this implication is sometimes present and often interpreted as such in Christian discussions of love. Given the originating biblical context of *agape*, such an implication is hard to avoid. Still, because of our always less-than-ideal experiences of marriage, it is the unique function of our figurative moral imagination of love to remind us of the inevitable distance we all experience between the ideal and the real, and that in this space the multiple manifestations of love appear to us nonhierarchically.

Against the rhetoric of our own origins, marriage is now a better model for even agapaic love than either consecrated virginity or celibacy, though some discussion in the Church—for example, required clerical celibacy—still implies the contrary. The concrete and material reality of a single other in marriage focuses our moral vision in a more intense way than models of consecrated virginity or dedicated celibacy. First we are loved and learn to love in the specific, then in general. This may partially account for why marriage has come to the fore as the Church's normative model. Virginity and celibacy still have their place in Christian life, but they occupy their position because of functional dedication to specific needs of the body of faith rather than because they model the "highest" form of love over all.

That the *specific other* needs to be different from ourselves is also epitomized and modeled most clearly and visually in heterosexual marriage. We should not make either too much or too little of this point. To say that heterosexuality is the only way to model the difference *agape* demands is to say too much. Not to recognize that heterosexual relations visualize such difference more clearly than homosexual relations is to say too little. What is at stake is where we look for the clearest normative model of the values necessary to effectively guide our sexual lives. As I have argued throughout, such a model does not automatically entail a specific heterosexual rule of life for all Christians.

Fidelity

The second pattern of virtue that immediately flows from love is *fidelity*. Fidelity comes from love insofar as the drive to reunion that most generally characterizes love creates obliging bonds with another. In relative degrees of intensity all love is decentering, turning us away from self toward an other, and, in this sense, self-transcending and self-liberating. Still the self must remain implicated in the dynamics of love. In being powerfully decentered by the experience of love, we experience strange dislocations but we do not become alien to the experience. In order for the self and the other to remain implicated in the experience of love, the bond of fidelity is necessary—being tied to the other in a faithful communion.

Such bonds of fidelity also require *constancy, honesty* and *singularity*. Constancy is required for faithful love because coming to reunion with one different from the self requires time and effort. The journeys to loving reunion make no promises of being easy or over only familiar terrain. Familiarity is not only what we seek but also difference and new discovery. Such journeys are difficult, engaged only over time, and never accomplished in any given instance. Only the naive envision love without constancy. Now being fully implicated in the fabric of culture and Church, the norm of marriage models faithful constancy for all loving sexual relationships.

Fidelity also requires honesty. Our journeys toward the other are too difficult and fraught with too much danger to allow for anything short of truthfulness and honesty. I have already suggested a difference between brutal frankness and truthfulness. Truthfulness pertains to our posture of openness and honesty toward the other, avoiding "pretense, evasion and deception" (Kosnik: 92–93). Honesty suggests a posture of openness within all the dimensions of love: openness about our physical needs and desires as well as our passions and dreams. Under the dimension of *philia*, friends remain friends only when they are honest with each other. Certainly sexual complexities in general, as well as the specific burdens of modern marriage, make honest friendship often the most difficult moral pattern for heterosexual marriage to model. Modern culture has not been very successful at modeling friendship at all and between the sexes in particular, with marriage faring no better. Often our best and most open and honest friendships are with those of the same sex. It also may very well be that this moral pattern of responsible life is now being effectively modeled as often by homosexual relations as heterosexual ones. At the same time, heterosexual marriage still holds great potential for such modeling even as it now fails so abysmally. If honest and equal relationships can be modeled even across significant gender differences and barriers, then the values and goods of honest friendship in modern societies will have much greater prospects for being rehabilitated. It is hard to calculate the enormity of the loss to our moral sensibilities and character because of the erosion of friendly relations in private and public life.

Fidelity and honesty in our sexual relations raise the important question of singularity. In terms of sexual relations, must we be monogamous? It certainly is not necessarily the case that we must have only one "best friend," or only one person with whom we can be "totally" honest. Though often, if we are fortunate, this is the case. Still, I argue for singularity and monogamy in our sexual relations. In order to make this point, we will have to discern what is unique about sexual relations and marriage—different in fact from other forms of human relationship where singularity is not as clear or even an appropriate requirement. Here, perhaps more than any other place, we must broach the theological dimensions of sexuality and marriage. In sum, our argument must be framed upon the horizon of the biblical commitments to monotheism.

Like everything else historical, Judaism and Christianity developed in their understanding of the relationship of singular and monogamous sexual behavior and their commitments to one God. Throughout biblical texts, however, images and mythic narratives were drawn to relate such a God intimately to the people. The constant thematic in biblical religion is that God is historically and intimately present among the people in all dimensions of their lives. Thus, it was not a great strain of imagination to configure such faith commitments also in terms of the intimate relations of sexual activity. As we are joined to each other sexually, God is joined to us; and as God is joined to us, so we are joined to each other. Such a configuration of images also helped to bring sexual expression within the orbit and norms of the particular faith community and culture. Even as sexuality was made sacred according to the religion of a particular community, it was desacralized from its manifestations in other religious beliefs and practices considered unfaithful and profane in terms of the new monotheism. In associating sexual practice with "their own" and only one God, the people of the Bible brought it into their orbit of religious meaning and truth, implicating it in their life and culture. Gradually the implication of biblical monotheism created an entailment of singularity and monogamy in sexual relations. As they were to relate religiously in covenant to only one God, and one God alone, so were they to relate to one other person sexually. In the Christian dispensation similar images were configured in interrelating marriage and the sexual union with Christ's love and union with the Church (*Ephesians*, 5). Augustine, like so many others, argued precisely that the sacramental "vinculum," or bond of marriage, was singular and indissoluble as a sacred obligation and sacred sign because it referred and pointed to "the mystery of the unity existing between Christ and his Church" (Schillebeeckx: 1965: 281–83). There is one God; there is one Christ and Church; there is one *other* in marriage.

Certainly the values of singularity and monogamy have been easier to proclaim than accomplish (see Brundage). The Church struggled for ages over the question of polygamous concubinage. Some forms of concubinage were tolerated and even accepted at times without formal sanctions under the aegis of other dedicated relationships. The Catholic Church's own requirements for what was necessary for a valid marriage remained in great flux until the late middle ages before diversifying again in the Reformation and refocused in the Counter-Reformation. Nonetheless the ideals of monogamy and singularity are and have been the broadest theological and moral frames among all the traditions for Christian teaching on marriage. One could add—with less confidence—psychological and sociological factors that suggest more likelihood of depth of feeling, constancy, and at least putative honesty in singular rather than plural or multiple relations, though these factors too are more ideals that data in modern life. Be that as it may, the fact remains that in the Christian theological relation of sexual activity and intimate mono-theism—*God with us*—the Church now intends to model in marriage the values of singular and monogamous sexual relations as effective guid-ance for all forms of sexual activity. This rules out on a prima-facie basis promiscuity, adultery, and all forms of "open marriage" relationships for Christians whether agreed to by the couple(s) involved or not.[26]

In terms of monogamy and singularity, the question of the moral possibility of divorce needs only a brief treatment here. If we expand the phenomenon of marriage from a *sign* of and pointer to the unity existing between God and God's people and Christ and the Church to that of an effective sacramental *symbol*, we can argue that *failed marriages*—that is, those that have failed without reasonable prospect of recovery to effect singular, faithful, and honest love—have ceased to be normative. Ceasing to be *good* in the lives of the persons involved and in the Church at large, the sacramentally effective place of this marriage and its obliga-tions of service to the wider body of the faithful have also ceased. These marriages are no longer regulative in the lives of these people nor are they performing the work of a norm in the Church. Responsible divorce, while never engaged lightly and always within the dimensions of loss and failure, is always a recognition of what has already happened.

Even though I have said that the theological and moral possibility of divorce demands brief treatment in argument here, the debilitating effects of divorce is a major concern. All juridical procedures of denomi-nations with respect to marriage and divorce ought to be oriented toward responding constructively to this most destabilizing element of Christian sexual morality. If the Church is depending on marriage to model morally responsible sexual behavior over all, then neither puni-tive nor only perfunctory procedures with respect to divorce are called for. Rather the denominations must find ways to help counter the growing instability of the norm and institution of marriage. If the Church's discourse is constantly deflected to a single-minded concentra-tion on the violations of Christian sexual standards among nonmarried and homosexual Christians, the attention that marriage deserves and needs will not be forthcoming. Without going any further along this tack, such obsessive conversations most often disclose personal and institutional fears and humiliations now projected onto others. If our standards of sexual morality are deteriorating, it is finally because our marriages are deteriorating.

Creativity

The third and final pattern of values and virtue modeled by heterosexual marriage is *creativity*. I choose the term *creativity* precisely because of its generality and its ability to include more values and goods than the more specific, but often used, *generativity*. For example, creativity frames better the values of "social responsibility" mentioned by Kosnik (1977: 93–94). As these authors indicate, marriage is not only ordained for the couple or family involved but also, as an act of the Church, for the wider community as well. In bringing values to effective realizations as goods in the wider community, marriage models virtues of social responsibility. Nonetheless, the sexual realities of marriage require that we find the proper relation of creativity and generativity. These value relations are often disregarded or confused in the Church's contemporary conversations on sex.

If we connect creativity and generativity with the value of life, we find the difference and possible relations between them. Creativity implies that our sexual relations must be "life-serving" (Kosnik, 1977: 94). This is to say that all of our sexual relations share a unique burden of promoting life under the dimension of creativity. Our experiences of sexual pleasure, erotic desires for reunion, and communions of friendship and other-regarding love all frame obligations to create forms and structures of life wherein others can come to similar and vital participation. In this same vein, our obligations of creativity are to be most especially engaged for those who suffer from unjust exclusions from life's pleasures and joys, passions, and communions—others who have become not prior in social intercourse but the least and most marginal. In this way sexual love creatively serves justice.

Still, the work of creativity has its limits. The unique obligation of our sexuality and sexual behavior to be informed by creativity is embodied most clearly and intensely in the specificity of generativity than in the generality of creativity. Many areas of life stand under general obligations of creativity; but only sexual relations frame adequately the values of generativity.[27] Because of the association of sex and biological life, our sexual relations can become central and informing metaphors and symbols for the enhancement of life overall. Because we know that human life is generated sexually, sexual generativity becomes an epitome for an entire array of life-serving values. It is because the sex act is generative that it can become a metaphoric and symbolic figuration of the values and goods of life itself. In sum, it is creativity that gives us the general dimension we need for guidance overall and generativity that gives us the concrete specificity. Confusing this role and relationship can lead to certain difficulties.

If we argue that the generality of creativity is all that is necessary for the disclosure and effectuation of values that promote life, both individually and in the public realm, we run the risk of abstraction. There are many forms of creativity, and we have no way of knowing what is unique about the life-serving creativity of sexuality. If we make the specificity of generativity alone obligatory, we gain the concrete relation to sexuality, but we lose the breadth necessary for disclosing other values of creativity than the physical production of new life. We narrow our sexuality to its traditional and relatively singular association with children and lose the gains we have made in emphasizing creative intimacy, communication, and friendship so necessary for responsible sexual behavior. What is important here is that we keep clear the relationship between creativity and generativity, though we may start with either pattern-set. Creativity is the normative umbrella so to speak—the widest range of a value-set that guides the virtuous achievement of an entire range of goods. Sexual activity is bound by obligations of creativity whether or not children are intended or biologically possible. Nonetheless, it is in the specific generation of children that we can *visualize* most intensely and clearly the concrete manifestation of what *new life* means—its epitome, root metaphor, and designating symbol. To make generativity the overarching value-set is to narrow the range of values disclosed. To leave creativity as the only value set at stake in sexual relations is to run the risk of abstracting generality.

We can say, for example, that marriage is a form of *creative communication* without much further concrete specification. On the one hand, if "communication" is used as metonymy, we speak more reductively and imply that all that is needed for responsible sexual expression is honesty and sincerity. If, on the other hand, "communication" is used as a synecdoche, especially when qualified by "dialogic," we speak expansively and can gain a fruitful and apt figure of speech for framing the entire range of values, virtues, and goods at stake in responsible sexual behavior. Surely we learn much about love when we speak of it as an intimate and deep dialogue between free and equal moral persons. We learn, more specifically, that under dialogue's "asymmetrical symmetry"—of speaking *and* listening—an agapaic communion is one where there is a reciprocating exchange of priorities of others. We learn, as well, that sexual intimacy is not only a form of "touching each other," but in a significant way, where we learn much about "staying in touch" with each other.

To be sure, sex is a form of deep human communication, but its unique physicality disclosed by generativity still suggests that sexual communication cannot simply be conflated with all other forms of communication. While phenomenologically related to the praxis of dialogic speech in general, physical sexual communication has unique dimensions. Communication remains a rich image for sexual ethics, but it also remains limited by its generality. Whatever else of a positive nature is disclosed in all figures of speech of sex as *communication*, there remains a strong tendency to over-generalize and lose the unique phenomenological and physical context of sexual communication upheld in generativity.[28]

If we keep the proper relationship between the values of creativity and generativity in mind, we need not argue that birth control, or the inability of either heterosexual or homosexual couples to "generate" children, or even for couples to decide not to have children at all necessarily violates the value of creativity in marriage or sexual practice in general. Even though children are intrinsic to the normative model of marriage and sexuality, our obligations of creativity are broader than only having children, and, as I have indicated in my analysis of an ethical norm, those who do not have children are not to be understood as "abnormal." Most often in terms of nonmarital relations, and combined with obligations for "safe-sex" practices in general, creativity obliges us morally to take appropriate precautions not to generate new life. On the other hand, to never consider the core dimension of generativity at all, and to suggest that creativity in all of its generality is enough to guide our sexual relations in the context of values, is to remain aloof from the specific physicality of sexuality itself. Whatever else sex is about, it is also about bringing children into the world. We serve no particular and constructive moral purpose by deflecting our arguments and our behavior from this reality.

Combining both value-sets of creativity and generativity, heterosexual marriage is still the best model for morally informing our sexual behavior. Once again, however, we find serious strains. When, against our own deep Christian memory, the Church's teaching on marriage remains insulated from social and political realities, the promise of creativity is stifled. Christian marriage is also implicated in the life of its own cultures and societies, and, to remain creative, cannot be separated from them. At the same time, when we fail to take adequate notice of generativity and turn against the value of children in our lives and in the lives of our society, allowing them to linger in tragic conditions of impoverishment, abandonment, and abuse, we cannot claim that our sexual activity or our marriages are adequately moral. Whether we ourselves engage in the generation of children or not, their value is inestimable and our treatment and policies on their behalf is a true gauge of the moral state and future of any culture, society, and community.[29]

## Nonmarital Sexual Expression

If heterosexual marriage is the Church's centering norm for modeling and guiding all forms of sexual behavior, then there is some rationale for the term "nonmarital." Again, however, this does not imply that those who are not married are "abnormal" in any social-psychological sense or that their sexual behavior is always beyond or outside of the norm in any moral sense. I have argued that norms disclose and designate a set of values for the purpose of effectively demonstrating them as goods amid the various and plural conditions of social life. Such processes must be modeled visually and practically in culture and society for these functions to be performed. I have suggested that despite serious fractures and fissures, marriage is still performing these tasks, and it is the hope of the Church that it can continue to do so. Consequently, we should not think of the norm of marriage as a scale model, or schematic analogue, or only noetically theoretic, but rather as a metaphoric and symbolic re-presentation of values that have the continuing possibility and sometimes the reality of functioning as an effective sacrament. As such, marriage is a concrete *configuration* of values and goods visible to the community of faith. In this sense the norm of marriage remains figurative rather than literal: no single couple or the entire range of married couples embody the norm itself. Rather they participate in a sacrament that, when functioning effectively as a model of virtue, gives the community a glimpse of the ideal values necessary for the guidance of responsible sexual life and demonstrates them as goods.[30] In this figurative and tropological sense, any given marriage, both historically and in the present day, stands under "the sign of the Analogue." Particular marriages bring only a familiarity of necessary values and goods to the life of the Church rather than a literal and identifying embodiment. All particular marriages operate in the dialectical space of analogy: they reveal, at the same time, both their closeness and distance from the ideals of the norm. Even as they more directly engage in the obligation of modeling the normative values of responsible sexual behavior for all, married Christians are themselves always "off the norm." Only in this context ought we to discuss the moral situation of the unmarried.

Single Heterosexual Christians

Single heterosexual Christians can fall under a number of categories and places in life. Some are desirous of being married, and when it comes to sexual expression and behavior we often speak of "premarital sex." Some have been married and are either divorced or their spouses have died. Others decide not to marry or for some other reason do not marry. Some unmarried Christians are sexually active, some are not for any given time or overall. And while in any complete discussion of these states of life an entire array of unique and specific issues would need to be raised, I will suggest a broad overture to discerning responsibility in sexual behavior for single heterosexual Christians. I will raise only those specific issues—for example, age and maturity—that have a direct impact on this broad frame. I emphasize in this discussion those Christians for whom the question of morally responsible sexual behavior has occupied their minds and been pressed upon their character. At the end of this discussion, I will make comments about those who have either chosen or accepted a state of sexual celibacy in a religious context.

Applying my arguments about the normative status of marriage to the situation of unmarried Christians is not difficult. In principle, for responsible sexual behavior the values disclosed by marriage need to be present as goods in their lives. Evaluating substantive claims of the possibility and reality of these values and goods in specific relationships is more complex, both for the couple involved and for those whom they seek for advice and guidance.

First, all will want to know how the value-sets of love, fidelity, and creativity can be effectively mediated as goods in nonmarital relationships. In short, we need to describe a habit of virtue for the unmarried Christian who is challenged with the question of responsible sexual behavior. The same discriminations of love we discussed with respect to marriage must be applied here. Therefore such relationships, framed by sexual desire and the passionate desire and quest for friendly companionship among equals, also come to maturity when the *other* in the relationship gains priority. Along with the other dimensions of love, Christian marriage is obliged to mirror and model an agapaic relationship. In the relationships of unmarried Christians as well, the sign of freely engaged other-regarding love is necessary for responsible sexual behavior. It follows that such relationships must be faithful. This means that they must be honest, constant, and monogamous. Finally, such relationships must be creative, producing constructive and life-affirming effects for the couple and in the social world. I argued above that, while necessary lest our ethics of physical sexual expression become overly spiritual and abstract, generativity ought to be framed upon the broader moral horizon of creativity. For unmarried Christians, as in a more limited way for the married, the value of generativity has both negative and positive dimensions. Because morally responsible sex is a free physical act that not only embodies intimate relations of faithful, honest, constant, and singular love but also can biologically generate children, the value of generativity—and by extension the value of children themselves—obliges the unmarried, in almost every case, not to bring children into the world. I suggest "in almost every case" to recognize the possibility and the fact that on occasion the unmarried can provide a stable, nurturing, and loving environment for children. There are cases where the care and virtue expressed in the lives of unmarried parents is truly admirable. Still, the harder social facts are that some of the most difficult and poverty-ridden circumstances of life in any culture are exhibited in the lives of unmarried women with children. Many of these women, often abandoned by their male partners, exhibit significant moral heroism. It is, however, a heroism marked by tragedy. In a more positive vein, the value of generativity ingredient in the physical act of sex itself obliges the unmarried and sexually active Christian in a special way to take an interest in and act for the welfare of children, so many of whom are abused and functionally abandoned both in and out of marriage. Both creativity and generativity function as value-signs for responsible sexual relations also among unmarried Christians.

Certainly it may be more difficult for such relationships to realize these values without the social, religious, and moral structures of marriage. The specific difficulties of single relationships must be part of any responsible interpretation of their moral status. But it is also important to note the difference in role, function, and obligation of nonmarital relationships in the Church. We will not get very far in argument or practice if we depict and engage them as "mini-marriages" left in midair without foundational supports. Even though the same values and goods disclosed by marriage are at stake in a life of virtuous sexual behavior among the unmarried, their obligations with respect to the Church's norm are not the same as married Christians. I have argued that married Christians take on a unique public and ecclesiastical obligation and responsibility to actively uphold and support the Church's norm directly. Unmarried Christians have the obligation to *receive* the values and goods for responsible sexual behavior that marriage discloses, designates, and sometimes effectively demonstrates and live them out virtuously in the world. Sexual behavior among unmarried Christians does not directly entail an obligation to uphold the Church's norm of marriage in this way. Rather these relationships indirectly participate in the norm by learning to live by the values, virtues, and goods disclosed by marriage and developing their characters in their light. It is the special ecclesiastical role and obligation of formally married Christians alone to uphold the revelatory sacramental praxis of marriage and secure its special place in the Church. This is why we should speak of the special *office* that married Christians occupy in the Church and why, all other biblical and doctrinal reasons not withstanding, we should speak of marriage as a *sacrament*. This is also the reason why ritual and sacramental marriage engaged in public remains of vital importance. We err when we argue that the main difference between being married and being not married pertains always to the quality of our commitment and love for each other. Given the necessary set of responsible values, virtues, and goods, however, the difference is often more ecclesiastical, social, and cultural. Married and unmarried Christians occupy different ecclesial and social roles and functions. In this sense it is only marriage that is the specific sacramental act of the Church. Being implicated in the community and the world by the obligations of baptism, marriage, like ordination, marks Christians with a special office and ministry.

Finally, conditions of maturity often discerned according to age and experience have much to do with the prospects of responsible sexual behavior among the unmarried. It is only prudent to accept that gaining the values, virtues and goods of responsible sexual relationships demand a certain level of adult maturity. Biologically, in terms of our species, sex is also an adult act. At issue, too, are the facts that both our sexuality and the conditions and criteria of adulthood exist within the contexts of culture and society and therefore are more than just biologically determined, though our biology is never absent nor, in the sexual generation of children, ever without moral significance. Thus as cultures develop in complexity, biological maturity and social and moral adulthood become more separated in time, and the developmental processes toward an integrated maturity take much longer. This hiatus has been most pronounced in technologically advanced cultures like our own where the social and cultural entrance to adulthood is postponed longer than more traditional agrarian societies. Consequently, given the argument that sex is more than only a biological act, we are often left with a problem of determining when an adequate level of maturity has been reached for the adult engagement of responsible sexual behavior. If we add to these biological and cultural facts the high level of symbolic and sacramental significance that the Church attaches theologically to acts of sexual relations, our problem becomes more complex. If this is a significant issue for unmarried Christians, a fortiori, marriage itself would also require a significant degree of social and moral maturity. Attempting to "solve" problems of irresponsible sexual activity among the unmarried by marriage only compounds the moral, social-psychological, and, often, economic difficulties.

For responsible sexual behavior among unmarried Christians, the Church will be comforted by greater rather than lesser maturity. To keep this from becoming only a truism it is important to remember the practical common sense that ought to ground the Church's rhetoric of sex. And while common sense and practice alone does not indicate moral rectitude, critical moral interpretations cannot be only theoretic but rather must emerge from and return to the common realities of everyday life. Since significant levels of sexual behavior among single Christians has little prospect for abatement, if we can grant with conscientious integrity the formal moral possibility of responsible sexual behavior for unmarried Christians, we can become more focused on the values, virtues, and goods necessary for their guidance. Being less distracted about the formal possibility for responsible sex, we can concentrate, in this case, on moral maturity as one important condition for the substantive occurrence of responsible sex. In our guidance of the young, instead of stopping all discussions with a peremptory "no," we will be able to engage them in a more comprehensive discussion about their own level of social and moral maturity. In such discussions, young persons can come to a decision about sexual relations in the context of their own states of character development. Moreover, in such constructive conversations, they will also have been instructed and taught precisely in the context of the Church a good deal about what responsible sexual behavior requires in the life of a Christian. Both the freedom of moral decision and the obligation of ecclesiastical instruction will have been upheld. In such conversations parents, pastors, and teachers must accept the possibility of disagreement, at least initially. It is not unusual and is often part of the nature of transitional states—even those postponed in "advanced" societies beyond the traditional assignments of age—to desire and thus claim more maturity than one actually possesses. In such situations, especially given the new physical dangers of unsafe sexual activity, parents and teachers need to avoid alienating young persons from continuing discussions of responsible sexual behavior. This also raises the question of how serious in the life of the person and in the Church is morally irresponsible sexual activity among the unmarried.

I have already argued that the most significant negative effects upon sexual morality in the life of the Church come from morally irresponsible marriages, and that in the failure of such marriages these effects are transmitted to the unmarried. In terms of the vulnerabilities of the individual persons involved, all sexual irresponsibility can be serious, though I do not think that the traditional approach of the Roman Catholic confessional manuals that sexual sins are "mortal sins *ex toto genere suo*, i.e., sins which according to their nature can never be venial" (Jone, 1953: 47) is necessary or helpful.[31] The primary reason why sexual irresponsibility is serious in Christian life is that, whatever other moral issues it may involve, and there are many, sexuality and sexual behavior also involve a sacred and obliging *sacramentum*—a seal, sign, and symbol—of the free, constant, and loving intimacy of the divine-human relationship. However unsuccessful our efforts, it is upon this horizon that we are obliged to relate to others, including our sexual relationships. Consequently, in terms of an adequate Christian theology of sex, the formal gravity of sexual sin as well as the formal celebration of sexual virtue, require a level of mature engagement of Christian faith itself. We can neither become adequately virtuous nor deeply sinful in our sexual relationships without this core involvement. Reconstructed Catholic moral theology has tried to indicate this dimension of mature responsibility and sin with the term "fundamental option."[32] Such a term is somewhat of a misnomer, however, insofar as we seldom, if ever, *will* core involvements of our personality through single acts, though single acts may be signs of deeper orientations. Rather, over time, we gain or not the maturity to engage intersubjective life within a posture of moral sensitivity and responsibility—in the case of sexual behavior, specifically and most pointedly by being *in love* with another. Still, not every act of sexual affection and intimacy involves what the Catholic manuals term, "grave matter," nor need they involve core levels of our personality. However, the *moral horizon* of sexuality, and thus, taken *en masse*, of sexual activity, pertains to the deepest core of our personality, and our most intense acts of sexual intimacy ought to be responsive to that core.

John Mahoney also points out the danger of thinking of "fundamental option" in an overly agential and subjective way: "it places too much credence in the moral resources of the individual and in the last resort discounts the amount of objective wrong and harm which the individual may perpetrate in his single minded pursuit of self-fulfillment." Mahoney goes on to argue that the only way to answer such serious objections lies in highlighting the intersubjective dimension of individuality wherein the moral person lives in "a kingdom" of other subjects. It is this context of communal intersubjectivity that allows us to respect and contribute to the "collective wisdom of the Christian community," and at the same time to respect "the experience and wisdom of other individuals in the community, as well as of the community as a whole" (1989: 221–22).

Mahoney highlights the final point we need to consider in a discussion of the gravity of sexual sin. If the formal gravity of sexual sin as well as the accomplishment of sexual virtue pertain to the level of our general moral orientations to human relationships in general, and to our sexual relationships in particular, the substantive gravity—as Mahoney puts it, "the amount of objective wrong and harm"—also demands consideration. If sexuality finally involves deep and core levels of our personality, then the potential of sexual behavior for "objective harm" is always present even when the formal requirements for serious sin and virtue are not. There is much indication—psychological, sociological, and anthropological—that even trivial and banal sex in individuals and culture indicate deeper fear and anxiety that only come from some implication of the core of our personalities.[33] Certainly individuals can engage in sexual activity in superficial ways, but if our general needs and expectations indicate more importance to sex than this, the potential to harm ourselves and others because of this superficiality remains. This is especially the case if our superficial approach to sex goes on too long or is misplaced in the cycles of our own psychosocial development—if we, in fact, fail to "grow up" sexually.

With respect to the important area of sexual behavior short of intercourse, especially in dating relationships, I can only point out that no one in the moral life comes to levels of maturity and core involvement with respect to any particular dimension easily or overnight. Thus dating is a very important venue for developing the necessary habits of virtue for mature and responsible sexual relations. Nor does such a developmental process end when we marry or arrive at some putative adult age. Aristotle's classical notion of virtue as habit that can be taught indicates that even with all the advances in the psychology of moral development, how we learn to relate to each other when we are young has effects on moral maturity in later life. And while it is true, as Aristotle could never have suspected, that a good deal of this potential to learn comes from our earliest experiences in infancy and childhood, in one way or another, such learning must be modeled. This is also a further contextualization for my argument that marriage, and now parenting in general, models the psychosocial and moral worlds wherein the young will learn to relate to each other as adults. In this sense, a life of virtue must be modeled for us with our potential for moral maturity varying according to that modeling from the earliest periods of our life.[34] There is freedom of development, conversion, and change with respect to a life of virtue, as there are limits and determinisms. What we must *demand* from ourselves and others are minimum levels of moral adequacy—for example, not being harmed or harming others deliberately or through crass moral ineptitude. What we *hope for* is continual growth in caring, honest, and just relationships.

The Church has strong obligations in educating young Christians in moral responsibility especially in the area of sexual behavior. And while marriage, woven as it is for good and for ill in the fabric of society, will be the primary teacher and model, the Church cannot assume that becoming married will magically orient young Christians to moral responsibility. As I have indicated, periods of dating relationship, whether of the young or not, are crucial times for this ongoing learning. Without being either moralistic or naive about the promise or risk, the Church must accept that the entire range of sexual activity will be present in the dating relationships of single Christians. The same context of values, virtues and goods we have been discussing must be brought to their moral instruction rather than staying with our present functional abandonment of especially the young under the faulty morality of the peremptory "no." As a final note, especially for the young and relatively inexperienced, it is often the case that sexual intercourse changes relationships in one way or another—decenters and destabilizes them offering proximate prospects for both growth and decline. This also must be taken into account for responsible sexual behavior among the unmarried.

Lastly, a word is necessary about those who through a self-conscious religious promise, vow, or choice of some kind intend to remain sexually celibate. No matter how understanding our rhetoric, it is tempting to at least privately think of such celibate Christians as either somehow abnormal or to raise them to heights of spiritual adulation. Neither is the case. All the conditions and obligations of love, fidelity, and creativity apply to religious celibates as to all relationships of the Christian life. Sexual desire and its needs remain. In this dimension, celibates are impoverished—in the words of Charles Davis, "empty and poor for Christ" (1966). But they need not remain impoverished in their own passions for community and cause. *Eros* seeks and accomplishes reunion in friendly relations and other dedications. The requirements of fidelity to others pertain to celibates, not just in the abstract, but in faithful dedication to a cause in the context of Christian values.[35] There obligations of creativity and generativity are engaged in working for that cause and effecting new life in the process. Still dedicated celibacy is often a lonely state. As in all dimensions of Christian existence, there will be suffering in such loneliness but there will also be, in responsible celibacy, a communion with others. Those others are always prior in the life of dedicated celibates and contribute meaning and form to the larger *agapaic community*. Without such loyalty and dedication to a cause, even with self-conscious acceptance and strong attempts at integration of the emptiness and loneliness that celibacy always to some degree entails, the lives of celibates can be tragically dysfunctional. When religious celibates use others, leading them into intimate relationships inappropriate to their state only to pull back in hiding behind their vow or promise or when their celibacy becomes a way of fleeing from such dedication and passionate intimacy with the cause of others, they act irresponsibly.

Homosexual Christians[36]

I have used the example of homosexual behavior throughout to explicate many of the points I wished to make about the proper historical and analytic contexts for understanding ethical norms and engaging in moral practices. I have also indicated that the present level of obsessive and compulsive speech about sex, especially with respect to homosexuality and to homosexual Christians in particular, is not necessarily a sign of healthy concern but can be a deflection from the real issues at stake in the "decline" of sexual morality. The homosexual community is in somewhat of a double-bind. To speak openly of their lives and values, to talk about what it means to be and act as a gay and lesbian Christian, is crucial if these fellow Christians are to be brought from the moral margins of Church and culture. No adequate and complete analysis can be engaged until this happens. At the same time, and more importantly, it is because homosexual persons have been so long on these margins that the most egregious violations of love and justice have been visited upon them. Often living at the margins of society, they have had to tolerate abuse from people and institutions who have been functionally indemnified. However, now that homosexual persons are becoming more vocal, and at times militant in asserting their value and rights, they run the risk of moral and political backlash.[37]

As important as our obligations are to counter homophobic violations of love and justice, homophobia ought not to be the subject of intense moral argument. These moral issues are clear. The challenge and subject of the Church's response to homophobia is to discern through discussions of the meaning of Christian faith and human personality why these evils are not also clear in the minds of many Christians, including Christian leaders, and to find ways to engage and promote social and moral policies that no longer partake of such clear evil. I will present a framework for inclusive, competent, and undistorted moral debate in the next chapter. Here I will only discuss some of the issues that pertain to the moral theological interpretation of homosexual behavior in light of the norm of heterosexual marriage.

In the Church's debates on homosexual behavior, we cannot conflate homophobic violations of love and justice and the debate about the morality of homosexual acts. No matter how pastorally sensitive some denominational stances proclaim to be, no amount of sensitivity can resolve in itself the moral questions about homosexual behavior as such. The core issue at stake, though it has many ramifications, is whether the Church can faithfully accept homosexual rules of life among a significant population of its membership. In the context of the Christian value-sets I have proposed, my arguments and examples to this point indicate that I believe that the Church can and must do so. At the same time I argued against a discourse that proclaimed parallel norms—one heterosexual and the other homosexual. Heterosexual and homosexual relationships do not phenomenologically appear and thus sacramentally image exactly the same realities. There are surely significant continuities between heterosexual and homosexual relations, but there are also significant discontinuities and differences. Some of this visual difference is often experienced with shock by heterosexual persons. But this should not lead us to confuse visceral and emotive reaction with adequate moral argument and faithful confession. I have argued that feelings have their place in moral argument and decision, but alone are inadequate guides. It is also important to understand that often the public behavior of surely a minority of the homosexual community that shocks heterosexual persons the most can be explained in large part as a reaction-formation to their marginal status and a parody of the worst of heterosexual fears. Often the most outrageous public behavior of some homosexual persons functions as street-theater that only thinly masks a poignant cry for acceptance. I do not suggest that the dynamics of public parody is always intentional and has no deleterious effects in the lives of homosexual persons, or always promotes their cause. Coming to a mature and stable sexual identity and moral responsibility is difficult for heterosexual persons with all the social, cultural, and religious supports available to them. Harder still will it be for many homosexual persons when they have been rendered marginal and closeted in a necessary secrecy for their own protection.[38]

Nonetheless there is a phenomenological difference in the appearance of heterosexual and homosexual relationships in culture and society. Formally, homosexual relationships seldom if ever have functioned as equally parallel models to heterosexuality,[39] nor do they now or have they ever occupied the same place of normative significance in the Church as heterosexual marriage. This is not to say that homosexual relationships image and model nothing of value. To the contrary, as I have indicated and as only one example, it may very well be that with the significant erosion of "friendly love" in married states, and in light of the the extreme difficulty we are having in establishing friendships between the genders, that homosexual relations have a great deal to contribute to upholding and revealing the values of *philia*. This special contribution does not obviate the value and virtue sets of love, fidelity, and creativity discussed previously. These can and do come to bear as goods in the lives of many homosexual couples. I will not rehearse those arguments here.[40] But I will point out again the special importance of keeping clear the distinction and proper relation between creativity and generativity, since confusions here are often used as arguments against the possibility of a morally responsible rule of homosexual life.

For the sake of a faithful Christian life, the same obligations of morally responsible and virtuous sexual behavior I noted for unmarried Christians also pertain to homosexual Christians. Consequently, in terms of the present state of Christian faith and life, heterosexual marriage functions in a normative way for homosexual Christians just as for the unmarried. Homosexual Christians are obliged to receive and live responsibly the values, virtues, and goods disclosed, designated, and sometimes demonstrated by the normative model of heterosexual marriage. In this way, heterosexual marriage remains a sacrament for all.

Finally, if my arguments hold, and given the presence of loving, faithfully constant, monogamous, and creative homosexual relationships, the question arises whether the Church should admit them for sacramental and ritual recognition—in effect "to bless" dedicated and committed homosexual unions. This question remains complex even if arguments are sustained and accepted for the moral and historical integrity of such unions. Given the moral responsibility of some homosexual unions, the case can be made that unless the Church admits them to some sort of religious approbation and public liturgical acceptance, homosexual Christians are unjustly burdened. On the one hand, the Church requires a requisite level of Christian sexual responsibility. On the other, it withholds from homosexual couples much of the very liturgical and communal support that, as committed Christians, they desire and need for maintaining Christian responsibility—support that is at least offered in principle to heterosexual Christians through the liturgical celebration and communal approbation of marriage. It is both a curiosity and a tragedy, as well as a sign of its present inability to articulate a viable Christian ethic of homosexuality and homosexual behavior, that many still express more moral disapproval of committed homosexual relationships than of the immature and irresponsible heterosexual practices of some unmarried Christians, or of abusive spousal relations in marriage. Consequently our questions become even more pointed about whether we ought to consider such committed and dedicated homosexual couples ready to marry or, in effect, to be married and recognize them as such sacramentally. These questions of "blessing such unions" are some of the most vexing in the Church's entire discourse on sexual morality.

I accept the argument, and it is certainly implied in my own, that dedicated relationships of this kind ought to have some kind of liturgical and communal approbation and support. And I think it is the responsibility of the Church and its denominations to provide it. However, the so-called *pastoral* ramifications of even a limited public and officially sanctioned liturgical blessing are important and may for some time to come be burdensome to the somewhat fragile state of denominational and parochial communities with respect to this question. Therefore, with a reminder that I am speaking here of formal, official, and public liturgical celebration of homosexual unions and not of the question of the moral responsibility of such unions, I hesitate at present to make a blanket recommendation before the debates of Church and, to some extent, society reaches an acceptable level of competent communication and argument. In fact, precipitous action across the board might very well be counterproductive for those homosexual Christians who will endure further backlash, as well as confusing to the body of the faithful who have not often received good instruction on this point or on sexual morality in general. Until that time, those denominations and groups within denominations who have attained such a level of competent analysis and argument serve the Church and its homosexual membership, often at some ecclesiastical risk to themselves, when they offer such "blessings" either openly or, when necessary, more discretely.

According to my argument of the singular status of the norm of heterosexual marriage, however, I am not prepared to recommend that such "blessings" be engaged at the same level of sacramental marriage—to in fact "be sacramental marriages" in the general sense of the term. If my analysis of the present state of the Church is accurate in this respect, then we cannot do so coherently. Coherence here has more to do with accuracy and integrity of the Church's historical memory and present self-understanding than with any great and untoward fear that were we to "sacramentalize" such unions, moral corruption of the community would ensue. We have over time become dependent on heterosexual marriage as our single norm for modeling the values, virtues, and goods necessary for a sexually responsible Christian life. As I have argued, there will always be under this single norm, a plurality of responsible rules of sexual life. Such rules of life, however, cannot replace or be confused with the norm. As we have seen, norms develop and grow over time and sometimes, if left unattended, become dysfunctional and die. However, being historically mediated, faithful remembrance means that they are not subject to simple *choice*, even of a significant group or of the body itself. Offering a ritual of liturgical blessing to homosexual relationships that formally equates it with sacramental marriage is not, in my judgment, a present historical and theological possibility for either Church or society. Nor am I convinced that much would be gained if we were to do so, while I think a great deal would be lost.

Trying to impose primary burdens of disclosure, designation, and the effective modeling of values upon a form of Christian life and relationship that at present does not have either the historical or cultural/societal foundation to bear them, is to program "homosexual marriages" to inevitably fail at these ecclesiastical and social/ethical tasks. It is important to remember that in these tasks, it is not just the moral integrity of the way of life that it is at stake but also their symbolic and heuristic integrity. For metaphors, symbols, and models to reveal and re-present moral ideas, an audience is required to receive them. I have already argued that with all extant historical, sociocultural, and ecclesiastical support, heterosexual marriage is itself often failing as a sacramental model of Christian sexual values but that it has more prospect for rehabilitation than what I think will be a failed project of building a new and parallel normative sacramental model. In applying my arguments about the role and function of ethical norms to this particular issue, I do not find dedicated homosexual relationships having the same role in the life or expectation of Christian denominations as heterosexual relationships and thus do not find parallel obligations with respect to the designation of formal sacramental marriage. I have deliberately avoided the use of rights language with respect to this question since it is not central. The right to be with those we love—whether heterosexual or homosexual—within the context of Christian values is not at issue here. Such a right can be asserted and sustained. Since I have argued, however, that to enter the state of formal *sacramental marriage* is essentially to enter an *ecclesiastical office* with attendant and special tasks, burdens, and responsibilities for a particular service to the body of the faithful and to society overall, rights language is not the best mode of moral theological discourse to engage the issue of liturgical blessing for same-sex relationships. At some levels of personal piety and communal life, the blessing of same-sex relationships can function, in more traditional language, as "a sacramental," or occasional service, but unless the level of historical, sociocultural, and ecclesiastical reality change rather radically, such unions *will not be able to perform the tasks of a fully sacramental model.* Something of a historical corollary can be made with respect to consecrated virginity and promised celibacy to the extent that these are no longer parallel or "other" and higher norms for fully modeling the values, virtues, and goods of sexual life. Despite our ancient Christian origins, and the contributions of other rules of life, heterosexual marriage now occupies the central moral stage.

Still, I have argued that marriage is somewhat in disarray. It lies at its present state in danger of becoming dysfunctional in its work. Trying to "create," as it were, another and parallel norm, whether homosexual or any other, offers no better prospect for modeling a sexually responsible life, but rather significant prospects for worse. Self-consciously "chosen" and radical variety at foundational levels of character identification of a given community or tradition eventually leads either to moral chaos or an eventual splitting and change of core identity. It may seem strange to some to consider heterosexual marriage part of the core identity of the Church, but I am convinced that a fair reading of our historical past and a critical gauge of the interest, indeed vehemence, in the present debate indicates that this is so. Skeptics on this point should not be so convinced that only creedal or doctrinal issues can occupy core levels of Christian identity. Often concentrating only on our creeds and doctrines at the expense of similarly and sometimes more identifying patterns of virtuous moral practice functions as a self-serving distraction. Can we not say that sexism, racism, antisemitism, and homophobia corrupt Christian identity just as much if not more than any putative heresy?

Finally and more specifically, the Church's memory—the reality of its historical past—does not offer any prospects at all for stability in such a choice. Still further, we can hardly support the norm we have much less another. Nor should this argument be taken as a sign of further abandonment of homosexual Christians. Their place in the Church can be secured under the norm of heterosexual marriage and whatever particular liturgical blessing and approbation necessary for their religious and communal support. The *ekklesia* has many tasks, with diversity of gift, role, function, and obligation. The role and obligations of married

Christians are unique in the Church's memory and present experience. Such diversity, however, should not be framed hierarchically and, consequently, the place of married and heterosexual Christians is not higher nor the place of homosexual Christians and their dedicated relationships lower than that of any other member of the body. The deepest challenge for the Church's argument on homosexuality is to discern the unique place and role of homosexual Christians as they serve the body of the faithful in our common work of the Gospel. This will not be accomplished by a splitting of identifying normative models; but it will be aided in more adequate and competent moral discourse by a Church that faithfully and courageously engages its tasks in the world in which it finds itself.

## The Liabilities and Limitations of Argument

I said at the outset of this discussion that the question of "blessing" same-sex unions and the sacramental status of homosexual unions was complex and difficult. I pointed out in the Introduction that rational arguments are never wholly satisfactory or without loose ends or dangers of misapplication and abuse. My argument here is open to two important counters in terms of possible and even likely misapplication. In raising issues of pastoral prudence with respect to the Church "not being ready" for even a blessing of same-sex unions and thus the necessity for discrete liturgical celebrations of such unions, I bring on legitimate comparisons with the recent history of civil rights for African-Americans. Here we find a common and illegitimate counsel of patience for the proper time for full civil rights for black persons. Given my argument for the possibility of morally responsible rules of homosexual behavior, I do recognize a certain formal similarity on the matter of blessing same sex unions and the dangers of overly cautious counsels of patience in the face of clear obligations to do the right thing. While I think that the claim upon the Church to support liturgically dedicated same-sex unions is strong and our obligations great, I am giving such counsel at the present time and call for careful discretion with respect to private or public ceremonies. I, however, certainly do not counsel the same patience with respect to the full acceptance of gay and lesbian Christians within the Christian Church and its denominations. Nonetheless I argued that the realistic situation of denominations, parishes, clergy, and laity seems to call for such discretion insofar as we must first work to overcome the egregious violations of love and justice with respect to homosexual Christians before we can entertain, across the board, the public and joyful celebrations of their dedicated unions. To this extent, with respect to the question of such public "blessings," my argument intends to be a pragmatic and practically prudent one—in an Aristotelian sense, an exercise of *phronesis* or practical life-wisdom—but still one that may indeed be a misreading of the practical possibilities and strong moral obligations of the situation.

The second problem raised by my arguments pertains to the question of diversity of obligations with respect to the burdens and function of sacramental designation. In arguing that heterosexual marriages are now singularly normative in the Christian Church but with a diversity of rules of authentic Christian sexual life, I have run the risk throughout of being understood as suggesting that other rules of life are "abnormal" or "less than" heterosexual marriage. I have tried to counter such interpretations of my argument but recognized their likelihood. In may very well be that Christian history, in both Catholic and Protestant varieties, has been so foundationally envisioned hierarchically—from God, king, and priest *above* to earth and subject *below*—that it may be functionally impossible to remove such a vertical and linear imagination short of profound conversion. Thus when I argue, in a Pauline sense, for difference and diversity of function, task, and obligation without hierarchical designation—in short within a horizontal rather than a vertical imagination and cosmology—the risks of misinterpretation are great.

As a formal subset of the problems noted above, if misunderstanding and misapplication of any argument may be so pervasive then my attempts to apply the general arguments of this book consistently on this point must be given further consideration. Formal arguments, and theory itself, must always be aware of the procrustean temptation to impose consistency upon unique particularity. While consistency in argument is a virtue, it is not the only virtue of good argument. The possibility remains that such a negative and obsessive logjam has arisen with respect to the theological and moral rhetoric of the status of homosexual Christians in the Church that only a radically particular and perhaps inconsistent response is called for. That is to say, at least in terms of the major Christian denominations, that while I still think that historical, ecclesiastical, and sociocultural accuracy and function suggest an argument that the place and role of the dedicated relationships of homosexual Christians is not that of formal sacramental marriage—even with the caveats I have noted—it may very well be that the present obligations of love and justice are stronger and now demand their full acceptance and sacramental recognition by the Christian community.[41]

Rational arguments have their liabilities and limits. They require legitimation as being right and good as well as verification as being true. Furthermore, I am not at all sanguine about claims that an argument is "true" no matter what its consequences are in the lives of others. We have to take great care with immediately and facilely translating a rational "victory" in theory and argument into a moral obligation. Finally, I believe that it is practice that legitimates theory and that human needs and interests drive knowledge, not the reverse.

# 7

## Building Communities of Moral Discourse

### The Moral Intentions of Rationality

Even though rational argument has its limits and liabilities, I have argued throughout that in discussions about moral questions it is incumbent on individuals and communities to continue rational debate until those limits are reached or until the liabilities of harming others makes continuing the conversation itself illegitimate. Becoming proficient in rational argument, with all of its variety, is an obligation of human being itself and of our associations with others. Philip Wheelwright suggests that at the heart of our obligations to intend rational speech is not just the practice of contriving syllogisms or manipulating "mental counters." Rather, "the heart of the axiom" that we are "rational animals" concerns our "ability to reach 'intentively' beyond the here and now. Such intentionality is of two basic kinds, corresponding to the familiar Aristotelian distinction between Practical and Contemplative Reason." On the one hand, we make decisions and reflect upon ends and purposes, even ultimate ones, and "remake" ourselves in light of these reflections. On the other hand, we use rational discourse to symbolize and "hold up some particular patch of experience, sensed or imagined...not for what it is but for what it indicates or suggests" (1954: 17). I have argued that both forms of rational discourse are necessary in ethics. Consequently we can say that speaking about moral concerns is an exercise of our rational natures both of individuals and communities. In rational moral discourse we engage the proximately possible with the remotely ideal. We talk both of strategies and imaginations. We anticipate in conversation what we will later effect in decision and action. We speak as well as act intentionally. Wheelwright continues his description of these two dimensions of rational intentionality:

> In the one there is the intention in the popular and dynamic sense of the word—a reaching out toward the future in an act of delib-

erate choice, a striving toward a still unrealized possibility which lies somehow within our power to effect. In the other there is "intention"...where the mind's outreach is not in the time dimension but from the sensuously grasped particularity to the something more which it is taken to symbolize or adumbrate." (1954: 17–18)

I have already noted Richard Weaver's claim that rational speech that intends to persuade is "a kind of love" (1965: 14). In other words, when we come together to critically and fairly engage others in rational debate, when we project possible decisions as well as impossible ideals and listen to the projections of others, we engage life within the perspective of commonality and community. Nor should we be chagrinned that we are attempting to influence each other. The absence of any intention at all to rationally influence another, as well as our receptivity to such influence, signals the victory of solipsistic isolation of individuals from each other and the neutering of all passion for achieving the right and the good. Of all disciplines, ethics is the most appropriate for engaging in the fair and honest rhetoric of rational persuasion precisely because the necessary moral affections for critical ethical reflection require that we care about the right and the good, care about our neighbor's welfare as well as our own, and may, in speaking together about our mutual needs and interests, come to love one another.

But it is just here that we become anxious again. In coming "to love" those we engage in rational moral speech, perhaps we will become too obliged to them—indeed care too much about them and become forever enmeshed in the complexities of their lives. And so we retreat from these complexities of both rationality and morality and attempt to render our language simple and one dimensional. In so doing, as Kenneth Burke maintains (1945: 90), we eliminate from our speech all elements of "exhortation or command" and narrow the "circumference" of our discourse "to a point where the principle of personal action is eliminated from language, so that an act would follow from it only as a non-sequitur, a kind of humanitarian after-thought" (quoted in Weaver, 1953: 70).

Moral Discourse and the Nature of the Church[1]

In Robert Bolt's play *A Man for All Seasons*, Cardinal Wolsey gives a final piece of melancholic advice to Sir Thomas More:

If you could just see facts flat on, without that horrible moral squint;
with just a little common sense, you could have been a statesman.[2]

In the Church's contemporary engagements with moral questions
and dilemmas, we are more often like Wolsey than More. Surely, we
think, some moral questions are settled as *facts* of our sociocultural and
ecclesial life. To engage in vigorous argument about such facts is only to
disrupt the body of the faithful and cause confusion. I do not doubt that
some moral issues are not debatable at any and all times in the Church's
life. I have argued that racism, sexism, and homophobic interpretations
and actions are examples of such issues. To be involved in these negative
moral postures, even in debate, creates fractures at the very heart of our
Christian identity. Many Christians, however, do not always understand
themselves to be self-consciously proclaiming racist, sexist, or homophobic attitudes or do not see such rhetoric and its attendant actions as
violations of clear moral facts. We have become more subtle about our
bigotries. What we lack, and what Wolsey failed to engage, is "that
horrible moral squint." Even when there is a certain stability of moral
understanding and consensus at any given time in the Church's life,
norms and rules seldom appear as simple facts but demand ongoing
attempts at critically constructive conversation and debate—times and
places where the Church exercises its moral vision and dynamic of character, first set in motion by our moral squints.

When the Church is being self-consciously historicist and modern,
understanding its claim to revelation not as only the reception of simple
and positive facts but rather as time-full engagements of life in multileveled and rich confessions, narrations, and imaginations, we maintain
the critical squint necessary for fidelity. We hold up More and not Wolsey
for emulation precisely because More exercised his character by refusing
to take as given the moral assumptions of his society and age. He
engaged in conscientious questioning and exercised his moral squint.
Nor, in principle, would one need to necessarily agree with More to
admire his posture of character integrity.

The character of institutions, societies, and communities are under
the same obligations of critical inquiry and conscientious rational debate.
When the Church has been most faithful to its informing heritage, it has
engaged in vigorous debate about its obligations in any and all times and
places, refusing to reduce itself to a forum for only the discourse of
"statesmen" who see "facts flat on."

Part of what has been lacking in the Church's rhetoric on sexual
morality has been this critical squint. We have been assuming that the

basic facts of sexual morality are settled despite every indication that our norms are unravelling and single dimensional rules of life are not working for the promotion of responsible sexual behavior. Because many of our denomination leaders and teachers have been functioning more as diplomats than leaders in critical debate, the body of the faithful has often been left in confusion and without the guidance it has every right to expect and demand. Moral discourse and decisions are risky, often messy, and cannot be adequately engaged by those who desire to shy away from controversy because it does not suit some self- or institutionally-serving political purpose.

Even though our bigoted violations of love and justice have become more subtle, necessitating new and more critical moral vision and debate, we also cannot allow ourselves to be seduced by interminable and overly fastidious debates or by false appeals to diversity of viewpoint or manipulative accusations of "political correctness." It is an inestimable liability of late modernity that *political* and *moral correctness* have become so disjunctive in both our rhetoric and our actions. In seductive efforts to deflect the critical and open debates and judgments necessary for difficult moral questions, it seems at times that, especially in our ecclesiastical institutions and adjudicatory bodies, a false rhetoric of pluralism, civility, and decorum in discussion has led the Church itself to become the last, best refuge for scoundrels. In any examination of the nature of rational speech, it is vitally important to understand the difference and relation between "only theoretic" and practical moral debates. While theory always has its place, and when presented well always has practical origins and consequences, practical moral questions are more proximate in their effects. Consequently, we do not often have the time or leisure, much less the moral sanction, to engage proximate and pressing moral questions as if they were "only theoretic," especially when people are being harmed immediately by negating words and actions—for example, of a racist, sexist, or homophobic nature. As I have argued throughout, these violations must be opposed immediately on their own grounds as well as on the grounds of the systematically distorting effects they have on all further rational discourse. Only then will any subsequent "theoretic debate" about causes and strategies for response, including better moral education, gain even initial legitimacy.

Thus, while authentic decorum and friendly relations are always normative, reducing the rational and moral conversations of the Church to the institutionally self-serving interests of only diplomats and "statesmen" is a radically unfaithful posture that has serious negative effects on the state of Christian faith and life. The Church has always claimed an intimate connection between a faith confessed and a life lived, not just for "professional ecclesiastics" but for the entire body of the faithful. It is precisely the moral question that brings this obliging nexus of faith and life to its most profound crisis. Part of what it means to be the Church—an essential *mark*, if you will—is our practice of legitimately critical moral debate. Without such discourse, faith and life will inevitably become disjunctive, with faith and doctrine hovering in an ethereal and abstract atmosphere above the vicissitudes of our historical existence and our moral behavior lacking adequate guidance and ecclesial integrity. Moral questions are always also ecclesiological questions pertaining to the character integrity of the community of faith.

I have suggested that at some level the denominations understand the relation of sexual morality and ecclesiastical character and that this understanding has been part of the informing horizon of the Church's debate on sexual morality. However, what is often missed is that the character integrity of the Church, whether manifest in sexual or any other morality, is itself not adequately understood as a simple fact of ecclesiastical diplomacy or functionalist conformity. We cannot see adequately the multidimensional obligations and stress and strains of character by single vision. Character integrity does not emerge only homogeneously nor is homogeneity the single sign of a stable and responsible character. Rather our vision of character itself must also be refracted by the heterogeneous dimensions of the Church's life. We must constantly refocus our ecclesiological and moral vision, not for some facile and perverse motive to disrupt and cause confusion but because we must be assured that our faith and life are being brought into critical relationship in the times and places in which we find ourselves. Indeed, the Church is also an institutional system with functional needs for stability and order; yet such needs are neither primary nor foundational. Before the Church is an institution, it is a vital community of people who are challenged to live lives in light of their core confessions of character identity and to allow these challenges to inform, develop and, at times, counter any previous assumptions of their moral character. Character identity is not stabilized by being static. A vital character is always as critically responsive to the new as it is to the old. Nor can there be any structured hierarchy here, though there will always be risk. It is always possible that in our struggles of character—to know who we are at any time and place as persons and as a Church—we will become *converted* so to speak. Conversion and change rest as the constant horizon of possibility for vital character. The character identities of people and communities have boundaries and limits that once crossed create new characters. Such changes can be for moral good or ill. Vital character integrity knows no stability beyond this core moral risk. This too is part of the risk of the Church's modern discourse on sexual morality, but one that must be taken self-consciously if the connection between faith and life is to be maintained in this vital dimension of the lives of the faithful.

Perhaps more than in any area of the Church's life our sacramental commitments to what Kenneth Leech has called "the carnality of grace" (1991) ought to be manifest in the Church's rhetoric of sex. If we are unable to discuss critically the theology and morality of sex, the Church stands at significant risk of failing to make the necessary connections between faith and life in general. Failing in constructive moral discourse about sex, we will fail more profoundly to be a vital Church in the late modern and postmodern ages. Oddly enough, we are losing the passion of constructive debate about our own passions. Often functionally equating sex and sin, we diminish the appearance of both and wind up simply not knowing what we are talking about, or worse yet, not having enough fellow-feeling to come to consensus. In so doing, we come to grave risk of losing our character integrity as a community of moral speech and action.

In his essay, "The Church: A Community of Moral Discourse," James Gustafson calls the Church to a deeper and broader self-understanding. Gustafson describes this ecclesiological designation as a "normative theme" but one that we can no longer assume to be the purview of the clergy alone since "any oracular power they might have had in the past no longer exists" (1970: 83; 84). Indeed, the discourse of the Church about moral questions is a task, obligation, and *mark* of the whole body, one way among others (we need no hierarchy here) of identifying and building up the character of the community. Gustafson is clear about what he means:

> By a community of moral discourse I mean a *gathering of people with the explicit intention to survey and critically discuss their personal and social responsibilities in the light of moral convictions about which there is some consensus and to which there is some loyalty* (1970: 84).

The reason why we must gather seriously for such debate is because of our loyalties to the tradition in which we stand, a tradition that makes no facile separations between faith and life—a tradition of sinners and saints whose very lives and practices were in every way tied to their informing confessions. Within the informing dimension of faith, we must use, and use precisely and with adequate moral sensitivity, the language of ethics. Gustafson continues:

> If the language of salvation, self-fulfillment, relief from guilt and
> anxiety, in short the language of what religion can do for you (i.e.,
> your self-interest) dominates, the purpose of the church is askew....
> (People)...in the Christian and Jewish traditions are *moralists*: we
> are concerned with the right ordering of human relationships, we
> seek the *good* of the neighbor (1970: 89, parens added).

And, as Gustafson emphasizes, we are obliged to do this—to engage in
empathic conversation and debate with each other—precisely because
we have been called to "serve the good of the near and distant neighbor,"
to preserve and cultivate "the goodness that God created for (us)" (1970:
95).

There is, however, a final distraction and seduction from this
obliging task of our faith. When faith and the moral life become segmented from each other, we run the great risk of assuming a form of
moral fideism. We think that the strength of present or prior "belief" and
moral conviction is enough. We substitute assertion for argument, with
the strongest and loudest assertion becoming "orthodox"—the one that
claims the most popular support or satisfies our own individual tastes
and needs. Our discussion and debates become "systematically distorted."[3] Understandably, in such a state the Church will experience a
great deal of anxiety. But this too is often misplaced. Gustafson concludes:

> I am not anxious about the orthodoxy and unorthodoxy of the
> language: I am anxious that the religious community engage seri-
> ously and responsibly in its duties and opportunities to serve the
> temporal good (1970: 95).

### Framing Constructive and Effective Debate:
### The Praxis of Communicative Action

If the Church is to adequately envision itself as a community of
moral discourse, more than claims are required. Attention must also be
given to the development of an adequate theory to inform a praxis of
"communicative action." The most significant work toward the development of such a theory is being done by the social philosopher Jürgen
Habermas, and it is to his work that I will now turn for an introduction
to some of the significant issues at stake.[4] I will only raise the foundational issues and claims informing Habermas's project that serve to
introduce a theoretic frame for advancing this ecclesiological self-

understanding. Habermas's work is developmental in the sense of emerging over time in a long series of research and reflections that build toward what he now calls a theory of "discourse ethics." However, it is important, at the outset, to locate Habermas within the general debate between cognitivists and noncognitivists in ethics. Like my own approach in this book, Habermas is oriented toward the cognitivist view. That is to say, while cognizant of the vital role of the affections in rational inquiry, he is convinced that adequately verified and practical moral judgments can be accomplished through rational conversation that is an exercise of competent and nondistorted communication. Further, such conversation can be formally legitimated through rational debates that are guided by the norms and rules of discourse ethics. However, Habermas is not naive about the fact that much of our rational debates are systematically distorted and that final criteria for the substantive legitimation of our conclusions must come from the experiences of material historical life. Thus, as I will indicate, while having a general Kantian flavor, his cognitive approach is a radical re-visioning of Kant through the reconstruction of material-historical pragmatics.[5]

In his article "Discourse Ethics" (1990: 43–115), Habermas's general point of departure is from the observation that human beings in communal and discursive relationships do on regular occasions come to effective and rational moral judgments. This empirical and cultural "fact" compels us to investigate the logic of practical speech that makes such occasions of communicative success possible (Habermas, 1990: 62). If we can find an adequate theoretic understanding of the foundational logic and ethic of such conversations, then we can gain both epistemological perspective and moral guidance for overcoming the systematic distortions of our rational speech situations in general. Such distortions are far more than coming up with the "wrong answer" but also have profoundly negative impact on our abilities to sustain responsible and constructive relationships as cultures, societies, and communities. Distortions in our rational speech situations create distortions in our abilities to live together as communities: distorted speech fractures our intersubjective connections with each other and the integrity of our social character.

Justifying his own conviction about the ability of cognitive moral discourse to inform and foster such substantive character integrity both in our specific decisions and our social groups, Habermas engages in debate with "noncognitivists"—i.e., those who suggest that rational moral speech under any claim and norm of universality at all finally winds up as an exercise of "blind emotional attitudes and arbitrary decisions" (1990: 43). Rather than being cast upon a universal cognitive horizon, our moral speech is best understood as semantic codes for felt needs and preferences whose possibility for coherence and consensus is particular to smaller homogeneous cultures rather than to the more pervasive heterogeneity that afflicts human reason itself. Thus noncognitivists promote the possibility of moral consensus, not upon the ability of reason to render impartial judgments of practical questions based on better reasons but upon the balance of common needs and emotions or through "negotiating a compromise" of wills in a contest wherein "the idea of a *balance of power*" tries to "strike a balance between conflicting particular interests" (Habermas, 1990: 43; 72).

However, Habermas is aware that at least part of the reason for the reaction of the noncognitivists in ethics has to do with the hubris of certain modern conceptions of rationality, "notably its stubborn tendency to narrow down to the cognitive-instrumental domain the domain of questions that can be decided on the basis of reasons"(1990: 45). In this way, ethics is reduced to an instrumentalist determination of action toward a purposive end within the uncritical moral assumptions of a functionalist social institution and system. Still, Habermas considers this critique of modern rationality to be "one-sided"(1990: 45)—that is to say only part of the self-understanding of the age. He is convinced that modernity also discloses a more adequately grounded model for discursive rationality than only the instrumental reason and narrow purposive rationality of technocratic culture. In fact, the liberating and critically inquisitive environment of enlightenment modernity has disclosed the possibility of elucidating moral phenomena "in terms of a formal pragmatic analysis of communicative action, a type of action in which the actors are oriented to validity claims."(1990: 44).[6]

Moral Norms and Moral Truth

If an adequate justification of cognitive moral speech is to be accomplished against the criticisms of the noncognitivists, we will have to demonstrate how moral discourse relates to truth. For it is an essential claim of cognitive speech in modernity to say something true about the world. If moral cognitivism fails on this point, then the way is set for the noncognitivist to always submit our normative moral speech to only a philosophical *therapy* of clarification and reduction—that is, that we could always say better what we falsely think of as claims to truth in moral speech by reducing such claims to what they really are, experientially descriptive sentences and evocative utterances. If this is so, Habermas argues that none of these types of sentences can serve as a vehicle for making a truth claim or for making any claim to validity that requires argumentation. That is why, on this view, the belief in the existence of moral truth is construed as an illusion stemming from the intuitive understanding of everyday life. In short, with a single blow noncognitivist approaches deprive the sphere of everyday moral intuitions of its significance (1990: 55).

Furthermore, noncognitivists argue that "disputes about basic moral principles ordinarily do not issue in agreement" and, consequently, cognitive moral speech fails in "all attempts to explain what it might mean for normative propositions to be true." (Habermas, 1990: 56). If these noncognitivist positions are accurate, then all communities of moral discourse, including the Church, would simply be exercising diplomacy and "pastoral prudence" in order to balance competing interests and negotiate a compromise, usually in favor of the majority and never working to achieve a common interest based on cognitive consensus about the truth and right of their conclusions and judgments. Habermas argues that "participants in a practical discourse strive to clarify a common interest, whereas in negotiating a compromise they try to strike a balance between conflicting particular interests." Moreover, if in our practical moral speech we begin to replace cognitive argumentation with "will formation," we will pay the high price of giving "up the distinction between the validity of norms and their de facto acceptance in society" (1990: 72). The validity of our norms and the legitimacy of our rules will be robbed of both their cognitive and moral significance (Habermas, 1990: 72; 74). In the absence of the cognitive, the way is open for only the imperative and for an overly voluntarist understanding of morality and law with the will and intention of the law-giver given supremacy (see Mahoney, 1989: 224–58). The noncognitive approach to practical moral speech becomes attractive to those who long for easy "consensus," agreement, and obedience in the face of substantive pluralism. Nonetheless, such attractiveness is seductive. The problems of substantive pluralism are not solved but only postponed in the noncognitivist and voluntarist approaches. Formal compromise or "loyal obedience" to the will and judgment of the authority, in effect, reduces the substantive issues at stake to a level of practical value-neutrality. All cognitive speech that intends the redemption of validity claims is short-circuited and we conflate "validity claims and power claims" and reduce "the obligatory character of norms to the obedience shown by followers confronted with the power to command and the power to threaten sanctions" (1990, 72; 73). The moral authority of a norm is not rooted in the power of its enforcement: "a norm does not enjoy validity simply because it is linked to sanctions that enforce compliance" (Habermas, 1990: 73). Thus the norm of heterosexual marriage will not enjoy validity simply because the juridical authority of the Church or any denomination *says that it does*, but rather because the discourse of the Church has *found* it to be so. This is why the juridical authority can legitimately claim this norm in the first place.

Habermas trusts the intuitions of common moral speech more than the noncognitivists. If we are successful in interpreting more systematically what in fact goes on in successful moral debate and argument, then we are in a position to show how substantive and cognitive agreement in moral argumentation is possible in principle, no matter how counterfactual and dysfunctional any particular conversation may be. Though our success at such cognitive consensus is only occasional and distortions abound, through an adequate theory of communicative action we can come to an understanding of how such consensus can and does occur. Thus the noncognitivist complaints of impracticality and failure will lose much of their force. Further, and precisely on the point of the truth value of normative claims, Habermas argues that we must give up the counter-intuitive premise of the noncognitivists that "normative sentences, to the extent to which they are connected with validity claims at all, can be valid or invalid only in the sense of propositional truth" (1990: 56).[7] Such a premise cannot be proven unless moral truths are reduced to uncritically described facts. But this is precisely what is counter-intuitive, since we commonly make claims for the truth of our normative utterances that are beyond the claims of descriptive propositions. Furthermore, when we raise such claims, we imply that we can defend them cognitively—that is provide reasons for them that are more than only our feelings or tastes. We assume similarly that our efforts to defend and verify our claims will not be merely arbitrary or an exercise of only private opinion. We trust that in our practical moral discourse we will be able to distinguish a right norm and command from a wrong one (Habermas, 1990: 56). Finally, on more substantive grounds, we reject even a limited identification of moral and propositional truth, since in the context of technocratic modernity, to reduce morality to only claims that can be verified by empirical and objective descriptions is to submit moral discourse to the uncritical impositions of instrumentalist reason serving the power interests of dominant groups. Critical morality loses its necessary tension between the ideal and the real, and practical moral speech becomes only a submission to the "facts" of everyday life. We become robbed of our critical moral squint, and virtue ceases as a habit that can inform an age.[8]

If moral truth and the truth of moral norms cannot be simply identified with propositional truth, while, at the same time, truth engaged as a descriptive and indicative proposition about the "facts" of the world has become the epistemological benchmark of the modern scientific age, then we are cast back again into our familiar dialectic between similarity and difference—the same and the other. We will therefore look again for such truth under *the sign of the Analogue* (Ricoeur, 1984a). Habermas argues in this vein:

> But if normative sentences do not admit of truth in the narrow sense of the word "true," that is, *in the same sense* in which descriptive statements can be true or false, we will have to formulate the task of explaining the meaning of "moral truth" or, if that expression is already misleading, the meaning of "normative rightness" in such a way that we are not tempted to assimilate the one type of sentence to the other. We will have to proceed on a weaker assumption, namely that normative claims to validity are *analogous to truth claims* (1990: 56).

This transfer of our norm for moral truth from either a sign of similarity with respect to propositional truth or from a sign of a radically different "truth" of our will and affections to *the sign of the Analogue* will open the way for a discussion of the unique type of practical cognitive discourse that engages us when we take up moral questions for discussion and decision. We will, as Habermas indicates, take up Stephen Toulmin's (1969: 64; 74) basic questions: "What kind of argument, of reasoning is it proper for us to accept in support of moral decisions?" and "What kinds of things make a conclusion worthy of belief?" With these kinds of question we can make "the transition to the level of a theory of argumentation." (Habermas, 1990: 56–57).

A Theory of Moral Argumentation: Basic Concepts

The goal of Habermas's theory of argumentation is to show that in the case of practical moral discourse, our ordinary justifications come from the force of better cognitive argument—that is to say that we will ordinarily accept better reasons for our moral decisions based on the premise that "real argument makes moral insight possible" (1990: 57). Such argument, however, ensues not from the isolated thinking subject but from what Habermas calls the standpoint of "communicative action."

> I call actions *communicative* when the participants coordinate their plans of action consensually, with the agreement reached at any point being evaluated in terms of the intersubjective recognition of validity claims (1990: 58).

Coming to a discursive agreement grounded in communicative action involves three sorts of validity claims: *claims to truth* about something in the objective world expressed in propositional statements, *claims to truthfulness* about something in the subjective world of the speaker "to which one has privileged access," and *claims to right* about "something in the shared social world (as the totality of the legitimately regulated interpersonal relationships of a social group)" (Habermas, 1990: 58). While our true representations of external reality, as well as our expressions of honest sincerity about our "internal" lifeworlds are necessary in competent speech situations, the "truth-claims" of practical moral discourse are centered most proximately in our claims for legitimated interpersonal relations or "shared value orientations" (Habermas, 1979: 29). Furthermore, such speech is more "communicative" than "strategic."

In mature moral discourse,[9] we are more interested in achieving a rationally motivated consensus (*communicative action*) than influencing behavior toward a specific and narrowly determined end through "threat of sanctions or the prospect of gratification" (*strategic action*). In communicative action we depend on the "binding/bonding effect" of the "illocutionary speech act" (Habermas, 1990: 58). Following J. L. Austin (1962), Habermas understands the term "illocutionary" to indicate that in practical moral discourse we make assertions and claims about the world of social relations within the speech situation itself. Illocutionary language is performative in the sense that we "do things by saying something" (Habermas, 1976: 34), and bind ourselves with further performative obligations to enter into a discursive process of practical consensual validation of the claims we make. Thus we can speak here, most specifically, of the performative power of "speech acts."[10] Within a situation of competent practical moral discourse, the generative power of an illocutionary speech act calls forth an interpersonal relation among the participants for the purpose of reaching a consensual understanding. Thus the action engaged is communicative. Such an ethos and norm of interpersonal communicative action frames and guides the cognitive argument for the purpose of regulating the speech situation. When in the mind of any participant or group of participants, strategic action, and its attendant ideology, takes the place of communicative action as the normative guide and rule of competent moral speech, the conversation becomes systematically distorted. The single and overriding motive of particular and strategic action through either *threat of sanction or prospect of gratification* distorts the normative ethos of discourse ethics—i.e., of reaching an understanding through cognitive consensus.

Discourse ethics obliges the speaker—the one who makes claims for legitimate norms of interpersonal relations—to engage in a process of consensual validation. It is this obligation of communicative rather than strategic action alone that initially ties a community of discourse together. Competent speakers give each other mutual guarantees of submitting their claims to the process of rational validation and consensus.

> In the case of claims to truth or rightness, the speaker can redeem his guarantee discursively, that is, by advancing reasons; in the case of claims to truthfulness he does so by consistent behavior. (A person can convince someone that he means what he says only through his action, not by giving reasons.) (Habermas, 1990: 59).

Only within a competent speech situation of mutual obligation and guarantee for discursively redeeming all of our claims about the normative and regulative quality of our interpersonal relationships can communities of moral discourse and action continue (Habermas, 1990: 59).

Even though Habermas argues that with respect to moral norms our "claims to truth" reside only in our speech acts, the "locus of normative claims to validity" reside primarily in the norm itself (1990: 60). That is to say that we must have a "resource" prior to our speech situations that provides the substantive content of our conversations and the formal claims we make. As I have argued, we cannot *create* the norms that we subject to our consensual recognition in practical moral discourse. Thus my previous arguments about the locus of the metanarrative of history for the primary disclosure and ultimate justification of moral norms do not contradict Habermas's emphasis on the logic and ethics of moral argumentation. I did not suggest that time itself discloses and justifies our norms by some sort of automatic historical revelation; nor did I argue that time was redemptive. Rather I indicated that *human history was time and place engaged by human intelligence* and our critical hermeneutic and argumentative powers. In this sense we can discern the necessary transit from a concentration on the general metapraxis of history to the actual and specific practices of communicative action. Substantive and "time-full" interpretations of our *historical situation* will provide the subject/content of our practical speech—the *locus* of our normative claims—while our *communities of moral discourse* will provide the venue for *exercising* our normative claims and our obligations to submit them to discursive validation. It is precisely because, as Habermas indicates, historical lifeworlds provide the substantive and plural horizons for the disclosure and justification of our norms, "prior to any reflection," that we must submit them to conversation and argument in the first place.[11] It is this social and historical reality that we address in the claims. Thus our normative validity claims are necessitated by and "built into" the material-historical universe of moral norms (Habermas, 1990: 58; 60–61).

This relationship between the *claims* and *locus* of practical moral speech creates a unique mark of objectivity for consensually validated claims. If moral norms "are dependent upon the continual reestablishment of legitimately ordered interpersonal relationships" (Habermas, 1990: 61)—i.e., are regulative both in the sense of effectively and legitimately establishing the relations of discourse as well as those of the social world—then their *objectivity* will be determined on the basis of whether such complementary relationships have in fact been established. In other words norms become "objective" not because they exist as quantities that can be measured but because they exist as qualities and models of interpersonal life that can be observed and experienced. Even though I have gone further than Habermas and made thematic for determining the "objectivity" and legitimacy of a moral norm what I have called its "sacramental efficacy," he does indicate that norms "would assume a utopian character in the negative sense and lose their very meaning if we did not *complement* them, at least in our minds, with actors who might follow them and actions that might fulfill them" (1990: 61).

Yet ambiguity remains in determining the unique objectivity and validity of the moral norm. Norms may exist "objectively" in the social world as models whose intention is to disclose and designate values for informing and finally regulating our behavior while still not being adequately verified discursively in any given time and place. Conversely, norms that have been discursively verified by competent moral speech and argument may not be accepted as informing and regulating in the social world of any culture, society, or community. Habermas argues:

> While there is an unequivocal relation between existing states of affairs and true propositions about them, the "existence" of social currency of norms says nothing about whether norms are valid. *We must distinguish between the social fact that a norm is intersubjectively*

*recognized and its worthiness to be recognized.* There may be good
reasons to consider the validity claim raised in a socially accepted
norm to be unjustified. Conversely, a norm whose claim to validity
is in fact redeemable does not necessarily meet with actual recognition or approval (1990: 61, emphasis added).

It is the ongoing discursive redemption of their claims to validity in
historical communities of moral discourse *and* action that gives norms
their legitimacy. "In the long run the social currency of a norm depends
on its being accepted as valid in the group to which it is addressed"
(Habermas, 1990: 62). Loyalty demands legitimacy; and legitimacy must
be continually tested over changing material-historical circumstances
and ever-expanding and changing social groups.

Habermas's stress on the logic and ethics of practical speech
advances our discussion toward a theoretic perspective on what the
Church would look like when it engages in practical moral discourse for
the verification and legitimation of its moral norms. The fact that historical insight and practice undergo change suggests that competent
conversations about moral norms and subsequent rules of behavior
must go on in the Church in every generation. I have emphasized more
than Habermas has how a major part of the discursive redemption of
validity claims of moral norms and their subsequent legitimation must
also include interpretations and judgments on how the norm is working
in everyday life—whether it is being "sacramentally" effective or not.
Thus the reasons we advance in argument must find a wider material-
historical coherence and validation than that of the confines of any *particular* moral theory or narrow province of meaning and experience. This
raises the final part of the theory of moral argumentation that we will
consider: the question of universality.

The Principle of Universalization Informing a Rule of Argumentation

Habermas suggests a fairly severe revision of the principle of
Kantian universality for informing a rule of competent moral debate.
The principles of universalization and universality we seek to inform
rules of competent moral speech are always related to the plurality of
experiences we bring from the horizon of our material-histories. Thus we
will use not such principles to offer an *ultimate* standing point, or from a
Kantian perspective, a posture *sub specie aeternitatis*. Rather we must
consider formal principles of universalization in ethics as a bridge to a
consensus of "all concerned" rather than the triumph of the particular
position of any person or power bloc . That is to say that what we gen-

erally mean and intend by a principle of universality is "that valid moral norms must be generally teachable and publicly defendable" (1990: 63–64; 65). Consequently, Habermas, argues that

> it is not sufficient...for *one* person to test whether he can will the adoption of a contested norm...or whether every other person in an identical position could will the adoption of such a norm. In both cases the process of judging is relative to the vantage point of *some* and not *all* concerned. True impartiality pertains only to the standpoint from which one can generalize precisely those norms that can count on universal assent because they perceptibly embody an interest common to all affected. It is these norms that deserve intersubjective recognition. Thus the impartiality of judgment is expressed in a principle that constrains *all* affected to adopt the perspectives of *all others* in the balancing of interests (1990: 65).

This principle of universalization intends to inform a rule of "the *universal exchange of roles*," or what George Herbert Mead (1934) called "ideal role taking" or "universal discourse" (Habermas, 1990: 65). Adequate communities of moral discourse, then, require an ethos of full rather than partial participation. Such full participation informs "real-life argumentation" (p. 66) rather than only abstract and procrustean impositions of inadequate theories and unverified assumptions upon those subject to the obligations of moral norms. A principle of universalization also guards against monologic distortions of a fully communicative and dialogic interaction. The need for a new and more comprehensive discursive validation of norms emerges most pointedly when consensus has been disrupted and conversation distorted. With no expectations of ultimate and absolute closure, dialogic cooperation in discourse oriented toward consensus becomes a way of reestablishing a community of intersubjective recognition for either the revitalization of the norm or the recognition of its demise. "What is needed" and what communities of moral discourse provide when framed by the principle of universal and dialogic participation,

> is a "real" process of argumentation in which the individuals concerned cooperate. Only an intersubjective process of reaching understanding can produce an agreement that is reflexive in nature; only it can give the participants the knowledge that they have collectively become convinced of something (Habermas, 1990: 67).

This universality principle is therefore not the same as the "perspective of eternity" informing the Kantian categorical imperatives, though it shares much of the Kantian intent. As Thomas McCarthy indicates (1978: 326), "the emphasis shifts from what each can will without contradiction to be a general law, to what all can will in agreement to be a universal norm" (in Habermas, 1990: 67). The horizon of material-historical pragmatics replaces the standpoint of the thinking subject alone and we are obliged to engage in real cooperative dialogue rather than in the "monological form" of, ironically, *hypothetical* thinking occurring through *categorical imperatives* framed "in the individual mind" (Habermas, 1990: 68).[12] Within the universe of common moral speech and communicative action expressed in the material-historical circumstances of culture and society, Habermas finds the possibility of a "transcendental-pragmatic" analysis of the universal conditions of competent speech. "Every person who accepts the universal and necessary communicative presuppositions of argumentative speech and who knows what it means to justify a norm of action implicitly presupposes as valid the principle of universalization"(1990: 86).[13]

Habermas is aware of the "performative contradictions" of his depiction of competent speech and argument and that "in all cases we have to be content with approximations" (1990: 91). The participants in such conversations are "not Kant's intelligible characters," but are rather "real human beings" who inhabit particular times and places, contexts and circumstances who are "driven by other motives in addition to the one permitted motive of the search for truth" (1990: 92; 105–9). The speech itself must be organized in terms of topic, time, and other empirical limitations—in sum, institutionalized. All ideals are counterfactual in part, and the principle of the universalization of consensus provides an ideal perspective to aid, "in principle"—if our discourse is open and long enough—a practical and effective ethic of argumentation under empirical conditions. The principle of universality is formal only in this sense (1990: 92; 105; 103).[14] Thus Habermas's claims for an "ideal speech situation" of competent speech are not derived from "a transcendental deduction in the Kantian sense," but must always "be checked against individual cases" (1990: 95; 97). Nor is anything lost in denying that the transcendental-pragmatic justification is an ultimate one. At this point in its formal development—though eventually this will be necessary—discourse ethics does not need to foundationally justify the moral intuitions and common practices of everyday life, but to clarify them and bring them to some systematic and coherent vision by means of adequate theory (1990: 98).

## "Discourse Ethics"

Habermas intends that the "discourse ethics" that informs his theory of argumentation aid in the formation of the ideal of an "'unrestricted communication community'" (1990: 88). However, even if we could relatively remove ourselves from "membership in the community of beings who argue" we would still find the demands and obligations of critical discourse remained in terms of our "shared socio-cultural form of life." He argues that we cannot reject "the ethical substance (*Sittlichkeit*) of the life circumstances in which (we) spend (our) waking hours" nor "extricate (ourselves) from the communicative practice of everyday life." In such circumstances we are continually drawn into situations of rational speech and communicative practice where we are obliged to respond discursively. The question is only whether we will become self-conscious and morally aware of such circumstances so that our conversations can be adequately guided by the ethics of discourse—action that is oriented toward understanding and consensus among mutually recognized and equal competent subjects (1990: 100; 101). Since our lifeworlds in the socialization and social integration of culture and communities are mediated symbolically, we have no real choice in rejecting communicative action. To mediate effectively, and thus to inform and create communities, such symbols demand the praxis of critical interpretation and judgment in the forum of discursive and cognitive speech situations: "There is no other, equivalent medium in which these functions can be fulfilled." Without such "action oriented toward reaching an understanding" (Habermas, 1990: 102), our communities of intersubjective integrity will devolve and fracture. Nor if distorted communication goes unattended for too long, can such fractures be contained. Not only will particular subgroups become dysfunctional within a larger community, but the very tradition and heritage of the community itself will erode. Losing the horizon of communicative action, the concrete historical "reality" of the meaning and function of the community will give way to narrow provincialism and competing strategic interests. The character identity of the whole will become splintered, and the general will to remain together as a heritage and tradition will be lost.

These dangers are most prominent in the distorted speech of communities with respect to ethical norms and moral practices. I have already indicated Habermas's insistence that we do not generate norms by our particular conversations alone but merely bring their claims to competent testing. Our practical moral discourses are always related to the wider material-historical horizons of what is being brought forward from our historical past toward an effective future—i.e., to *Tradition* itself. I have also indicated that the need for competent practical speech emerges most pointedly when there is a serious disturbance of consensus with respect to a norm and attendant practices. As Habermas argues: "Practical discourses are always related to the concrete point of departure of a disturbed normative agreement. These antecedent disruptions determine the topics that are up for discussion" (1990: 103). However, if these disruptions and the topics they engender for discussion are not handled competently, then the traditions that inform the identity of a particular community and culture are eventually brought to a crisis in legitimation (see Habermas, 1975). In such a state outside of the principle and rule of universalization, we might continue for a time along the path of a provincialism of regions of competing and strategic moral discussions with narrow and distorted applications of meaning.[15] But such segmentation will not provide the recovery of the balance we need. Contested norms destabilize institutions and traditions and "upset the balance of relations of intersubjective recognition" (Habermas, 1990: 106). Struggles over moral norms are also struggles to come to an adequate recognition of the character of the community and its members. Thus the imperatives of discourse ethics have ramifications beyond the particular topic of the discussion narrowly conceived. Habermas warns:

> Practical discourses resemble islands threatened with inundation in a sea of practice where the pattern of consensual conflict resolution is by no means the dominant one. The means of reaching agreement are repeatedly thrust aside by the instruments of force. Hence, action that is oriented toward ethical principles has to accommodate itself to imperatives that flow not from principles but from strategic necessities (1990: 106).

Without an adequate ethics and practice of competent conversation and debate, communities lose their moral horizon: the necessary ideal moral vision is lost in a sea of assumptions of facts and narrow interests and needs. Our lifeworlds become too close for adequate critical vision and we lose both our viewpoints and the rights and obligations of our points of view. We assume again a relatively premoral naivete about the normative power of the factual and lose our ability to envision a critical moral ideal to inform new ways of life and transform old ones. As I have indicated, in such a state we are not even able to receive for critical reconstruction and transmission the values embedded in our heritage and, having difficulty distinguishing "the good life from the reproduction of

mere life," we lose our ability to engage in the ongoing project of character identification that always demands the translation of our moral
insights into moral action (Habermas, 1990: 108; 107–9).

### Moral Intuitions and the Vulnerability of Sociocultural Life

These dangers of distorted communication indicate a vulnerability
in persons and communities based on the linguistic nature of our relations with each other. This vulnerability, rooted in language, pertains to
character-integrity itself and indicates the importance of our obligations
of competent speech and the need for an adequate "discourse ethic." In
his article "Morality and Ethical Life" (1990: 195-215), Habermas argues
that the origin and role of human moral intuitions are rooted in this
intersubjective vulnerability, first of the *other* and then, reciprocally, of
the self. Self and other are socialized as individuals through a linguistically engaged intersubjective lifeworld. In turn, the lifeworld of a
community of discourse recapitulates this larger matrix of character
identity and formation: the lifeworlds of the individual and the collective are interdependent. In the process of character individuation, we
become more differentiated from the group yet remain still dependent
upon the collective for affirmation and ongoing development. "The
more the subject becomes individuated, the more he becomes entangled
in a densely woven fabric of mutual recognition, that is, of reciprocal"
exposure "and vulnerability" (Habermas, 1990: 199). Thus, the entire
process of individuation and relationship indicates a vulnerability of
both the individual and the collective and a constant need for thought-
fulness and consideration. Unless subjects externalize themselves "by
participating in interpersonal relations through language," they are
"unable to form that inner center" of personal identity. Habermas
continues: "This explains the almost constitutional insecurity and
chronic fragility" of the identity of the person (and the group)—"an insecurity that is antecedent to cruder threats to the integrity of life and
limb.... Our moral intuitions...instruct us on how best to behave in situations where it is in our power to counteract the extreme vulnerability of
others by being thoughtful and considerate." Sympathy and compassion
defend the integrity of the individual and preserve "the vital fabric of
ties of mutual recognition through which individuals *reciprocally* stabi-
lize their fragile identities" (1990: 199; 200).

Thus sympathy and compassion also become normative principles
for informing rules of competent speech. Since our basic moral intuitions
serve to protect "the fragility of human beings individuated through

socialization," sympathetic and compassionate moral discourse and argument must serve the interests of protecting both "the inviolability of the individual by postulating equal respect" and also of protecting "the web of intersubjective relations of mutual recognitions" wherein we can "survive as members of a community." Such an ethos of "equality of respect, solidarity, and the common good" is protected and fostered, in Habermas's view, by the praxis of communicative action (Habermas, 1990: 200; 201).

> In other words, the common core of all kinds of morality can be traced back to the reciprocal imputations and shared presuppositions actors make when they seek understanding in everyday situations.... Discourse generalizes, abstracts, and stretches the presuppositions of context bound communicative actions by extending their range to include competent subjects beyond the provincial limits of their own particular form of life (Habermas, 1990: 201–2).

Consequently, even if any particular theoretic configuration on the one side of discourse ethics fails to justify an adequate within which our rational and moral speech are to be formally practiced, on "its other side," discourse ethics, rooted existentially in the vulnerability of both our private and public lives, always enforces metaethical commitments of sympathy, fellow feeling, care, and mutual respect for the practical ethical guidance of all speech situations. In this way discourse ethics gains its completion in the full praxis of communicative action among free and equal subjects.

Consensus and Community:
Toward a Moral Theology of Communication

Habermas's description of the praxis of communicative action and his consensus model for competent speech and moral discourse offers the Church a promising foundation for building an adequate moral theology of communication.[16] If the Church is a community of moral discourse, then it will need to engage an adequate line of theoretic vision toward the development of an ethic to order and regulate its conversations. Both formally, and in light of the present state of our substantive conversations, the Church's rhetoric of sexual morality indicates the weight as well as the opportunity of this burden of our character. All too often our conversations about sex have become distorted by provincial and competing power interests, by a reduction and exclusion of competent subjects, and by a variety of arguments against the modern age itself based upon failed ecclesiastical visions of a Church of times past, or of a segmented remnant, or of an aestheticist cloud of unknowing hovering above the fray. Not paying enough attention to our obligations and practices of competent and cognitive speech, we make major mistakes in our understanding and use of moral terms and concepts as well as in misunderstanding the role that norms rooted in our historical past must play in contemporary life. All of these failures, however, do not leave us without hope. Our current fractious debates on sex can provide us with an opportunity to raise again the ancient rhetoric of the Church as a community of sympathetic and compassionate persons who, before any particulars of theological and moral debate, understand ourselves as a *koinonia* community of critical interpreters and communicative actors in the social world. John Mahoney argues the Church as *koinonia*—the "communion of all Christian believers" who "partake" of the Spirit of God in Christ—

> is a hospitable concept, embracing all who have gone before in the history of the Christian community and sensitive to that tradition without being fixed in it or being unaware of its historical limitations. It is coming to embrace in increasing awareness those who, despite tragic disunities within the fellowship, share "the *koinonia* in the gospel" (*Phil.* 1: 5) (1989: 345; 341–47).

Upon this confessional horizon of *koinonia* companionship, our debates on sexual morality must be framed within an ethos and ethic of communicative consensus. Consensus does not require total agreement on every "letter of the law" but rather first a "feeling together" (*consentire*). The Church as a *koinonia* community partakes of a Gospel proclaimed by, perhaps, our premier controversialist, that obliges us first "to treat each other in the same friendly way as Christ treated you" (*Romans* 15: 7). The final and tragic irony of the internal and external fractures of the Church's rhetoric of sex is that we have become distracted from this core value of friendship. While the forms of love are many, the love of friendship must center our passions with each other. It is here in the *koinonia* communion of friends that we will find the foundation of an adequate moral theology both of sex and communication in the body of the Church.

# Appendix

## THE RHETORIC OF MORAL DISCOURSE

### *ACTION*

| Styles of Speech | Levels of Moral Discourse | Forms of Disciplines |
|---|---|---|
| | **Emotive Appeal**<br>Affective Appeals to Particular Action | |
| *Evocative* | *Ideology*<br>*Passionate Persuasion* | *Rhetorical/Homiletic* |
| | **Moral Rule**<br>Rational "Ought Statements" in Particular Situations | |
| *Argumentative* | *Theory*<br>*Rational Coherence and Understanding* | *Systematic* |
| | **Ethical Principle**<br>General Declaration of Normative Values | |
| *Imaginative* | *Critique*<br>*Making Fundamental Suppositions Problematic* | *Foundational Inquiry* |
| | **Metaethical Foundations**<br>Individual and Communal Confessions; Narrative Histories; Character Identifying Metaphors, Symbols, Models | |

### *REFLECTION*

## SPECIFIC TERMS OF MORAL/ETHICAL DISCOURSE

| Values | Virtues | Goods |
|---|---|---|
| *Intentionally Obliging Moral Meanings* | *Habits of Interpretation and Response* | *Positive States of Affairs* |

A value is *something of worth* (L.,*valere*: "to be strong, of worth"]

Values are the critical hermeneutic ground of moral discourse. If something *appears* and is *interpreted* and *named* a value, there arises a *prima facie* obligation to bring that value to positive realization as a good. "Intentional" here refers to (L.) *intendere*, "to stretch toward." In this usage, values always stretch toward their own realization as *goods*.

Virtues *join* and *mediate* values and goods.

As *Habits*, virtues ground the phenomenon of character and center the moral life.

Virtues share in the *prima facie* obligation of bringing values to realization as goods.

Goods *accomplish* and bring values to *social* and *political realization* via the mediation of virtues.

As the *terminus* or *intentional goal* of moral discourse, goods disclose and make concrete the material-historical nature of moral discourse and the moral life.

Consequently, what is brought to positive realization and claimed as *good*, in turn can criticize the prior value-meanings.

### Motives

*That which moves us to act.*

Motives are *reflexive*. What from *past experience* (e.g. obliging duty) as a moral person (character in a life-world) moves us to act in this situation [L., *movere*, "to move")? The principal hermeneutic activity in the discernment of motive is *remembrance*.

### Intentions

*That which is intended or sought.*

The *goal* or *consequence* we seek to accomplish. Intentions are *projective* (L., *intendere*, "to stretch toward"). The principal hermeneutic activity in the discernment of intention is *anticipation*.

### Rights

*Obliging claims of self* (individual/ group) *upon another* (individual/ group)

### Duties

*Obliging claims of another* (individual/ group) *upon the self* (individual/ group)

*Obliging* here and throughout means the right or duty ought to be met—the claim satisfied. The question of whether the claim has been verified and legitimated (i.e., is actually rationally and morally obliging) is the question of the validation of the right and duty—whether the right and duty has been sustained by moral argument, cultural/anthropological expectation, and moral policy and law; and whether all of these can be grounded adequately at metaethical levels of intersubjective experience (L., *Obligare*, "to bind or tie;" "to bind back;" "to bind forward").

| Norms | Principles | Rules |
|---|---|---|
| *An Ethical/moral norm is an historical, cultural, and societal figuration for the disclosure of moral values.* | *Ethical principles are linguistic statements of ethical/moral norms.* | *Moral rules are measures and regulations for practical guidance in the actual and contextually specific situations of moral decision making.* |
| As *figurative speech*, norms display qualities and functions of a *metaphor* and *symbol*, and when mature, are displayed in history, culture, and society as *models*. | The ethical principle is most often stated by way of a declarative sentence. | The proximate purpose and function of rules are to bring values to realization as goods in *actual and specific states of affairs.* |
| Norms are figurative speech since moral/ethical norms do not simply describe states of affairs statistically or demographically, that is, *how things are*, but engage in a counterpoint between how things are and how things ought to be. This counterpoint between the *is* and the *ought* is the *metaphorical* quality and function of ethical/ moral norms. | *Ethical principles* are the foundations of systematic moral argument. | As contextually specific and sensitive, adequate moral rules must be more *flexible, plural* and *variable* than moral norms and ethical principles. |
| When the obliging values disclosed by the | | |

metaphorical counter-
point become *sedimented
and routinized* in terms
of moral expectations
and ritualized moral
behavior and practices
in culture and society,
norms achieve the level
of *symbol.*

When such values
become systematized in
*analogical paradigms and
patterns* of ways of life,
norms become *models.*

As figures of disclosure,
norms are necessarily
general and distant
from the challenge of
actual moral decision,
but function to orient
that decision in the
journey of value to
good. Since norms are
embedded in the figura-
tive discourse of history,
culture and society—in
heritages of moral tradi-
tion—norms cannot be
simply chosen, but
rather must be identi-
fied. Within any specific
community or culture of
discourse and character
identification, norms
function in a singular
way. A change in char-
acter-identifying norms
involves a change in the
character of the group
itself as well as of individuals within the
group.

**THE TEMPORAL PATTERN OF MORAL/ETHICAL REFLECTION
AND DISCOURSE**

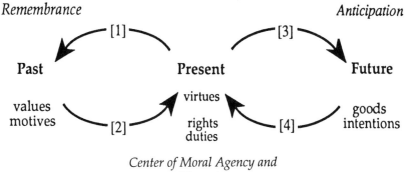

*Center of Moral Agency and
Character*

The phenomenal experience of moral character—the *feeling of being* situated in place and time in intersubjective relation to others—centers the moral life. This is the experience of *moral agency*—being an actor with others in the dramas of moral obligation and action; being a character in the ongoing narratives of history, culture, and society; a participant/traveler on historical journeys. These phenomenal experiences are grounded in the hermeneutic/historical acts of remembrance and anticipation through which we gain a moral *habit of being* through the *praxis of virtue*.

# NOTES

## Introduction

1. Throughout the first section, I will offer a context for the modern debate about the continuing possibility of substantive and constructive rational discourse in ethics in general and sexual morality in particular. For an alternative view and a strong criticism of the enlightenment heritage of modernity with respect to rational moral discourse, see Alasdair MacIntyre (1984; 1990).

2. In describing as "inadequately faithful" what I will call later the anti-modern "neosectarianism" and "melancholic traditionalism" of some denominations with respect to sexual morality, I do not mean to be moralistic or personally indicting of any individual or group. I am using the term "fidelity" here to mean teaching that bears the faith and life of the Church forward to meet constructively the challenges of any age. Certainly our attempts to return to what we take to be more coherent worlds of traditional teaching does express in part a concern for an orderly and responsible life in our sexual relations. Also I remain aware of the contributions of classical sectarian Christianity, especially in its prophetic indictments of false and irenic accommodations to contemporary cultures and societies. In this faithful service, the radical sectarian traditions have often been contemporary despite their protests to the contrary. However, I will argue that the specific question of a "neosectarian" ecclesiology and moral posture by mainline denominations that are not classically and radically sectarian is more complex. This selective and essentially bourgeois sectarianism as well as the melancholic traditionalism noted above all suffer from a combination of inadequate ecclesiology, innervating anxiety about modernity, and fundamental confusions in moral argument finally rooted in a misunderstanding of the historicity of the Church's faith and life.

3. I will take up the question of pluralism and modernity in the next three chapters. I will also discuss the necessity of both discontinuity and continuity with the past for an adequate understanding of history and tradition. I will argue against the assumption that fidelity is always or mainly cast with only the continuities of history and tradition. An inadequate understanding of tradition has greatly contributed to the current inability of the Church to present both a faithful and contemporary sexual ethic.

4. Often this pragmatic "intuition" of the Church has been closer to what can be called the "preconscious" or "subconscious" than the cognitive—in less psychological terms, closer to our foundational faith confessions than to our

systematically articulated theology and ethic that often have only this "conserving" cast. Still it is one of the tenets of radical and modern historicism that we cannot escape the confines of contemporaneous time and circumstance no matter how much we try. One could argue that the attempted "escapes" from history I have been discussing are negative engagements with modernity—part of the Church's own recurring "crisis mentality." The purpose of this book, however, is to suggest and search for positive and constructive engagements with historicist modernity rather than to only describe the malaise. The present rhetoric of Christian sexual morality can be seen as a focus of the wider problems the modern Church is having with fidelity and contemporaneity overall. Such a rhetoric of crisis of the Church in the modern world may be understandable at the end of a century and millennium as well as, perhaps, an age. We should take care, however, that this rhetoric does not substitute our own needs for catharsis for our obligations of worldly engagement.

5. After Freud, the relation of sexuality and anxiety is now commonplace. Freud's "discovery" of repression in sexual matters is hardly debatable. Nor need this anxiety-ridden repression be manifested only in the psyche of individuals. With some ambivalence, Freud argued that the life of civilizations, cultures, institutions in general, and religion in particular, recapitulated the psychosexual dynamics and vicissitudes of the individual. Freud's major works in this area are essays published in 1912–1913 and collected later under the title *Totem and Taboo* (1950); *The Future of an Illusion* (1927); *Civilization and Its Discontents* (1930); *Moses and Monotheism: Three Essays* (1939). For these references, see James Strachey, ed., *The Standard Edition of the Complete Psychological Works of Sigmund Freud.* Vols.. 13; 21; 21; 23, respectively. (1953–1974)).

6. The schematic for such "time-fullness" starts from and always returns to the point of contemporary experience. The first act of critical hermeneutic remembrance indicates a loop of retrieval of the past—the past being brought to present experience in acts of *remembrance*. Following that, a second loop of *anticipation* casts us toward the future. While both loops begin and end in the present, both are necessary for the experience of "time-fullness." While neither remembrance of the past nor anticipation of the future have normative and criteriological priority, the loop of remembrance is phenomenologically prior. That is to say that our quests for biographical identity as individuals and groups seem to be initiated by our remembrances. See the Appendix for a diagram of this schematic.

7. The etymology of the word homosexuality can be ambiguous. The Latin root *homo* is often translated by the noninclusive *man* but means *human being*, or now less precisely, "generic 'man.'" Note also the OL, *hemo* from *humus*—the *earthy one* and *earth born*; and *nemo*, or "nobody" in particular (see Partridge, 292). When Latin intends to be precisely gender specific, the word *vir* is used for man. However, the Greek (*homos/homoios*) means *same* or *like*. In this book, I will combine the most generic Latin and Greek roots and use the term

*homosexual* to refer to same-sex orientations/relations of both genders. However, it remains important to understand that male and female homosexuality (or lesbianism) display significant psychological and sociological differences that ought to be addressed in any thorough study of human sexuality. I will give an argument for my decision not to use the more popular term "gay" with reference to same-sex orientations and relations in Chapter Six.

Unless otherwise indicated, definitions, etymologies, and word studies here and throughout are from *Webster's Third New International Dictionary of the English Language Unabridged* (1986); *Webster's New World Dictionary of the American Language* (1978); *The Random House College Dictionary* (1979); Eric Partridge, *Origins: A Short Etymological Dictionary of Modern English* (1983); and F. E. Peters, *Greek Philosophical Terms: A Historical Lexicon* (1967).

8. For a modern classic on rhetoric as persuasion, see Richard Weaver who, as I have indicated, in his *The Ethics of Rhetoric* (1965), considers such speech "a kind of love" (p. 14) Weaver further argues that "it is 'love' because it is something in addition to bare theoretical truth. That element in addition is a desire to bring truth into a kind of existence, or to give to it an actuality to which theory is indifferent" (p. 25). For other works whose intent is to recover the philosophy and art of substantive discourse and persuasive argument, see: Wayne C. Booth (1974; 1979); W. V. Quine and J. S. Ullian (1978); Stephen Toulmin (1964; 1969); and Ronald Dworkin (1993).

9. See, for example, Carol Gilligan, *In a Different Voice: Psychological Theory and Women's Development* (1982); Mary F. Belenky, et al., *Women's Ways of Knowing* (1986); and Eva F. Kittay and Diana Meyers (eds.) *Women and Moral Theory* (1987). For an important debate about these and related matters within the feminist movement, see Elizabeth Fox-Genovese, *Feminism Without Illusions: A Critique of Individualism* (1991).

10. See David Tracy's adoption of Wallace Stevens's poetic line "Blessed rage for order"—from "The Idea of Order at Key West"—as the signature theme for his book in fundamental theology, *Blessed Rage for Order* (1975).

11. See Tom L. Beauchamp and James F. Childress, *Principles of Biomedical Ethics* (1983, p. ix–xii). For a discussion of the difficulties in the pursuit of ethical and moral perfectionism both in argument and in life, see Isaiah Berlin (1988).

12. For the notion of the plenitude of understanding in all acts of historical interpretation and judgment, and in history itself, see Hans-Georg Gadamer, *Truth and Method* (1975); and the second and revised translation (1991).

13. The title and theme "The Church: A Community of Moral Discourse" is James Gustafson's (1970). I will deal with this theme more directly in Chapter Seven.

Chapter 1. Sexual Discourse and the Problem of Modernity

1. For a good presentation of the relationship between theological discourse and reflection and cosmological orientation, see Max Wildiers (1982).

2. Though Heidegger can be used as only one partial reference for my "historicist" approach in this book, I do not follow him all the way. Despite his so called "turn to history," Heidegger finally engages in an "aestheticism" I will criticize later in this chapter. Heidegger also engages in a strong critique of modernity on transcendental/idealist grounds of ontological retrieval and the quasi-mystical disclosure of being. Kolb describes Heidegger's approach as one that suggests that "the price of immersion in events was too high; it would hinder the step back, which is the essence of thinking" (1988: 208). In this, Heidegger also participates in at least a quasi-geneticist view of the priority of origins and a rather paradoxical nostalgia for the return of the future of being to its destiny in land, culture, and nation (see also Michael E. Zimmerman, 1990).

For a discussion of Heidegger's aestheticism in general, see Alan Megill's *Prophets of Extremity* (1985: 142-180). Both Megill and Kolb note that the dangers of Heidegger's aestheticist romanticism are displayed in his marginal location of reflection and rational discourse. Megill goes on to suggest that "Heidegger is a poor guide for those who want to grasp how the 'ordinary' world operates" (1985: 180). My own approach concentrates more on the material content and practical moral implication of history's conversations and narrations than Heidegger's transcendental eschewal of the "details" of history found in the "naivete" of the "natural attitude" (see Kolb, 199–200). Despite the continuing importance of his philosophical work, Heidegger's general ontological organicism and romantic transcendentalism oriented him to what we now know as more than merely an initial and passing acceptance of National Socialism. Jürgen Habermas indicates that Heidegger's moral breakdown was not just personally characterological: "Even Richard Rorty misses the point that the problem is not the relation between person and work, but the amalgamation of work and world view " (1989b: 436 n15). In this regard, see also Richard Rorty (1988); Thomas Sheehan (1988); Victor Farias (1989); Arnold I. Davidson, ed. (1989); Luc Ferry and Alain Renaut (1990); and Richard Wolin, ed. (1991).

3. I know of no better treatment of the challenge of self-conscious historical contemporaneity in theology and ethics in terms of confessional fidelity than H. Richard Niebuhr's *The Meaning of Revelation* (1960, first published, 1941).

4. For the categories of continuity and discontinuity, I am indebted to Nicholas Lash's "Continuity and Discontinuity in the Christian Understanding of God" in Nicholas Lash, *Theology on Dover Beach* (1979: 27-44). Lash argues that it is the mystery of faith in the plenitude of God's involvement amid any and all changes in human history that frames both the dynamics of continuity and discontinuity in Christian theological and moral understanding.

5. While associated historically with the classical theory of "natural law," the existential utility of the terms "nature" and "human nature" in Christian ethics are not limited to that theory or its critically reconstructed underpinnings. I have indicated that for moral experience in general and for the primary motivation to engage in rational public moral discourse, "nature" or some functional equivalent must be used to articulate a ground of ordered participation in a larger whole—a sense of worlds of meaning and experience that tie us together as individuals and groups in environments of existential obligation.

I am not suggesting that "nature" is always the best or only term to use to articulate this necessary sense of ordered participation. Nor do I suggest that its continuing crass physicalist discrimination over against the "unnatural"—as in "birth-control or homosexuality are unnatural"—is adequate, especially in sexual ethics. Nor does any term for "order" need to indicate a total historical continuity without break or change. Furthermore, this is not an attempt to rehabilitate that often-invalid logical transference from "what is" to "what ought to be." And while any logical witness to such an invalid transference is only relative to its undergirding cosmology and epistemology, the invalidating witness of sociopolitical history to this sort of "naturalist fallacy" is more universal. Rather, I am suggesting that the reason why the term "nature" has had such a long run in the history of ethics and why it survives today in common moral speech and conscience, however uncritically, is because it articulates an intuition that the experience of participation in larger and relatively ordered worlds is necessary lest morality become only individual taste, norms only statistical averages, and moral discourse only a logical game played by disconnected and warring intellects and wills. Other philosophies and theologies will use other terms for ordering character and world. Nonetheless, our quests for ordered location and presence amid dislocation and absence remain necessary for the event of moral character. The ubiquity of the use and abuse of the term "nature," and its correlatives "natural" and "unnatural" in arguments about sexual morality can be understood in this light. In this regard, see also Robin Lovin (1991) and John Courtney Murray, "The Doctrine Lives: The Eternal Return of Natural Law," in Curran and McCormick, eds., (1991: 184–220).

6. It may very well be that my own particular Roman Catholic tradition informs me here, at least initially, as much as anything else. Since my tradition came late to modernity so to speak, I am loath to "give up" this cosmology without a critical fight.

7. Marshall Berman (1982: 21) quotes Karl Marx's description of modern times: "All fixed and fast frozen relations, with their train of ancient and venerable prejudices and opinions, are swept away, all new-formed ones become antiquated before they can ossify. All that is solid melts into air, all that is holy is profaned, and men at last are forced to face…the real conditions of their lives and their relations with their fellow men" ("Speech at the Anniversary of the *People's Paper*").

8. For further discussion of the problem of moral analysis and judgment in postmodern deconstructionism, see Peter Hodgson (1986) and Richard Kearney (1984). For a postmodernist criticism of historicist approaches, see Jean-François Lyotard's "The Postmodern Condition" (1987: 73–94). Lyotard defines postmodernity "as incredulity toward metanarratives" (p. 74).

9. A very important and good treatment of the discourse of the early Church on sexual theology and morality is Peter Brown's *Body and Society: Men, Women and Sexual Renunciation in Early Christianity* (1988).

10. For the influence of Hellenism in Hebraic thought, see Martin Hengel, *Judaism and Hellenism*, Vols. I & II (1981).

11. It is important to note again that there did exist a more radical sexual theology and ethic of renunciation that informed most of the writings on sex up to the time of Jerome and Augustine (see Peter Brown, 1988). Much of this rhetoric was drawn specifically from the apocalyptic cast of the religious mentality of those ages. Because of his intention to trace the ethics and law of *sexual behavior*, Brundage does not pay sufficient attention to this earliest phenomenon and, indeed, "norm" of Christian sexual ethics. For many of these earliest Christian writers and teachers, the classical age was coming to an end and a renewed, more "spiritual," cosmos was in the offing. That this did not happen in the ways they expected led to the need for the development of the more specific norms, rules, and codes of sexual behavior that Brundage investigates. Interestingly enough, the rhetoric of crisis of that earliest age is not in form totally different from some of what we are currently experiencing in our own (for example, see Hauerwas and Willimon: 1989; and Monti: 1993). I will discuss further the relevance of this period for developing a contemporary Christian sexual ethic in Chapter Six.

12. Thomas Kuhn's *The Structure of Scientific Revolutions* (1970) is familiar in this context insofar as it emphasizes the pragmatic interests and purposes that inform dominant theoretic and practical paradigms as building blocks for cosmological worlds.

13. This conflict over historicism has plagued the Church from the origins of modernity and continues to be a major issue in the modern discourse on sexual morality. The fundamental question is whether fully critical theology and ethics can be articulated faithfully by the Church within the full context of modernity—that is, articulated in a way that depends on no implied methodological priority of past, present, or future but is fully dialectical, dialogical, and materially historicist. Such a thoroughly modern theology and ethic would take the questions and answers of its own time with as much seriousness as all past and possible future times. Or is Christian theology in general so rooted in historic and communal myths, stories, and symbols of origin to be in one way or another geneticist and antimodern? The approach I am taking in this text suggests that I do not think we need necessarily remain within such a dilemma of fidelity and

contemporaneity—one not even adequately noticed when, in our interpretations of scripture, doctrine, and the moral life, we relatively collapse the meaning of fidelity into a return to past origins.

14. Douglas John Hall offers a critique of Christianity in North America as a religion of optimism rather than hope—a religion whose theology of resurrection has been born at the expense of its theology of the cross. Along with the work of Metz (1980; 1984) and others, Hall's is one of the better in a growing list of theological reflections on the failure of modernist progressivism to ground an adequate ecclesiology (1976; 1988; 1989; 1993). However, while Hall and Metz have strong criticisms to make of the assumptions of enlightenment reason, and partake of the growing rhetoric of crisis that surrounds the debates about late modernity and postmodernity, it would be a mistake to classify them as antimodernists. For a more directly antimodernist perspective in ecclesiology, see Stanley Hauerwas and William Willimon, *Resident Aliens: Life in the Christian Colony* (1989); and Stanley Hauerwas, *After Christendom?* (1991). For further discussion, see Anthony Battalgia (1988: 128–42).

15. Gellner gives an example of what he calls the "Fallacy of the Gauls:" "It is said that in the French colonial empire, elementary education, like other things, was centralised and homogeneous. Hence children in outposts of empire used textbooks similar to those used in Lille or Dijon. Apparently one of the elementary textbooks spoke of 'our ancestors the Gauls'...and thus little Berber, Senegalese, Malagasy or Tahitian children solemnly repeated: 'Our ancestors the Gauls....'" (1978: 15; 28). In this regard, see also Paulo Freire, *Pedagogy of the Oppressed* (1970).

16. Hall (1976) describes this crisis in modernity as the anxiety produced in the disjunction between *expectation* and *experience*—that is modernity failing to deliver what it has promised. When such a condition prevails in more discriminate social systems, as Jürgen Habermas argues (1975), a crisis in legitimation occurs. However, as we participate and even revel in the false promises of such ages and systems, such self-conscious notice and discrimination is not easily attainable. Consequently when such crises occur they are marked—often for long periods—by a slowly developing feeling of malaise along with an attendant anxiety-ridden and often nondiscriminate rhetoric of crisis.

17. For my criticism of what I consider the neo-sectarian agenda of Stanley Hauerwas and William Willimon expressed in their *Resident Aliens* (1989), as well as a version of the same argument I use in this book against the new sectarian ecclesiology in general, see my "Dangerous Times and Obliging Places" (1993).

18. In this regard, see Max Horkheimer and Theodore W. Adorno, *Dialectic of the Enlightenment* (1972) and Jürgen Habermas's analysis in "The Entwinement of Myth and Enlightenment: Max Horkheimer and Theodor Adorno" (Habermas, 1987: 106–30).

19. Ironically enough, in light of my previous depictions of the rise of the artisan-self and agent-centered conscience in the Renaissance and early modernity, neo-sectarian moral rhetoric on this point is more modern than it thinks.

20. The categories of "internal and external history" are from H. R. Niebuhr's *The Meaning of Revelation* (1960: 59–66). The phrase "to give birth to oneself" is from Robert Bellah, et al. (1985: 82).

21. Much of the present debate over the priority of *lex orandi* (the law/order of prayer) and *lex credendi* (the law/order of belief) is misplaced. Prayer and belief—including the obligations and commitments of the moral life—must remain vitally interactive in a continuing dialectical exchange amid the continuities and discontinuities of the Church's historical life. If liturgy is to function as a ground for religious and moral lives, it will fail to do so if the relationship is monologic—that is, *lex orandi* simply leading to *lex credendi*—and abstracted in its rituals from the material-historical realities of contemporary experience. For good discussions of the relationship of liturgy to theology and ethics, but still under the relative priority of *lex orandi*, see Geoffrey Wainwright (1980) and Timothy Sedgwick (1987).

22. For example, from the Christian perspective, Jewish-Christian conversations, especially after the Holocaust, are not only for mutual understanding but are also for an increased and renewed "self-understanding" for Christians based on a non-negating Christology. In this approach, Judaism is the "other" who calls Christianity to a renewal and reformation of its own identity. See my *Who do you say that I Am? The Christian Understanding of Christ and Antisemitism* (1984).

23. For my initial approach to the phenomenological priority of the other in the paradigm of dialogic conversation, see my *Ethics and Public Policy: The Conditions of Public Moral Discourse* (1982). See also Stephan Strasser, *The Idea of Dialogal Phenomenology* (1969). For a discussion of the decentering effect the other has on the ego and another critique of "egological" orientations in ethics, see Thomas Ogletree, "Hospitality to the Stranger: The Role of the 'Other' in Moral Experience" (Ogletree, 1985: 35–63).

24. See, for example, Rollo May, *Love and Will* (1969) and *Power and Innocence* (1972). See also, Herbert Marcuse, *Eros and Civilization* (1966); and Ernest Becker, *Escape from Evil* (1975).

25. Art and aesthetics do not necessarily involve these motives of release and "self-creation." My point here is to note that these interrelated motives are often part and parcel of art as it functions as a radical critique of modernity in crisis—i.e., in at least a relative postmodern frame. Some premonition of this can be found in *A Portrait of the Artist as a Young Man* (1964), where James Joyce depicts Stephen Dedalus's flight from the encrustation and enslavement of religion and Church to enjoy the freedom and creativity of art. In Chapter Five,

Joyce describes both art and the artist in terms of a radical aestheticist release and self-creation.

> The personality of the artist, at first a cry or a cadence or a mood and then a fluid and lambent narrative, finally refines itself out of existence, impersonalizes itself, so to speak. The esthetic image in dramatic form is life purified in and reprojected from the human imagination. The mystery of esthetic like that of material creation is accomplished. The artist, like the God of creation, remains within or behind or beyond or above his handiwork, invisible, refined out of existence, indifferent, paring his fingernails (p. 215).

For the notion of the artist as "Godlike" in Steven Dedalus and James Joyce, I am indebted to J. Mitchell Morse (1959: 127–39).

26. The theological work of Karl Rahner is only one, but perhaps the most significant in this century, which takes seriously the relationship between the ever-present but ever-receding anthropological horizon of rational inquiry and the theological depths of faith. See, for example, Rahner's *Foundations of Christian Faith* (1982).

27. I will develop this point later in what I call the "norm of content" in moral discourse. But an example may be helpful now. In discussions of how victims of AIDS are to be assisted or how we are to respond to this epidemic as a major threat to life in our own time, even critical conversations about the ethics of sexual practices can be materially misplaced. Sexual morality may be legitimately discussed, but only as it materially pertains to this wider discussion about life and death—i.e., we ought not to engage in sexual practices that can kill. The presenting conversation is not about sexual morality per se, but about living and dying in terrible ways. Guided by the material content and historical reality of AIDS as a proximate threat to life, in this context no central discussion of sexual morality as such has any real prospect of being productive since it will be a misplaced conversation, and, though relevant in other times and places, in this conversation it ought to be to be deferred. In the present moral debate about AIDS, ordinary questions of sexual morality have been transformed into a discourse about our responsibilities and obligations of life and death. Therefore, whatever a denomination may argue about homosexuality, the use of condoms, or nonmarital sexual practice in general, information and policies that promote what is currently understood as "safe sex" ought to be encouraged unless the denomination could sustain an argument to the contrary on grounds of life and death and not of sexual morality.

28. I have been instructed here by Walker Percy's discussion of the literature of alienation in his *The Message in the Bottle* (1975: 83-100). In this oxymoronic way, the literature of alienation—as literature—is neither in text nor author a participant in real alienation.

29. In this context, John E. Smith's reminder of the significant difference between statements such as "humans seek freedom" and "humans are freedom" is important (1984: 52; 43–54).

30. Aestheticist understandings of art as worldly release and "self-creation" create special strains for confessionally incarnational religions. For example, a comparison can be made of the lives and work of Thomas Merton and James Joyce, both artists by autobiographical identification. If as I noted above (see Note 25), the encrustation of James Joyce's Irish Catholicism required a flight from religion to art, Merton's *The Seven Storey Mountain* (1948) describes a reverse flight from unbounded aesthetic freedom to the bonds of religion, church, and world. The failure of either the Church or the age to account for the new, the different, and the other—what was not "allowed" to be said or written—makes Joyce's motive of aestheticist release from such encrusted worlds and the search for the new freedom of radical criticism understandable and a necessary "therapy." Nevertheless, Merton's lesson is more complete and historically sustaining: the freedom of release is finally justified by the desire and practice of "return," with aestheticist self-creations giving way to new and worldly re-creations. Certainly Merton eventually found in an essentially anti-modern monastic tradition, as well as in himself and his American culture, much of the same debilitating encrustation of Joyce's youthful Catholicism. The lesson of Merton's life is that both critical art and religion finally must engage what it finds rather than seeking release to more ethereal levels of "creativity."

31. The major proponent of the deconstructionist critique in philosophy and literature is Jacques Derrida: see, for example, Derrida's *Speech and Phenomena* (1973); *Of Grammatology* (1976); *Writing and Difference* (1978). For an introduction to the use of the deconstructionist critique in religion and theology see, Thomas Altizer, ed. (1982); Mark C. Taylor (1982; 1984); Charles E. Winquist (1986).

32. For a full discussion of the meaning of the deconstructionist neologisms of *altarity* and *différance*, see Mark C. Taylor (1987: xxi–xxxiv; 1982: 99–103).

33. I will take up the question of competent moral discourse across the wide body of the Church in a more direct way in the last chapter. However, even here it is important to note Jürgen Habermas's reminder of the necessary problematic of expertise in the engagement of critical public discourse: "The vindicating superiority of those who do the enlightening over those who are to be enlightened is theoretically unavoidable, but at the same time it is fictive and requires self-correction: in a process of enlightenment there can only be participants" (1974: 40).

34. All typologies are heuristic. Consequently we can expect mixtures and recombinations of the various types amid the paradoxes and vagaries of the Church's historical life. Still, a further rational ordering may be attained that is a deeper heuristic grounding for the typologies themselves. For example, with all

of their variety of recombination and expression, all of these forms of antimodern and postmodern theological and moral rhetoric can be related under the common depiction of "postliberal" antifoundationalism. Hans W. Frei (1992) describes the antifoundationalist approach when Christian theology is viewed as "exclusively a matter of Christian self-description. External descriptive categories (or foundations) have no bearing on or relation to it at all." Functioning in specific contexts only and under its own "internal logic," "Christian theology is strictly the grammar of the faith, a procedure in self-description for which there is no external correlative" (p. 4; parens added). The neo-sectarian reduction of the Church's discourse to an internal grammar and logic of faith and the moral life clearly exhibits a form of antifoundationalism, as does the aestheticist intention of gaining release through the deconstruction of external referents of discourse and text. The rhetoric of melancholic nostalgia can become a variant of antifoundationalism more by default than intention. When our debates and arguments become radically anachronistic, we tend to be content with having conversations with only those of like anachronistic mind. We become satisfied with only the internal logic of the speech itself, and among ourselves, rather than concerned about its reception and external performance in terms of wider worlds and audiences. In this regard also, see the hermeneutic proposal of "intratextuality" of George A. Lindbeck (1984).

## Chapter 2. The Historicity of Faith and Life

1. Note here Johann Metz's powerful discussion of the "memory of the dead" and "the dangerous memory of Jesus Christ" in *Faith in History and Society* (1980).

2. I interpret the work of Jürgen Habermas in this light—i.e., as research responding to what he calls "systematically distorted communication" in the modern age. I will discuss the relevance of Habermas's theory of "communicative action" for informing competent nondistorted communication and "discourse ethics" in Chapter Seven.

3. More traditionalist Roman Catholic leaders, as well as traditionalists in other denominations, often claim that the Church is not a "democracy" nor authentic religion a "cafeteria line" where we can pick and choose what suits our taste. In any extreme utilitarian sense of moral decision by crass majority vote of taste and preference, their claims are true. Yet it was precisely the intent of the Second Vatican Council to democratize the administration and decision making of the church, at least insofar as collegial participation was to be the norm rather than the exception to the rule. Some gains have certainly been made with the work of national conferences of bishops and local clergy and parish councils. However, as long as episcopal and clerical conferences and councils remain overly homogeneous, and as long as consultation of the faithful is only solicited

at the margins, the necessary critical mass for a fully participatory and collegial discourse will be lacking. Finally, even though the Roman Catholic Church has a better record than most, if not all, denominations in its regular use of theological expertise in its teaching documents, the recent renewal of intimidating and punishing measures for the ordinary exercise of theological research, teaching, and writing on sexual morality will remain troublesome for a full engagement of new constructive conversations. In this regard see Charles E. Curran (1986), and Curran and Richard A. McCormick, eds. (1988).

4. For a discussion of antimodernism in general in a significant period of American cultural life and its unintended effects, see T. J. Jackson Lears's *No Place of Grace* (1981). Lears is a good reminder that antimodernism as a cultural and societal movement is more complex than my own use of the category as part of a heuristic typology to organize varieties of discourse in specific conversations about sexual morality.

5. For a discussion of the theme "saving the appearances" in history, culture, and society, see Owen Barfield (1965). My use of the term "phenomenological" in this context is aptly described by Paul Tillich, who understands a phenomenological description "as one which points to a reality as it is given, before one goes to theoretical explanation or derivation" (1976: 17). The phenomenological approach and methods have been significant attempts to understand and organize the radical pluralism of modernity.

6. In his *Truth and Method* (1975), Gadamer argues against understanding "methods" of inquiry as only an array of arts or techniques (p. xvi) among which we pick and choose according to some predetermined desire or end. Rather, in Gadamer's view, the "progress" of history grounds critical hermeneutic inquiry as the praxis of human understanding itself. In this sense, critical historicist "method" is not just one option among many (pp. 274; 431–33).

7. My discussion of modernist, antimodernist, and postmodernist rhetoric on sexual morality has some relation to H. Richard Niebuhr's typologies in *Christ and Culture* (1951): i.e., the overt antimodernism of "Christ Against Culture;" the subtle antimodernism in the continuity of a moribund classical synthesis in "Christ Above Culture;" the mixture of modernist, antimodernist, and at least an early promotion of postmodernist themes in "Christ and Culture in Paradox;" the acceptance of many popular modernist self-understandings in "Christ of Culture;" and the more selective acceptance of modernist understandings of progress in "Christ, the Transformer of Culture." However, none of Niebuhr's models adequately reflect the full dialectical praxis of mutual transformation of question and answer—of both Christ and culture—required in the decentered spirals of fully historicist conversation.

8. In *The Social Sources of Denominationalism*, H. Richard Niebuhr argues that it is not simple diversity that creates the evils of denominationalism but the phenomenon of loyalty to caste and the failure of the denominations "to resist

the temptation of making their own self-preservation and extension the primary object of their endeavor" (Niebuhr, 1963b: 21).

9. Substantive criteria for judging the range of necessary participants and adequate subjects in fully critical conversations are often difficult to determine in practice. Theoretically, the horizon of such critical-practical discourse covers the range of human history itself—history as "the grand convention," the "gathering together" of humankind in conversations and narrations about subjects of substantial weight, serious moral interest, and practical import. However, what is "only theoretic" and impossible to fully attain is often not without practical effect. The ideal of universal historical discourse about the meaning and practice of human life in the world suggests an ongoing and normative horizon for critical inquiry. Such an ethos of foundational critique knows, in Gadamer's terms, that there is always more to say than has been said, more to know than has been known (1975; 250–53; 325–41), and that efforts to include those who have been traditionally excluded from such discursive "conventions" are required for even initial and formal criteria of legitimacy and verification (See Habermas, 1975; 1990). Still, with all of the practical effects of such a universal ideal, even relative achievement among the ideological power-blocs of modernity is uncommon. Nonetheless, the radical pluralism of historicist modernity presents a normative horizon that while disclosing failure also offers new promise for deeper understanding rather than an only excuse for further fracture.

10. John G. Gibbs writes: "Though Paul neither produced cosmogonies nor used the method of a *theologia naturalis*, his thought was not confined to the realm of redemption, the church, or the interior of the pietistic soul. The cosmic dimension of Christ's lordship is present in Romans (5: 12–21; 8: 19–23, 38–39), I Corinthians (8: 6; 15: 21–22, 45), and Philippians (2: 6–11). The hymn in Colossians and the introduction to Ephesians, far from being aberrations in the *corpus Paulinum*, develop further this earlier and undoubtedly Pauline motif" (1971: 466). I have engaged the question of Christology, including this cosmic dimension, and Jewish-Christian relations in my *Who do You Say that I Am? The Christian Understanding of Christ and Antisemitism* (1984).

11. Mistakes are sometimes made in concentrating on the form of stories and dramas at the expense of their content. And while interpreting forms is a way to understanding content, it is the content we seek. For example, though framed as stories told to and by the people of Israel, biblical narrations of God's ways with the world were not stories told only about or for that people. Thus the story of God's particular covenant with Israel must be cast upon the horizon of a larger more universal story of God's covenant with the world. Similarly, stories about the ethics of Jesus told in and for the New Testament communities do not continue as stories whose coherence and obligation remain rooted as a history and heritage of only those particular people. No matter how particular and focused the form of their telling, biblical narratives are not insulated from the

existential challenges involved in telling and retelling their tales to and for larger worlds. For an introduction to theology that takes both of these polarities seriously and makes them thematic, see Douglas John Hall (1989). See also my "Dangerous Times and Obliging Places" (1993).

12. I have been describing my constructive understanding of modernity through the adjective "historicist" rather than under the more common rubric of "historicism." Historicism is a notoriously ambiguous term that, on the one hand, attempts to encompass under one umbrella a variety of substantive interpretations of history, all of which have significantly different implications in gauging the historicity of knowledge and values. On the other, historicism sometimes simply means the radical turn to history in modernity. Consequently, historicism can be equally too "thick" and too "thin" a term to be very helpful in gauging the self-understanding of the modern age. Maurice Mandelbaum (1971: 41–49) suggests that "given the variety of characterizations of 'historicism' which already exist, the usefulness of any other definition will depend on how well it unifies and clarifies the phenomena with which others have also dealt" (p. 41). He then goes on to attempt such a definition: "Historicism is the belief that an adequate understanding of the nature of any phenomenon and an adequate assessment of its value are to be gained through considering it in terms of the place which it occupied and the role which it played within a process of development" (p. 42).

Even if we accept Mandelbaum's formal definition as a useful clarification of historicism, it does not provide any substantive criteria for deciding among the wide range of meanings available. As Mandelbaum indicates, the radical quality of historicism lies in seeing individuals and events—truths, values, and norms—as part of a process of change and development, a moving stream, rather than as continuities of given natures (pp. 42–43). And yet how one (and the age) sees and images history's "process," "progress" and "development"—what constitutes the dynamics of its "stream"—gives the variety of substantive meanings to the term historicism. Thus, under the thin and formal definition of historicism noted by Mandelbaum, I have argued more substantively that modernity's self-understanding of history's *progress* is best clarified under the what I have depicted as the historicist model of a moving and decentering conversational spiral.

13. The major philosophical and theological criticism of the modernist spirit of reason is wide ranging and issues from a variety of sources. As I indicated in Chapter One, the most insightful theological criticism emerges as a critique of evolutionary progressivism, which is seen as coextensive with the history of rational discourse and the growth of "scientistic" and technocratic consciousness and instrumentalist reason in first-world bourgeois cultures. At the same time, under the aegis of a more radical crisis, other voices have emerged to catalogue the failures of modernity itself as a meaningful cosmological home for critical intellectual and moral enterprises. See Allan Megill's discussion of "modernist" reason under the theme of the *crisis of modernity* and the rise of post-

modernity in Nietzsche, Heidegger, Foucault, and Derrida (1985). However, while all cosmologies have risks and dangers, there is in this rhetoric of the crisis of modernity special dangers of an overly romantic and aestheticist antimodernism as in the case of Martin Heidegger and National Socialism. In his article "The Normative Content of Modernity," Jürgen Habermas notes that "The radical critique of reason exacts a high price for taking leave of modernity" (1987: 336: 336–67).

14. I have already referred to Allan Megill's (1985) tracing of the interconnecting thread of aestheticism in the response of Nietzsche, Heidegger, Foucault, and Derrida to *the crisis of modernity*. My point about "literary philosophies," or more precisely, philosophy as only literature-criticism is another reference to the deconstructionist movement led by the French philosopher, Jacques Derrida. The phrasing of my criticism should not mislead. Derrida is engaging in a serious philosophical engagement of dominant understandings of modern rational discourse, although he suggests, with "playful seriousness," that his work is "nonsensical" and that he is taking the risk of not wishing to say or mean anything (see Megill, 1985: 259). As I have indicated, my initial concerns about the deconstructionist project pertain to its tendency to formally reduce rational discourse that is substantively responsive to material-historical issues and problems to a relatively unbound literary aestheticism. When this happens, legitimate and pressing moral concerns become absorbed through an infinite deferral of interpretation and meaning—become in fact lost in the text. Here I am also influenced by Jürgen Habermas's argument in "On Leveling the Genre Distinction between Philosophy and Literature" (1987: 185–210).

15. The Christian paradigm for such a material-historical context for divine speech and human response is foundationally Christological. Consequently, an adequate theological model for revelation will be neither theocentric nor anthropocentric but rather Christocentric. The implications of a fully incarnational Christology not only frame the radical and material-historical content of Christian revelation but also frame and ground it's *Method* of theological articulation and moral engagement. In substance and form, Christian revelation theology is Christocentric, historicist, and materially worldly. For my criticism of theocentrism in theology and ethics, see my review (1986) of James Gustafson's, *Ethics from a Theocentric Perspective: Volume I: Theology and Ethics.* (1981).

16. This approach to covenant theology begins with the single covenant of creation framed historically and materially between God and world—a covenant that invites all to a dwell in worldly circumstances with God and each other. Such a single and universal covenant with the material-historical world is made manifest in the histories and ongoing narratives of particular people. The biblical manifestations and revelation of such a universal covenant is made most particular in the heritage of Jewish and Christian images, symbols, and stories, many of which pertain to the divine recommitment after human sin. As our individual and communal biographies are not interchangeable neither are the

covenantal manifestations of our religious heritages. However, the point of such particular stories and the communities they engender is to reveal a more universal and ongoing tale of God's material interest and intentions for the created world itself. In covenant theology, the plural *dimensions* of particularity are cast against a horizon of historical universality. It is the earth and its peoples that has been *chosen* by God in creation to be the time and place of the divine dwelling.

17. In *Reaping the Whirlwind: A Christian Interpretation of History* (1976), Langdon Gilkey uses the categories of fate and destiny to demarcate the eschatological horizon that informs the biblical view of history. Still, notions of a "particular destiny" like those of "being particularly chosen" are always morally dangerous. As history demonstrates, the hopeful destiny of one group of people often involves the despairing fate of another. Merely to mention the correlative situations of the peoples of Israel/Palestine, the situation of Northern Ireland or, closer to home, the ongoing "fate" of Native American peoples when faced with the "manifest destiny" of the so-called "new nation," should be example enough to ground this point. Claims of a destiny that creates hope for individuals or communities cannot be spoken faithfully except under criteria of verification and legitimation grounded in the material histories of those fated others.

18. According to the chronology of Niebuhr's own developing work and the dates of their original publication, these works are *The Social Sources of Denominationalism* (1929) and *The Kingdom of God in America* (1937); *The Meaning of Revelation* (1941); *Christ and Culture* (1951); *The Purpose of the Church and Its Ministry* (1956); *Radical Monotheism and Western Culture* (1960); *The Responsible Self* (1963); and the recent posthumous publication of *Faith on Earth* (1990), written in the mid-1940's placing it between *The Meaning of Revelation* and *Christ and Culture*. Dates for current editions are given in the bibliography.

## Chapter 3.  History, Interpretation, and the Moral Life

1. Along with his conviction of Christian life and Church as permanent metanoia, Niebuhr (1960) also maintains the modern historicist, but not evolutionist, notion of progress.

> A revelation which furnishes the practical reason with a starting point for the interpretation of past, present and future history is subject to progressive validation. The more apparent it becomes that the past can be understood, recovered and integrated by means of a reasoning starting with revelation, the more contemporary experience is enlightened and response to new situations aptly guided by the imagination of the heart.... (p. 97).

2. My understanding of the fundamental interaction of meaningful history and the praxis and labor of critical interpretation has been influenced by

Hans-Georg Gadamer's *Truth and Method* (1975; 1991). Those familiar with Gadamer's work will recognize certain key categories and concepts of his hermeneutic ontology of understanding that I have applied to this project: the historicity of understanding and hermeneutic distance; the linguistic and conversational nature of tradition; the dialectic of question and answer and the dual moments of historical interpretation; dialogic conversation and the nature of prejudice as prejudgment; the plenitude of meaning that frames the finite dynamic of all acts of critical hermeneutic retrieval; and the normative dynamic of "historical effectiveness." For a more detailed application of Gadamer's hermeneutic ontology to the challenges of competent public moral discourse in general, see my *Ethics and Public Policy* (1982). For "A Gadamerian Response to Deconstructionism," see G. B. Madison (1988: 106–22).

3. It is the classical and reconstructed modern versions of history as metanarrative that are challenged most severely by the postmodernity thesis. In this regard, see Lyotard (1987: 73–94). In terms of the classical and quasi-classical versions of the metanarrative of history, as well as of the evolutionary progressive version of much of modernity, I agree with the incredulity and deconstructive intent of the postmodernity thesis. I have suggested an alternative version of history in modernity as a metanarrative that demands attention to discontinuities as well as continuities—attention to the dynamic of decentering all assumptions of a linear and progressive coherence grounded by the interests and narratives of dominant power groups. Such a decentering casts our attention to the narratives and life experiences of those at the margins of our traditional historical stories and brings them to a center they have seldom, if ever, occupied.

4. Bearing history's burden of critical interpretation is not easy for individuals or for the Church, but it is threatening and often terrifying. I have argued that modernity is still a possible home for virtuous character and rational moral speech, but like all ages of history, it is not, in its own uncritical and presumptive "modernisms," an easy or nonlaborious home. As Niebuhr writes:

> All reasoning is painful and none more so than that which leads to knowledge of the self. In the Christian community we do not use our revelation faithfully but seek by a thousand devices to escape from the rational understanding of ourselves. By means of dogmatism which assures us that nothing more is necessary to our knowledge than the creeds supply, or by means of scepticism which declares all things unintelligible, we seek to evade the necessity of illuminating and reconstructing our memories and acts. Sometimes we regard revelation as though it had equipped us with truth in such measure that no further labor in historical and psychological searching is necessary; sometimes we dismiss it as offering no basis for the reason of man. Fundamentalism in its thousand historic forms escapes in one way; modernism, which exists in many disguises as there are climates of opinion, escapes by applying to life the short and narrow ideas of some present moment. Emotionalism reduces the historic revelation to a dema-

gogic device for arousing fear, anger and pity in the service of some petty cause. The figures of the Christian drama are even made to act out the puerile and vicious farces of racial, nationalistic and ecclesiastic imaginations. But revelation is not the source of such irrationality and absurdity. We become fools because we refuse to use revelation as the foundation of a rational moral life (Niebuhr, 1960: 96).

5.  Along with my debt to H-G. Gadamer, I owe a similar debt to Jürgen Habermas's work in critical theory. I have found critical conversations between hermeneutic theory and critical theory to be foundational for setting the proper historicist and hermeneutic conditions for constructive moral discourse— discourse that leads to systematic ethical argument, critical judgment, and a legitimate and effective practical rhetoric of moral persuasion. Those familiar with the work of Habermas will find here and throughout his influence in an array of categories, concepts, and approaches equal to that of Gadamer: the material-historical conditions of knowledge and its human interests; communicative competence and systematically distorted communication; the critique of prejudice as ideology; crises in the verification and legitimation of rational speech and its communities, institutions and societies; and the praxis of communicative action. For my initial interpretation of Habermas's project for ascertaining further critical conditions of public moral discourse, as well as for an exposition of the informing debate between Gadamer's hermeneutic theory and Habermas's critical theory, see my *Ethics and Public Policy* (1982).

6.  I have argued that in the full dimensions of historical time, past, present, or future have no logical or moral priority in our efforts to understand and identify ourselves either individually or communally. However, for historically interactive characters, there is an initiating phenomenological and biographical priority of the past. This is to say that our first, but by no means our final, act of character identification is remembrance. Remembrance and the stories, values, and norms it engenders, is the initiating phenomenological moment of our inclusion as rational and moral characters in history's metaconversation and narrative. In this sense we can say that critical interpretation begins within the phenomenological dimension of remembrance of the past. Consequently, how we image the reality of our orienting and grounding past will have great significance to the process of character formation and its identifying norms. Drawing from Paul Ricoeur's analysis in *The Reality of the Historical Past* (1984a), I will discuss in Chapter Six a variety of ways in which moral discourse remembers and images the Church's historical norm of heterosexual marriage, brings it to its present state of historical effectiveness, and anticipates its future.

7.  Still, in allowing for even some *admission to conversation* arguments against the ordination of women based on reasons that may not be initially and self-consciously sexist, I may be being too patient and inappropriately tolerant— postures I am not willing to accept with respect to racism. It is likely that my own biography as a southern white man makes the record of racist violence easier for

me to see and hear than the violence of sexism, though I have no doubts that sexist violence is as real and virulent. On this point it is necessary to hear from women, especially women of color. Thus, my own *internal* biographical story and understanding will be challenged and augmented by those *external others*. It also needs to be reiterated that admitting an argument to discourse only implies that it is *competent*, not correct, and that its engagement will not systematically distort the conversation.

8. My main intention in using the term "homophilia" here is to name, generically, a variety of historical and contemporary feelings, attitudes, and understandings that suggest, in one way or another, that same-sex relationships are on a "higher" or "purer" plane, are less complicated by gendered differences and thus capable of being more intensely engaged. (For a discussion of this phenomenon with respect to male homosexuality in classical Greece, see A. W. Price, 1989.) It is only in this limited sense that homophilia parallels homophobia. In the material histories of homophobia and homophilia, the assaults and violations of love and justice experienced by homosexuals persons are not paralleled by heterosexual persons. As in the histories of racism and sexism, here we have an asymmetrical historical narrative.

9. This raises the notion of "political correctness" now occupying the popular debate. In the general public forum, and with appropriate prohibitions of speech that deliberately incites and provokes violence, especially in language that demeans other persons or groups, no extraordinary and prohibitive rules and laws ought to be placed upon our human penchant to be foolish, silly, or even generally insulting. However, this does not mean that under false appeals to "freedom of speech" we need accept any and all forms of speech as equally serious contributions to conversations that intend constructive rational engagement with issues and affairs. Thus, for example, foolish and insulting racial, ethnic, and sexual slurs have no place in academic conversations or its communities—communities whose reason for being is serious rational inquiry and competent debate. Nor does it mean, moreover, that the discourse of the Church or its institutions should tolerate without comment speech that violates its informing commitments to love and justice.

10. Aristotle (1925) sets the proper material-historical foundation for ethics and moral discourse in general—what I am calling here *the norm of content*. This classical wisdom is quite contemporary given our modern penchant for abstracting moral debate in flights of idealist and ideological fancy.

> Our discussion will be adequate if it has as much clearness as the subject matter admits of, for precision is not to be sought for alike in all discussions, any more than in all the products of the crafts.... We must be content, then, in speaking of such subjects and with such premises to indicate the truth roughly and in outline, and in speaking about such things which are only for the most part true and with premises of the same kind to reach conclusions that are no better. In the same spirit, therefore, should

each type of statement be *received*; for it is the mark of an educated man to look for precision in each class of things just so far as the nature of the subject admits. (*Nicomachean Ethics*, Book I: 1094b12)

11. Jürgen Habermas (1971) argues that there is not only a formal but a substantive connection between knowledge and material-historical human interests. "The analysis of the connection of knowledge and interest should support the assertion that a radical critique of knowledge is possible only as social theory. This idea is implicit in Marx's theory of society, even though it cannot be gathered from the self-understanding of Marx or of Marxism" (Habermas, 1971: vii).

12. For an example of a moral argument that engages its subject self-consciously under [to use in a different context John Rawls's term (1971)] a significant "*veil of ignorance*," see my "Abortion: The Status of Fetal Life" (1991a).

13. Paul Tillich calls all critical theology a necessarily *dangerous* endeavor (1959: 7). Similarly, Johann Metz suggests that the shortest definition of religion is *interruption* (1980: 171).

## Chapter 4. Ethical Norms and Moral Rules

1. I am not unaware of the irony of returning to the very venue of common discourse in which I have claimed such confusion has abounded, especially in the area of sexual morality. Throughout this book I concentrate on the role of the Church as moral teacher and guide. Given this concentration, the confusion in the Church's conversations on sexual morality is now focused among the ecclesiastical teachers and theorists. Much like the phenomenon of physician-induced illness, if the teachers and leaders of any community are confused, so too will be those who look to them for guidance. At the same time enough common wisdom may yet abide in the body of the faithful to counter such confusion, or at least to indicate that something is wrong. As I have noted, "in a process of enlightenment there can only be participants" (Habermas, 1974: 40).

2. Following this example, the norm of truthfulness in the narrative stories of cultures, societies, nations, and institutions can erode over time, often without notice, until a crisis in moral legitimation becomes too great to ignore. Thus special attention needs to be paid to both formal and informal patterns of speech and communication. Maintaining norms of openness and truthfulness, and telling the truth overall, are foundational for social and moral legitimacy. Maintaining an adequate critique of the penchant for obfuscation and distortion of all speech, especially of those with power, is fundamental for maintaining the norm of truthfulness. For a discussion of truthfulness and the future of the Church, see Hans Küng (1968).

3. In the same vein, Gibson Winter argues that social character and the moral life emerge in a "pre-given" world, and thus, "ethical reflection does not start in a vacuum; values are the pre-given stuff of social process.... The 'lived' world is a horizon of meanings, valued relations, and possibilities" (1966: 218). In "Values as Principles for Action" Georges Gusdorf develops this point further:

> It appears that value is found to be present everywhere in man's conduct. It is value that determines its orientation and its structures. In each situation, regardless of what it may be, man's freedom will never be undifferentiated freedom.... Thus, the most general definition of value would characterize it as a reality structure that is immanent to our action, as a manner of meeting the world and of qualifying it as a function of our constant or momentary exigencies.... Values thus intervene in our concrete existence as instigators of action, a prospect of engagement, as the reason for our behavior and our expression in the universe, as the key of intelligibility (in J. Kockelmans, 1972: 223–24).

For further discussion see my *Ethics and Public Policy* (1982: 27–32; 81–84).

4. Writing in ethics often makes a distinction, not always consistently, between the terms *moral* and *ethical*. In general, the term *moral* is shaded by the entire range of practice with respect to both discourse and action. Whereas the term *ethical* is shaded by the entire range of systematic theory and argument. Still the discipline itself remains notoriously ambiguous in its use of terms with the assumptions of any particular ethical theory often substituted for actual and common usage in the discrimination of the meanings of terms. Consequently, analytic therapies for the language of moral discourse remain necessary in ethics and as far as possible ought to be theory-neutral.

5. Building upon Aiken, I will offer my schematic diagram of the levels of moral discourse in the Appendix.

6. Norms and principles are often grouped together in the language of ethics. Aiken tends to do this and thus we find them together in his paradigm. While I think that norms and principles are closely related in common usage, I will offer some further discriminations between these terms.

7. Aiken's distinctions are as follows: "(a) The conventional use of words as vehicles for the expression of emotion; (b) the varying degrees of intensity and rhetorical force of such expressions; (c) the expressive or 'venting' relation holding between the speaker and the expression itself; (d) the symptomatic relation in virtue of which the expression functions as a natural sign to an interpreter; (e) the incitive or rhetorical effect of the expression upon an interpreter, in virtue of which we speak of a relation of communication between him and the speaker; and (f) the intentions of the speaker in thus giving vent to his emotion" (1962: 69).

8. The understanding of critique as making our basic suppositions problematic belongs to Alvin Gouldner (1976). For good discussions of ideological

speech and its function in culture, see Gouldner (1976) and Clifford Geertz, (1973). See also my *Ethics and Public Policy* (1982).

9. The following case reported in the *St. Louis Post Dispatch* (September 1979) calls this dilemma to mind. A Jehovah's Witness couple refused an ordinary maternal transfusion in a childbirth trauma, and with the acquiescence of her physicians, the woman died while giving birth to her third child, who was born alive. The couple had devised a code and the woman "winked twice to doctors who asked her if she would permit a transfusion. Two winks was her code for 'No.'... 'We have great respect for life and want to try to keep living and healthy as long as possible,' said the husband.... 'The only restriction we have to abide by is that, as God told all of us in the Bible, to abstain from blood.'... As he waited almost four hours, he said, doctors asked him four times to allow them to administer blood, but he refused. 'I understood how serious it was each time, but God is serious too.'"

10. For a further discussion of abortion and the status of fetal life see my "Abortion: The Status of Fetal Life" (1991a). Ronald Dworkin's (1993) case against the status of fetal life as logically centering the public debate on abortion discloses interesting facets of that debate but finally remains unpersuasive to me. My own view is that while the question of fetal life remains central, it is not one that can be resolved completely at levels of moral/ethical argument but retains a necessary meta-ethical confessional and thus pluralistic character. It is for this reason that our public and legal policies on abortion must finally be resolved in a generally liberal manner.

11. In Catholic moral theology a distinction is commonly made between the material and formal dimensions of sin. A "material sinner" is one who has committed an act that, in one way or another, has been judged sinful by the Church or in retrospect by the person—i.e., the *act* is sinful. A "formal sinner" has the requisite knowledge, intention, and freedom to have done otherwise, with the person at least putatively *guilty* of the act. At the same time, even though the obligation to follow the church's teachings is considered strong, such traditions teach that accusation of formal sin can finally be made only by the person involved—that is, a "self-accusation" of a properly formed conscience most often made in sacramental confession. This latter point is often forgotten in the recent debates on sexual morality of denominations formed by the Catholic moral theological traditions.

12. I say "generally" here because of the conflict in the example I offered above (see Note 9) where we found a tension between the good of saving someone's life and the at least putatively equal good of respecting one's freedom of conscience because of the value and principle of human autonomy. It would be hard to argue that physical life is an absolute value that takes priority as a good in any and all circumstances. In the Jehovah Witness example, we have two abiding values and prima facie principles and goods in severe conflict.

13. In the next chapter I will provide a rationale, at least in terms of an analytic discussion of moral argument, for my adoption of the unusual term "sacramental" to describe this third functional characteristic of mature ethical norms. In a book directed toward the Church, the fact that this term has a history of familiar ecclesiastical use and meaning probably increases my risk of being misunderstood.

14. For a discussion and discrimination of logical, phenomenological, and ontological-pragmatic sense in rational discourse, see Robert O. Johann's "The Nature of Philosophical Inquiry" in Johann (1968: 35–53).

15. I will discuss a revision of the principle of universalization informing a rule of argumentation on more specific moral-political grounds in Chapter Seven.

16. However, in this discussion of "ethical competence" it is also important to understand the value of being "successful" in the moral life—that is, to be successful in achieving the good rather than in only being dutiful. In other words, we not only want to be motivated by the right and intend the good but also accomplish the goods we seek—i.e, to be skillful in our ethics. For a discussion of the related point of the classical understanding of moral intentions not only to do the right things but also to "fare well," see Alasdair MacIntyre (1966).

17. See Aiken's rendering of this Kantian logic ( 1962: 83).

18. "Two things fill the mind with ever new and increasing admiration and awe, the oftener and more steadily we reflect on them: the starry heavens above me and the moral law within me. I do not merely conjecture them and seek them as though obscured in darkness or in the transcendent region beyond my horizon: I see them before me, and I associate them directly with the consciousness of my own existence. The former begins at the place I occupy in the external world of sense, and it broadens the connection in which I stand into an unbounded magnitude of worlds beyond worlds and systems of systems and into the limitless times of their periodic motion, their beginning and their continuance. The latter begins at my invisible self, my personality, and exhibits me in a world which has true infinity but which is comprehensible only to the understanding—a world with which I recognize myself as existing in a universal and necessary...connection, and thereby also in connection with all those visible worlds" (Immanuel Kant, Critique of Practical Reason, 1956: 166).

19. Even though I claim to go beyond Aiken's stopping point in this discussion, I will necessarily stop short as well. Any adequate job of probing the grounds of moral obligation in general, and Christian moral obligation in particular, is the work of other books. In this book I have given what I consider the location of such a task and some of the terrain that must be explored.

## Chapter 5. The Origin, Structure, and Function of Ethical Norms

1. I intend the terms "ideal" and "real" in an analytic context of ordinary speech. In this sense, *ideal* means an image—an accomplishment of the imagination—of a paradigmatic and relatively archetypal vision of fully moral conduct. Our ideals indicate how we ought to be if all our values, virtues, and goods were understood and lived out to their fullest measure—a type of "perfection," if you will, whose etymological root (*perficere*) means "to make or do thoroughly" (Partridge,1983: 485). In contrast to the *real*, by which I mean the "facticity" of everyday life, the ideal is necessarily only a relative accomplishment of the imagination. Few would argue that according to the "facts" of everyday life, we make or do anything thoroughly or perfectly. With respect to the *real* (the material *res*, or "thing"), I am not talking about the scholastic and metaphysical *realitas* (Partridge, 553). Furthermore, I do not mean to suggest that images and the imagination do not "partake" of *realitas*, however it is understood or determined; nor am I suggesting that the "real facts" of everyday life are brute or crass, available to us without interpretation. At the same time, we ordinarily understand the "facts"—not necessary "the complete truth"—to be attained by the letter (*littera*), or through a literal description and measurement of the "surface" of an event— indeed by "perception" as a form of initial and primary "interpretation" in a narrow sense. I am contrasting the imaginative ideal as a type of refiguration and reconstruction of the surface appearance and the literal—i.e., a quest for a "deeper" truth by way of a "thicker" interpretation (see, for example, Geertz, 1973: 3-30). In contrast to the *real* then, the *ideal* is a longer, wider, and deeper vision—*idein*, "to see;" *idealis*, "archetypal, ideal," and with more of a phenomenological than Platonic or neo-Platonic implication, *eidos*, "that which is seen, hence the form or shape, hence a figure" (Partridge, 303). In ethics and the moral life, the *real* and the *ideal* are dialectically engaged. As imaginative "ideals," ethical norms remain dependent on the literal "facts" of the material-historical life: literal facts are transformed into moral projects by normative ideals.

2. I do not mean to suggest that social sciences as disciplines are always reduced to this sort of statistical measurement. In fact, what has come to be called "critical theory" in sociology is precisely a strong critique of any tendencies toward such a reduction. See, for example, Martin Jay (1973) and Alvin Gouldner (1971).

3. Rollo May (1969: 228) points out this important etymological root of "intentionality" (*in-tendere*, "to stretch"). For a further discussion of my understanding of the dialectical and dialogic quality of intentionality, see my *Ethics and Public Policy* (1982).

4. As I have indicated, even though the term "sacrament" has mainly theological and ecclesiastical usage, and I take some risk of being misunderstood according to some particular rather than the generic use I intend, *sacramental* accurately depicts this particular dimension and function of an ethical norm. The classical theological notion of a functioning sacrament is that it "effects what it

signifies." This is the precise intention of an ethical norm—that is, to *demonstrate* and *effect* the values *disclosed* metaphorically and *designated* symbolically as goods of everyday life. However, there will not be total continuity with this classical usage. A norm does not effect values as goods merely by the act of disclosure or signification. Analytically envisioned, the metaphorical and symbolic disclosures and designations of norms are *incomplete sacraments* waiting to be effected as goods. Furthermore, if my analysis stands, and the sacramental quality of ethical norms is established, then there will be formal analytic and practical reasons for considering marriage a "sacrament" whatever the state of more theoretic doctrinal debates.

5. See, for example, David Tracy's discussion of the metaphorical quality of religious discourse in terms of "limit-language" (1975; 1981).

6. In a postmetaphysical world, it is inevitable that one will speak metaphorically in describing the most critical functions of metaphor. The new meanings and truths disclosed by metaphor do not reside or exist as essences in any speculative metaphysical sense, but rather arise from and depend on the failure of literal speech to communicate what we experience in everyday life.

7. While moral discourse and ethics need not be openly religious, much less theological, there may be both more and less convergence than is commonly admitted. Certainly, one can be adequately, even profoundly, moral without being avowedly religious. However, if my argument about our universal dissatisfaction with literal description holds, then the ordinary practice of metaphorical disclosure may provide a common ground for both religious and moral sensibilities. In this sense, in both religion and morality, there is "something more going on than meets the eye"—for example, an *other* power, value-ideal, or in theistic religion and theology, narrowly understood, an *Other Person* upon whom we depend to gain sense and meaning in our lives and to ground our claims for truth and right. Thus religion and morality would have a common critical—though not negating—stance toward the literal that initiates them into the illusive worlds of metaphor and symbol. And while both religion and morality must make "sacramental returns" to the social and political worlds of everyday life for verification and legitimation of their claims, any informing *literalism* or *fundamentalism* makes them stillborn from the beginning. See also David Tracy's analysis of the religious dimension through the concept of limit (1975: 91–118).

8. Merely describing the limits of ordinary literal speech, of course, does not verify the cognitive status of the new meaning disclosed by the metaphorical utterance. Donald Davidson is pointedly critical of the new predicative function of metaphor promoted by Black, Ricoeur, and others and argues: "We must give up the idea that a metaphor carries a message, that it has a content or meaning (except, of course, its literal meaning)" (1978: 45). Davidson goes on: "I have no quarrel with these descriptions of the effects of metaphor, only with the associated views as to *how* metaphor is supposed to produce them. What I deny is that metaphor does its work by having a special meaning, a specific cognitive

content." Metaphor can make us "appreciate some fact—but not by standing for, or expressing, the fact" (1978: 46). In response, Max Black accuses Davidson of finally holding a discounted view of metaphors as "cryptic substitutes for literal similes"(1979: 140).

Implied in Davidson's challenge, however, is the point that a metaphorical utterance cannot be totally discontinuous with the literal facticity of its origin. The challenge of the tension and interaction theories of Ricoeur and Black is to indicate how the discontinuity established between the literal and the figurative maintains enough continuity to transform the literal into new meaning with cognitive content and practical implication. Thus, to function predicatively with respect not only to the self—in this case the speaker and/or writer—but also to the world and to have cognitive as well as emotive content, the metaphorical utterance must remain dependent on the literal description and the limiting dissatisfaction it promotes. To remain dependent and connected to this *bios*, the *logos* of metaphor will require the work of symbol.

9. For an analysis of this crisis of modern sciences see Edmund Husserl (1970).

10. I am aware of the current popularity of speaking of the work of metaphor, symbol, paradigm, and model in science. Such work is necessary and important for the foundations of science and for informing and understanding the structure of scientific investigation. When scientific instruments of literal description lag behind scientific inquiry and research, as they inevitably will, science becomes dependent on imaginative models. And in the philosophy of science, the entire range of the genres of critical speech can be engaged. Nonetheless, now fully wedded to technology, functioning science in late modernity is finally centered in literal and functional description and is not a form of critical language at least as now used in the speech of religion, poetry, morality, and the other critical imaginative disciplines. When these critical disciplines speak of "sorting out" and "digging deep" into the surface or "searching the heights and depths" of reality, they are speaking metaphorically. When functioning science speaks in a similar way, while inevitably and relatively dependent for a time—perhaps for long periods—on imaginative figuration, it is finally speaking literally and descriptively.

We will not gain an adequate understanding and appreciation of the disclosures of metaphor, symbol, and myth by attempting to render figurative speech primary once again. As we have seen, there is finally both a relation and a difference between critical figurative speech and the speech of literal description. We need not fear such differences or seek to collapse them in some sort of universal field theory of experience and knowledge. For example, I may be more than satisfied with the literal regularities of my surgery and want my surgeon to operate directly and with literal efficiency. The launching and return of space vehicles ought to proceed in the same "literal" manner. However, if something goes tragically wrong I will finally not be satisfied with only a literal description. Nor will I be satisfied when science claims to have within its own structure and function enough moral imagination and critical figures of moral discourse to alone determine what is morally responsible research and technological development, or suggests, conversely, that the production of scientific knowledge is to be held aloof from questions about its moral use.

11. In this comment, Ricoeur mirrors some of the concerns I expressed in Part One about the dimensions of "permanent release" and negation that seems to infect deconstructionism with respect to the work of social, political, and moral judgment amid the literal realities of everyday life. As a radical form of dissatisfaction with the speech of both literal description (the priority of *bios*) and figurative imagination (the priority of *logos*), deconstructionism attempts to permanently stand between them both, not as a constructive ordering of language for practical use, but as a deconstructive disordering of language at the margins of meaning and understanding. Thus deconstructionism challenges all substantive rational claims for verifying and legitimating judgments of truth and right. In this way, as others have indicated in different contexts and arguments, deconstructionism may provide a "therapy" for language as it approaches any postmodern age wherein the dissatisfactions with rational discourse could become so pronounced that the "biocentric" language of literal description and the "logocentric" language of imaginative figuration become separated rather than interactive. In such a topsy-turvy world we would surely not know the difference between up and down, what is meaningful and absurd, or the sense of any claim of truth and error, right and wrong at all. Indeed, as Ricoeur indicates, all language would have left to predicatively celebrate is itself and its own permanent deconstruction of both the literal and the figurative.

Short of such a profound crisis in reason and language, rather romantically affirmed—indeed sometimes celebrated—by the rhetoric of deconstructionism, deconstructionist theory can remind us of the problematic tension that exists between *bios* and *logos*, between the speech and language of literal description and that of figurative imagination and the increasing challenge of finding their coherent, meaningful, and practical-cognitive interrelation. In being a therapy for language, deconstructionism can become a therapy for the judgments that language is finally asked to make within the material-historical irregularities of everyday life. In this way, even in its radical deconstructive moments, language could become a more careful and intense celebration of the world in all its alterity rather than of only itself.

Certainly Jacques Derrida (in Kearney, 1984: 105–26) is not unaware of the pressure of the moral and political upon any deconstructionist project. Derrida suggests that the moment of affirmation in the radical negation of deconstructionism is more by way of a "vocation" for the celebration of alterity (for Derrida, *altarity*)—i.e., of what and who is different from the self and its own judgments and affirmations. This, Derrida proposes, is the precondition for any critical questioning at all and for philosophy in particular. Still Derrida is hesitant to describe such a vocation as a prophetic one—preparing the way for those who will "call down" political and moral judgments, however critical, upon any particular place and time. He confesses "that I have never succeeded in directly relating deconstruction to existing political codes and programmes.... I try where I can to act politically while recognizing that such action remains incommensurate with my intellectual project of deconstructionism" (Kearney 1984: 118; 119; 120).

12. The etymology of *mimesis* does suggest "mimicry and imitation." F. E. Peters indicates that with some ambiguity in Plato such imitation generally suggests that any mimetic activity, such as language and art, effect and disclose "worlds of meaning" that are so dependent on the original *eidos* that "one point is clear: the activity known as *mimesis* has as its product an entity whose ontological status is inferior relative to that of its model" (1967: 118). Taken in a generally Platonic sense, a distinction, reminiscent of simple substitution theories of metaphor, emerges between "a 'true' reality and a mimetic reality.... True knowledge (*episteme*) will be of the 'originals,' while opinion (*doxa*) is the best one can hope to attain in confronting imitative being" (Peters, 119).

However, in his connection of *mimesis* and *poiesis* (*poieín*, to make; "to act, action;" *poietike*, "productive science, art" [Peters, 1967: 162]), Ricoeur rejects the Platonic notion of a lesser status of the *productions* of the mimetic/poetic activity of metaphor in the sense that metaphor imitates the productive activity of meaning in ordinary language by "transposing the meaning of ordinary language into *strange* uses" (Ricoeur, 1978a: 148). When *mimesis* functions in this way of "fabrication, construction" and "creation"—functions as *poiesis*—contra Plato, it makes "human actions," indeed human meanings, "look *better* than they actually are" (Ricoeur, 1978a: 148). Thus, while always connected and bound to ordinary descriptive language, the metaphorical/imaginative quality of the ethical norm discloses putatively *higher* and *better* worlds of ethical value and moral relationship.

In being identified with *poiesis*, *mimesis* both participates in and advances the *dynamis* ("active and passive capacity, hence power" [Peters, 1967: 42–45]) and *energeia* ("functioning, activity, act, actualization" [Peters, 1967:42–45; 55–56]) of ordinary language. In this Aristotelian sense of *energeia*, along with the other forms of nondescriptive speech, both *mimesis* and *poiesis* complete the work of language. At the same time, the productive and constructive work of *poiesis* is not, in an Aristotelian sense, *techne*, which as Peters indicates is a generalized craft and skill that can be taught (1967: 190–91). Ricoeur has already indicated that the work of metaphorical construction cannot be so regularized. However, the generalization of individual experiences of meaning implied by *techne* is one of the marks of the transition of metaphor to symbol that I will indicate below. In this sense, the symbolic designations and demarcations of the moral life of character and virtue, regularized in a culture, society, and community can be taught—often through the effective demonstrations of normative models. The dynamic and constructive metaphoric disclosures of ideal value meanings, and the regular symbolic designations and demarcations of how those meanings are to run their virtuous course toward the good, ground the structure and function of an ethical norm as a model of practical life-wisdom—what Aristotle calls *phronesis* (Peters, 1967: 157). For Aristotle especially, and now metaphorically and symbolically for us, the *seat of phronesis* as the practical life-wisdom of virtuous character and the moral life is in the activity of the heart—*kardia* as "the *arche* of life, movement, and sensation" (Peters, 1967: 96–97, 157). I have argued throughout that the life of virtue and moral character are combinations of habits of mind and heart. In the formation and structure of the ethical norm, the work of metaphor and symbol participate in both.

13. In *The Symbolism of Evil* (1969: 5), Ricoeur points out the transforming and constructive effect of modernity on myths and their narrations:

> For us, moderns, a myth is *only* a myth because we can no longer connect that time with the time of history as we write it, employing the critical method, nor can we connect mythical places with our geographical space. This is why the myth can no longer be an explanation; to exclude its etiological intention is the theme of all necessary demythologization. But in losing its explanatory pretensions the myth reveals its exploratory significance and its contribution to understanding, which we shall later call its symbolic function—that is to say, its power of discovering and revealing the bond between man and what he considers sacred. Paradoxical as it may seem, the myth, when it is thus demythologized through contact with scientific history and elevated to the dignity of a symbol, is a dimension of modern thought.

14. Other interpreters of metaphor theory may be even shier than Wheelwright and want to make no ontological claims at all, which seems to be the case with Max Black when he says: "we lack an adequate account of metaphorical thought" (1979: 143). Nor do I intend to attempt an account in this book beyond what I am indicating about how ideal value images first emerge metaphorically in the ethical norm. I have, however, suggested that in one way or another, accounting for the fact of our dissatisfaction with literal description and the anthropological universality of metaphor and symbolic speech in general will simultaneously be an account of our own quest for identity and personality as interactive and intersubjective characters in the world. The foundational questions for ethics here are how we come to be obliged in terms of imaginative ideals and in our relations with others.

15. I am using the terms "disclose" to describe the work of metaphor and "designate" to describe the work of symbol. The terms are not totally satisfactory since *disclose*—"open up" and "reveal"—initiates for many complicated ontological discussions of the interrelation of being and language. Thus, the critique (for example, in Derrida's deconstructionism) of any ontological and "logo-centric presence" abiding in reality and waiting to "reveal itself" can and does become at the same time a critique of metaphor theory. It could, however, very well be that there is, as Wheelwright says (1968: 162), only a "shy ontological claim" in much of metaphor theory (for example, in Wheelwright and Ricoeur). Furthermore, just as Ricoeur talks of the necessity of speaking metaphorically about metaphor (1978c: 145), perhaps "being," and ontological discourse itself,

function analytically as a metaphor for the totality, and indeed, irregularity of how what we count as *reality* appears and is experienced in general in any particular historical and cosmological age. Such a similarly "shy ontology" would be more phenomenological, practical, and material-historical than metaphysical and speculative, with all of the subtle reappearances of metaphysics in the modern age not withstanding. In any event, I will not develop this point further in this book though such a discussion would be necessary in foundational ethics.

Similar dissatisfaction also remains with the term *designation*—"marking out" and "delimiting"—as a description for the work of symbol since it is also found in the work of metaphor, just as symbols also "disclose." My intention is to focus on the central work of both metaphor and symbol with a recognition that, although there are dimensions of close interaction and mergence, there are also significant differences between metaphor and symbol that are important for understanding the structure and function of the ethical norm.

16. Though somewhat of an oxymoron, these characterizations of "true" and "false knowledge" are still accurate. "True knowledge" is knowledge whose claims have been verified. However, according to its own intentional dynamic toward persuasion to specific action, ideology will always initially resist moving to more systematic and critical levels of even formal verification—i.e., to theory and critique. At the same time, as the language of passionate persuasion, ideology is inevitable and necessary. Overall, ideology alone can be called "false knowledge" insofar as it both discloses and obscures important truths about individuals and groups. Consequently, ideological speech—the speech of political rhetoric and of the homilist—remains dangerous. Furthermore, just as knowledge needs to be verified as true, it also needs to be legitimated as good. This raises the parallel but plaguing and complex Faustian question: Is there any such thing as "evil knowledge?" (For a schematic diagram of the place of ideology among the levels of intellectual and moral discourse, see the Appendix.)

17. Clifford Geertz is suspicious of what he calls *consensus gentium* theories insofar as they are most often "empty" categories only vaguely associated with "underlying realities." Without an adequate empirical case being made for *universals* that render all "cultural particularities" of "secondary importance," Geertz finds such theories unpersuasive (1973: 39). To say that "'religion,' 'marriage,' or 'property' are empirical universals...is to say that they have the same content, and to say that they have the same content is to fly in the face of the undeniable fact that they do not" (Geertz: p. 39-40).

Even though Geertz is undoubtedly right about the empirical diversity of the actual forms of marriage across history and culture, and thus, not an empirical universal in this "thick" sense, marriage can still function as a hermeneutic universal and an archetypal symbol in a "thinner" sense. That is to say that, with all its significant diversity, heterosexual and monagamous marriage may be developing into a universal interpretive model with metaphoric and symbolic dimensions for identifying, understanding, and judging the life of a culture and society. The importance of the *consensus gentium* approach in this sense is in its description of the state of married and family life as one foundational criterion for identifying the character of a culture and society. As at least a quasi-arche-typal model, heterosexual marriage may be functioning as a moral anchor and benchmark for the sexual life and behavior of cultures.

Nonetheless, it would be too much to say, as Geertz indicates (pp. 37–43), that the substantive differences in cultural understandings and societal practices of marriage have no effect on the moral reality. Monogamy and polygamy are not the same things nor are the canons of intimate and committed love applied to marriage, if at all, the same in all cultures. We therefore must still wait for more ethnological reports about the course of marriage toward the status of an arche-typal moral symbol and model. For further discussion of these matters from the perspective of ethical theory, see Gene Outka and John P. Reeder (1993).

18. Taking the literal with more sacramental seriousness in the way I am suggesting does not obviate the problematic status of figurative speech. As I have indicated, in the context of scientific modernity, giving an adequate account of the cognitive status of the figurative in relation to the literal remains somewhat illu-sive. However, in a passage reminiscent of William James's depiction of the "stern personality" (1961), Owen Barfield suggests the confessional and characterolog-ical core of the problem, both for the individual and the age, and implies the metatheoretic and phenomenological discourse that must be engaged.

It will, I believe, be found that there *is* a valid connection, at some level however deep, between what I have called 'literalness' and a certain hard-ness of heart. Listen attentively to the response of a dull or literal mind to what insistently presents itself as allegory or symbol, and you may detect a certain irritation, a faint, incipient aggressiveness in its refusal. Here I think is a deep-down moral gesture. You may, for instance, hear the literal man object suspiciously that he is being 'got at.' And this is quite correct. He is. Just as he is being 'got at' by his unconscious through the symbolism of his dreams. An attempt is being made, of which he is dimly aware, to undermine his idols, and his feet are being invited on to the beginning of the long road, which in the end must lead him to self-knowledge, with all the unacceptable humiliations which that involves. Instinctively he does not like it. He prefers to remain 'literal.' But of course he hardly knows that he prefers it, since self-knowledge is the very thing he is avoiding.... To idolatry an event is *either* historical or symbolical. It cannot be both (1965: 162–63; 168).

Barfield suggests further that the positive side of the acceptance of symbolic and figurative language and thinking indicates "a certain humble, tender *receptive-ness* of heart which is nourished by a deep and deepening imagination and by the self-knowledge which that inevitably involves" (p. 163).

19. For more discussion of this point see my "Dangerous Times and Obliging Places" (1993).

20. See H. Richard Niebuhr's powerful relation of soteriology and ethics in his understanding of Christ's *redemption* of God from the *power* upon whom we absolutely depend to the *Person* in whom we can absolutely trust (1963a; 1989). As God's relation with us is the primary and paradigmatic model for all relationships in religious ethics, a similar *redemption* is necessary at the foundations of a responsible moral life—*others* transformed from the status of impersonal powers and alien threats to interpersonal and interactive agents. Similar transfigurations and "redemptions" are involved in most religious traditions.

21. In a more analytic vein, Isaiah Berlin writes:

The notion of the perfect whole, the ultimate solution, in which all good things coexist, seems to me to be not merely unattainable—that is a truism—but conceptually incoherent; I do not know what is meant by a harmony of this kind. Some among the Great Goods cannot live together. That is a conceptual truth. We are doomed to choose, and every choice may entail an irreparable loss (1988: 15).

## Chapter 6. The Norm of Heterosexual Marriage

1. My analysis in this section is drawn principally from Paul Ricoeur, *The Reality of the Historical Past: The Aquinas Lecture, 1984* (Milwaukee: Marquette University Press, 1984a). But see also Ricoeur's work in *Time and Narrative, Vols. I* (1984b); *II* (1985); *III* (1988), especially Chapter 6, "The Reality of the Past" (pp. 142–56), and Chapter 10, "Towards a Hermeneutics of Historical Consciousness" (pp. 207–40) where he examines more completely the relationship between narrative and temporality.

2. Ricoeur continues with a counter to any suggestion of ethically neutral action in art and literature—a counter, in fact, to only aestheticist and deconstructionist reading. While he is speaking here most directly about fiction, Ricoeur's argument pertains also to all critical historical narratives and to their necessary figurative and tropological mediation of the past.

Aristotle's *Poetics*...presupposes not just 'doers' but characters endowed with ethical qualities that make them noble or vile. If tragedy can represent them as 'better' and comedy as 'worse' than actual human beings, it is because the practical understanding authors share with their audiences necessarily involves an evaluation of the characters and their actions in terms of good and bad. There is no action that does not give rise to approbation or reprobation, to however small a degree, as a function of a hierarchy of values for which goodness and wickedness are the poles. When the time comes, I shall discuss the question of whether a mode of reading that would entirely suspend all evaluation of an ethical character is possible. What, in particular, would remain of the pity Aristotle taught us to link with unmerited misfortune, if aesthetic pleasure were to be totally disassociated from any sympathy or antipathy for the characters' ethical quality? We shall see that this possible ethical neutrality has to be conquered by force in an encounter with one originary and inherent feature of action: precisely that it can never be ethically neutral.... The actual order of action does not just offer the artist conventions and convictions to dissolve, but also ambiguities and perplexities to resolve in a hypothetical mode. Many contemporary critics, reflecting on the relation between art and culture, have emphasized the conflicting character of the norms that culture offers for poets' mimetic activity.... But, at the same time, does not such ethical neutrality of the artist suppress one of the oldest functions of art, that it constitutes an ethical laboratory where the artist pursues through the mode of fiction experimentation with values? Whatever our response to these questions, poetics does not stop borrowing from ethics, even when it advocates the suspension of all ethical judgment or its ironic inversion. The very project of ethical neutrality presupposes the original ethical quality of action on the prior side of fiction. This ethical quality is itself only a corollary of the major characteristics of action, that it is always symbolically mediated (1984b: 59).

3. Despite the generic intent of this depiction of history as "men in time," in this case, as I will indicate, the gender-exclusive usage cautions us to pay special attention to histories, especially of sexuality, written for the most part by men.

4. Ricoeur has in mind R. G. Collingwood's approach in *The Idea of History* (1956) and he quotes Collingwood's claim: "All thinking is critical thinking: the thought which re-enacts past thoughts, therefore, criticizes them in reenacting them" (Ricoeur, 1984a: p.41 n.8).

5. Ricoeur finds the idealist approach of Collingwood (1956) unable to address adequately the *alterity* of the past. "The notion of re-enactment expresses the audacious effort to resolve the otherness of repetition in terms of the identity of reflection" (Ricoeur, 1984a: p. 14).

6. See again Ernest Gellner's example of ethnocentric bias in education depicted as "the fallacy of the Gauls" (1978: 15; 28).

7. Though a valuable study, I think John Boswell's *Christianity, Social Tolerance, and Homosexuality* (1980) is flawed in this way. As his overarching theme, Boswell adopts "intolerance as a historical force" in the specific instance of homosexuality (pp. 4–39). While the themes of intolerance and, indeed, persecution are required in any study of homosexuality, no long historical record demonstrates only one theme. Intolerance of homosexuality is a pervasive and deadly memory to be sure, but left as a single theme of investigation other more deeply embedded or more subtle memories will be missed and a good bit of the

story of Christian homosexuality left untold. By adopting the single theme of intolerance, Boswell tends to conflate the separate histories of Europe's oppressed minorities (p. 15) as well as present, in general, an historical analysis that implies one-to-one correspondence with the contemporary experience of homosexual Christians. In so doing, he tends to sublimate the differences among the stories of homosexual Christians under a single homogeneous history. In Ricoeur's terms, Boswell abolishes "the difference between others of today and others of yesteryear" and "obliterates the problematic of temporal distance and eludes the specific difficulty related to the survival of the past in the present" (1984a: 17). Still, part of my criticism of Boswell may have to do with the ambivalent way he has depicted the subject of his book. If he is writing about intolerance in this specific instance, then he has written a relatively good history of the Church's record of intolerance. If, on the other hand, he intends a remembrance of the reality of homosexuality in the Church's past, he has written a rather flawed history of Christian homosexuality and homosexual Christians. Both types of history are necessary for aiding the Church's discourse on this matter and Boswell's book, as it stands and as it has been received, is somewhat confused both methodologically and substantively. For criticism of some of Boswell's substantive historical interpretations of homosexuality as such, see David Greenberg, *The Construction of Homosexuality* (1988).

8. In this instance, my understanding of the specific literary tropes of *metaphor* and especially *metonymy, synecdoche,* and *irony* has been guided by Ricoeur's discussion on pp. 30–31, and pp. 48–49 n.32. in *The Reality of the Historical Past* (1984a).

9. The dangers of perfectionism and of over-burdening marriage and married Christians are great at this point in my argument, even though I am discussing more of the symbolic ideal than the literal fact. Without any attendant perfectionism, symbolic ideals and the obligations they imply are necessary for the work of ethical norms. Later, I will argue that there may be certain values necessary for sexual responsibility that are often being modeled better by other rules of life—for example, friendship (*philia*) in some homosexual and nonmarital relationships, and radically "other-regarding love" (*agape*) in some rules of celibate life. On the dangers of perfectionism in marriage and Christian sexual ethics overall, see Kenneth Leech, "'The Carnality of Grace': Sexuality, Spirituality, and Pastoral Ministry" (1991: 81–90).

10. For a discussion of this issue, see "Symposium: Toward a Theology for Lesbian and Gay Marriages" in Richard Wentz (ed.), the *Anglican Theological Review*, Vol. LXXII No. 2 (Spring 1990). For my contribution to this symposium, see "The Norm of Heterosexual Marriage" (pp. 165–67).

11. Brown argues: "We should not forget the presence of a 'silent majority' of married persons in the large churches of the East. By 300 A.D. there may have been as many as five million Christians scattered throughout the Roman world. Yet they are shadowy figures, hardly visible on the edge of the

bright limelight in which the vivid and articulate few argued so vehemently and with such deadly consequentiality.... It is they that now line the shelves of our libraries" (1988: 138).

Brown gave similar cautions and insights in an earlier work, *The Making of Late Antiquity* (1978). There he warned against investing "the religious and social changes associated with the making of Late Antiquity with a false air of melo-drama" (p. 2). Rather, the inhabitants of the small towns of the Mediterranean world "had long possessed a finely articulated and embracing *koiné* of religious and social experience" (pp. 3; 7). Because of this intimate connection between the religious and the social in the ancient world, historical understanding requires attention to "the slow moving religious life of the city, the *quartier*, and the family" (p. 6). And in a point that is beginning to be taken more seriously by historical research in general, Brown argues: "The religious historian, just because he is a religious historian, must be 'concrete and fastidious.' He needs a sense of life lived twenty-four hours in the day.... Compared with the flesh and blood that the religious historian demands, much of the conventional political and administrative history of the Later Roman Empire is an airy wraith" (p. 6). Like religion itself, all history is finally embedded in the material circumstances of everyday life.

12. Brown indicates that "throughout this period, Christian men used women 'to think with' in order to verbalize their own nagging concern with the stance that the Church should take to the world. For ancient men tended to regard women as creatures less clearly defined and less securely bounded by the structures that held men in place in society. She was both a weak link and a bridgehead. Women allowed in what men did not permit to enter"(1988: 153).

13. With respect to gender relations, Brown makes the interesting and relevant point that "pious women did not share the urgent need of male ascetics to create for themselves a man-made 'desert,' by destroying all bonds of kinship and former friendship. Virgins, tended, rather, to coagulate into small groups in a more frankly organic manner. Intense friendships between female companions played an essential role" (1988: 265).

14. Brown points out that "when Tertullian spoke of *castitas* he did not mean virginity; he meant sexual activity whittled away to a minimum in marriage and abandoned totally after marriage" (1988: 149).

15. Despite the subtleties in Origen's thought, strong negative suspicions remained. Brown considers the relation and difference between the Platonism of Origen and that of Plotinus to be a significant example of the parting of the ways between Christianity and paganism in later antiquity: "Origen's anxious sense of the threat of a 'counter-sensibility,' his fear that the soul's capacity for spiritual delight might be subtly and irreparably coarsened by the experience of physical intercourse, was notably lacking in Plotinus. For Plotinus, the physical embraces of the married couple were a very distant mirror, indeed, of that primal joining; but he never treated them as a tarnished and distorting mirror" (1988: 178–79).

16. I do not doubt that with respect to sexuality and sexual morality Augustine's shadow upon Christian history is ambivalent and often dark. Our memories of Augustine, however, are often selective. To essentially "blame" Augustine for most of our negative orientations toward sex—our long Augustinian detour so to speak—is to misread both Augustine and our own history. I find some of this in Elaine Pagels's *Adam, Eve and the Serpent* (1988). For example, Pagels argues that: "Augustine, one of the greatest teachers of western Christianity, derived many of these attitudes from the story of Adam and Eve: that sexual desire is sinful; that infants are infected from the moment of conception with the disease of original sin; and that Adam's sin corrupted the whole of nature itself" (p. xix). As I will indicate, Brown argues more critically that while sex became a melancholic and dark horizon upon Augustine's mind and soul, it was always a manifestation of something deeper—our originally disordered will. Brown is a much better guide to Augustine on these matters than Pagels (see Brown, 1967 and 1988). In terms of the influence of Augustine's "negative anthropology" and attendant voluntaristic orientations in parts of Roman Catholic moral theology, especially in connection with the rise of the relatively singular will of the legislating magisterium in moral matters, see John Mahoney (1989: pp. 37–71; and 224–58).

17. Augustine held a double understanding of freedom and the human will. *Liberum arbitrium* is our ability to make free choices and thus is subject to the *discordiosum malum*, with *libertas* being the higher freedom of the will's simple and clear orientation to virtue and the final good. *Libertas* is now present as a graced vision and horizon of the future "city of God" (See Vernon J. Bourke (ed.), *The Essential Augustine*: 176). In that city

> "the spirit shall will nothing which is unbecoming either to the spirit or to the body.... Neither are we to suppose that because sin shall have no power to delight...free will must be withdrawn. It will, on the contrary, be all the more truly free, because set free from delight in sinning to take unfailing delight in not sinning. For the first freedom of will which man received when he was created upright consisted in an ability not to sin, but also in an ability to sin; whereas this last freedom of will shall be superior, inasmuch as it shall not be able to sin. This, indeed, shall not be a natural ability, but the gift of God" (Augustine, *The City of God*: 1950: 864–65).

18. For a discussion of the "Penitentials" and the influence of auricular confession in general, see Pierre J. Payer (1984); John. T. McNeill and Helena M. Gamer (1990); and John Mahoney (1989).

19. The decree *Tametsi* also led to a hardening of the Roman Church's position on the proper form for a valid Christian marriage overall. Even though beyond the specific intentions of the council, the church, in effect, began to claim that marriage between any and all baptized Christians, Catholic or not, had to be performed in the presence of a priest and two witnesses. Even so, as Edward Schillebeeckx points out (1965: 367), not until *Ne Temere* of 1907 was the priest

required to be more than a passive witness and "to hear the consensus himself." This position was the result of a long process of development in the meaning and role of marriage in the Church. Schillebeeckx indicates that the marriages of the earliest converts to Christianity were "blessed," so to speak, simply by their baptism with no other ceremony required. Even for Christians who wished to marry, at first no specific ecclesiastical ceremony was deemed necessary apart from that required by secular authority. When the Church did begin to require specific celebrations of marriage, they were often those of popular custom accepted by the Church (1965: 233). Between the fourth and eleventh centuries, when more emphasis was placed on these particular Church celebrations, there was still no implication that they were necessary for validity (p. 260). From the eleventh to the thirteen centuries, the jurisdiction of the Church over marriage became complete and the idea of the sacramental nature of marriage was hotly debated. The issue in question was how marriage was a *sacramentum*, or "sacred sign" of the mystery of Christ and the Church. It was concluded that the life-long bond of marriage was rooted in this *sacramentum*, which not only pointed to the reality of divine commitment and permanence but effected it in the lives of the couple. The only distinction in question was whether the permanent sacramental bond was effected intrinsically or extrinsically—latent in the act itself (Patristic view), or made efficacious in the ecclesiastical contracting (view of the "schoolmen") (pp. 280–87). Further debates surrounded what act precisely constituted the marriage—i.e., consent or consummation—and the related question of at what moment was the sacrament effected. All finally agreed that the full *sacramentum* came into effect with both *consent and consummation* and not with the mere intention to marry, or betrothal, and consummation—a view that had prevailed among some canonists with the ecclesiastical ceremony being a celebration of a *fait accompli*. Still as Schillebeeckx points out, "the principle of indissolubility was not dependent on the fact that the marriage had been contracted *in facie Ecclesiae* (i.e., solemnised by a priest); or on the fact that local customs had or had not been observed, although clandestine marriages were strongly condemned once more" (pp. 296–97; 287–302). The necessity of a priest as witness for validity was only regularized with the decree *Tametsi* of Trent (pp. 361–67) and not during the time when "the *sacramentum* of marriage was accepted simply as something experienced" (p. 303). But it is important to recall again that not until *Ne Temere* of 1907 was the priest required to be an active participant (p. 367).

Thus the issues of the sacramentality of marriage and the question of the Church's jurisdictional control, though closely related historically, ought not be conflated theologically. The reformers had rejected the claims of sacramentality as a protest against jurisdiction and not as a protest against the sacredness or sign/symbol of the action (Schillebeeckx, 1965: 316; 359–61). For both Catholics and Protestants, marriage was in some manner a sacred mystery. And as later history indicates, the reformer's position was not without cause. In the Roman manner of law, *Tametsi* also required promulgation. As Schillebeeckx indicates, this led to a "mixed bag" of "valid" and "invalid" marriages in countries where the decree was promulgated and where it was not, as well as variety—through dispensation, privilege and the like—in the church's recognition of purely "protestant marriages" and "mixed marriages" (1965: 365–70). The reformers' rejection of the sacramentality of marriage may not have had full theological foundation (Schillebeeckx, 1965: 316–19), but their suspicion of the dangers of the complications of power with a relatively unbound juridical control of the church over marriage seems to have been somewhat born out. The problem continued to be finding the proper relation between the secular reality and sacred mystery of marriage. Present Roman Catholic canon law certainly "recognizes" the sacramental marriage of other Christian denominations, and certain conditions being met, the marriage of a Catholic and "non-Catholic" no longer requires the presence of a priest (Canon Law Society of America, 1983: *Code of Canon Law*: Book IV, Title VII: Can. 1055–1062; 1124–1129). For further discussion of "the indissoluble marriage" in Western culture, see Philippe Ariès (Ariès and Béjin, 1985: 140–57).

20.  On the other hand, commentary upon the recent encyclical on moral theology of John Paul II, *Veritatis Splendor* (John Paul II, 1993), suggests some expectation that this encyclical would raise the status of the Church's teaching on birth control to the level of "infallibility." Without mentioning the profound theological problems that plague this "doctrine of infallibility" in general, that this did not take place suggests both pastoral prudence as well as continuing ambivalence of the possibility of such teaching on specific and practical moral matters of this kind, or in doing so in an "ordinary" encyclical letter. Encyclical letters, coming in varying degrees of scope and regularity in different papacies, are considered exercises of the authentic but *ordinary* teaching authority of the magisterium, while "infallible" pronouncements are *extraordinary*, for the universal Church, and precisely directed—albeit by the ambiguous phrase—to *necessary* "faith and morals" (*fides et mores*)—i.e., that which has been believed, asserted, and practiced continuously by the Church. It is also important to add, however, that this particular encyclical reasserts the magisterium's prohibitive teaching on birth control more strongly and unambiguously as an "intrinsic evil" than any document since and including the Second Vatican Council.

21.  Certainly an inadequately critical conservatism in form and substance in the Church's discourse on sex is not only a problem with the Catholic traditions. In general, there appears to be a lack of any significant change in the debates of either Protestant or Roman Catholic traditions after the Counter-Reformation until well into the present century. Either my reading of these times is faulty, or in the European Enlightenment, the critical discourse on sex shifted largely to secular arenas. If this is so—and I am convinced that it is especially, for example, with respect to the role of women—the Church is now in late modernity challenged severely to catch up.

22.  I have commented in the Preface about the attitude of Christian ethics toward the possibility of morally responsible sexual practice without love.

However, in this book I have made the assumption that most, if not all, of the discourse of the Christian denominations considers love an informing value of sexual behavior at least in the mature ideal. I have also assumed a direct Western cultural context for my discussions. Relating love to the indissolubility of marriage, Philippe Ariès comments: "The outstanding fact in the history of western sexual behavior is the persistence, over many centuries and right up to the present day, of the pattern of marriage, as a binding tie, monogamous and indissoluble." Ariès goes on to indicate that this fact cannot be assumed in the history of other cultures where "the form of marriage in which a man can repudiate his wife and remarry is undoubtedly the most widespread"—i.e., "dissolve the union and start again" (Ariès and Béjin, 1985b: 140).

23. See Partridge, (1983: 146–47), and Rollo May, (1969: 223–45).

24. Tillich's understanding of the Greek term *ek-stasis* ("*existanai*, to put [*histanai*] out of [*ex-*] place, to derange, whence *ekstasis*" [Partridge: 661]) has relevance here and for his theology of *the spiritual presence* in general. Faith is "ecstatic" to the extent that it decenters us and draws us outside of ourselves, with love drawing us back in again toward the object/subject of that faith. Both faith and love participate in the dynamic decentering and "derangement" of the self (see Paul Tillich, *Systematic Theology III*, 1976: 129–44).

25. Thomas Ogletree (1985: 35–63) criticizes Tillich's understanding of love as being generally "ego-logical" in orientation and points to the important work of Emmanuel Levinas (See 1969; 1987; 1990a; 1990b ) as a corrective. But even in this criticism, Ogletree still notes that one cannot stress alterity to the point where the "other" becomes so disconnected from the self as to become alien. The self must still be implicated even in the alterity of other-regarding *agape*. I do not find Tillich as vulnerable on this point as does Ogletree. See also Tillich's discussion in his systematic theology (1976: 134–40). See also, Paul Ricoeur, *Oneself as Another* (1992); and Charles Taylor, *Sources of the Self* (1989).

26. I have not intended and thus will not discuss these and related questions in terms of a moral theological case-method approach. Before the complexity of cases and the margins of moral responsibility can be discussed adequately, including the "exceptional case," foundational contexts of both an analytic and substantive nature must be laid out. This has been my major intention in this book rather than a specific moral theology of particular cases of sexual behavior.

27. The new technologies of biological generation raise serious concerns in terms of their effects on upholding the necessary interpersonal moral framework for maintaining adequate values of physical generativity. Such technologies need not always be ruled immoral, but for moral adequacy they must be performed in the context of interpersonal love and mutual need rather than for the purposes of abstract experimentation or demonstrations of technocratic power. Recent experiences in the new birth-technologies demonstrate the

inevitability of serious moral conflict even in terms of our basic informing metaphors and designating symbols. Are embryos and children produced in this new technology still "gifts of God" or are they (also) "property" subject to contractual regulation like any other commodity? As "gifts," legal contracts for "surrogacy," for example, seem morally inappropriate; yet legal contracts may be the only way to ensure the necessary protections for all concerned, especially for the child.

28.  While presenting interesting and insightful analyses of sexual expression as deep human communication, I believe James Nelson's *Embodiment* (1978) suffers to some degree from this over-generalization and reductionism.

29.  See John Boswell's historical study of the abandonment of children, *The Kindness of Strangers* (1988).

30.  Some comparison can be made of the normative function and obligations of sacramental marriage with the relation of the body of a Christian assembly and the celebration of the Eucharist or Lord's Supper. The Christian Eucharist and Supper stand as sacramental "celebrations" that also disclose, designate, and purportedly "demonstrate" a way of Christian life in communion with others and the world. No particular Christian group or the body as a whole epitomizes in their own lives all that is disclosed in the eucharistic symbols and rites. They *participate* in these values, virtues, and goods and have special obligations, as Christians, to promote their realization. But no individual Christian or particular assembly *becomes* the eucharistic norm of communion. As in marriage, here too we are all "off the norm."

31.  For reconsiderations and reconstructions of this approach in Roman Catholic moral theology and in general, see Charles E. Curran (1977: 165–90). For the place of the "manualist" tradition in the history of Roman Catholic ethics, see Mahoney (1989).

32.  For a point of departure for the discussion of "fundamental option," see Josef Fuchs (1971: 92–111).

33.  Whatever criticism can be brought to bear upon Freud's so-called "pansexualism," his sexuality thesis implicates the dimension of sex at the core of the human personality. Besides his clinical evidence and metapsychological theories, Freud claimed sexuality to be the materially embodied ground of both the human psyche and the science of psychology. Much of the reason for Freud's break with C. G. Jung concerned the sexuality thesis that Freud felt was not only indicated by the clinical evidence but required to keep the new psychological science from lapsing into flights of occultist fancy. Rejections of Freud and psychoanalysis in general on the basis of religion and morality because of the sexuality thesis are unfounded. In an interesting letter to Jung in 1906, Freud writes:

> Transference provides the impulse necessary for understanding and translating the language of the ucs. (unconscious); where it is lacking, the

patient does not make the effort or does not listen when we submit our translations to him. Essentially, one might say, the cure is effected by love. And actually transference provides the most cogent, indeed, the only unassailable proof that neuroses are determined by the individual's love life (in McGuire, 1974: 12–13, parens added).

In theological terms, Freud's insistence on the sexual embodiment of the psyche can serve understandings of the sacramental nature of human life in the world.

34. Aristotle's *Nicomachean Ethics* (1925) and Aquinas's "Treatise on Virtue" in the *Summa Theologiae* (1969) ground much of the classical Christian ethics of virtue. For examples of contemporary psychological approaches to moral development and moral education, see Kohlberg (1973; 1981); Gilligan (1982); Knowles and McLean (1986); and Stern (1985).

35. Though not in the specific context of dedicated chastity and celibacy, H. Richard Niebuhr's discussion of dedication and loyalty to a cause is pertinent here (1963a: 83–84; 74–89).

36. I have used the term "homosexual" and "homosexuality" almost exclusively to refer to persons oriented to and involved in "same-sex" sexual relationships. I described the etymology in the Introduction. For a further discussion of this etymology, and with criticism of the continuing use of the single adjective "homosexual" for all references, see Boswell (1980: 41–46). It is clear that many homosexual persons prefer the term "gay," with sometimes a further discrimination of "gay" for males and "lesbian" for females. It is certainly the case that persons and groups have a right of preference in their own naming. Boswell makes good points in his discussion leading to the conclusion that a change to common usage is a "concession of speech…which scholars can make at very little cost to themselves" (1980: 46). The problem I discern, however, and the only reason I have resisted the popular usage in this book, is the somewhat diminutive implication of especially the term "gay" among some in the heterosexual population. As Boswell indicates, the term "gay" can be most proximately derived from the French *gai*, used in the thirteenth and fourteenth centuries to refer to courtly love and "troubadour eroticism," sometimes with explicit homosexual reference (p. 43 n.6). Partridge (1983: 248) finds an earlier Frankish root in *gahi*, meaning "impetuous, sudden, sharp." An ordinary dictionary definition of modern meaning indicates that "gay" suggests "a lightness of heart or liveliness of mood that is openly manifest." With respect to sexuality and sexual expression, "gay" could indicate that there is a joy and openness among the manifest gay community with respect to the rather grave traditions of heterosexuality. On the other hand, in the context of what many heterosexual persons perceive to be the "nature" of "gay persons," this usage could also reinforce the presumption that homosexual persons lack seriousness and maturity and are showy, vain, and ostentatious. Even though I think that for most gay and lesbian persons these assumptions are wrong, I am concerned that the term "gay" has often been taken pejoratively and promoted the alien marginality of this population. Thus, I

believe that the term itself has had subtle deleterious effects upon the efforts of gay and lesbian persons to come to the center of the serious moral and political debates of Church and society. That the term "homosexual" also carries derogatory implications for many pertains more to the remaining burdens of our conversations about same-sex intimacy than to the etymological history of the term. In this book I have adopted the more generic usage because of what I perceive to be these remaining burdens. Still words have a cultural life of their own and will follow their course despite all individual protestations to the contrary. Perhaps all that I can do here is to promote more awareness among heterosexual persons of a possible diminutive implication when they use the term "gay."

37. Note Susan Faludi's (1991) analysis of this phenomenon with respect to women and the feminist movement in general.

38. The analytic psychology of homosexuality is complex and I will only make a comment about responsible research and the moral implications of the data. In light of the difficulties of the modern moral discourse on homosexual orientation and practice, and the historic abuse and persecutions visited on homosexual persons, research and writing in this area have become problematic. From both so-called "conservative" and "liberal" postures, research is often received, if not engaged, from uncritical ideological perspectives. Uncritical assumptions of radical deviance stress the discontinuity between homosexuality and heterosexuality. While often well-intended, motivations of "liberal acceptance" sometimes stress the total continuity between homosexuality and heterosexuality. In the first instance, homosexual persons are rendered *alien* to ordinary and "normal" human sexual expression and often promote, intended or not, homophobic social and moral policies. In the second instance, the particular and unique processes and burdens of psycho-sexual development of homosexual persons tend to be ignored for the sake of social and moral acceptance. Thus their own particular needs for understanding themselves and finding assistance when necessary—burdens shared equally by heterosexual persons—are ill-served. I have suggested that there are both continuities and discontinuities between homosexual and heterosexual development and behavior. I have also suggested that any differences discerned through research and clinical evidence between homosexuality and heterosexuality require no *prima facie* moral discrimination. Responsible research in this area should first be descriptive. If this becomes our *norm* of research, then accurate data can be used to advance more responsible and critical moral discourse and argument on the subject.

Still, the "moral-politics" of such good research remains vexing. For example, it is becoming commonplace to fixate on research that may indicate a physiological basis for homosexuality as well as other practices and habits of behavior that have traditionally been understood as rooted in a morally disordered will, such as alcoholism. Certainly, such research ought to continue, but we need to be cautious in assuming that this is the only way to accomplish an adequate moral understanding and acceptance of such persons and their orientations and situations. In terms of sexual orientation, as I have argued in another place: "It is simply not the case that we need to find a physical origin of this kind to establish the *non-moral* status of sexual orientation. Paradoxically, at primary levels, developmental and psychodynamic orientations are in the long run more resistant to amelioration and change than many conditions of material-physical origin." (Monti, 1990: 165). It would be difficult to imagine any point in our lives where we simply chose our sexual orientation. In our research and evaluations of homosexual orientations and practice, we need to continue neither with archaic assumptions of deviance nor deny the developmental psychodynamics of sexuality, and its burdens—especially with respect to the clinical evidence of what appears as unique in the lives of some homosexual persons.

I do not assume that every homosexual person will bear a unique psychological burden over and beyond what all persons must endure, except insofar as social marginality and secrecy are often particularly deleterious to personal growth and character development. I do assume that all sexuality has a psychodynamic dimension and that growth toward character integrity and maturity in this area of our lives is difficult for all. While our efforts to understand the homosexual dimension of human experience must be multifaceted, including the narratives of the lives of well-integrated and successful homosexual persons, clinical evidence ought not be discounted. With respect to these and related matters of clinical theory and evidence, see Robert J. Stoller, *Observing the Erotic Imagination* (1985), and Elaine V. Siegel, *Female Homosexuality: Choice Without Volition* (1988); and for an historical account of the developments of psychoanalytic theories and approaches, Kenneth Lewes, *The Psychoanalytic Theory of Male Homosexuality* (1988).

39. Even in classical cultures where some homosexual practices were more publicly accepted, there was not a simple correspondence between heterosexual and homosexual practices. The acceptance and approval of male homosexual practices were often implicated in the patriarchy and slavery that dominated the heterosexual world. With respect to Greek culture, Brown indicates that it caused little surprise that "men might wish to caress and penetrate other beautiful men.... What was judged harshly was the fact the the pursuit of pleasure might lead some men to wish to play the female role, by offering themselves to be penetrated by their lovers: such behavior was puzzling to the doctors and shocking to most people. No free man should allow himself to be so weakened by desire as to allow himself to step out of the ferociously maintained hierarchy that placed all free men, in all their dealings, above women and slaves" (1988: 30). In this regard, see also Paul Veyne, "Homosexuality in Ancient Rome" in Philippe Ariès and André Béjin (1985: 30; 26–35); Michael Grant (1989: 281). And for explicit reference to the general philosophical assumptions of classical culture with respect to homosexuality, see A. W. Price, *Love and Friendship in Plato and Aristotle* (1989: 223–35), especially with respect to the assumption of the perfection of male beauty in an order "unencumbered" by the physical prospect of procreation.

40. I have already indicated in Part One the use and misuse of traditional arguments of natural law. In the context of modernity's turn to the individual, to history and, more recently, to interpreting its moral life through adequate paradigms of intersubjectivity and principles of totality, overly "physicalist" interpretations of natural law based solely on a presupposed "unnatural" quality of particular human/physical acts have become untenable as the basis for single arguments against homosexuality and other sexual practices. For further discussion on natural law and of moral absolutes grounded mainly in the physical nature of the act, see Charles E. Curran (1985: 119–72); Charles E. Curran and Richard A. McCormick, S.J., eds. (1991); and John G. Milhaven, and Martin Nolan, in Charles E. Curran, ed., (1968: 154–85; 232–48).

41. For a discussion of the question of the relationship between the universal and consistent and the unique and particular in moral discourse and argument in terms of gender, see Eva F. Kittay and Diana T. Meyers, eds., *Women and Moral Theory* (1987). I am also grateful to Patricia Templeton for challenging my argument on this question and pressing for more clarity and comprehensiveness.

## Chapter 7. Building Communities of Moral Discourse

1. Some of the material in this section is taken from my "Foreword: 'The Church: A Community of Moral Discourse" (1993a) and is used with permission.

2. Quoted in Eric Mount Jr, *Professional Ethics in Context* (1990: 13).

3. This term and theme has been developed in the work of social philosopher Jürgen Habermas. For example, see Jürgen Habermas's "Systematically Distorted Communication" in Paul Connerton, ed. (1976: 348–62), and in *Inquiry* (1970: 205–18); "Toward a Theory of Communicative Competence" in Hans Peter Dreitzell, ed. (1970b: 115–48); and Habermas: 1979: xii–xiii; 169; 208n–209n.

4. Even though Habermas deals with this project in a variety of writings, I will concentrate mainly upon his essay. "Discourse Ethics: Notes on a Program of Philosophical Justification" in Jürgen Habermas, *Moral Consciousness and Communicative Action* (1990: 43–115).

5. For an introduction to Habermas's theory of "Discourse Ethics," see Thomas McCarthy's "Introduction" to *Moral Consciousness and Communicative Action* (1990: vii–xiii); and Habermas's essays "What is Universal Pragmatics?" and "Toward a Reconstruction of Historical Materialism," in Jürgen Habermas, *Communication and the Evolution of Society* (1979: 1–68; 130–76). For a general Introduction to Habermas's work, see Thomas McCarthy, *The Critical Theory of Jürgen Habermas* (1978). For my relation of Habermas's work to the problem of public moral discourse, see my *Ethics and Public Policy* (1982).

6. For more complete discussions of Habermas's interpretations of both the problems and possibilities of the modern age, see *The Philosophical Discourse of Modernity* (Cambridge, MA: The MIT Press, 1987).

7. Habermas notes the quasi-cognitivist claim that in practical discourse, "we utter normative statements in the indicative mood, indicating thereby that normative statements, like descriptive ones, are open to criticism, that is, to refutation and justification" (1990: 52). If we take these common intuitions and cultural speech practices to be our points of departure, then we may have a substantive material-historical practice to adjudicate the claims of our moral discourse. However, Habermas warns that going down this initially plausible path based on, as I have indicated, the common speech practice of uttering ethical principles in the declarative mode, still leads to the unwarranted assumption that "normative statements can be true or false in the same way that descriptive statements can be true or false. Intuitionism is an example of a theory that assimilates normative statements to such predicative statements as 'This table is yellow,' 'All swans are white, etc." (p. 52).

8. In this regard, Habermas criticizes Alasdair MacIntyre's, *After Virtue* (1984) as being one-sided in its negative criticism of the enlightenment project of "a morality free of metaphysical and religious assumptions" (1990: p. 43). I have already criticized MacIntyre's conclusion that we must revert to smaller and more coherent worlds of rational moral discourse where virtue can be "born again." Stanley Hauerwas has been influenced by MacIntyre on this point, and his neosectarian ecclesiology suffers from this same one-sided criticism of enlightenment modernity. For further criticism of Hauerwas's ecclesiology see my "Dangerous Times and Obliging Places" (1993).

9. Habermas's emphasis on the Enlightenment commitment to the "mature autonomy" (*Mündigkeit*) of free and equal citizens engaged in responsible and competent speech about the meaning and practice of their lives has been thematic in his work. He argues that "the human interest in autonomy and responsibility is not mere fancy, for it can be apprehended a priori. What raises us out of nature is the only thing whose nature we can know: language. Through its structure, autonomy and responsibility are posited for us" (Habermas, 1971: 314). He continues: "In a certain way, mature autonomy (*Mündigkeit*) is the sole idea which we have at our disposal in the sense of the philosophical tradition...for in every speech act the *telos* of reaching an understanding (*Verstaendigung*) is already inherent. 'With the very first sentence the intention of a general and voluntary consensus is unmistakably enunciated'" (Habermas, 1974: 17).

10. See John R. Searle, "What is a Speech Act?," in Max Black, ed., *Philosophy in America* (1965: 221–39), and *Speech Acts* (1969); and J. L. Austin, *How to Do Things With Words* (1962), and "Performative Utterances," in *Philosophical Papers* (1970: 233–52).

11. Habermas continues: "The attempt to ground ethics in the form of a logic of moral argumentation has no chance of success unless we can identify a special type of validity claim connected with commands and norms and can identify it on the level on which moral dilemmas initially emerge: within the horizon of the lifeworld.... If claims to validity do not appear in the plural there in contexts of communicative action and thus prior to any reflection, we cannot expect a differentiation between truth and normative rightness to occur on the level of argumentation either" (1990: 57–58).

12. In "Freedom and Morality from the Standpoint of Communication" (1976; 45–60) Robert O. Johann discriminates three fundamental starting points for moral discourse that stand in concentric relation in terms of increasing comprehensiveness. Johann argues that "to speak of a standpoint is to speak of a disposition of an experiencing subject which in some way determines what is given in his experience" (p. 46). The first standpoint is from the one engaged in thinking. In this standpoint, the thinker takes as "given and evident" only that which pertains to the narrow activity of his or her thoughts. "Whether or not there exist anything beyond these thoughts to which they may be referred and by which they may be tested is problematic" (p. 48). The second standpoint is of the agent/actor who reflects in terms of a "hand to hand" transaction with another for the purpose of action and change (p. 48). The third and most comprehensive standpoint is beyond the isolation of the thinking subject, or the "hand to hand" transaction, but rather is a "face to face encounter" with another for the purpose of communication and understanding. "I am engaged with the other face to face as well as hand to hand. From this standpoint, the other exists for me, nor merely as a co-factor in an objective transaction, but as a co-source of dialogue. He is a partner with me in a shared experience" (p. 49). Johann's thesis is "that much of the contemporary and seemingly hopeless confusion about ethical matters results from the fact that the standpoint from which they are investigated is inadequate to the task" (p. 43).

13. The principle of universalization also raises the fundamental methodological procedure that Habermas claims for his theory of adeqaute moral speech and argument. In taking the occurrence of common and effective moral speech as given, Habermas has been led to a particular form of transcendental analysis—that is to say, to research into the conditions for the possibility of competent speech in general, and in this article, of moral discourse in particular. Because the transcendental methodology that informs his project is not directly pertinent to my use of Habermas in this chapter, I will only offer a few indications of his position. In general, it is clear that Habermas's form of "transcendentalism" is far more materially historical and pragmatic than Kant's. Habermas argues that an adequate theory of moral argument can be ascertained by examining the conditions for the possibility of communicative action overall (1990: 81). In other words, quoting Karl-Otto Appel (1987), Habermas understands his transcendental method as indicating "those transcendental-pragmatic presuppositions of argumentation that one must always (already) have accepted,

if the language game of argumentation is to be meaningful" (in Habermas, 1990: 82). This particular understanding of "transcendental method" is also captured by R. S. Peters (1974) who sees it as "pointing to what any individual *must* presuppose in so far as he uses a public forum of discourse in seriously discussing with others or with himself what he ought to do.... These arguments would be concerned not with prying into individual idiosyncrasies, but with probing public presuppositions" (in Habermas, 1990: 84). Habermas concludes: "only those *public* presuppositions are comparable to the transcendental preconditions on which Kantian analysis was focused. Only of them can one say that they are inescapable presuppositions of irreplaceable discourses and in that sense universal" (1990: 84).

14. Habermas argues: "Practical discourses are always related to the concrete point of departure of a disturbed normative agreement. These antecedent disruptions determine the topics that are up for discussion. This procedure, then, is not formal in the sense that it abstracts from content. Quite the contrary, in its openness, practical discourse is dependent upon the contingent content being fed into it from outside. In discourse this content is subjected to a process in which particular values are ultimately discarded as being not susceptible to consensus" (1990: 103).

15. With respect to the question of particular and prudent application, Habermas argues that the dynamic toward universality makes clear the dangers of "partiality and selectivity of applications. Applications can distort the meaning of the norm itself; we can operate in a more or less biased way in the dimension of prudent application. *Learning processes* are possible in this dimension too" (1990: 105).

16. For an effort to develop a general political theology of communicative action in the context of the development of the late modern sciences, and with special attention to Habermas's understanding of communicative rationality, see Helmut Peukert, *Science, Action, and Fundamental Theology: Toward a Theology of Communicative Action* (1984). For further philosophical efforts in making communicative praxis and action thematic, see Calvin O. Schrag (1986).

# BIBLIOGRAPHY

Aiken, Henry David
1962    *Reason and Conduct: New Bearings in Moral Philosophy.* New York: Alfred A. Knopf.

Altizer, Thomas. J. J. (ed.)
1982    *Deconstruction and Theology.* New York: Crossroad Publishing Company.

Appel, Karl-Otto
1980    *Towards a Transformation of Philosophy.* London: Routledge and Kegan Paul.

1987    "The Problem of Philosophical Foundations in Light of a Transcendental Pragmatics of Language." Pp. 250–90 in Kenneth Baynes, James Bohman, and Thomas McCarthy (eds.), *After Philosophy.* Cambridge, MA: The MIT Press.

Aquinas, Thomas
1969    *Summa Theologiae: Virtue* Vol. 23 (Ia2ae). Edited by W. D. Hughes, O. P. New York: Blackfriars/McGraw-Hill.

Ariès, Philippe
1985a    "Love and Married Life." Pp. 130–39 in Philippe Ariès and André Béjin (eds.), *Western Sexuality: Practice and Precept in Past and Present Times.* Translated by Anthony Foster. London: Basil Blackwell.

1985b    "The Indissoluble Marriage." In Philippe Ariès and André Béjin (eds.), *Western Sexuality: Practice and Precept in Past and Present Times.* Translated by Anthony Foster. London: Basil Blackwell.

Aristotle
1925    *Nicomachean Ethics.* Translated by W. D. Ross from *The Works of Aristotle*, Vol. IX, W. D. Ross, (ed.). Oxford: Clarendon Press.

1973    *Rhetoric.* Translated by W. Rhys Roberts from *Introduction to Aristotle*, 2nd ed. Richard McKeon, (ed). Chicago: University of Chicago Press.

Augustine
1950    *The City of God.* New York: Random House.

Austin, J. L.
  1965    *How to Do Things With Words*. Oxford: Oxford University Press.

  1970    "Performative Utterances." Pp. 233–52 in J. L. Austin, *Philosophical Papers*. Oxford: Oxford University Press.

Barbour, Ian G.
  1976    *Myths, Models and Paradigms: A Comparative Study in Science and Religion*. New York: Harper & Row.

Barfield, Owen
  1965    *Saving the Appearances: A Study in Idolatry*. New York: Harcourt, Brace, Jovanovich. 2nd ed. Middletown, CT: Wesleyan Press, 1988.

Barth, Karl
  1961    "The Doctrine of Creation" Part 4 in *Church Dogmatics* Vol. III. Translated by A. T. MacKay, et al., Edinburgh: T. & T. Clark.

  1968    *On Marriage*. Philadelphia: Fortress Press.

Batchelor Jr., Edward (ed.)
  1982    *Homosexuality and Ethics*. 2nd ed. New York: Pilgrim Press.

Battalgia, Anthony
  1988    "'Sect' or 'Denomination': The Place of Religious Ethics in a Post-Churchly Culture." *Journal of Religious Ethics* 16(1) (Spring): 128–42.

Baum, Gregory and John Coleman (eds.)
  1984    Sacred Congregation of the Faith. "Declaration on Certain Questions Concerning Sexual Ethics." Pp. 93–102 in *The Sexual Revolution*. Edinburgh: T. & T. Clark.

Beauchamp, Tom L. and James F. Childress
  1983    *Principles of Biomedical Ethics*. 2nd ed. New York: Oxford University Press.

Becker, Ernest
  1975    *Escape from Evil*. New York: Free Press.

Belenky, Mary F., et al.
  1986    *Women's Ways of Knowing*. New York: Basic Books.

Bellah, Robert, et al.
  1985    *Habits of the Heart: Individualism and Commitment in American Life*. Berkeley: University of California Press.

Berger, Peter L.
  1969    *The Sacred Canopy: Elements of a Sociological Theory of Religion*. New York: Doubleday.

Berger, Peter, Brigitte Berger, and Hansfried Kellner
    1973    *The Homeless Mind: Modernization and Consciousness.* New York:
            Random House.

Berlin, Isaiah
    1988    "On the Pursuit of the Ideal." *The New York Review of Books.* 35(4)
            (March 17): 11–18.

Berman, Marshall
    1982    *All That is Solid Melts into Air: The Experience of Modernity.* New
            York: Simon and Schuster.

Bernstein, Richard J. (ed.)
    1985    *Habermas and Modernity.* Cambridge, MA: MIT Press.

Black, Max
    1962    *Models and Metaphors: Studies in Language and Philosophy.* Ithaca,
            NY: Cornell University Press.

    1965    (ed.). *Philosophy in America.* Ithaca, NY: Cornell University Press.

    1979    "How Metaphors Work: A Reply to Donald Davidson." *Critical
            Inquiry*: 6(1): 131–43.

Blenkinsopp, Joseph
    1969    *Sexuality and The Christian Tradition.* Dayton, OH: Pflaum Press.

Booth, Wayne
    1974    *Modern Dogma and the Rhetoric of Assent.* Chicago: University of
            Chicago Press.

    1979    *Critical Understanding: The Powers and Limits of Pluralism.* Chicago:
            University of Chicago Press.

Boswell, John
    1980    *Christianity, Social Tolerance and Homosexuality.* Chicago: Uni-
            versity of Chicago Press.

    1988    *The Kindness of Strangers: The Abandonment of Children in Western
            Europe from Late Antiquity to the Renaissance.* New York: Pantheon
            Books.

Bourke, Vernon J. (ed.)
    1974    *The Essential Augustine.* 2nd ed. Indianapolis, IN: Hackett
            Publishing Company.

Brown, Peter
    1967    *Augustine of Hippo.* Berkeley and Los Angeles: University of
            California Press.

1978       *The Making of Late Antiquity*. Cambridge, MA.: Harvard University Press.

1988       *The Body and Society: Men, Women and Sexual Renunciation in Early Christianity*. New York: Columbia University Press.

Brundage, James A.
1987       *Law, Sex, and Christian Society in Medieval Europe*. Chicago: University of Chicago Press.

Burke, Kenneth
1945       *A Grammar of Motives*. New York: Prentice-Hall.

1967       *The Philosophy of Literary Form: Studies in Symbolic Action*, 2nd ed. Baton Rouge: Louisiana State University Press.

Canon Law Society of America
1983       *Code of Canon Law: Latin-English Edition*. Washington, DC: Canon Law Society of America.

Carey, John. J., et al.
1991       *Presbyterians and Human Sexuality*. Louisville, KY: The Office of the General Assembly of the Presbyterian Church (U.S.A.).

Cohen, Ted
1978       "Metaphor and the Cultivation of Intimacy." *Critical Inquiry* 5(1): 3–12.

Collingwood, R. G.
1956       *The Idea of History*. Oxford: Clarendon Press.

1972       *The Idea of Nature*. Oxford: Oxford University Press.

Curran, Charles E.
1968       (ed.) *Absolutes in Moral Theology?*: Washington, DC: Corpus Books.

1977       *Themes in Fundamental Moral Theology*. Notre Dame, IN: University of Notre Dame Press.

1985       "Natural Law." Pp. 119–72 in Charles E. Curran, *Directions in Fundamental Moral Theology*. Notre Dame, IN: University of Notre Dame Press

1986       *Faithful Dissent*. Kansas City, MO: Sheed and Ward Press.

1988       *Tensions in Moral Theology*. Notre Dame, IN: University of Notre Dame Press.

Curran, Charles E., and Richard A. McCormick (eds.)
1988       *Dissent in the Church*. New York: Paulist Press.

1991    *Moral Theology No. 7: Natural Law Moral Theology.* New York: Paulist Press.

Davidson, Arnold I. (ed.)
1989    "Symposium on Heidegger and Nazism." *Critical Inquiry* 15(2) (Winter).

Davidson, Donald.
1978    "What Metaphor Means." *Critical Inquiry* 5(1): 31–47.

Davis, Charles
1966    "Empty and Poor for Christ." *America* 115(15) (October 8): 419–20.

Derrida, Jacques
1973    *Speech and Phenomena and Other Essays in Husserl's Theory of Signs.* Translated by D. B. Allison. Evanston, IL: Northwestern University Press.

1976    *Of Grammatology.* Translated by G. Spivak. Baltimore: Johns Hopkins University Press.

1978    *Writing and Difference.* Translated by Alan Bass. Chicago: University of Chicago Press.

1982    *Margins of Philosophy.* Translated by Alan Bass. Chicago: University of Chicago Press.

Dworkin, Ronald
1993    *Life's Dominion: An Argument About Abortion, Euthanasia, and Individual Freedom.* New York: Alfred A. Knopf.

Ellison, Marvin M.
1990    "Reflection; Common Decency: A New Christian Sexual Ethics." *Christianity and Crisis* 50(16) (November 12): 352-56.

Faludi, Susan
1991    *Backlash: The Undeclared War Against American Women.* New York: Crown.

Farias, Victor
1989    *Heidegger and Nazism.* Edited by Joseph Margolis and Tom Rockmore. Translated by Paul Burrell and Gabriel Ricci. Philadelphia: Temple University Press.

Ferry, Luc and Alain Renaut
1990    *Heidegger and Modernity.* Translated by Franklin Philip. Chicago: University of Chicago Press.

Foley, Barbara
1985    "The Politics of Deconstruction. Pp. 113–34 in Robert Con Davis and Ronald Schleifer, eds. *Rhetoric and Form: Deconstruction at Yale.* Norman: University of Oklahoma Press.

Foucault, Michel
    1980    *The History of Sexuality: Vol. I: An Introduction*. Translated by
            Robert Hurley. New York: Vintage Books.

Fox-Genovese, Elizabeth
    1991    *Feminism Without Illusions: A Critique of Individualism*. Chapel Hill:
            University of North Carolina Press.

Frei, Hans
    1992    *Types of Christian Theology*. Edited by George Hunsinger and
            William C. Placher. New Haven, CT: Yale University Press.

Freire, Paulo
    1970    *Pedagogy of the Oppressed*. Translated by Myra B. Ramos. New
            York: Seabury Press.

Fuchs, Eric
    1983    *Sexual Desire and Love: The Origins and History of the Christian Ethic
            of Sexuality and Marriage*. Translated by Marsha Daigle. New York:
            Seabury Press.

Fuchs, Josef
    1971    *Human Values and Christian Morality*. Translated by M. H. Heelan
            et al. London/Dublin: Gill and Macmillan.

Gadamer, Hans-Georg
    1975    *Truth and Method*. Translation edited by Garrett Barden and John
            Cumming. New York: Seabury Press.

    1977    *Philosophical Hermeneutics*. Translated and edited by David E.
            Linge. Berkeley: University of California Press.

    1991    *Truth and Method*, 2nd rev. ed. Translation revised by Joel
            Weinsheimer and Donald G. Marshall. New York: Crossroad
            Publishing Company.

Geertz, Clifford
    1973    *The Interpretation of Cultures*. New York: Basic Books.

Gellner, Ernest
    1978    *Thought and Change*. Chicago: University of Chicago Press.

Gibbs, John G.
    1971    "Pauline Cosmic Christology and Ecological Crisis." *Journal of
            Biblical Literature* 90 (December): 466–79.

Gilkey, Langdon
    1976    *Reaping the Whirlwind: A Christian Interpretation of History*. New
            York: Seabury Press.

Gilligan, Carol
    1982    *In A Different Voice: Psychological Theory and Women's Development.* Cambridge, MA: Harvard University Press.

Gouldner, Alvin
    1971    *The Coming Crisis of Western Sociology.* New York: Avon Books.

    1976    *The Dialectic of Ideology and Technology: The Origins, Grammar and Future of Ideology.* New York: Seabury Press.

Grant, Michael
    1989    *The Classical Greeks.* New York: Charles Scribner's Sons.

Green, Garrett
    1989    *Imagining God: Theology and the Religious Imagination.* San Francisco: Harper & Row.

Greenberg, David F.
    1988    *The Construction of Homosexuality.* Chicago: University of Chicago Press.

Gula, Richard M.
    1989    *Reason Informed by Faith: Foundations of Catholic Morality.* New York: Paulist Press.

Gusdorf, Georges
    1972    "Values as Principles of Action." Pp. 222–49 in *Contemporary European Ethics: Selected Readings.* Edited by Joseph J. Kockelmans. New York: Doubleday-Anchor Books.

Gustafson, James M.
    1965    "Context Versus Principles: A Misplaced Debate in Christian Ethics." *Harvard Theological Review.* 58(2) (April): 171–202.

    1970    "The Church: A Community of Moral Discourse." Pp. 83–95 in James M. Gustafson, *The Church as Moral Decision-Maker.* Philadelphia: Pilgrim Press.

    1976    *Treasure in Earthen Vessels: The Church as a Human Community.* Chicago: University of Chicago Press (Midway Reprint).

    1978    *Protestant and Roman Catholic Ethics.* Chicago: University of Chicago Press.

    1981    *Ethics from a Theocentric Perspective: Vol. I: Theology and Ethics.* Chicago: University of Chicago Press.

    1984    *Ethics from a Theocentric Perspective: Vol. II: Ethics and Theology.* Chicago: University of Chicago Press.

Habermas, Jürgen

    1970a    *Toward a Rational Society.* Translated by Jeremy J. Shapiro. Boston: Beacon Press.

    1970b    "Toward a Theory of Communicative Competence." Pp. 115–48 in *Recent Sociology No. 2.* Edited by Hans Peter Drietzel. New York: Macmillan.

    1971    *Knowledge and Human Interests.* Translated by Jeremy J. Shapiro. Boston: Beacon Press.

    1974    *Theory and Practice.* Translated by John Viertel. Boston: Beacon Press.

    1975    *Legitimation Crisis.* Translated by Thomas McCarthy. Boston: Beacon Press.

    1976    "Systematically Distorted Communication." Pp. 348–62 in *Critical Sociology.* Edited by Paul Connerton. New York: Penguin Books.

    1979    *Communication and the Evolution of Society.* Translated by Thomas McCarthy. Boston: Beacon Press.

    1984    *The Theory of Communicative Action. Vol. One: Reason and the Rationalization of Society.* Translated by Thomas McCarthy. Boston: Beacon Press.

    1987    *The Philosophical Discourse of Modernity.* Translated by Frederick Lawrence. Cambridge, MA: MIT Press.

    1989a    *The Theory of Communicative Action. Vol. Two: Lifeworld and System: A Critique of Functionalist Reason.* Translated by Thomas McCarthy. Boston: Beacon Press.

    1989b    "Work and Weltanschauung: The Heidegger Controversy from a German Perspective." Translated by John McCumber. Pp. 431–56 in Arnold I. Davidson (ed.). *Critical Inquiry* 15(2) (Winter).

    1990    *Moral Consciousness and Communicative Action.* Translated by Christian Lenhardt and Shierry Weber Nicholsen. Cambridge, MA: MIT Press.

Hall, Douglas John

    1976    *Lighten Our Darkness: Toward an Indigenous Theology of the Cross.* Philadelphia: Westminster Press.

    1986    *Imaging God: Dominion as Stewardship.* Grand Rapids, MI: Eerdmans.

    1988    *The Stewardship of Light in the Kingdom of Death.* Grand Rapids, MI: Eerdmans Press.

1989    *Thinking the Faith: Christian Theology in a North American Context.* Minneapolis: Augsburg Press.

1993    *Professing the Faith: Christian Theology in a North American Context.* Minneapolis: Augsburg/Fortress Press.

Hanigan, James P.
1988    *Homosexuality: A Test Case for Christian Sexual Ethics.* New York: Paulist Press.

Hauerwas, Stanley
1983    *The Peaceable Kingdom: A Primer in Christian Ethics.* Notre Dame, IN: University of Notre Dame Press.

1991    *After Christendom?* Nashville, TN: Abingdon Press.

Hauerwas, Stanley and William H. Willimon
1989    *Resident Aliens: Life in the Christian Colony.* Nashville, TN: Abingdon Press.

Häring, Bernard
1966    *The Law of Christ Vol III: Special Moral Theology.* Translated by Edwin C. Kaiser. Westminister, MD: Newman Press.

Hazo, Robert G.
1967    *The Idea of Love.* New York: Frederick A. Praeger.

Hengel, Martin
1981    *Judaism and Hellenism Vols. I & II.* Translated by John Bowden. Philadelphia: Fortress Press.

Hodgson, Peter C.
1986    "Review Article: *Erring: A Postmodern A/theology* by Mark C. Taylor." *Religious Studies Review.* Vol. 12(3/4) (July/October): 256–59.

Hoehn, Richard A.
1983    *Up from Apathy: A Study of Moral Awareness and Social Involvement.* Nashville, TN: Abingdon Press.

Horkheimer, Max, and Theodore W. Adorno
1972    *Dialectic of Enlightenment.* Translated by John Cumming. New York: Seabury Press.

Husserl, Edmund
1970    *The Crisis of European Sciences and Transcendental Phenomenology.* Translated by David Carr. Evanston, IL: Northwestern University Press.

James, William
1961    *The Varieties of Religious Experience.* New York: Collier.

Jay, Martin
    1973    *The Dialectical Imagination: A History of the Frankfurt School and the Institute of Social Research*. Boston: Little, Brown and Company.

Johann, Robert O.
    1968    *Building the Human*. New York: Herder and Herder.

    1976    "Freedom and Morality from the Standpoint of Communication." Pp. 45–60 in Robert O. Johann (ed.), *Freedom and Value*. New York: Fordham University Press.

John Paul II
    1993    "Veritatis Splendor." *Origins: CNS Documentary Service*. 23(18) (October 14): pp. 297–336.

Jone, Heribert and Urban Adelman
    1953    *Moral Theology*. Westminster, MD: The Newman Press.

Joyce, James
    1964    *A Portrait of the Artist as a Young Man*. New York: Viking Press.

Kant, Immanuel
    1956    *Critique of Practical Reason*. Translated by Lewis White Beck. Indianapolis, IN: Bobbs-Merrill Company, Inc.

    1968    "On a Supposed Right to Lie for Altruistic Motives." Pp. 120–26. In James M. Gustafson and James T. Laney (eds.), *On Being Responsible: Issues in Personal Ethics*. New York: Harper & Row.

Kittay, Eva F., and Diana T. Meyers (eds.)
    1987    *Women and Moral Theory*. Savage, MD: Rowan and Littlefield

Knowles, Richard T., and George F. McLean
    1986    *Psychological Foundations of Moral Education and Character Development: An Integrated Theory of Moral Development*. Lanham, MD: University Press of America.

Kohlberg, Lawrence
    1973    *Collected Papers on Moral Development and Moral Education*. Cambridge, MA: Moral Education Research Foundation, Harvard University Press.

    1981    *The Philosophy of Moral Development: Moral Stages and the Idea of Justice*. San Francisco: Harper & Row.

Kolb, David
    1988    *The Critique of Pure Modernity: Hegel, Heidegger and After*. Chicago: University of Chicago Press.

Kosnik, Anthony, et al.
    1977    *Human Sexuality: New Directions in American Catholic Thought*. New York: Paulist Press.

Kuhn, Thomas
  1970    *The Structure of Scientific Revolutions*, 2nd ed. Chicago: University of Chicago Press.

Küng, Hans
  1968    *Truthfulness: The Future of the Church.* New York: Sheed and Ward.

Lash, Nicholas
  1979    *Theology on Dover Beach.* New York: Paulist Press.

Lawler, Ronald and Joseph Boyle Jr.
  1985    *Catholic Sexual Ethics: A Summary, Explanation, and Defense.* Huntington, IN: Our Sunday Visitor, Inc.

Lears, T. J. Jackson
  1981    *No Place of Grace: Antimodernism and the Transformation of American Culture, 1880-1920.* New York: Pantheon.

Leech, Kenneth
  1991    "'The Carnality of Grace': Sexuality, Spirituality, and Pastoral Ministry." *Sewanee Theological Review.* 35(1) (Christmas): 81–90.

Lemming, Bernard
  1960    *Principles of Sacramental Theology*, 2nd ed. Westminister, MD: The Newman Press.

Levinas, Emmanuel
  1969    *Totality and Infinity: An Essay on Exteriority.* Translated by Alphonso Lingis. Pittsburgh: Duquesne University Press.

  1985    *Ethics and Infinity.* Translated by Richard A. Cohen. Pittsburgh: Duquesne University Press.

  1987    *Collected Philosophical Papers.* Translated by Alphonso Lingis. Dordrecht: Martinus Nijhoff.

  1990a   *Nine Talmudic Readings* by Emmanuel Levinas. Translated and with an Introduction by Annette Aronowicz. Bloomington: Indiana University Press.

  1990b   *Time and Other and Other Essays.* Translated by Richard A. Cohen. Pittsburgh: Duquesne University Press.

Lewes, Kenneth
  1988    *The Psychoanalytic Theory of Male Homosexuality.* New York: Meridian.

Lindbeck, George
  1984    *The Nature of Doctrine: Religion and Theology in a Postliberal Age.* Philadelphia: Westminster Press.

Lovin, Robin
    1991    "The Persistence of Natural Law." *The Christian Century*. 108(27) (October 2): 869–70.

Luhmann, Niklas
    1986    *Love as Passion: The Codification of Intimacy*. Translated by Jeremy Gaines and Doris L. Jones. Cambridge, MA: Harvard University Press.

Lyotard, Jean-François
    1984    *The Postmodern Condition: A Report on Knowledge*. Translated by Geoff Bennington and Brian Massumi. Minneapolis: University of Minnesota Press.

    1987    "The Postmodern Condition." Pp. 73–94 in *After Philosophy*. Edited by Kenneth Baynes, James Bohman, and Thomas McCarthy. Cambridge, MA: MIT Press.

MacIntyre, Alasdair
    1966    *A Short History of Ethics*. New York: Macmillan.

    1984    *After Virtue*, 2nd ed. Notre Dame, IN: University of Notre Dame Press.

Madison. G. B.
    1988    *The Hermeneutics of Postmodernity*. Bloomington: University of Indiana Press.

MaGuire, Daniel C.
    1968    "Moral Absolutes and the Magisterium." Pp. 57–107 in Charles Curran, (ed.), *Absolutes in Moral Theology?* Washington, DC: Corpus Books.

Mahoney, John
    1989    *The Making of Moral Theology. A Study of the Roman Catholic Tradition*. Oxford: Clarendon Press.

Mandelbaum, Maurice
    1971    *History, Man, and Reason: A Study in Nineteenth-Century Thought*. Baltimore: Johns Hopkins University Press.

Marcuse, Herbert
    1966    *Eros and Civilization*. Boston: Beacon Press.

May, Rollo
    1969    *Love and Will*. New York: W. W. Norton.

    1972    *Power and Innocence: A Search for the Sources of Violence*. New York: W. W. Norton.

McCarthy, Thomas
  1978    *The Critical Theory of Jürgen Habermas.* Cambridge, MA: MIT Press.

  1990    "Introduction" Pp. xi–xiii in Jürgen Habermas. *Moral Consciousness and Communicative Action.* Translated by Christian Lenhardt and Shierry Weber Nicholsen. Cambridge, MA: MIT Press.

McFague, Sallie
  1982    *Metaphorical Theology: Models of God in Religious Language.* Philadelphia: Fortress Press.

McGuire, William (ed.)
  1974    *The Freud/Jung Letters.* Translated by Ralph Manheim and R. F. C. Hull. Princeton, NJ: Princeton University Press.

McNeill, John T., and Helena M. Gamer
  1990    *Medieval Handbooks of Penance.* New York: Columbia University Press.

Mead, George Herbert
  1934    "Fragments on Ethics." Pp. 379–98. In G. H. Mead, *Mind, Self and Society.* Chicago: University of Chicago Press.

Megill, Allan
  1985    *Prophets of Extremity: Nietzsche, Heidegger, Foucault, Derrida.* Berkeley: University of California Press.

Melton, J. Gordon, (ed.)
  1991    *The Churches Speak on Sex and Family Life: Official Statements from Religious Bodies and Ecumenical Organizations.* Detroit: Gale Research Inc.

Melton, J. Gordon, and Nicholas Piediscalzi, (eds.)
  1991    *The Churches Speak on Homosexuality: Official Statements from Religious Bodies and Ecumenical Organizations.* Detroit: Gale Research Inc.

Merton, Thomas
  1948    *The Seven Storey Mountain.* New York: Harcourt, Brace and Company.

Metz, Johann
  1980    *Faith in History and Society: Toward a Practical Fundamental Theology.* Translated by David Smith. New York: Seabury Press.

  1984    "Productive Noncontemporaneity." Translated by Andrew Buchwalter. Pp. 169–77 in Jürgen Habermas, (ed.), *Observations on "The Spiritual Situation of the Age."* Cambridge, MA: MIT Press.

Milhaven, John G.
    1968     "Moral Absolutes and Thomas Aquinas." Pp. 154–85. In Charles
             Curran, (ed.), *Absolutes in Moral Theology?* Washington, DC:
             Corpus Books.

Monti, Joseph
    1982     *Ethics and Public Policy: The Conditions of Public Moral Discourse.*
             Washington, D.C.: University Press of America.

    1984     *Who do you Say that I Am? The Christian Understanding of Christ and
             Antisemitism.* New York: Paulist Press.

    1986     "Review Article: *Ethics from a Theocentric Perspective: Volume I:
             Theology and Ethics* by James Gustafson." *The Saint Luke's Journal of
             Theology* 29(4) (September): 293–305.

    1990     "The Norm of Heterosexual Marriage." *Anglican Theological
             Review* 72(2) (Spring): 165–67.

    1991a    "Abortion: The Status of Fetal Life." *Sewanee Theological Review.*
             35(1) (Christmas): 39–56.

    1991b    "Foreword: 'The Church: A Community of Moral Discourse.'"
             *Sewanee Theological Review.* 35(1) (Christmas 1991): 9–11.

    1993     "Dangerous Tmes and Obliging Places: A Response to the New
             Sectarianism" *Quarterly Review* (Winter 1993): 71–87.

Moran, Gabriel
    1983     *Religious Education Development: Images for the Future.* Minneapolis:
             Winston Press.

Morse, J. Mitchell
    1959     *The Sympathetic Alien: James Joyce and Catholicism.* New York: New
             York University Press.

Mount Jr., Eric
    1990     *Professional Ethics in Context.* Louisville, KY: Westminster/John
             Knox Press.

Murphy, Francis X.
    1981     "Of Sex and the Catholic Church." *The Atlantic Monthly.*
             (February): 44–57.

Murray, John Courtney
    1991     "The Doctrine Lives: The Eternal Return of Natural Law." Pp.
             184–220 in Charles E. Curran and Richard E. McCormick, (eds.).

Nelson, James B.
    1978     *Embodiment: An Approach to Sexuality and Christian Theology.*
             Minneapolis: Augsburg.

Nelson, James B., et al.
  1989    *Sexual Ethics and the Church: A Christian Century Symposium.* Chicago: The Christian Century Foundation.

Niebuhr, H. Richard
  1951    *Christ and Culture.* New York: Harper & Row.

  1956    *The Purpose of the Church and Its Ministry.* New York: Harper & Row.

  1960    *The Meaning of Revelation.* New York: Macmillan.

  1963a   *The Responsible Self: An Essay in Christian Moral Philosophy.* New York: Harper & Row.

  1963b   *The Social Sources of Denominationalism.* Cleveland, OH: World Publishing Company.

  1970    *Radical Monotheism and Western Culture.* New York: Harper & Row.

  1989    *Faith on Earth: An Inquiry into the Structure of Human Faith.* Edited by Richard R. Niebuhr. New Haven, CT: Yale University Press.

Nolan, Martin
  1968    "The Principle of Totality in Moral Theology." Pp. 232–48 in Charles E. Curran (ed.), *Absolutes in Moral Theology?* Washington, D.C.: Corpus Books.

Norman, Richard
  1971    *Reasons for Action: A Critique of Utilitarian Rationality.* New York: Barnes & Noble.

  1983    *The Moral Philosophers: An Introduction to Ethics.* Oxford: Clarendon.

Norris, Christopher
  1982    *Deconstruction: Theory and Practice.* London: Metheun.

Nygren, Anders
  1953    *Agape and Eros*, rev. ed. Translated by Philip S. Watson. London: S.P.C.K.

Nozick, Robert
  1981    *Philosophical Explanations.* Cambridge, MA: Belknap Press of Harvard University Press.

Ogletree, Thomas W.
  1985    *Hospitality to the Stranger: Dimenisons of Moral Understanding.* Philadelphia: Fortress Press.

Outka, Gene and John P. Reeder, Jr., (eds.)
  1993    *Prospects for a Common Morality.* Princeton, NJ: Princeton University Press.

Pagels, Elaine
    1988      *Adam, Eve and the Serpent*. New York: Random House.

Partridge, Eric
    1983      *Origins: A Short Etymological Dictionary of Modern English*. New York: Greenwich House.

Payer, Pierre J.
    1984      *Sex and the Penitentials: The Development of a Sexual Code 550–1150*. Toronto: University of Toronto Press.

Percy, Walker
    1975      Walker Percy. *The Message in the Bottle*. New York: Farrar, Straus & Giroux.

Peters, F. E.
    1967      *Greek Philosophical Terms: A Historical Lexicon*. New York: New York University Press.

Peters, R. S.
    1974      *Ethics and Education*. London and Atlanta: Scott, Foresman, 1967.

Peukert, Helmut
    1984      *Science, Action and Fundamental Theology: Toward a Theology of Communicative Action*. Translated by James Bohman. Cambridge, MA: MIT Press.

Price, A. W.
    1989      *Love and Friendship in Plato and Aristotle*. Oxford: Clarendon Press.

Quine, W. V. and J. S. Ullian
    1978      *The Web of Belief*, 2nd ed. New York: Random House.

Rahner, Karl
    1982      *Foundations of Christian Faith*. Translated by William V. Dych. New York: Crossroad Publishing Company.

Ramsey, Ian
    1973      *Models for Divine Activity*. London: SCM Press.

Rasmussen, David M.
    1974      *Symbol and Interpretation*. The Hague: Martinus Nijhoff.

Rawls, John
    1971      *A Theory of Justice*. Cambridge: Belknap Press of Harvard University Press.

Ricoeur, Paul.
    1969      *The Symbolism of Evil*. Translated by Emerson Buchanan. Boston: Beacon Press.

1973a    "Creativity in Language: Word, Polysemy, Metaphor." Translated by David Pellauer. *Philosophy Today* 17: 97–111.

1973b    "Ethics and Culture: Habermas and Gadamer in Dialogue." Translated by David Pellauer. *Philosophy Today* 17: 153–65.

1976    *Interpretation Theory: Discourse and the Surplus of Meaning.* Fort Worth: Texas Christian University Press.

1977    *The Rule of Metaphor: Multi-disciplinary Studies of the Creation of Meaning in Language.* Translated by Robert Czerny, Kathleen McLaughlin and John Costello, S. J. Toronto: University of Toronto Press.

1978a    "Metaphor and the Main Problem of Hermeneutics" Pp. 134–48 in *The Philosophy of Paul Ricoeur,* edited by Charles E. Reagan and David Stewart. Boston: Beacon Press.

1978b    "The Hermeneutics of Symbols and Philosophical Reflection." Pp. 36–58 in *The Philosophy of Paul Ricoeur,* edited by Charles E. Reagan and David Stewart. Boston: Beacon Press.

1978c    "The Metaphorical Process as Cognition, Imagination, and Feeling." *Critical Inquiry* 5(1): 143–59.

1984a    *The Reality of the Historical Past: The Aquinas Lecture, 1984.* Milwaukee: Marquette University Press.

1984b    *Time and Narrative Vol. I.* Translated by Kathleen McLaughlin and David Pellauer. Chicago: University of Chicago Press.

1985    *Time and Narrative Vol. II.* Translated by Kathleen McLaughlin and David Pellauer. Chicago: University of Chicago Press.

1988    *Time and Narrative Vol. III.* Translated by Kathleen Blamey and David Pellauer. Chicago: University of Chicago Press.

1992    *Oneself as Another.* Translated by Kathleen Blamey. Chicago: University of Chicago Press.

Rorty, Richard
     1988    "Taking Philosophy Seriously: A Review of *Heidegger et le Nazisme* by Victor Farias." *The New Republic* 198(15) (April 11): 31–34.

Schillebeeckx, Edward
     1965    *Marriage: Human Reality and Saving Mystery.* Translated by N. D. Smith. New York: Sheed and Ward.

Schrag, Calvin O.
     1986    *Communicative Praxis and the Space of Subjectivity.* Bloomington: Indiana University Press.

Searle, J. R.
    1965    "What is a Speech Act?" Pp. 221-239 in Max Black (ed.), *Philosophy in America*. Ithaca, NY: Cornell University Press.

    1969    *Speech Acts: An Essay in the Philosophy of Language*. London: Cambridge University Press.

Sedgwick, Timothy
    1987    *Sacramental Ethics: Paschal Identity and the Christitian Life*. Philadelphia: Fortress Press.

Sheehan, Thomas
    1988    "Heidegger and the Nazis." *New York Review of Books*, 25(10) (June 16): 38–48.

Siegel, Elanie V.
    1988    *Female Homosexuality: Choice Without Volition*. Hillsdale, NJ: Analytic Press.

Silverman, Hugh J. and Don Ihde (eds.)
    1985    *Hermeneutics and Deconstruction*. Albany: State University of New York Press.

Smith, John E.
    1984    "The External and Internal Odyssey of God in the Twentieth Century." *Religious Studies* 20 (March): 43–54.

Stern, Daniel
    1985    *The Interpersonal World of the Infant: A View of Psychoanalysis and Developmental Psychology*. New York: Basic Books.

Stoller, Robert J.
    1985    *Observing the Erotic Imagination*. New Haven, CT: Yale University Press.

Strasser, Stephan
    1969    *The Idea of Dialogal Phenomenology*. Pittsburgh: Duquesne University Press.

Stratchey, James (ed.)
    1953–    *The Standard Edition of the Complete Psychological Works of*
    1974    *Sigmund Freud*. London: Hogarth Press.

Taylor, Charles
    1989    *Sources of the Self: The Making of Modern Identity*. Cambridge, MA: Harvard University Press.

Taylor, Mark C.
    1982    *Deconstructing Theology*. New York: Crossroad Publishing Company and Scholars Press.

1984    *Erring: A Postmodern A/theology*. Chicago: University of Chicago Press.

1987    *Altarity*. Chicago: University of Chicago Press.

Theunissen, Michael
1984    *The Other: Studies in the Social Ontology of Husserl, Heidegger, Sartre, and Buber*. Translated by Christopher McCann. Cambridge, MA: MIT Press.

Tillich, Paul
1959    *Theology of Culture*. New York: Oxford University Press.

1967    *Love, Power, and Justice*. New York: Oxford University Press.

1976    *Systematic Theology III*. Chicago: University of Chicago Press.

Toulmin, Stephen
1964    *An Examination of the Place of Reason in Ethics*. Cambridge: Cambridge University Press.

1969    *The Uses of Argument*. Cambridge: Cambridge University Press.

Tracy, David
1975    *Blessed Rage for Order: The New Pluralism in Theology*. New York: Seabury.

1981    *The Analogical Imagination: Christian Theology and the Culture of Pluralism*. New York: Crossroad Press.

Tucker, Robert C.
1963    "Marx and Distributive Justice." Pp. 306–25 in Carl J. Friedrich and John W. Chapman (eds.), *Justice: Nomos VI*. New York: Atherton Press.

Veyne, Paul
1985    "Homosexuality in Ancient Rome." Pp. 26–35 in Philippe Ariès and André Béjin (eds.), *Western Sexuality: Practice and Precept in Past and Present Times*. Translated by Anthony Foster. London: Basil Blackwell.

Wainwright, Geoffery
1980    *Doxology*. New York: Oxford University Press.

Weaver, Richard
1953    *The Ethics of Rhetoric*. Chicago: Henry Regnery Company.

Wentz, Richard (ed.)
1990    "Symposium: Toward a Theology for Lesbian and Gay Marriage." *Anglican Theological Review* 72(2) (Spring): 134–74.

Wheelwright, Philip
    1954    *The Burning Fountain: A Study in the Language of Symbolism.*
             Bloomington: Indiana University Press.

    1968    *Metaphor and Reality.* Bloomington: Indiana University Press.

White, Hayden
    1973    *Metahistory: The Historical Imagination in Nineteenth Century Europe.*
             Baltimore: Johns Hopkins University Press.

    1978    *Tropics of Discourse: Essays in Cultural Criticism.* Baltimore: Johns
             Hopkins University Press.

Wildiers, Max
    1982    *The Theologian and His Universe: Theology and Cosmology from the
             Middle Ages to the Present.* Translated by Paul Dunphy. New York:
             Seabury Press.

Winquist, Charles E.
    1986    *Epiphanies of Darkness: Deconstruction in Theology.* Philadelphia:
             Fortress Press.

Winter, Gibson
    1966    *Elements for a Social Ethic.* New York: Macmillan.

Wolin, Richard (ed.)
    1991    *The Heidegger Controversy: A Critical Reader.* New York: Columbia
             University Press.

Zimmerman, Michael E.
    1990    *Heidegger's Confrontation with Modernity.* Bloomington: Indiana
             University Press.

# INDEX

abortion, 129–133, 308n.10
adultery, 235
aestheticism, 40–42, 55, 57, 186,–189, 191; 301n.14; escapist, 71; nihilistic, 54; postmodern, 42, 50–57, 59; release, 53
aesthetics
    and religion, 244–245n.25, 296n.38
African–American,
    stories of, 68
*agape*, 229–232, 320n.9
age,
    cosmological, 36
agent(s),
    rational moral, 52
AIDS, 143, 295n.27, 295n.27
Aiken, Henry David, 8, 122–146, 307n.7, 309n.17
alterity, 204, 228; *altarity*, 55–56, 296n.32; and moral praxis of history, 90–91
Ambrose, Saint, 220
amoral, 120
analysis,
    an analytic mistake, 115–121, 119; moral, 108
anarchism, 110
anthropology,
    negative in Augustine, 322n.16
anticipation,
    historical, 61–62
antifoundationalism, 296–297n.34
antimodernism, 8, 40–42, 50, 65, 69, 72, 298n.4
antiquarianism, 99
antirationalism, 49
antisemitism, 107

appearance,
    phenomenological, 67
Appel, Karl-Otto, 332–333n.13
Aquinas, Thomas, 327n.34
argument, xii, xiii, 7–13, 27, 37, 52, 55, 97, 103–107, 123–24, 140, 142; and gender, 11–12; claims of truth, truthfulness, and right 269–270; communicative action, 269; critical, 18, 124; defined, 123; limitations and liabilities of, 253–255; making sense, xi–xii, 10–12, 309n.14; moral, 18; moral/ethical, ix,–xi, 4–8, 11, 25–28, 40, 42, 92, 96, 97, 108, 120–124, 127, 133–135, 138 142–144, 151; persuasive, 53; place of ethical, 121–146; role of ignorance, 306n.12; strategic action, 269; systematically distorted, 100–107, 142–143; theory of, 269–272; verification and legitimation, 255
Ariès, Philippe, 324–325n.22, 329n.39
Aristotle, 83–84, 245–246, 257, 305–306n.17, 318–319n.2, 327n.24
asceticism, 214
Augustine, 27, 220, 221–224, 234, 322nn. 16, 17
Austin, J. L., 269, 331n.10


Barfield, Owen, 160, 172–173, 298n.5, 317n.18
Barthes, Roland, 162
Beardsley, Monroe, 157
Beauchamp, Thomas L., 289n.11
Becker, Ernest, 174
behavior, 9, 131, 166, 168; sexual, ix, x, 3, 8–9, 12, 26–27, 59, 71, 78, 122, 129,